Encyclopaedia of the
MODERN
BRITISH ARMY

Encyclopaedia of the
MODERN
BRITISH ARMY

3rd edition

Terry Gander

Guild Publishing London

Then it's Tommy this, an' Tommy that,
  an' 'Tommy, 'ow's yer soul?'

But it's 'Thin red line of 'eroes'
  when the drums begin to roll.
                                   Kipling.

This edition published 1986 by Book Club Associates
by arrangement with Patrick Stephens Limited.

Title pages *Challenger in action. During exercises, a red flag is
flown from each vehicle when weapons are loaded.*

Printed and bound in Great Britain

Contents

Introduction

This is the third edition of this book but so much has changed in the Army in the years since 1980 when the first edition appeared that it seems to be almost a new book. Almost as soon as the first edition appeared the Army went into a veritable thrash of re-organisation, much of it imposed rather than chosen, and a major campaign has been fought and won. The Army has also had to accept its share of a reduction in public spending just at a time when it needed more to re-equip and prepare for the future. It would be fool-hardy to suggest that this period of relative uproar has ceased, for it certainly has not, but further major re-organisation seems unlikely (unless yet another formation has to be brought back to the United Kingdom from Germany) and the bulk of the re-equipment programme is under way.

The events of the past few years have meant a drastic re-write of many of the sections of this book, not the least of which has been the organisational side itself. Re-organisations within the various arms and services of the Army have also resulted in some almost total re-writes, not least in the section dealing with the armoured regiments for they have undergone some significant alterations in structure and size since the first edition was finished. So this third edition presents itself as a substantial change from the original edition.

Looking back at the introduction to the first edition some remarks made then are still apposite. The Army still seems to suffer from a generally bad 'Press' despite all its efforts to change matters, and many still see the Army as at best a huge national joke or at worst an unnecessary expense. Much of this still stems from a general lack of realisation of exactly what role the Army has to play in the life of the nation. It is no longer a refuge for those who could not fit into normal civilian life, nor is it a refuge for authoritarian maniacs who love to order people around. Anyone who has had even the most fleeting dealings with the modern Army will have learned this but there are still

Her Majesty the Queen, Commander-in-Chief, reviewing 4 Division, 1 (BR) Corps at Sennelager on July 7 1977.

whole sectors of the population who go out of their way to misunderstand almost every aspect of the Army's methods, role and costs. In some small way this book sets out to explain some of these factors, but it seems to be an uphill struggle for the truth is that the Army is only appreciated when it has failed in its ultimate duty, and that is to persuade an enemy that there is no point in becoming actively aggressive.

The Army today spends a great deal of time and resources trying to inform the nation as to its activities. However, mention was made in the first edition of this book of the legacy of the old Army, and that legacy is with us still. Reinforced by the memories of National Service, the Army is still seen in terms of what it was years ago, and needless to say no-one remembers the positive aspects of those days. The modern Army is now vastly different. It has a much more enlightened outlook on all aspects of life from the utilisation of modern technology to attempting to present its case. One aspect of its structure has still not changed, though, and shows no sign of doing so, and that is the retention of many old traditions and especially the regimental system.

The regimental system of the Army—in which the members of any regiment or corps look upon themselves as one form of 'tribal family' into which no intrusion is allowed—is with us still. It has tremendous strengths in forming internal alliances at all levels but it does not allow for a great deal of operational flexibility on the battlefield. Many other armies now use a more flexible system of cross-posting and cross-training which allows *ad hoc* formations to be assembled and used at short notice in action, but the British have repeatedly rejected any such system and cling instead to their time-honoured regiments. It is also very true that many other armies envy the 'tribal' affiliations of the British Army and attempt to produce their own equivalents. Perhaps, therefore, it cannot be all bad but, even so, the regimental system is still looking rather dated. Only a revolution will change it, though.

The second edition of this book made much mention of the numbers factor. Even though the Army operates as part of a much larger NATO force, it is still short on numbers. The old adage that 'God is on the side of the big battalions' is still true and when one starts to look at the numbers of men and weapons available to the Warsaw Pact even in times of peace one wonders if three armoured divisions will be able to do very much in an emergency. They certainly will have something to do with the eventual outcome if the men involved have anything to do with it, for the Army has many excellent officers and men of all ranks. There can have been few times in history when the Army has been better served by the quality of its manpower. In all aspects of military abilities, leadership, education, character and social graces, the Army has never been so well provided for. Working with such people has made the writing of this book a positive pleasure and the author can only offer his thanks to all who have put up with his questions and requests during the compilation of this third edition.

Other people also deserve my thanks, not the least of whom are the many and various people in Defence Promotions and Facilities (Army) at the Ministry of Defence. They have been a constant source of assistance and information. Other individuals who must be mentioned include Ken Musgrave for updating his excellent four-view drawings and producing new ones at short notice, Christopher Foss who has been so liberal with his advice and information, and Peter Guiver who has also put up with many requests for information. Paul Beaver was of considerable assistance with reference to the AAC side of things so my particular thanks to him.

A final word of thanks must also go to Bruce Quarrie yet again. He planted the seed of this book many years ago, on a Canadian prairie as I like to remind him, and his editorial contributions and patience while waiting for the finished product in the form of this third edition means that this book is now very much his as well as mine.

Terry Gander
Billingshurst, 1986

The British Army since 1945

There is an old maxim that states 'History always repeats itself'. Whether it is true in a general sense is a matter for debate, but for the British Army it has a very ominous ring. Twice in this century the Army has been through a cycle of general neglect and lack of appreciation of its proper role and worth, and twice it has had to suffer appalling losses and experiences as a result of that neglect. Twice it has had to expand its numbers and powers to unheard-of limits, and twice it has emerged victorious from the worst historical and social upheavals the world has known. But for the Army the worst that history has had to show is that twice it has been relegated to its former state of acceptability in a nation reluctant to accept the true cost of defending all they profess to hold dear.

As these words are written the British Army is still a major component of the fabric of the British nation but in numbers and capabilities it is a mere shadow of its former self. Thus in a number of senses history has repeated itself, for the years since 1945 have seen a gradual and insidious decline in numbers and roles of the Army. It is true that in equipment, striking power and general expertise the Army has never been stronger but its position in society and national esteem has reverted once again to that which it has occupied for centuries, a role of that of an almost closed society that seemingly devours a larger slice of the national cake than many would wish.

The fallacy of this situation has been disproved so many times that it is one of the major faults of the British character and social make-up, but it is still with us nevertheless. For centuries the Army has been regarded as little more than a necessary evil that was called upon to convert the decisions of the executive body into the physical occupation of foreign soil, while at home it was handy for the suppression of an unruly populace. While the overseas forays were greeted with acclaim and honours, these symbols of acceptance seldom lasted long and in the (infrequent) periods of peace the numbers in

the ranks were slashed to the absolute minimum and elaborate and cheap systems of reserve or volunteer semi-trained civilians were kept in being ready for any future conflict. By the late 1800s the Army system had become a small segment of the expanding British economy but it was starved of funds just the same, despite the fact that it was in a very large part responsible for the huge areas of the globe that were coloured red in the school atlases read by an increasingly literate population.

The Cardwell Reforms of 1860 perpetuated the traditions built up over the years by an Army that was organised and led on a social system little changed from the Middle Ages. Landowners' sons led working class soldiers into battles where initiative and innovation were regarded with suspicion. The tiny British Army of 1914 crossed the Channel to France to fight the invading German hordes but in so doing they were the unwitting vanguard of a new move in British history which reversed the policies of a century by once more bringing the physical evidence of a new British involvement in Europe. The Great War transformed not only Europe, it transformed the United Kingdom and its Army. Between the years 1914 and 1918 the Army ceased to be a closed society by virtue of the sheer weight of human numbers imposed by the seemingly insatiable demands of trench warfare. The Army received an infusion of all that the best of the British nation could provide and despite the efforts of the hidebound high-ranking establishment, it was never to be the same again.

After the massive victories of late 1918 the Army lost little time in reverting to its former social order and its former enclosed self. But the seeds of change had been sown deep by the passage of the masses of 1914 to 1918. It had (grudgingly) accepted the needs of large-scale mechanisation, it had accepted the need for new weapons and equipment and it had already started to become a fully professional force abreast of technological change. Between 1920 and

Ferrets in the ruins of Beirut, 1983 (UKLF).

1935 the main restrictions on the role of the Army came not from within but from the national purse. The dreadful demands of the Great War on the British economy and nation led to the wishful delusion that the 'War to end all Wars' had been fought and there was no further need for the Army other than to provide imposing garrisons for the numerous colonies. Consequently the 1920s and early 1930s were years of financial starvation and regression as units once more paraded and disported themselves in formations that employed tactical methods proved obsolete by the machine-gun and the aeroplane. Horses wheeled and charged in ranks that ignored the battlefields of France, and infantry trudged on weary route marches made unnecessary by the advent of the motor lorry. But there were many who had learned the lessons so dearly imposed in France and elsewhere, and many high-ranking officers used what little funds there were for experimentation and new equipment.

With the coming to power of Hitler and the NSDAP in Germany in 1933 the political climate of Europe began once again to change for the worse. After 1919 it had become an unstated British political policy not to become involved in the structure of Europe, as had France, but this reluctance to accept a political role had led to the gradual emergence of Nazi Germany to occupy the power vacuum left by the collapse of Whilhelmine Germany and the old Austro-Hungarian Empire. By 1935 the British attitude to Germany and Europe as a whole was gradually changing, and with the change came reluctant acceptance of the fact that any involvement with Germany would once more include the need to send an armed force over to Europe. But to expand a small well-intentioned garrison Army into an expeditionary force no longer involved the passing of a Bill in Parliament along with the resultant recruiting campaign and the issuing of uniforms. Modern warfare had changed all that into the expensive and time-consuming training and equipping of a new type of Army, an Army that depended on radio and motor traction. New weapons had to be hastily obtained or made, new bases had to be constructed and Home defences contrived and brought into use. The years after 1935 saw a gradual but growing importance of the Army in the United Kingdom establishment, even if it was behind the Admiralty and the Air Ministry in the allocation of what funds a Parliament inclined to appeasing dictators was wont to release. The 1938 Munich fiasco came as a welcome return to reality to the military and political scene in the United Kingdom as a whole, and from then onwards the Army began to prepare for war.

It prepared surprisingly well, in retrospect. The little BEF which crossed to France in September 1939 was the only fully-mechanised contingent in *any* of the warring European armies and its equipment levels were high. It suffered from the fatal weakness of being emotionally and practically equipped for the Great War and not for the fast-moving onslaught it had to face. It also suffered from not having any practical reserve, for after the Battle of France virtually all its mobile and heavy equipment and weapons were lost. Overseas, enemy pressure was everywhere desperate but weapons and equipment came from America and the old Empire provided men. These were insufficient to prevent the loss of many colonies in the Far East when Japan entered the war in late 1941. By that date the British Army and the Allies were out of Europe and everywhere the Axis forces seemed triumphant. The Army had suffered overwhelming defeat, or so it seemed, and a great deal of criticism was directed at the Army and its leaders from all quarters. The truth was that the Army was taking the brunt of the blame that should have been directed to the British nation as a whole for their years of failing to accept that nationhood imposes responsibilities as well as benefits. The failure of the United Kingdom to assume a European role after 1918 was a direct cause of the holocaust of 1939 to 1945 with its costs, not only in lives but in the bankruptcy of the British nation after about 1941. The Army took the blame for all this in 1941 as it was the instrument that had to convert years of financial and social neglect into practical terms on the battlefield. Not suprisingly it often failed. What is surprising is that in many ways it managed to do so well. The build-up of a new effective Army in the years after 1940 was an achievement of major magnitude.

After 1941 the worst was over. But the Great War still cast its long shadow by the reluctance of the General Staff to become involved in the types of campaign epitomised by the messy slogging matches of Flanders and the Somme. The Army had to be built up into an instrument capable of crossing the Channel to take the war into Europe once again. In the meantime trained formations were sent to North Africa to take part in the Western Desert campaign, a venture that has now grown into a major part of British legend. In truth, the campaign provided an excellent forming and training ground but its eventual conclusion aided the general Allied war effort but little. For all its dramatic to-ing and fro-ing it was a sideshow in the overall framework of the eventual defeat of Nazi Germany.

After 1941 the United Kingdom was no longer fighting alone. In the United States and the USSR it had two allies who ensured the eventual victory, a victory that was considerably aided by the most extreme example of German military tactical excellence taking precedence over strategic sense. That example was provided by Hitler's decision to invade the Soviet Union, a campaign that came to overshadow all the others that took place later. It was in the Soviet Union that the attrition of the Great War trenches was replaced by the sheer scale and enormity of total war to the death between nations. The affluence of the USA provided equipment, money and men to all, including the British Army, but after 1942 the British took less and less part in the overall conduct of the conflict. The Army took part in the type of slogging combat to which it was best suited along the mountainous length of the Italian peninsula, and it provided about one third of the formations used in the Invasion of Normandy in 1944 and the subsequent operations that led to the eventual defeat of Nazi Germany in May 1945. In the Far East units of the British Army joined with the old Indian Army to fight the long, bitter and seemingly forgotten war against the Japanese in Burma, while the American forces island-hopped across the Pacific Ocean. But to this day the British people are reluctant to acknowledge that by 1945 they had become a secondary power among the Allies. The war effort had bled the British economy white and the British nation no longer held effective sway over large tracts of its former overseas colonial (and wealth-making) territories.

At the end, the British forces were everywhere victorious. In Europe the Army was deep within Germany and in Italy the long slog through the mountains was over and the Army was on the Austrian borders. In Burma the Japanese were driven from their last strongholds, and a new force was being formed for the invasion of Japan itself.

En route to the Falklands, 1982 (UKLF).

The dropping of the first operational atomic bomb on Hiroshima ended that project, and for the first time for six years the Army was able to take stock of itself and its achievements. It had much to be proud of. From a small nucleus the Army had grown into a huge citizens' army that had mastered the arts of battle in the desert, the jungle and the mountains. It had developed new forms of transport into battle and had learned how to fight from the sky itself. It had also relearned the art of amphibious warfare and in so doing had raised the state of the art to new heights. It had also learned to harness modern technology and science for its overall aims, and it had played its part in transforming a peaceable population into a highly disciplined and skilled fighting force. In 1945 the Army was at the very peak of its powers and at the height of its achievements, but within a very few months nearly all of that had been swept away.

With the coming of victory the massive machine that the Army had become was soon in the process of being dismantled. The citizens' Army returned to its homes in large drafts but the post-war task of the Army was far from over. All over the world societies and peoples were in turmoil and chaos as the wake of war subsided. Nations overthrew their former governors and many others went through the painful and costly process of insurrection. Wherever the British Army was based it, often alone and unaided, had to bear the brunt of keeping an often fragile peace, and in many places (such as Greece) it often found itself taking up arms against people who only a few short months before had been allies. In the turmoil of post-war events this keeping of the peace passed almost unrecognised but it marked a major reversion of the Army's role from that of a fighting field force to that of 'action in support of a civil power'. The major field forces were kept in being and trained constantly for major war but after 1945 the Army more and more became an international policeman.

In the years following 1945 the gradual run-down of the Army's numbers continued apace, but the international situation for once prevented a general reversion to the pre-war strengths as had taken place so swiftly in 1919. In Europe the clash of ideology between the wartime Allies proved too strong for the alliance to survive more than a few months and the Cold War set in with the Churchillian 'Iron Curtain' dividing the continent into its mutually suspicious halves. The political and military threat provided by the presence of massive Soviet forces deep within Europe ensured that at last the Army had a European task imposed upon it and that task was accepted and carried out to the limit. It has been carried out so effectively that today the Army is not only still well installed on the European continent but its major forces have now been subordinated to an overall European ideal, that of a component in a European Army. The NATO Treaty was signed in Washington on April 4 1949 and as a direct result the United Kingdom provides a component of the NATO forces guarding the borders between themselves and those of their Eastern counterparts, the armies of the Warsaw Pact.

Outside Europe, the Army had a thankless role to carry out in the gradual dismantling of the old British Empire. The war years had accelerated the pace of withdrawal from Empire, and in many cases had initiated it, but it was a process that took place nevertheless. For the first time in history a major nation voluntarily handed over autonomy of its often hard-won possessions to their inhabitants. Often the hand-over did not run smoothly, or at a rapid-enough pace to suit all concerned, but it took place all the same and in nearly every country concerned the British Army had to bear the brunt of the difficult work. But nowhere was the task more deeply felt by the Army than in the withdrawal from India in 1947.

The old British Army had two homes. One, the smaller, had been in Ireland, but that had finally been lost in 1922 so that left only one, and that was the finest of all; it was India. India, the 'jewel in the crown' of the Victorian Empire, was the Army's spiritual home where it had drilled, fought and lived for over two centuries. The Home Army supplied it with men and equipment but it was in India that the old Army planted its roots, formed its traditions and kept its active skills finely honed by the endless skirmishes on the North-West Frontier. A whole string of colonial stations were established along the routes to India to keep the country supplied and, even more important, to guard the trade routes to and from the United Kingdom. But India was the heart, not only of the old Empire but also of its Army. When the Army left India it left not only its heart but a large piece of its very soul. The Army was never the same again after 1947—it had to find a new heart, a new reason for its existence, and much of the turmoil and evolution that has taken place within the Army since then can be traced directly to this cause. By the late 1970s the new home had been recognised at last, reluctantly by many, as being in Europe.

The withdrawal from India also led to a gradual withdrawal from the many stations on the route to India. After 1947 there was little reason or purpose in keeping them under British control, and the body politic retained them only for reasons that were understandable but historically invalid. The United Kingdom after 1945 was a nation reluctant to accept the true cost of victory. It was eager to return to the affluence and comforts of the pre-war years and at a loss to accept that the sources of cheap imports had vanished and that the long-term markets for Britain's staple industries were dwindling. We clung to the trappings of Empire in an attempt to turn back the historical clock but it was to no avail. Between 1947 and 1967 the bulk of the old Empire changed hands. Burma was one of the first nations to go, followed by Palestine, the Nile Delta and eventually by Aden, Cyprus and Malta. Even the hallowed Canal Zone in Egypt was handed over in 1954. In Africa the old colonies passed to their native political leaders one after the other; Kenya, Uganda, Tanganyika, the Gold Coast, Nigeria and many others changed from colonial rule to independence. The Army was involved in every hand-over and it alone often had to bear the burden of the transfer of power. In many cases the transfer did not take place rapidly enough to suit all and in many countries the hand-over of power was to the wrong political bodies or groupings, at least as far as political activists were concerned. Thus the Army took the brunt of the disruptions which often resulted. Political dissidents often took to the bomb or gun to accelerate the leaving rate of British government or to express their dissatisfaction at the planned methods of hand-over. The Army tried to keep the peace as its troops were attacked by terrorists or struggled to keep fighting factions apart. It was the common soldier who had to bear the constant threat of ambush or the stealthily lobbed grenade, and it was he who had to carry out the onerous and unwelcome searches, the tiresome roadblocking and the constant patrolling. When it finally left the Army was all too often the only organised body that stood for law and order during the last desperate days of hand-over. In many of the old colonies there were often many who mourned the Army's leaving as the first heady days of independence turned into power struggles, civil war and dictatorships.

Among all the post-war withdrawal from Empire the Army was able to claim one major achievement. That was the successful campaign carried out against the communist-inspired rebel forces in Malaya. To this day it is still the only such campaign to have been won by an established Army and government against the practitioners of revolutionary warfare, and it took place between 1948 and 1960. The Army took once more to the jungle and sought out and destroyed the communist guerrillas on their own ground and on their own terms. They fought a corresponding 'hearts and minds' campaign among the civil population to prevent the guerrillas finding their traditional refuges among the static settlements, towns and cities. When the Army left Malaya it was able to hand over the government to a democratically established nation.

Apart from the role of the colonial gendarme, the Army fought a major campaign in Korea. There a British brigade earned the admiration of all by its conduct in battle and the unflagging high spirits of its soldiers under dreadful conditions, not only in the front lines but also in the squalid conditions of the prisoner-of-war camps into which many British soldiers found their way.

But all the time the Army was gradually declining in numbers and the effectiveness of its equipment. The major impact of the Korean War for the Army was not to be found in the campaign itself but in the political realisation that the threat from the Communist Bloc was a real one and that steps would have to be taken to counter it. A re-armament programme was initiated, and steps taken to halt the run-down in numbers that had steadily taken place since 1945. By the mid-1950s the Army in Europe, by then well established as the British Army of the Rhine (BAOR), was ready to fight a defensive battle once again but time was to show that the measures taken were insufficient and too half-hearted to fully carry out the task that the Army was called upon to undertake.

The realisation came with Suez. The Suez campaign of 1956 had origins that are outside the scope of this book but basically the Army was called upon to play its part in an Anglo-French landing at Suez, an action which was called for because of, and created even more, political muddle, unclear objectives, and disorganisation. The Army was already stretched to its limits in Europe and elsewhere and the action took place over an over-extended period in which the rest of the world gradually combined to form a hostile reaction to the Anglo-French activities. Militarily the Suez landings were a disaster, as nearly all the dearly-bought lessons of 1940-1945 had been forgotten, and the supposedly large-scale operation was brought to a rapid halt before the full magnitude of the fiasco was demonstrated to all. While the politicians had to bear the bulk of the blame for Suez, the Army was shown to be overstretched and unable to carry out the type of operation that had once made the United Kingdom a world power.

The truth was finally recognised and out of the economic upheaval that Suez initiated came the realisation that the United Kingdom was no longer a major and independent world power but a secondary nation in need of allies and economic assistance. The Army finally turned its face to Europe and at the same time carried out the last of the major colonial policing operations in Aden. As it no longer had to provide garrisons for the old colonies and stations, the manpower levels could be run down to practical levels. A direct result of this was the ending of conscription in 1960, an event that had not only a social impact on the nation but also on the Army. Since 1945 conscription had ensured a steady flow of recruits for the ranks and the officer corps, and with them came the unwelcome chore of training the constant flow of bodies. But the constant flow also brought with it a healthy flow of ideas, attitudes and intellect that kept the Army more of a part of the mainstream of British society than it had ever been before. The Army, and the other armed services, became a factor of everyday life. Not everyone benefitted from the experience but as a general rule the nation gained from those who had 'done their bit' as they brought back into civilian life an independent outlook and education that often proved to be only slightly less effective than a university education. The Army gained through the understanding of its role, traditions and methods, as well as by the number of technically-minded and educated civilians who left their considerable mark. With the passing away of conscription the Army lost a great deal.

When the burden of conscription was removed, the Army reverted to what soon proved to be very much its former structure. It once more became a highly-trained professional body that rightly or wrongly gradually re-established itself as a closed society. With the withdrawal of a transient population, the long-term soldiers were again able to become more involved members of the family spirit and cameraderie provided by their regiments and corps. Gradually the old social patterns reappeared. The officer corps once more became a group that drew its carefully selected members from an elite formed by the upper echelons of the British class system, while the rank and file once again drew the bulk of their number from the established working class. Fortunately, the total withdrawal of the Army into its former social shell did not take place—it was not allowed to, and neither did the Army wish it to happen. Many factors combined to keep the Army a greater part of the general mainstream of British life. The Army had learned during World War 2 that public relations were important to ensure a stream of the right sort of recruits and also to put forward its political and financial messages. Perhaps the most important factor in the social change was that the Army became a married Army. In the old days prior to 1939 few soldiers were able to marry and obtain married quarters for their wives and families. But by the mid-1950s, the regular soldier was often a married man with a family. The Army had to provide not only married quarters but

schools, shopping centres and all the myriad medical and social services needed by garrisons at home and abroad. The huge civilian population that has gradually attached itself to the Army (not forgetting the thousands of civilians who now carry out jobs and roles once filled by serving soldiers) has ensured the Army has a sensibility to civilian needs.

The new 'civilian' stance of the armed service was to a great extent responsible for the fact that the Army has not reverted to the old 'huntin' and polo' days of the 1920s and 1930s, but it was not the only influence. The Army of the 1960s and 1970s soon showed itself to be far more professional and far more concerned with technical competence than its predecessors. The impact of the growth in general education made this improvement possible but it was a change imposed by the very nature of the role the modern soldier has to execute. He is now a highly-trained and competent technician in many fields, and the days when all he had to learn about were his rifle and foot drill have long since gone. His equipment is now so complex and expensive that he has had to learn many new techniques and skills derived from commerce and industry in order to remain abreast of the many changes in technology and man management that emerge year by year, and both in their turn have formed a bridge between the Army and the rest of the nation.

The main problem for the Army of the 1960s and the 1970s was that the new skills had to be learned in a period of constant turmoil and change, while at the same time the size and format of the Army were diminishing. Year after year, the manpower levels of the Army declined and progressive Defence spending cuts prevented the procurement of new equipment or facilities. Trained manpower gradually left the service and recruiting levels fell to the point where the Army reached its present level of about 160,000 men. For the Army the main problem was that they were still called upon to carry out many roles that had not been foreseen. It was at one time thought that the retreat from Empire had virtually ended after Aden, but it was not so. The Army was constantly being asked to provide formations to police various trouble spots all over the world, and to provide aid and assistance to all manner of bodies. In the Far East the Brunei and Borneo campaigns were typical of many 'Brushfire' conflicts, while on the other side of the globe, Central America was often a potential trouble spot. These constant forays abroad were a drain away from the main task of providing a meaningful presence in Europe and NATO, but to add to it all the events in Northern Ireland from late 1968 onwards necessitated the stationing there of a large permanent force of troops that has at times numbered some 21,000 men. Such numbers could only be achieved by the adoption of four-month tours (now $4\frac{1}{2}$-month) by all manner of combatant and non-combatant units which has greatly added to the problems of training and the establishment of fully-effective units.

To some extent the Army itself has added to its troubles by the retention of a regimental system that is now outmoded and inefficient. The regimental system built up by the British Army over many years has grown into an established form in which nearly every regiment and corps jealously guards its own particular honours, customs and idiosyncrasies. Based on what is very often a territorial recruiting area, each regiment or corps forms a family for its members and fosters a unit spirit that is almost impossible to intrude upon or break. While this system has many advantages in forming pride and a feeling of mutual trust within a formation it has inevitably led to a lack of co-operation between even different formations of the same divisions of the Army, and it has made inter-posting very difficult indeed. While many foreign armies regard the British regimental system highly, it is noticeable that few of them (other than the armies

established by the British themselves) have adopted it, and retain a corps establishment with unified training methods and mutual inter-dependability. Within the British Army the regimental system was at its most pronounced with the Infantry, but the rundown in manpower levels enforced the amalgamation of many fiercely independent regiments and the virtual abolition of some. Traditionalists both within and without the Army fought many hard campaigns to prevent the disappearance of famous regimental names, but the acceptance of the battle group as a combat formation further dictated the changes. In the end the Infantry adopted a typical British compromise. The regimental system stayed, but within a new structure of five administrative divisions. Within each division, the regiments, or such of them that remained recognisable, were regarded as mutually-supporting units, but only within their own particular division. Only the Guards and the Parachute Regiment remained outside the new reorganisation (at the cost of having their numbers attenuated)

Always in the front line, a member of the Ulster Defence Regiment manning a sentry post (AIS NI).

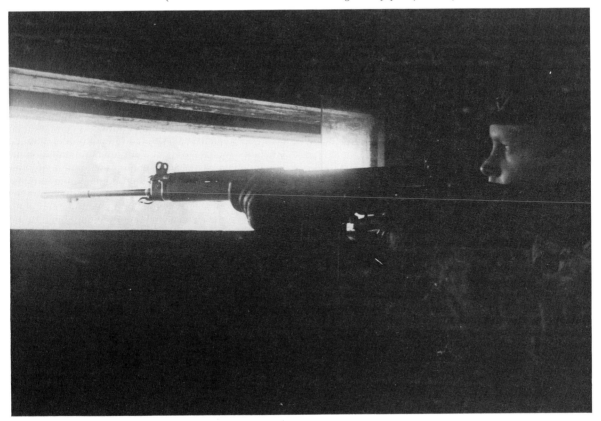

which took effect initially from 1958 to 1961, and the final touches were added during 1967.

The emergence of the battle group as a tactical formation also took place over an extended period, but it is now the established method of using Infantry and their supporting arms in modern warfare. Like so many innovations that were thrust upon the Army by a combination of tactical experience and financial strictures, the battle group and combat team concept has had a mixed reception, but its adoption has imposed its own command and administration difficulties. The old 'company, battalion, division, corps . . . ' hierarchy could not be adopted to suit the newer and more flexible battle group philosophy, so a new battle command structure was derived and is dealt with elsewhere in these pages. The new organisation was set in motion during the mid-1970s and received its first full test in large scale exercises within BAOR during 1976.

With the new structure came new command, communication and information systems, aimed not only at time-saving but also at savings in precious manpower. The four-armoured-division structure settled down to become the 1 (BR) Corps form, around which grew an established running and administrative routine to which future planning could be fixed. New communication and administration systems were designed and projected around the structure to the extent that when changes were imposed from without during 1981 the results were out of all proportion to those intended. The Thatcher government imposed strict restrictions on all facets of government spending and the defence establishment had to bear its share of the resultant cuts. In the event, the Army came off relatively lightly in cash terms, but it meant that one of the four armoured division headquarters had to be redeployed to the United Kingdom. In the upheaval, the armoured division concerned became an infantry division in the process and the carefully structured four-armoured-division Corps was transformed into three armoured divisions and one infantry division. With it, all future planning for such systems as Bates and Wavell were also put into uproar. The old system, which had been put to the test during the large scale international 'Crusader' exercises in 1980.

The Army then settled down to what promised to be a period of relative stability. Northern Ireland was no longer a major drain on resources and there were prospects that an end to any involvement in Belize was in the foreseeable future. New training areas in Kenya promised the chance of at least slightly more exotic locations than Minden and, despite all the spending cuts and the greater emphasis on personal fitness of all ranks, Service life seemed about to settle down to what passes for normal in the Army.

Then in 1982 it all blew up when Argentina invaded the Falkland Islands. Within days of the invasion virtually every sector of the Army was in uproar as men, supplies and equipment were hastily assembled for the expedition south. The units in Germany were relatively unaffected but what was then 5 Infantry Brigade was put on a combat footing and, after only a limited amount of training, travelled to the South Atlantic. The world now knows the course and nature of the Falklands' campaign but suffice to say it had, and still has, a profound effect on the Army. Men are still spending time there on their various tours and equipment changes discovered necessary in the aftermath of a 'shooting war' are still reaching the troops.

In retrospect the Falklands' campaign can be seen as a carry-over into the modern era of an old-style colonial campaign. In time-honoured fashion the Royal Navy escorted the expeditionary force to the battle area, the islands were duly invaded and under what top cover the Royal Air Force and Fleet Air Arm could supply, the Army duly marched across the islands and took the main objective, Port Stanley. The hapless Argentinian conscripts fought back with amazing ferocity at times, while on other occasions they seemed to be quite happy to give up after only a token struggle. Some of the feats of arms will go down into military history, the Paras' battle at Goose Green being perhaps the most remembered. But there were other equally hard slogs, especially in the final approaches to Port Stanley. When it was all over the celebrations gave the nation a real tonic for a while, but already the campaign appears to have submerged into the nation's long-term memory bank and references to the Falklands now deal mainly with the costs involved in keeping the garrison there. This is not entirely surprising for the problems are now almost all logistic, for everything has to be taken to the Islands along a very long chain and the expense involved is enormous.

In fact the word 'costs' seems to be cropping up more and more as the months go by, not only in relation to the Falklands but relating to the Armed Forces as a whole. In an era when military costs keep escalating, more and more queries are being raised about military spending, despite the fact that—as far as the troops are concerned—they are already running on a shoe-string. New equipment of all types is on the way but to pay for it the Army has had to make some drastic prunings, not only in the levels of equipment being supplied but in day-to-day operating methods. The recent operation 'Lean Look' has resulted in more men being taken away from the administrative 'tail' of the Army to be deployed nearer the 'teeth', but this has not yet resulted in a more efficient machine. It has rather had the opposite effect, although many would argue to the contrary. Army manning rates have for long been such that every man has had his important place to fill, and if for any reason that man is taken elsewhere it merely places an extra burden on those left behind. While it is encouraging to know that the new equipment now in use is being manned properly, one wonders exactly how that important administrative and logistic tail will function if it should ever be put under any more pressure than at present.

This last paragraph perhaps outlines what is now the Army's greatest weakness. It is superbly equipped, although there are still a few important and long-term gaps that need filling, and its fighting potential is considerable and far outweighs its relative shortfall in numbers. It is on the personnel side that the strain is still showing. The Army is today a highly technical Army, from the front-line soldier to the computer-wielding 'admin' personnel far to the rear. The Army is finding it increasingly difficult to obtain the right type of long-serving soldier to maintain even present manning levels, and quite as difficult as finding those men is simply keeping them. The present-day Army has some excellent men at every level but more and more of them are finding the attractions of civilian life hard to resist. It is not just a matter of money, for although current pay rates are not exactly over-lavish, they are no longer the source of mutterings that they once were. It is rather a reflection of the pace and manning levels that the Army has to endure. Long-term soldiers are leaving the Army, not from any deep-seated dissatisfaction with Service life but for a whole host of reasons which seem to be overlooked. The long-serving technicians that the Army so desperately wants to keep are leaving when they can for the sort of reason that comes to all after a long period of service. These types of soldiers (whatever their rank) are no longer attracted by long-term postings or detachments away from their families, which are caused by lack of manpower, to fulfil further tasks over and above their normal ones. They are increasingly disaffected by having to wait months for spare parts to get important items of equipment back into use. What is perhaps more important is that many soldiers feel that, despite the now-faded euphoria of the Falklands campaign, they are no longer valued by the nation as a whole. Instead, every one of their actions or requests for new equipment or facilities is being queried in ever more strident terms.

There is also the feeling, not often voiced from within, that the Army is too small for its many tasks. Leaving aside all the various overseas commitments, the modern Army *is* really too small for its operational role in Germany, or thus runs the argument. Even though the British Army operates as only a part of a much larger NATO Army, there is still the feeling that the troops on the ground are too few in number for their operational role. All too often the assumption seems to be made that the reserves and TA and the all-important Regular units based in the United Kingdom will have time to make the difficult journey to their combat areas during any period of tension. The prospect of defending the 1 (BR) Corps area with only the troops based in Germany appears to be increasingly overlooked. Instead, plans seem to be afoot to bring back even more men to the United Kingdom to save money (exactly how is never outlined). Once again the contribution of the Army to the way we live appears to be in danger of being under-valued and queried.

Soldiers are not automata and they can sense that already their importance to the nation as a whole is once more reaching the point that has so often prevailed in the past. They are seen as a constant cost to the exchequer, a cost that can only be borne by paring everything to the bone and keeping manpower down. So once again it seems that (with the Falklands' campaign fading into memory) the nation can quietly look the other way while numbers and equipment levels can gradually sink way below the safety levels that are known to exist. The parallels of 1914 and 1939 are not just prospects, they are with us now, and it is too much to expect that in any future conflict the ultimate victories of two World Wars will necessarily occur again. The old lesson that those who desire peace should prepare for war is one that is in danger of being forgotten once more; also being forgotten is the fact that in those same two World Wars it was the soldiers who had to pay for the omissions—with their lives.

Still, the Army is acquiring some excellent new equipment and its internal organisation is being constantly churned to meet commitments and present manpower levels. This third edition of the *Encyclopaedia of the Modern British Army* appears to be a very different book from the first which was prepared only a few short years ago, but it is basically the same under the array of new titles and gleaming new equipment. Let us just hope that the subject the book deals with never has to be used for the purpose it is maintained to fulfil, since any future war in Europe will be the last war any of us will know.

The Army in action since 1945

Trieste	1945-1954
Java/Sumatra	1945
Greece	1945-1947
Canal Zone/Egypt	1946-1954
India	1945-1948
Palestine	1945-1948
Aden	1947

Northern Ireland	1947-1948	Zanzibar	1963
Gold Coast	1948	Swaziland	1963-1966
British Honduras	1948	Cyprus	1963-?
Eritrea	1948-1951	British Guiana	1963
Malaya	1948-1960	Zanzibar	1964
Somaliland	1949-1951	Kenya/Uganda/Tanganyika	1964
Aqaba	1949	Radfan	1964-1967
Singapore	1950	Mauritius	1965
Korea	1950-1953	Oman	1965-1977
Aqaba	1951	Hong Kong	1966
Kenya	1952-1956	Seychelles	1966
British Guiana	1953	Hong Kong	1967
Cyprus	1954-1959	Libya	1967
Aden	1955-1958	Northern Ireland	1969-?
Singapore	1955-1956	Anguilla	1969-1971
Hong Kong	1956	Dhofar	1969-1976
Bahrein	1956-1957	Cyprus	1974
Suez	1956	Belize	1976-?
Belize	1957	Zimbabwe-Rhodesia	1979-1980
Muscat and Oman	1957-1959	Falkland Islands	1982-?
Togoland	1957	Lebanon	1983
Jordan and Lebanon	1958		
Gan	1959		
Cameroons	1960		
Jamaica	1960		
Bahamas	1961		
Kuwait	1961		
British Guiana	1962		
Belize	1962		
Malaysia/Borneo	1962-1966		

NB The above list is not complete as the Army has frequently been asked to assist various governments at times of crisis and it has often had to be called in to help after natural disasters when the efforts needed were often greater than those involved in a military campaign.

Organisation

In many publications, including the popular Press, it is usual to assume that the Army somehow organises itself along its own lines and functions in seeming isolation from outside influences. Not so. The Army has definite lines of command from which it assumes its direction, lines of command that reach up to Cabinet level where the Army receives its instructions as the instrument of an elected political executive. At Cabinet level the responsibility for defence matters rests with the Secretary of State for Defence but in practice his powers are delegated through a system of councils, boards and committees that form a tangle through which the lay reader would find it almost impossible to wade. I shall not attempt an outline of these delegated functions here other than to mention the Defence Council which is under the chairmanship of the Secretary of State and acts as the legal authority for the actual control of the three armed Services. This Council not only commands the three Services but is responsible for their administration and in turn advises the Cabinet on defence affairs. Each Service has its own Board of the Defence Council and the Army Board exercises control of the Army.

The professional head of the Army is the Chief of the General Staff, or CGS, and to him answer the three main members of the Army Council. They are the Officer Commanding Headquarters British Army of the Rhine (HQ BAOR), the Officer Commanding Headquarters United Kingdom Land Forces (HQ UKLF) and the Officer Commanding the Overseas Garrisons which stretch from Hong Kong to the Falkland Islands.

This division of the Army into its three main parts emphasises the important point that today it is no longer a purely British national army. It is part of a much larger defensive force organised under the auspices of NATO and in a global emergency would operate not solely in British interests but as part of a force defending Europe. To this end the bulk of the British Army is based not in the United Kingdom but in West Germany. Those formations resident in the United Kingdom would be used to reinforce the units already in West Germany or to supply them and generally act in their support. Only a relatively small proportion would be used for home defence. The strategy now adopted is that the United Kingdom can best be defended in Europe with the Army acting as part of the NATO forces. Thus, BAOR acts as the main operational element of the Army with the UKLF in support. The Overseas Garrisons are retained for various reasons of both local and national interest.

Within NATO the Army does not act in isolation: BAOR has been assigned a sector of the North German Plain to defend but even here it is acting as only part of a much larger plan. The sector assigned to BAOR is part of the domain of Armed Forces Central Europe, or AF CENT. In its turn AF CENT is but one of three defence groups (the others being AF NORTH and AF SOUTH) that report to Supreme Headquarters Allied Powers Europe (SHAPE) via the Supreme Commander European Region (SACEUR) with his base near Mons in Belgium. AF CENT Headquarters is at Brunssum in the Netherlands.

In AF CENT there are two Army Groups, Northern Army Group (NORTHAG) and Central Army Group (CENTAG). The British Army combat element of BAOR forms part of NORTHAG, and is known as 1 (BR) Corps. The NORTHAG headquarters are at Mönchengladbach and in time of war the Army Group would be commanded by the then current OC (officer commanding) BAOR. In peace every national element of NORTHAG remains under national control, apart from small elements who are permanently assigned to NATO staff functions, so only in an emergency would 1 (BR) Corps come under direct NATO control. Under such circumstances 1 (BR) Corps would be joined by similar formations from the Netherlands, West Germany and Belgium.

The NORTHAG operational area extends from Hamburg down to Kassel and from the Netherlands border to the Inner German Border (IGB) that marks

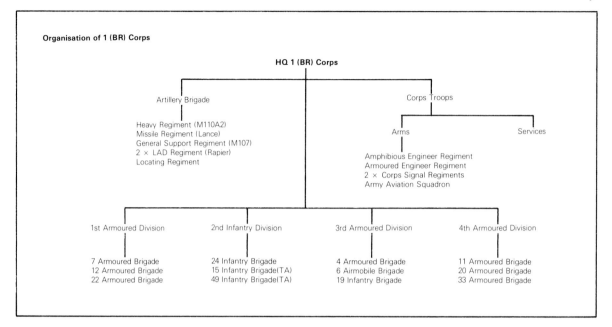

Organisation of 1 (BR) Corps

HQ 1 (BR) Corps

Artillery Brigade

Heavy Regiment (M110A2)
Missile Regiment (Lance)
General Support Regiment (M107)
2 × LAD Regiment (Rapier)
Locating Regiment

Corps Troops

Arms

Amphibious Engineer Regiment
Armoured Engineer Regiment
2 × Corps Signal Regiments
Army Aviation Squadron

Services

1st Armoured Division

7 Armoured Brigade
12 Armoured Brigade
22 Armoured Brigade

2nd Infantry Division

24 Infantry Brigade
15 Infantry Brigade (TA)
49 Infantry Brigade (TA)

3rd Armoured Division

4 Armoured Brigade
6 Airmobile Brigade
19 Infantry Brigade

4th Armoured Division

11 Armoured Brigade
20 Armoured Brigade
33 Armoured Brigade

the boundaries of East and West Germany. In the north is 1 (NL) Corps, headquartered at Apeldoorn, with 1 (GE) Corps next to its south (headquarters at Münster in peacetime). Then comes 1 (BR) Corps with its headquarters at Bielefeld. The southernmost formation of NORTHAG is 1 (BE) Corps with its headquarters at Köln-Junkersdorf.

The 1 (BR) Corps area extends from a line just north of Hannover down to a line just north of Kassel. The Corps area extends from the IGB back to a line just to the west of Soest but the BAOR boundary itself extends right back to Antwerp for BAOR has two main elements. One is the operational 1 (BR) Corps and the other Rhine Area. The latter is a peacetime organisation. If a war occurred it would become British Support Command, or BRSC. The BRSC supplies 1 (BR) Corps and guards the areas back to the ports through which the manpower for 1 (BR) Corps reinforcements would have to travel, along with all the logistic supplies for the Corps.

1 (BR) CORPS

1 (BR) Corps is the main combat formation of the British Army. Within the Corps are the bulk of the Army's combat elements and at any time the Corps could be made ready for action very quickly indeed. For prolonged combat it would require manpower from the United Kingdom, for recent defence expenditure re-arrangements have dictated that some of the Corps' manpower has to reside in the United Kingdom.

The main outline of 1 (BR) Corps organisation can

be seen in the accompanying organisation 'tree'. There are four main combat divisions—the 1st, 3rd and 4th Armoured Divisions and the 2nd Infantry Division. The 1st Armoured Division is head-quartered at Verden, the 3rd at Soest and the 4th at Herford. The 2nd Infantry Division has its head-quarters back in York, in the United Kingdom, and in an emergency it would have to travel with much of its equipment across to Germany where it would be used to guard 1 (BR) Corps' lines of communications and general rear areas. Part of 3rd Armoured Division also resides in the United Kingdom (19 Infantry Brigade at Colchester). The 2nd Infantry Division maintains a small forward headquarters at Lubbecke.

In time of peace the various units that make up 1 (BR) Corps are scattered in garrisons all over West Germany. In an emergency they would advance to their allocated combat positions with 1st and 4th Armoured Divisions forward (1st to the north) and 3rd Armoured Division to the rear in support.

1 (BR) Corps also has an Artillery Brigade, now known as HQRA 1(BR) Corps. Each of the four principal divisions described above have their own artillery increments of three Field Regiments apiece but the Artillery Brigade is held under Corps control and is allocated as thought fit by the Corps Com-mander. The Artillery Brigade is a powerful force for it contains the Corps' nuclear capability in the form of the Lance and M110A2 batteries. There are also two counter-battery M107 Regiments and two air defence regiments. A Locating Regiment

supplies artillery data for the entire Corps.

Also under direct Corps command are the Corps troops. These include two specialised Engineer Regiments, one amphibious for rapid bridging and the other armoured for combat engineer support for the armoured formations. There are two Corps Signal Regiments, one connecting forward to the front lines and the other to the rear, back to NORTHAG and beyond. There is also a Corps aviation unit.

When on a full war footing 1 (BR) Corps would number about 55,000 troops, over 600 tanks and 120 helicopters, to say nothing of the many armoured personnel carriers and other armoured vehicles. Backing them up would be numerous 'B' vehicles. These totals are dependent on manpower arriving from the United Kingdom, and additional personnel would arrive from Territorial Army sources.

The Armoured Division

The three armoured divisions all differ slightly from one another, as each has its own particular operational task and its own particular problems to face—for instance, the 3rd Armoured Division has one of its brigades located back in the United Kingdom. Each division has three armoured brigades and within these brigades (once known as 'task forces', a term that was never widely understood) are combat forces known as battle groups.

The armoured division uses the organisation shown in the 'tree' only for general administrative and other purposes. Once on the battlefield the three brigades split up into battle groups; however, the composition of a battle group is not easy to define for each is formed to meet a specific combat task over a particular piece of terrain. In theory each battle group is a balanced mix of armour, infantry and support but the actual balance and numbers involved will vary widely. For instance, some battle groups would have virtually no armour while others would have a proportionately larger armoured element. Some battle groups would be light on anti-tank defences while others would be almost entirely anti-tank orientated. Part of this disparity is due to the nature of the terrain in the Corps area. In the north it is largely open plain while in the south are the closer confines of the Harz

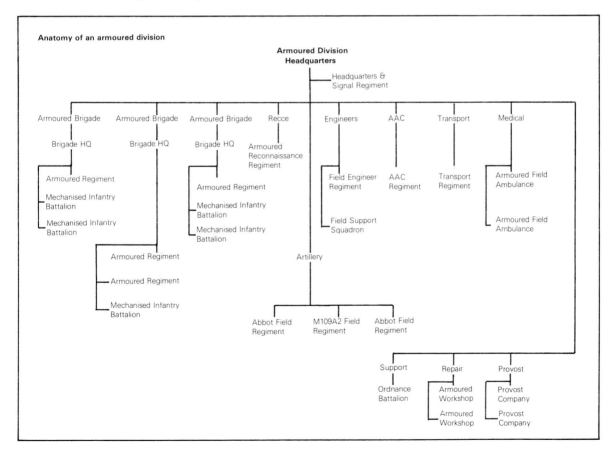

Mountains, both offering their own peculiar defence challenges.

The overall organisation of the armoured division and its three brigades is flexible to meet any likely scenario that might emerge. In theory battle groups can be augmented or re-structured as a local commander sees fit but in normal peacetime practice units can train to expect support and co-operation from other specific units. For instance, one particular artillery battery can expect to fire in support of one particular infantry battalion.

One special brigade within 1 (BR) Corps is 6 Airmobile Brigade, part of the 3rd Armoured Division. As an experiment this brigade has been equipped with a larger than usual complement of Milan anti-tank missiles (over 40 Milan firing posts to a battalion in place of the normal 26) to be moved by Puma or Chinook helicopters to any threatened sector of the battlefield. This will provide the Corps commander with a rapid-response anti-tank weapon. These mobile missile teams would be supported by artillery but the whole exercise depends on precious helicopters which may well be not available when needed, or alternatively may be used for the anti-tank defence team role to the extent that the other customers for the helicopters may suffer accordingly. As a result the 6 Airmobile Brigade concept is still experimental.

UKLF

United Kingdom Land Forces (UKLF) is the main supplier, trainer and personnel source for BAOR. It even acts as the base for BAOR units, namely the three Infantry Brigades of the 2nd Infantry Division and 19 Infantry Brigade. Other front-line combat elements of UKLF are 1 Infantry Brigade and 5 Airborne Brigade.

1 Infantry Brigade has a complex role for it is earmarked for the direct command of the Commander Allied Command Europe (ACE) who has his headquarters at SHAPE, near Mons. Under his command 1 Infantry Brigade acts as a central reserve for NATO but it also forms the basis of the United Kingdom Mobile Force (Land) or AMF(L). Based at Seckenheim, the AMF(L) is a multi-national force designed for the rapid reinforcement of the NATO flanks in Norway and Turkey. The British contribution to AMF(L) consists in the main of 1 Infantry Brigade plus a logistic support group and other elements. With ACE, 1 Infantry Brigade becomes part of the SACEUR Strategic Reserve, or SSR (SSR will also be allocated three SAS squadrons).

5 Airborne Brigade also has two roles. It used to be 5 Infantry Brigade and as such fought in the latter part of the Falkland Islands' campaign, after which it assumed the Airborne title to indicate its new role. It is primarily meant for the defence of the United

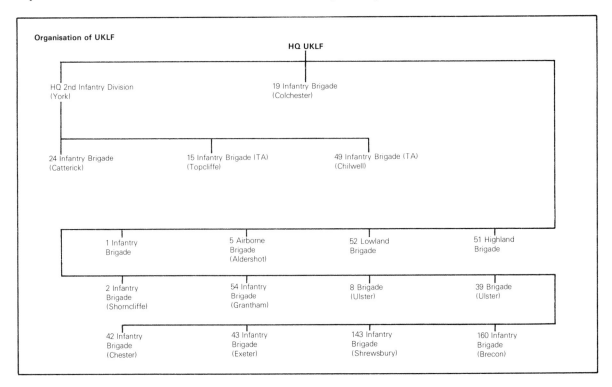

Kingdom but it also acts as a highly mobile 'fire-fighting' force for use whenever British interests might require its services. The Falkland Islands were an extreme example of this form of national interest but there might well be other smaller brushfire conflicts in remote parts of the world where a small armed force could do much to protect lives and property. Thus parts of 5 Airborne Brigade (headquartered at Aldershot) are on constant states of readiness for a sudden move virtually anywhere.

Within the United Kingdom a number of Military Districts are used to command and administer brigades within their boundaries. In order to create this District/Brigade command structure a number of brigades have been formed which can be seen in the accompanying UKLF organisation 'tree', the last of them being brought into existence during 1984. This structure is mainly for peace-time administration because in time of war the units within the District/Brigade boundaries would move away to their own particular allocations in BAOR, leaving the remaining home defence units, training schools and other units under District/Brigade command for local defence.

HQ UKLF is at Wilton, just outside Salisbury in Wiltshire. This headquarters commands the Military Districts as follows: London (HQ Horse Guards); Northern Ireland (Lisburn); North West District (Preston); Scotland (Edinburgh); Wales (Brecon); Western District (Shrewsbury); North East District (York—combined with HQ 2nd Infantry Division); South East District (Aldershot); and South West District (Taunton). Some of these Military Districts are co-located with one of the brigades under their command.

Overseas Garrisons

The British Army is still stationed at a surprising number of places around the world. One which must be mentioned right away is Berlin, where the Berlin Brigade is not part of BAOR but is maintained in the city as part of the 1945 Berlin Treaty. It remains in West Berlin together with a French and an American garrison and consists of some 3,000 soldiers organised as the Berlin Infantry Brigade. This brigade has three infantry battalions, an armoured squadron and a number of support units. It is not really part of the Overseas Garrisons structure but is treated as a special plum posting, mainly due to the special monetary rates of exchange which are still tied to the 1945 Treaty scales.

In Central America, Belize is still the location for an Army presence although at the time of writing the end of this commitment was considered to be foreseeable. Much of the manpower used in Belize is on a roulement basis with one infantry battalion plus a few companies on a tour from UKLF duties. In support there is an armoured reconnaissance troop, a Gunner battery, a Blowpipe Troop, a Royal Engineer Field Squadron and an AAC helicopter flight. Most units take the opportunity to combine guard and patrol duties with jungle-type training during their tours.

Cyprus is a much larger base but there the Army has two roles. Part of its strength is used to defend the Sovereign Base Areas that have been retained since 1960 when Cyprus became an independent nation. There are two of these Sovereign Base Areas (SBAs). The Eastern SBA contains Dhekelia and Ayios Nikolaios while the Western SBA contains Episkopi and Akrotiri. Within these SBAs the Army guards the SBAs themselves and provides troops and general support for UNFICYP (see below). They also generally look after NATO interests in their part of the Mediterranean and provide logistic support for the United Nations' Interim Forces and others operating in Lebanon (UNIFIL). In the SBAs are an infantry battalion plus two extra companies, an armoured reconnaissance squadron, an Engineer Support Squadron and an AAC flight.

The Army also acts as part of a United Nations Peacekeeping Force patrolling the dividing line between the Greek and Turkish areas of Cyprus. This is known as UNFICYP (United Nations Forces In CYPrus) and is separate from the SBA force. The UNFICYP contribution from the Army consists of an infantry battalion less two companies, an armoured reconnaissance squadron and an AAC flight. There is also a Royal Air Force Wessex helicopter flight.

At the opposite end of the Mediterranean the United Kingdom's long association with Gibraltar continues. On the Rock the locally recruited Gibraltar Regiment defends the Rock in its spare time alongside a full-time infantry battalion, a Royal Artillery surveillance battery and a Specialist Team Royal Engineers who continue to run many of the social amenities used by both the military and civil population (such as water supply). Gibraltar is still an important NATO communications and surveillance base.

In the South Atlantic the Falkland Islands still retain a sizeable Army garrison but at the time of writing the military population is in decline. Many of the major clearing-up and rebuilding tasks necessary following the 1982 campaign have now been completed and the new installations such as a radar surveillance system have been finished. The most important of the new constructions must be the airport at Mount Pleasant which will enable reinforcements to be flown to the Islands in an emergency so the past (and expensive) levels of manning will no longer be required. At times in the past the Falklands have been a major drain on manpower levels elsewhere but that period is now almost over and the Islands' garrison will probably be just a single infantry battalion, a gunner presence (air defence as well as field artillery), engineer support and an armoured reconnaissance unit. The AAC will no doubt retain a unit but these force levels are conjectures and hopefully they will never be called upon to be reinforced.

The largest Army Overseas Garrison is now in Hong Kong. However, much of the manpower involved is drawn from the Gurkha Field Force of four battalions together with Gurkha transport, engineer and signals support. Included in the Field Force is a single United Kingdom infantry battalion and an AAC squadron. (There is a further Gurkha battalion based in Brunei at the local Sultan's expense.) The Hong Kong Field Force is used for both internal and external security but is also usually involved in routine aid to the Civil Community of all kinds ranging from relief in the aftermath of a typhoon to arranging local water supplies and other utilities for the teeming local population.

That leaves Northern Ireland which is not, of course, an Overseas Garrison but part of the United Kingdom. Nevertheless, since 1969 the Army has been present in the Province in numbers well in excess of normal peacetime garrison duties and still the levels of violence prevalent in the Six Counties show no signs of diminishing to an acceptable level. The Army still has its own separate headquarters there for reporting purposes and maintains two brigades in the Province but the manpower involvement is now way below what it was about ten years ago. The disliked 'Operation Banner' roulement process has now all but faded away as the local police authorities assume many of the duties once carried out by the Army and in the main metropolitan centres the Army no longer has to carry out routine patrol duties. In the border areas, however, the Army is still called upon for patrols and guard duties and provides general support to the civil authorities.

On a more cheerful note the British Army currently has advisory or training teams in over 25 countries scattered around the world. They take with them the Army's outlook on training, operational methods and equipment and quietly act as low-key ambassadors. In return they usually enjoy the sort of military sense of adventure and variety that had seemingly all but passed away. Thus British soldiers still find themselves operating in desert regions, hacking their way through jungles and building bridges in remote wastes. Life in the modern Army is still not all boredom in German barracks or British garrison towns. Soldiers can still expect to see a bit of sun and unfamiliar terrain during their Service careers.

The Household Cavalry, The Royal Armoured Corps and the Yeomanry

What was once generally termed the Cavalry is now separated into three groupings. They are the Household Cavalry, the Royal Armoured Corps (RAC) and the Yeomanry. Between them they provide all the armoured components of the British Army, namely the armoured regiments and the armoured reconnaissance regiments. Within each grouping the regiments concerned are as follows:

The Household Cavalry: The Life Guards (LG) and the Blues and Royals (RHG/D);

The Royal Armoured Corps (RAC): 1st the Queen's Dragoon Guards (QDG), The Royal Scots Dragoon Guards (SCOTS DG), 4th/7th Royal Dragoon Guards (4/7 DG), 5th Royal Inniskilling Dragoon Guards (5 INNIS DG), The Queen's Own Hussars (QOH), The Queen's Royal Irish Hussars (QRIH), 9th/12th Royal Lancers (9/12L), The Royal Hussars (RH), 13th/18th Royal Hussars (13/18H), 14th/20th King's Hussars (14/20H), 15th/19th The King's Royal Hussars (15/19H), 16th/5th The Queen's Royal Lancers (16/5L), 17th/21st Lancers (17/21L), 1st Royal Tank Regiment (1 RTR), 2nd Royal Tank Regiment (2 RTR), 3rd Royal Tank Regiment (3 RTR) and 4th Royal Tank Regiment (4 RTR);

The Yeomanry: The Royal Yeomanry (RY), The Queen's Own Yeomanry (QOY), The Royal Wessex Yeomanry (RWxY), The Queen's Own Mercian Yeomanry (QOMY) and the Duke of Lancaster's Own Yeomanry (DLOY).

The above resounding array of titles tends to distract one from the fact that in the modern Army the role of the old Cavalry has changed drastically from the time when it carried out its historic tasks with panache and splendour, although many traditions remain. Today these regiments have to function within the framework of an organisational arrangement which has more in keeping with the distant past than the grim efficiency of today, but in recent years reshuffles and some amalgamations have enabled a working arrangement to be reached.

The Household Cavalry, the RAC and the Yeomanry have to provide the manpower for three types of battle formation, the armoured regiment, the armoured reconnaissance regiment and the light reconnaissance regiment—the latter is a matter for the Yeomanry. For the rest, regiments are likely to exchange their roles and equipments to fulfil either commitment, so it is not possible in a book of this nature to specify exactly which regiment will be

Cavalry badges. 1 *The Life Guards.* **2** *The Blues and Royals.* **3** *1st The Queen's Dragoon Guards.* **4** *The Royal Scots Dragoon Guards.* **5** *4th/7th Royal Dragoon Guards.* **6** *5th Royal Inniskilling Dragoon Guards.* **7** *The Queen's Own Hussars.* **8** *The Queen's Royal Irish Hussars.* **9** *9th/12th Royal Lancers.* **10** *The Royal Hussars.* **11** *13th/18th Royal Hussars.* **12** *14th/20th King's Hussars.* **13** *15th/19th The King's Royal Hussars.* **14** *16th/5th The Queen's Royal Lancers.* **15** *17th/21st Lancers.* **16** *The Royal Tank Regiment.*

involved in a particular role at any specific time. For instance, within the Household Cavalry, the regiments are either part of BAOR or are based in the United Kingdom (although other postings are possible). When in the United Kingdom they carry out their well-known ceremonial duties, but they also man an armoured reconnaissance regiment. As there are variations between the types of armoured formations they are best dealt with under separate headings.

The armoured regiment

There are now 13 armoured regiments in the British Army, of which 12 are based in BAOR. There is also a composite training regiment at Bovington. These armoured regiments are known as Armoured Regiments Type 57 or 43, depending on the number of main battle tanks (MBTs) they have; these days a MBT could be either a Challenger or a Chieftain.

The BAOR armoured regiments are distributed among the three armoured divisions of 1 (BR) Corps, but there is an extra armoured squadron equipped with Chieftains assigned to the Berlin Brigade. (The Berlin squadron's manpower comes from what would be the fourth squadron of one of the Type 43 regiments.)

The organisation and equipment levels of the Type 57 and 43 armoured regiments can be seen in the following table. Each regiment has a regimental headquarters (RHQ), a headquarters squadron (HQ Sqn) and four armoured squadrons (only three in a Type 43 regiment). The armoured squadrons are sometimes known as Sabre squadrons. Within each squadron there is the Squadron Headquarters

(SHQ—not to be confused with the headquarters squadron) with two MBT control tanks fitted with extra Clansman radio sets, one of which is usually fitted with a 'dozer blade. Each of the four Tank Troops (Tk Tp) has three MBTs. There is now no first line war reserve—all the MBTs a regiment has are kept with the regiment all the time. There are also administrative and REME light aid detachments (LAD) at both regimental and squadron levels.

The armoured regiment has three main roles in time of war, as follows: 1) Aggressive mobile action to destroy the enemy's armour; 2) Close combat in

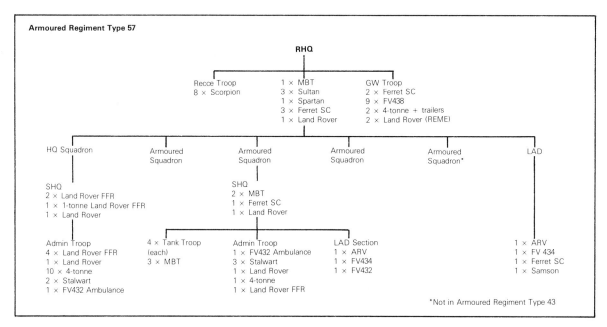

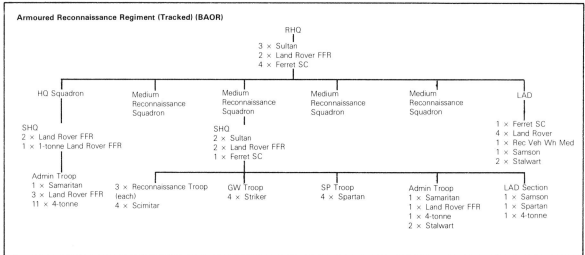

Chieftains moving up during an exercise in Germany.

conjunction with the Infantry; 3) The exploitation of shock action, ie, using to the full the primary tactical characteristics of the tank—firepower, protection, mobility and flexibility.

None of these roles can be fully carried out by the armoured regiment alone, so they are distributed under the control of task force commanders into battle groups. Within a battle group are the combat team, each of which is formed according to its particular role or the type of terrain it has to cover. The usual combat team consists of an armoured squadron combined with platoons of mechanised infantry and a troop of combat engineers. Thus the armoured regiments, within the battle group concept, have the following operational tasks: 1) Defensive operations, in both mobile and static situations; 2) Counterattack and counter-penetration; 3) Exploitation in support of nuclear warfare; 4) Covering force operations; 5) Advancing in contact with the enemy; 6) The assault and destruction of the enemy; 7) Penetration, exploitation and pursuit; and 8) Direct fire and other support of the Infantry.

The Armoured Regiment Type 57 incorporates several changes from the organisation which was in use until recently. One is that it now has its own integral reconnaissance troop of eight Scorpions, a factor which will warm the hearts of many 'tankies' who have for long had to rely upon reconnaissance from outside the regiment. This troop will be responsible for close reconnaissance rather than the broader battlefield reconnaissance provided by the armoured reconnaissance regiments. The other change is that each armoured regiment also has its own integral Guided Weapon (GW) Troop of nine FV438s armed with Swingfire, plus their support (to be withdrawn soon). Until comparatively recently the LRATGW role was carried out by the Royal Artillery, but this has now been switched to the RAC.

The armoured reconnaissance regiment

Compared to the straightforward organisation of the armoured regiments, the organisation of the armoured reconnaissance regiments is much more complicated. There are no fewer than three types of armoured reconnaissance and two types of Yeomanry reconnaissance regiment and all require some explanation. Before that is given, however, it would be as well to explain exactly what the roles of these formations are, for they are roles as old as warfare itself.

The primary role of the armoured reconnaissance regiments is to obtain accurate and useful information regarding the enemy and to pass this back to the appropriate command level in as short a time as possible. Any related information such as that pertaining to terrain, potential obstacles, etc, is dealt with in the same way. With this in mind, the armoured reconnaissance regiments have to rely on field craft, mastery of their equipment and good old-fashioned stealth to obtain their information—the use of firepower will often negate their intentions so firepower is thus a secondary consideration with regard to the vehicles and other equipment employed.

Whatever type of organisation each armoured reconnaissance regiment has, it has several tasks in a limited or a general war. They are as follows: 1) Covering defensive positions or withdrawals, usually in conjunction with other arms; 2) Observing obstacles; 3) Protection for the flanks of a formation; 4) Anti-helicopter or anti-airborne forces operations; 5) The advance to contact; 6) Independent raids and deep penetration missions; 7) Disruption in a pursuit situation; 8) Escort tasks for supply echelons and similar formations; 9) Major traffic control; and 10) Nuclear, Biological and Chemical reconnaissance.

The above tasks would be carried out during general warfare but the armoured reconnaisance regiments also have an important role to play during the various types of counter-revolutionary and counter-insurgency operations that now proliferate throughout the world. The light and handy vehicles involved in the reconnaissance role are also useful for a number of tasks in this demanding form of warfare, and in the British Army the FV721 Fox has shown itself to have considerable potential in this role. The major tasks anticipated for the reconnaissance regiments in counter-insurgency operations are: 1) Mobile patrolling, either by foot, vehicle or helicopter; 2) Manning observation points; 3) Road blocks and area cordons; 4) Escorting convoys, VIPs or important traffic; 5) General communications; 6) Crowd control and dispersal; and 7) Fire support for Infantry operations.

To return to organisation, perhaps the simplest to explain are the two armoured reconnaissance regiments that are part of 1 (BR) Corps. The exact organisation and equipment of these regiments can be seen in the accompanying table but it will be noted that each of the four Medium Recce Squadrons in each regiment has three Recce Troops, each with four Scimitars. Each squadron also has its own Guided Weapons Troop (GW Tp) of four Swingfire-armed Strikers, vehicles that merge very well with the others used by the regiment, and provide each squadron with a viable LRATGW role. There is also a Support Troop (SP Tp or Sp Tp) equipped with four Spartans.

These two 1 (BR) Corps regiments (at Herford and Wolfenbuttel) will be joined by a third from the United Kingdom in time of war for the support of the remaining armoured division. This regiment is known as the Armoured Reconnaissance Regiment (Tracked) (UK). The regiment concerned is based at Debden (Wimbish) and is one of two with identical equipment and organisation (see accompanying

table); the other regiment is based at Tidworth. These two regiments differ from their 1 (BR) Corps counterparts in having three Medium Recce Squadrons and a Guided Weapon Squadron—the GW Squadron has its own admin and LAD elements. Each of the Medium Recce Squadrons has four Recce Troops, each with two Scorpions and two Scimitars. There is also a Support Troop with five Spartans. The Tidworth-based regiment has to find one squadron for the ACE Mobile Force (Land).

There is still one more UK-based armoured reconnaissance regiment to mention and that is the Armoured Reconnaissance Regiment (UK) at Windsor. This is a dual-roled regiment that might be retained for Home Defence or assigned to some Out of Area task, and it has no LRATGW element. It has three Recce Squadrons, two wheeled (W) with FV721 Fox and the other tracked (T) with Scorpion. The exact organisation is, once again, provided in the accompanying table. It is this regiment that provides the armoured vehicles for the frequent anti-terrorist exercises held at London (Heathrow) Airport.

Before passing on to the Yeomanry there is one other Regular armoured reconnaissance squadron, based in Cyprus. This squadron has six troops each equipped with four Ferrets. This Cyprus squadron is the last operational unit still using the FV601(C) Saladin armoured car.

There are now five Yeomanry regiments, two known as Yeomanry Reconnaissance Regiments (BAOR) and intended for the reinforcement of units based in Germany. The other three regiments are light reconnaissance regiments for the Home Defence role only. They are known as Yeomanry Reconnaissance Regiments (UK) and are not armoured in any way, being based upon the use of civilian-model ¾-tonne Land Rovers.

The BAOR Yeomanry regiments are based on the FV721 Fox. By April 1986 both the Royal Yeomanry and the Queen's Own Yeomanry were to have four Recce Squadrons, each with five Recce Troops having four FV721 Fox each. There is also the usual Support Troop with five Spartans and the usual HQ Squadron and Admin, LAD, etc. One unusual addition to these regiments is the use of a small two-Ferret Intercommunications Troop under the control of the HQ Squadron. This troop has a purely liaison role both in and out of the regiment. (At the time of writing the Queen's Own Yeomanry had only three Recce Squadrons.)

The three Home Defence regiments each have three Recce Squadrons with the Royal Wessex Yeomanry having four. As will be seen from the table these regiments use civilian-model ¾-tonne Land Rovers (CLs) with only a limited number of 4-tonne trucks for back-up, one of which has to use its winch

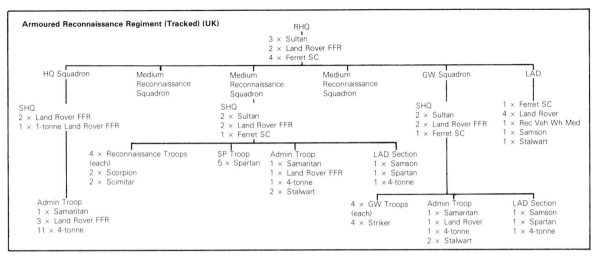

Armoured Reconnaissance Regiment (Tracked) (UK)

RHQ
3 × Sultan
2 × Land Rover FFR
4 × Ferret SC

HQ Squadron | Medium Reconnaissance Squadron | Medium Reconnaissance Squadron | Medium Reconnaissance Squadron | GW Squadron | LAD

SHQ
2 × Land Rover FFR
1 × 1-tonne Land Rover FFR

SHQ
2 × Sultan
2 × Land Rover FFR
1 × Ferret SC

SHQ
2 × Sultan
2 × Land Rover FFR
1 × Ferret SC

1 × Ferret SC
4 × Land Rover
1 × Rec Veh Wh Med
1 × Samson
1 × Stalwart

4 × Reconnaissance Troops
(each)
2 × Scorpion
2 × Scimitar

SP Troop
5 × Spartan

Admin Troop
1 × Samaritan
1 × Land Rover FFR
1 × 4-tonne
2 × Stalwart

LAD Section
1 × Samson
1 × Spartan
1 × 4-tonne

Admin Troop
1 × Samaritan
3 × Land Rover FFR
11 × 4-tonne

4 × GW Troops
(each)
4 × Striker

Admin Troop
1 × Samaritan
1 × Land Rover
1 × 4-tonne
2 × Stalwart

LAD Section
1 × Samson
1 × Spartan
1 × 4-tonne

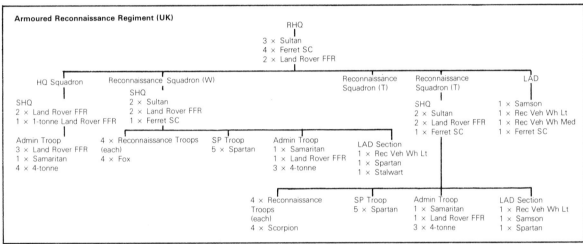

Armoured Reconnaissance Regiment (UK)

RHQ
3 × Sultan
4 × Ferret SC
2 × Land Rover FFR

HQ Squadron | Reconnaissance Squadron (W) | Reconnaissance Squadron (T) | Reconnaissance Squadron (T) | LAD

SHQ
2 × Land Rover FFR
1 × 1-tonne Land Rover FFR

SHQ
2 × Sultan
2 × Land Rover FFR
1 × Ferret SC

SHQ
2 × Sultan
2 × Land Rover FFR
1 × Ferret SC

1 × Samson
1 × Rec Veh Wh Lt
1 × Rec Veh Wh Med
1 × Ferret SC

Admin Troop
3 × Land Rover FFR
1 × Samaritan
4 × 4-tonne

4 × Reconnaissance Troops
(each)
4 × Fox

SP Troop
5 × Spartan

Admin Troop
1 × Samaritan
1 × Land Rover FFR
3 × 4-tonne

LAD Section
1 × Rec Veh Wh Lt
1 × Spartan
1 × Stalwart

4 × Reconnaissance Troops
(each)
4 × Scorpion

SP Troop
5 × Spartan

Admin Troop
1 × Samaritan
1 × Land Rover FFR
3 × 4-tonne

LAD Section
1 × Rec Veh Wh Lt
1 × Samson
1 × Spartan

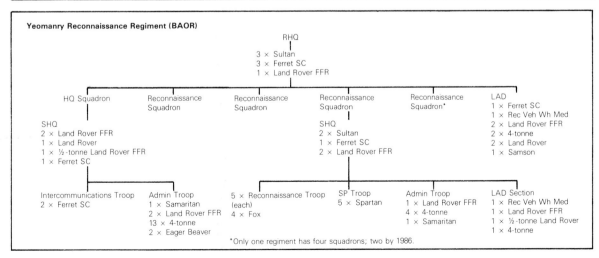

Yeomanry Reconnaissance Regiment (BAOR)

RHQ
3 × Sultan
3 × Ferret SC
1 × Land Rover FFR

HQ Squadron | Reconnaissance Squadron | Reconnaissance Squadron | Reconnaissance Squadron | Reconnaissance Squadron* | LAD

SHQ
2 × Land Rover FFR
1 × Land Rover
1 × ½-tonne Land Rover FFR
1 × Ferret SC

SHQ
2 × Sultan
1 × Ferret SC
2 × Land Rover FFR

1 × Ferret SC
1 × Rec Veh Wh Med
2 × Land Rover FFR
2 × 4-tonne
2 × Land Rover
1 × Samson

Intercommunications Troop
2 × Ferret SC

Admin Troop
1 × Samaritan
2 × Land Rover FFR
13 × 4-tonne
2 × Eager Beaver

5 × Reconnaissance Troop
(each)
4 × Fox

SP Troop
5 × Spartan

Admin Troop
1 × Land Rover FFR
4 × 4-tonne
1 × Samaritan

LAD Section
1 × Rec Veh Wh Med
1 × Land Rover FFR
1 × ½-tonne Land Rover
1 × 4-tonne

*Only one regiment has four squadrons; two by 1986.

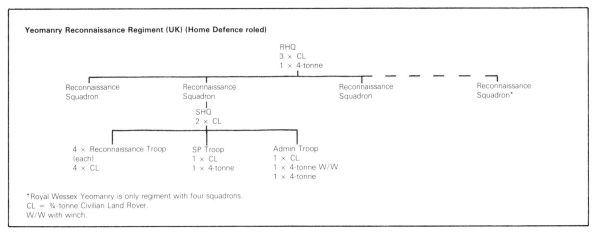

Yeomanry Reconnaissance Regiment (UK) (Home Defence roled)

RHQ
3 × CL
1 × 4-tonne

Reconnaissance Squadron — Reconnaissance Squadron — Reconnaissance Squadron — Reconnaissance Squadron*

SHQ
2 × CL

4 × Reconnaissance Troop (each)
4 × CL

SP Troop
1 × CL
1 × 4-tonne

Admin Troop
1 × CL
1 × 4-tonne W/W
1 × 4-tonne

*Royal Wessex Yeomanry is only regiment with four squadrons.
CL = ¾-tonne Civilian Land Rover.
W/W with winch.

for the recovery role. At the time of writing these light reconnaissance regiments were just being formed and more details of their armament and role are awaited.

The Infantry

'(physical occupation being ten points of the law in war, and infantry the bailiff's men)'

John Keegan, *The Face of Battle*.

Today, as always, the main manpower strength of the Army still rests in the Infantry battalions. The Army currently has 56 battalions of Infantry, all of them front-line units with the back-up of a further 35 TA Infantry battalions, in addition to which a further six battalions are currently being organised. For administrative purposes the retention of the Army's regimental system has been assured by the adoption of an organisational process known as the division. In order to maintain the advantages of the regimental system but partially combine them with the corps system in use with many other armies, the Infantry battalions are organised into these divisions within which some degree of commonality of working methods and cross-posting can be retained. It should be noted that the division mentioned here bears no resemblance to the armoured or Infantry divisions of BAOR. Here the division is a purely administrative term.

Of the divisions mentioned the Guards Division holds the same placing as the Household Cavalry does to the rest of the Cavalry units. To the general public this means red tunics and Trooping the Colour but that applies only to the London-based Guards battalions. The other Guards battalions not carrying out their ceremonial duties in London are usually in BAOR on a combat footing and rotate their combat and ceremonial duties in a similar manner to the Household Cavalry.

The battalions that make up the separate divisions are as follows:

The Guards Division: 1st and 2nd Battalions The Grenadier Guards (GREN GDS); 1st and 2nd Battalions The Coldstream Guards (COLM GDS); 1st and 2nd Battalions The Scots Guards (SG); 1st Battalion The Irish Guards (IG); 1st Battalion The Welsh Guards (WG).

The Scottish Division: 1st Battalion The Royal Scots (RS); 1st Battalion The Royal Highland Fusiliers (RHF); 1st Battalion The King's Own Scottish Borderers (KOSB); 1st Battalion The Black Watch (BW); 1st Battalion The Queen's Own Highlanders (QO HLDRS); 1st Battalion The Gordon Highlanders (GORDONS); 1st Battalion The Argyll and Sutherland Highlanders (A and SH).

The Queen's Division: 1st, 2nd and 3rd Battalions The Queen's Regiment (QUEENS); 1st, 2nd and 3rd Battalions The Royal Regiment of Fusiliers (RRF); 1st, 2nd and 3rd Battalions The Royal Anglian Regiment (R ANGLIAN).

The King's Division: 1st Battalion The King's Own Border Regiment (KING'S OWN BORDER); 1st Battalion The King's Regiment (KING'S); 1st Battalion The Prince of Wales' Own Regiment of Yorkshire (PWO); 1st Battalion The Green Howards (GREEN HOWARDS); 1st and 2nd Battalions The Royal Irish Rangers (R IRISH); 1st Battalion The Queen's Lancashire Regiment (QLR); 1st Battalion The Duke of Wellington's Regiment (DWR).

The Prince of Wales' Division: 1st Battalion The Devonshire & Dorset Regiment (D and D); 1st Battalion The Cheshire Regiment (CHESHIRE); 1st Battalion The Royal Welch Fusiliers (RWF); 1st Battalion The Royal Regiment of Wales (RRW); 1st Battalion The Gloucestershire Regiment (GLOSTERS); 1st Battalion The Worcestershire & Sherwood Foresters (WFR); 1st Battalion The Royal Hampshire Regiment (R HAMPS); 1st Battalion

The Staffordshire Regiment (STAFFORDS); 1st Battalion The Duke of Edinburgh's Royal Regiment (DERR).

The Light Division: 1st, 2nd and 3rd Battalions The Light Infantry (LI); 1st, 2nd and 3rd Battalions The Royal Green Jackets (RGJ).

The Brigade of Gurkhas: 1st Battalion The 2nd King Edward VII's Own Gurkha Rifles (2 GR); 1st and 2nd Battalions The 6th Queen Elizabeth's Own Gurkha Rifles (6 GR); 1st Battalion The 7th Duke of Edinburgh's Own Gurkha Rifles (7 GR); 1st Battalion The 10th Princess Mary's Own Gurkha Rifles (10 GR).

Also considered part of the Infantry but maintaining a separate grouping are the 1st, 2nd and 3rd Battalions of the Parachute Regiment (PARA).

The Battalion

After a lengthy period of re-organisation and internal heart-searching the Infantry are now undergoing a process of re-equipment and the first results of future operational projections. By the late 1980s the present appearance of the Infantry will have changed at virtually every level as new equipment comes into use and the battalion and company organisation outlined below may well have altered yet again. It should be emphasised again that, although the basic battalion structure is retained for peace-time administrative purposes, in war the battalion would re-align itself into a battle group and combat team structure in which the various companies will probably be broken up to go their separate ways.

There are at present three types of Infantry battalion; Mechanised, Type A and Type B. (MCV-80 Warrior battalions will be known as Armoured Infantry Battalions.) The Mechanised Battalion is used only within BAOR and 1 (BR) Corps in particular. As its name implies it is fully mechanised and moves on tracks, at present the basis being the FV 432, but these will be gradually supplemented by the

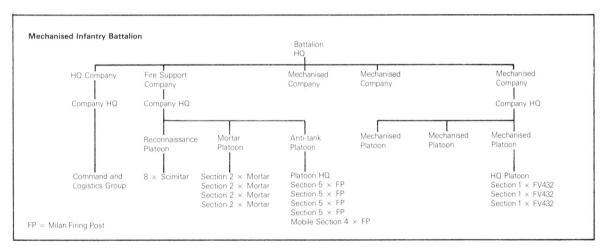

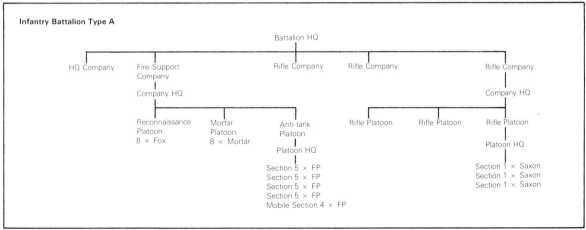

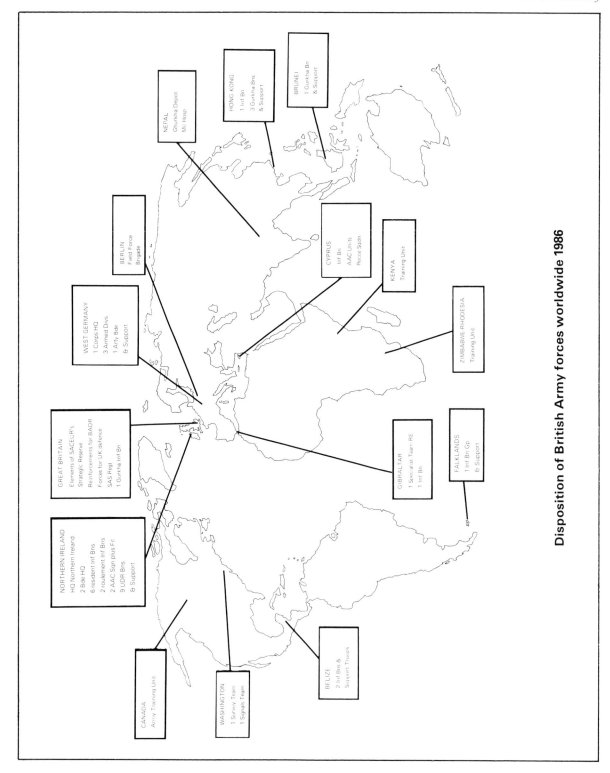

Disposition of British Army forces worldwide 1986

NEPAL
Ghurkha Depot
Mil Hosp

HONG KONG
1 Inf Bn
3 Gurkha Bns
& Support

BRUNEI
1 Gurkha Bn
& Support

BERLIN
Field Force
Brigade

CYPRUS
Inf Bn
AAC Units
Recce Sqdn

KENYA
Training Unit

ZIMBABWE-RHODESIA
Training Unit

WEST GERMANY
1 Corps HQ
3 Armed Divs
1 Arty Bde
& Support

GREAT BRITAIN
Elements of SACEUR's
Strategic Reserve
Reinforcements for BAOR
Forces for UK defence
SAS Regt
1 Gurkha Inf Bn

GIBRALTAR
1 Specialist Team RE
1 Inf Bn

FALKLANDS
1 Inf Bn Gp
& Support

NORTHERN IRELAND
HQ Northern Ireland
2 Bde HQ
6 resident Inf Bns
2 roulement Inf Bns
2 AAC Sqn plus Fit
9 UDR Bns
& Support

CANADA
Army Training Unit

WASHINGTON
1 Survey Team
1 Signals Team

BELIZE
2 Inf Bns &
Support Troops

MCV-80 Warrior. As will be seen in the accompanying organisational layout the battalion has five companies. The Headquarters Company is really a logistics organisation to support the other companies in the field. It does, of course, retain its headquarters function of commanding the other companies. It will be noted from the layout that the battalion now has three Mechanised Companies plus a Fire Support Company. For various reasons the old four-company structure was altered to the three-company plus Fire Support Company structure enabling the battalion to maintain, among other things, a Reconnaissance Platoon which, in the Mechanised Battalion, is equipped with eight Scimitars. The major change in the Fire Support Company has been the enlargement of its anti-tank guided missile strength. The Mechanised Fire Support Company has 24 Milan Firing Posts (FPs) organised into four Sections plus a Mobile Section using Spartans. The normal Mobile Section is made up of a Ferret Scout Car and a FV432 carrying the four FPs. Each section has 15 men in all. In the battalions of 6 Airmobile Brigade the Milan FP strength has been increased to over 40 but this is still in the experimental stage.

The Mechanised Company has three Mechanised Platoons, each commanded by an officer. The three Sections under his command are each ten men strong using three FV432s. Two of the Sections are armed entirely with the SLR but the other Section contains two men using the GPMG and another armed with a LAW. When SA 80 enters service it will be issued at the rate of three IWs to one LSW so it could well be that each FV432 Section will have two LSWs and up to eight IWs, for the driver normally stays with his vehicle. The LAW may continue to be issued to only one Section of the Platoon but one to each FV432 Section seems likely.

The Type A Battalion is based on the Saxon wheeled armoured personnel carrier and is slightly smaller in manpower strength than the Mechanised Battalion, primarily because the Saxon carries nine men as opposed to the ten of the FV432. The 24 Milan FPs are retained but the Reconnaissance Platoon uses the wheeled FV721 Fox. The Type A Battalions are used by 19 Infantry Brigade who would travel from the United Kingdom to Germany in their Saxons.

The Type B Battalion is used for home defence and is based on the use of trucks and 'B' vehicles for transport. In comparison to the other two types of battalion, the Type B is weak in anti-tank defence, having only six Milan FPs, and the manpower strength is less than in the other two types. The Rifle Companies use 4-tonne trucks for the bulk of their transport and the Reconnaissance Platoon is based on

the use of Land Rovers. Under the command of the Headquarters Company, the Type B Battalion has three Assault Pioneer Sections, each of eight men. The Type B Battalions are the only ones to have this increment, which may be a reflection of the fact that there will be few Sapper facilities available to support these battalions so they will have to provide a fair measure of their own. The Assault Pioneers are trained by the Royal Engineers. One section of the Type B Battalion that retains its full strength is the Mortar Platoon which remains at eight 81 mm mortars.

The Parachute Regiment is included among the Infantry (no doubt to their disgust) as, despite their adventurous method of reaching the combat area, once on the ground they function as Infantry. The parachute battalions of the Army (three Regular and three TA) are almost alone among NATO airborne forces in using normal Infantry weapons and equipment with few modifications for the airborne role other than packing. Recent years have seen a change in fortune for the Paras for, until the Falklands, they were seen as rear-area and raid troops that would not normally be used in front-line battles. With the introduction of 5 Airborne Brigade that has changed and recent years have seen a re-introduction of the support arms that the Paras once lacked. They now have their own artillery and engineer support along with signals and all the other support functions. The aircraft capacity to carry all these extras has also been made available by the Royal Air Force who now allocate enough C-130 Hercules to the Paras for two of the three parachute battalions to be para-trained at any one time. The Parachute Regiment Depot is at Aldershot.

The vanguard of the Infantry is still the Guards Division. As always, the Guards combine ceremonial and combat roles, usually on a three-year tour basis, but their long-established function is that of the Sovereign's personal escort, a function long overtaken by circumstances but cherished as a tradition. This function has now become a major attraction on the tourist scene in events such as the well-known Trooping the Colour and the daily Changing of the Guard at the London centres frequented by visitors, but on a more practical level this escort function can be seen by the positioning of the main Guards' barracks at Birdcage Walk, Chelsea, Windsor, Caterham and Pirbright.

The Brigade of Gurkhas includes its own signal, transport and engineer components with the five Gurkha Infantry battalions as the Brigade's main force. The main centre of recruiting is still Nepal while the bulk of the battalions are based in Hong Kong, the location of the Brigade Training Depot. One battalion is stationed in Brunei at the request and

Infantry badges. 1 *The Grenadier Guards.* 2 *The Coldstream Guards.* 3 *The Scots Guards.* 4 *The Irish Guards.* 5 *The Welsh Guards.* 6 *The Royal Scots.* 7 *The Royal Highland Fusiliers.* 8 *The King's Own Scottish Borderers.* 9 *The Black Watch.* 10 *The Queen's Own Highlanders.* 11 *The Gordon Highlanders.* 12 *The Argyll and Sutherland Highlanders.* 13 *The Queen's Regiment.* 14 *The Royal Regiment of Fusiliers.* 15 *The Royal Anglian Regiment.* 16 *The King's Own Royal Border Regiment.* 17 *The King's Regiment.* 18 *The Prince of Wales's Own Regiment of Yorkshire.* 19 *The Green Howards.* 20 *The Royal Irish Rangers.* 21 *The Queen's Lancashire Regiment.* 22 *The Duke of Wellington's Regiment.* 23 *The Devonshire and Dorset Regiment.* 24 *The Cheshire Regiment.* 25 *The Royal Welch Fusiliers.* 26 *The Royal Regiment of Wales.* 27 *The Gloucestershire Regiment.* 28 *The Worcestershire and Sherwood Foresters Regiment.* 29 *The Royal Hampshire Regiment.* 30 *The Staffordshire Regiment.* 31 *The Duke of Edinburgh's Royal Regiment.* 32 *The Light Infantry.* 33 *The Royal Green Jackets.* 34 *The Parachute Regiment.* 35 *The Brigade of Gurkhas.* 36 *2nd King Edward VII's Own Gurkha Rifles.* 37 *6th Queen Elizabeth's Own Gurkha Rifles.* 38 *7th Duke of Edinburgh's Own Gurkha Rifles.* 39 *10th Princess Mary's Own Gurkha Rifles.*

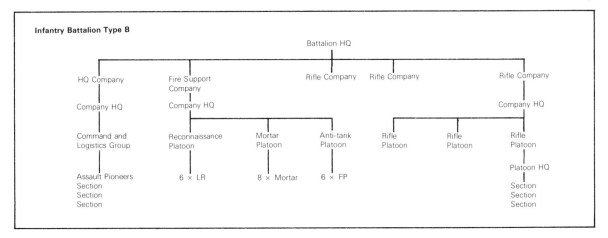

expense of the local government and another battalion is based in the United Kingdom at Church Crookham in Hampshire. The Gurkha base in Nepal is at Pokhara. Officers for the Brigade are no longer all-British but the formation is an integral part of the British Army and the friendships and traditions forged between the Army and the men from Nepal are still treasured and maintained on both sides.

Another tradition that has been retained can be seen with the retention of the Light Division. Within this Division the methods and history of the old light infantry battalions is still maintained by their brisk marching pace and drill, the use of the bugle to transmit orders and the use of field green uniform shades, black leatherwork, and so on. Once on the battlefield these traditions no longer have much value for operationally the Light Division operates along the same lines as the other divisions. Once off the battlefield the old traditions immediately take hold.

The backbone of the British Army may be stated to be formed by the old Regiments of the Line whose names can still be found in the battalions of the King's, Queen's, Scottish and Prince of Wales's Divisions. These battalions have served the nations well over the years and their dour and determined fighting qualities have been demonstrated all over the world. That they can still emulate the qualities of their forebears has been amply demonstrated in the Falklands and in Northern Ireland, much of this combat quality being formed by using the old regimental traditions as a basis. Despite all the re-organisations and upheavals of recent years, the Infantry battalions have endured much by using and maintaining their close familiar regimental bonds that are so much the strength and the inherent weakness of the British regimental system.

Perhaps the most valuable aspect of this close-knit system can be seen in the way that the Infantry itself has changed over the last few decades. The modern

Infantryman is no longer the docile rifle-carrying foot-slogger of the past but today is a highly skilled technician using equipment of the most advanced kind. The modern Infantryman has to be capable of driving a number of differing types of vehicle, use modern computers, operate and maintain all manner of electronic equipment from radios to surveillance devices and night-sights, and still train to a level of skill-at-arms that many other larger armies envy. Yet recruits still refuse to join regiments in which their fathers did not serve, and trained soldiers will still do their best to remain in the battalions that soon become as familiar to them as the homes which they left to sign on.

The Royal Regiment of Artillery & The Royal Horse Artillery

'The Infantry don't understand their orders, the Cavalry ignore them . . . the Artillery make their own arrangements.'　　　　　(Anon)

The Artillery component of the British Army is made up from two elements. By far the largest part of the Royal Regiment of Artillery is more commonly known as the Royal Artillery, the other element being the Royal Horse Artillery. In practical terms on the battlefield the two carry out the same functions and operate in the same manner, but the Royal Horse Artillery (RHA) is constituted as an élite force and works and acts accordingly. Officers for the RHA are carefully selected from the regiment as a whole; once they have been 'given their jacket' they spend a term with the RHA and then return to the Royal Artillery (RA). As the RHA standards are so high this procedure has the overall effect of raising the working

The new shapes of the air defence regiments, a Tracked Rapier in the background with a M548 carrier.

and operating standards of the Artillery as a whole.

The modern Artillery arm is a powerful and complex branch of the Army. It is the only section of the Army to employ nuclear weapons, the very weapons that are now 'Queen of the battlefield', and far outweigh any other single weapon type in destructive and disruptive impact. Thus, when the functions of the modern artillery are examined, the nuclear role must be afforded the overall priority, but the other functions of indirect fire and air defence cannot be overlooked or underestimated.

The functions of the Artillery are: 1) Nuclear warfare—to provide the capability of engaging selected targets with nuclear weapons at the appropriate stage of the battle; 2) Indirect fire—to a) Provide depth fire designed to disrupt, delay and destroy enemy forces before they can come into contact and in particular to destroy or suppress enemy artillery (the same application can be made against enemy forces not committed to battle); and b) to provide close support to battle groups in the destruction or neutralisation of enemy forces in the close contact battle; 3) Air defence—to provide the low-level air defence of the Field Army. The Long Range Anti-Tank Guided Weapon (LRATGW—Swingfire) function has now been assumed by the RAC.

The control of the Artillery as it is now practised is the outcome of a very long period of practical experience combined with pragmatic necessity. The present command and control arrangements have only recently been revised yet again following the switch of one of the four 1 (BR) Corps divisions to the United Kingdom and the transfer of the LRATGW to the RAC. The current organisation now encompasses weapons that range from the ultimate nuclear weapons down to one-man air defence missiles, but all of it has to be kept under close control without sacrificing the flexibility and speed of response that the modern battle will require.

The present control system is based on a flexible signal network combined with close personal contact at every command level. This can be seen in the BAOR Artillery command network where at every level the Artillery commanders liaise and work alongside the formation commanders. At HQ 1 (BR) Corps level, the Corps Commander has immediate and close access to the officer commanding all the artillery in the Corps. This officer, the Major General Royal Artillery (MGRA), acts as the Corps Commander's artillery adviser while at the same time commanding the 1st Artillery Brigade. At a lower level, each armoured division commander has his own artillery adviser who also acts as the commander for all the Artillery formations within the division. This officer, a Brigadier, is the Commander Royal Artillery (CRA) who commands his own HQRA and the three field regiments under his command plus any batteries that might be assigned to him. Each field regiment has its own Tactical Headquarters (TacHQ) with two Fire Direction Centres (FDCs), each of which is connected by radio not only to the TacHQ but also to the HQRA in each division. In this manner flexibility is built into the system to enable fire to be switched from one target to another so that one formation can provide fire for another, and fire concentrations can be rapidly switched from target to target—the advent of BATES (qv) will considerably assist these operations. Normally one FDC controls the artillery fire for one task force or battle group, but the Artillery control system enables the FDCs to switch their fire to support other formations than their own. The whole network has been devised to support the precept that artillery fire must always be used *en masse*, and never in dribs and drabs—one massed salvo from many guns has a far more destructive and disruptive impact than the same number of projectiles delivered by a single gun.

At 1 (BR) Corps level, what was once known as the Artillery Division has now been re-named the 1st Artillery Brigade. This is commanded by the MGRA who is now MGRA/Commander Artillery 1 (BR) Corps. The 1st Artillery Brigade is formed of 5 and 32 Heavy Regiments with their 175 mm M107s, 12 and 22 Air Defence Regiments with their mix of towed and Tracked Rapiers, and the three Lance batteries of 50 Missile Regiment, plus two RCT regiments in support. The M110A2 batteries of 39 Heavy Regiment will also continue to be controlled at Corps level and 94 Locating Regiment will continue to provide gunner information, although the M107 regiments now have their own locating batteries.

Most of the above regiments are gradually being centred at Dortmund although 94 Locating Regiment, RA, is based at Larkhill. Normally these regiments will be divided up among the various divisions with the bulk being centred on the armoured divisions, although it is anticipated that the Missile Regiment will be held in reserve under the command of the MGRA until it is definitely required.

The Divisional Artillery Group now comprises three field regiments, one with the 155 mm M109A2 and the other two with the 105 mm Abbot. Each of these batteries has eight guns organised into two troops to a battery. Each field regiment also has its own headquarters battery with the Abbot field regiment HQs having a troop of four Cymbeline mortar-locating radars. The M109A2 field regiment has

Javelin warheads and the Javelin guidance unit. This is one of the Royal Artillery's newest pieces of kit.

attached to it a troop using either Javelin or Blow-pipe—this attachment is for administrative purposes only as in action the troop will be allocated to the battle groups.

In time of war the Divisional Artillery Group would not operate alone. Alongside it could be a M107 battery, a M110 battery, a locating battery, a Rapier battery and possibly an extra field regiment from the TA using the 105 mm Light Gun. At least one of the armoured divisions would have a field regiment equipped with the towed 155 mm FH70 for there are only eight field regiments based in BAOR (2, 4, 19, 27, 40 and 47 Field Regiments, RA, and 1 and 3, RHA).

The United Kingdom is the base for a further eight field regiments (including two TA), and three Blow-pipe/Javelin-equipped air defence regiments, all TA. Three of these field regiments are equipped with the towed 155 mm FH70. 26 Field Regiment, RA, is at Thorney Island near Chichester, 45 Field Regiment, RA, at Colchester and 49 Field Regiment, RA, at Topcliffe. Then there are two 'specialised' field regiments. One is 7 RHA at Aldershot equipped with the 105 mm Light Gun. This is a three-battery field regiment plus a Cymbeline troop for the support of 5 Airborne Brigade—7 RHA is fully trained for the paradrop role and all personnel wear the red beret. The other 'specialised' regiment wears the green beret for it is 29 Commando Regiment, RA, based in the Citadel at Plymouth with one battery at Arbroath. Equipped with the 105 mm Light Gun, this regiment has a similar organisation to that of 7 RHA and provides support for the Royal Marine Commando Brigade—this regiment also has the support of a TA Commando Battery (289 Commando Battery, RA (V), based at East Ham in London).

There are two TA Light Gun field regiments. One is 100th (Yeomanry) Field Regiment, RA (V), and the other 101st (Northumbrian) Field Regiment, RA (V). They both have three six-gun batteries. Both would be assigned to BAOR in an emergency.

Then there are the UK air defence regiments. One of these is a regular unit, namely 16 Air Defence Regiment, RA, based at Kirton-on-Lindsay and equipped with towed Rapier. The other three air defence regiments are all TA and are equipped with Blowpipe/Javelin. They are 102nd (Ulster and Scottish) Air Defence Regiment, RA (V), 103rd (Lancashire Artillery Volunteers) Air Defence Regiment, RA (V), and 104th Air Defence Regiment, RA (V).

There is one more field regiment to mention but it has a far more complex organisation than the other field regiments. This is 14th Field Regiment, RA, based at the home of the Royal School of Artillery at Larkhill on Salisbury Plain. This regiment provides support for the School but also provides a battery of 105 mm Light Guns for the support of AMF(L). Also at Larkhill is 94 Locating Regiment, RA, by far the largest regiment in the RA in manpower terms. It has four batteries equipped with a whole gamut of specialised equipment varying from the Midge drones to sound locators and AMETS (qv). In simple terms, 94 Locating Regiment, RA, has to identify and analyse targets for future engagement by artillery fire, provide real time intelligence for various formations, and provide up-to-date meteorological information for use by RA and AAC units. It includes within its ranks the only mortar-locating battery in the Army—73 (Sphinx) Mortar Locating Battery, RA, equipped with Cymbeline (qv).

All the above are fully operational regiments but there is one other that must be mentioned even though it has a ceremonial and display role only. This is the King's Troop, RHA, based at St Johns Wood in London. The King's Troop is equipped with 13 pr guns from the Great War that are maintained in immaculate condition for saluting and display purposes. The Troop is organised around its horses and without a doubt it puts on one of the finest military displays to be witnessed anywhere. Competition to join its ranks is very keen and much of the specialist training involved with the King's Troop is carried out 'in house'.

The RA training organisation is based at the home of the RA at Woolwich, which is both the RA's Depot and also the home of 17 Training Regiment and Depot, RA, where basic recruit training and some other teaching is carried out. The Royal School of Artillery at Larkhill is obviously where much artillery training is carried out, but the RSA deals primarily with officers and instructors. The School has four instructional wings—Gunnery, Air Defence, Tactics and Signals—plus a REME wing and a Young Officers' Branch. The School also provides general courses for battle group commanders from all other branches of the Army. The Junior Leaders' Regiment, RA, trains the future senior NCOs of the RA. It is located at Bramcote in Warwickshire and is organised into four training batteries.

The above listing covers most of the major units within the RA but there are more. For instance, at Gibraltar there is 8 Surveillance Troop, RA, using its various radars to keep an eye on the border with Spain. In the UK the Honourable Artillery Company supplies the personnel for observation posts (as well as maintaining a very efficient Infantry battalion) and other TA units provide more observation post personnel, while yet others provide personnel for various headquarters functions. Apart from providing music, the Royal Artillery Band would convert to driving heavy trucks in an emergency.

A 105 mm Light Gun of 29 Commando Regiment, RA, on exercise in Norway (Royal Ordnance).

The Artillery is one branch of the Army that never seems to remain still for long. New equipments and operating methods arrive on the scene every year, bringing with them new organisational upheavals and revised working methods. Hovering in the wings at present is BATES which will bring with it a totally new operational approach to artillery control and make the resources available to the Artillery in 1 (BR) Corps considerably more effective. Then there is new equipment. MLRS will be on the scene by 1988—the first four training equipments arrived in 1985. When it arrives it is expected that it will be organised into two regiments based at Dortmund. Even further off at the time of writing is the 155 mm SP70. The future of this long-awaited weapon still seems uncertain but it has been going on for so many years that the RA is still making plans for its arrival into service, since the 105 mm Abbots are now long overdue for replacement. Instead, the international development and production teams battle it out to decide who is to get the main share of the production and other facilities. In the meantime the Tracked Rapier re-equipment programme continues, and research into enhanced range and specialised projectiles proceeds along well-established lines.

The Artillery is now one of the most scientific branches of the Army, dealing with all manner of skills and equipment from computers to survey and from meteorology to communications. To add to this array of skills, self-defence is not neglected. With equipments such as MLRS and Phoenix to look forward to and with BATES about to be put to use, the future of the Royal Artillery certainly looks lively.

Royal Artillery survey and observation

For the Artillery, survey has more than one function. Not only does it supply the essential information as to the enemy's position but it also provides the equally valuable information as to the precise location of one's own forces and equipments. To this end, survey is a vitally important part of the Artillery and considerable pains are taken to ensure its accuracy and relevance. Each major Artillery formation has its own survey troop which forms part of the locating battery, and this troop is responsible for the Artillery survey on the battlefield, using maps supplied by the Royal Engineers. The methods used by the troop follow conventional civilian survey practice but their equipment is generally more robust than the commercial equivalents. Numerous different instruments are issued from the basic steel measuring tapes up to the Tellurometer (MRA5), the Gyroscopic Orientor (GS908) and the Surveying Theodolite (Watts Mocroptic No.2 Mark 4). Some of the survey tasks will soon be supplemented by PADS but the survey troops will still be responsible for the important survey points that enable PADS to function.

The Royal Artillery Observation Post (OP) is the home of a number of other specialised instruments which have gradually been evolved into a common 'package'. A Forward Observation Officer (FOO) has to observe and correct the fall of artillery fire and give corrections back to his battery to ensure hits. For this purpose he must know exactly where he is (here PADS or survey once more come into play), but to determine exactly where the target is relative to his position a whole host of aids are ready to be mobile on an FV432 or an FV103 Spartan. All these vehicles can carry a device known as a Head Angulation Sighting Equipment (HASE), which is an instrument table giving survey angle related to its orientation (if used from a static position, the HASE is mounted on a Medium Level Tripod, or MLT). On to the HASE goes a Laser Rangefinder (LRF) and to add to the bulk, a Night Observation Device (NOD) can be added for night or low visibility use. Very basically the LRF is used to determine the range and angle of the target from the HASE. From these the enemy

The FOO 'Christmas Tree' mounted here on a FV432.

range and bearing can be assessed accurately and relayed to the battery in a very short space of time. The system, if correctly set up and surveyed, is very accurate and in past exercises opening rounds have landed within 60 metres of the lased target on 80 out of 100 occasions—subsequent corrections can then be made with a minimum of time and projectile wastage.

Lasers have another important function in that they can be used as target designators for ground attack aircraft. In this role a Laser Target Marker (LTM) is aimed at the selected target and a long burst of laser radiation is then 'fired'. The reflected beam can be picked up from up to 10,000 metres away by the attacking aircraft and the marker information is fed directly into the pilot's head-up display. In this manner a strike aircraft can attack a ground target without seeing the target itself.

Artillery fire is not directed by the methods outlined above in isolation. There are many other factors to be taken into account such as the meteorological conditions (data provided by AMETS), and the various ballistic data (individual gun muzzle velocities provided by PACER, charge temperatures, propellant lots, etc). Much of this technical detail these days is calculated by the FACE computer, but a skillful OP will also rely on good old-fashioned experience.

Field Artillery Computer Equipment (FACE)

The fire control of modern field artillery is a complex business which no longer has time for the old, 'fire-for ranging, fire-for-effect' orders. Instead artillery fire has to be capable of ranging on to targets that present themselves for fleeting instances, using artillery with variables such as differing projectiles and ranges, and with differing equipment. Fire orders have to be given to the guns quickly and accurately with any delays cut to an absolute minimum. Thus the days when all the variables involved were laboriously worked out by hand or from massive tables before any fire orders could be given are now over—the computer age is with us, and to the Artillery the computer is now an invaluable aid. The Royal Artillery uses one well-tried and reliable system known as the Field Artillery Computer Equipment, but more generally referred to as FACE.

FACE was first considered as an adjunct to the Artillery in about 1963 when the commercial computer was still in its relative infancy. Several industrial and Ministry agencies were involved but the final contract went to Marconi as their Marconi-Elliott 920B computer formed the heart of the final production model. The first examples were issued to the Army in 1969.

FACE has two main artillery tasks. The first is survey, in which it computes all the variables involved with the meteorological data required by modern artillery, and can even make allowances for the earth rotation effects and differing latitudes. But the main task of FACE is fire control in which role it acts as a rapid processor for the mass of variables involved in firing artillery. The usual issue of FACE is one to a battery, whatever its nature, but when some batteries have to be split into components for various tasks, this issue is increased. A usual arrangement is one FACE to two troops. Normally two men man the computer, one actually operating the console and the other either operating the associated teleprinter/paper punch and the signal equipment—sometimes an extra man is used for this role. The operation of the FACE console is fairly straightforward as the computer is programmed to operate in a set sequence or drill which reduces operator error to a minimum.

To explain FACE operation it is perhaps best to follow a battery into action. Once in position the FACE is switched on using a 24 volt supply. A paper tape outlining all the information relevant to the type of gun (or rocket) in use is fed into the computer, followed by another tape with all the relevant weather and survey data. Once the tapes

have been fed in the manual data is then inserted. This includes a pre-set sequence of information such as the centre of the battery position, the siting of the guns from that point, and the temperature of the ammunition charges to be used (such variables as muzzle velocity variations for each gun are already in the computer memory bank). Any meteorological variations are then fed in and the next information is the target data. This comes in the form of the target position (on a grid location), the types of projectile to be used, and the charges selected. The FACE then computes all the fire information needed for each gun, which in turn is displayed ready for voice transmission to the guns via land line or radio or, if it is in use, AWDATS (Artillery Weapon Data Transmission System). AWDATS presents the fire information to each gun on a display console next to the gun layer. Corrections, observed by the Forward Observation Officer (FOO), can be quickly fed into the computer and corrections are then made for each gun.

As well as these 'variable' targets, fire plans can be stored in FACE ready for use—up to 40 pre-planned targets can be stored ready to use, and of these, ten are automatically updated as meteorological variations are fed in. Each FACE can handle fire control orders for up to three batteries at their different locations and each of those batteries can be of up to eight guns.

The usual vehicle used for FACE installations within BAOR is the FV432, although some have been installed in the FV103 Spartan. Towed batteries usually have their FACE installations in Land Rovers

A FACE installation in a FV103 Spartan.

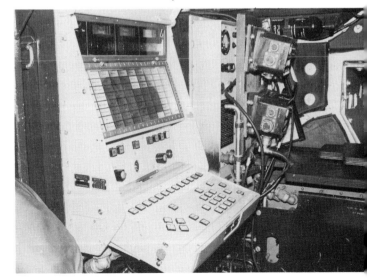

and installations have also been made in Bv202 Over-Snow vehicles. However, there are unlikely to be future installations in new types of vehicle for two reasons. One is that the introduction of BATES will involve a phasing out of FACE altogether, and secondly there is the introduction of Gunzen.

Gunzen is a companion equipment to the mortar-orientated Morzen. It is a hand-held computer device rather like an oversized pocket calculator and it can carry out all the functions of FACE in a much more portable form. Each Gunzen uses a read-only memory chip that goes through every stage of fire control in a set sequence and it can also be used for survey and meteorology. Gunzen can be used with every type of artillery weapon employed by the RA, including Lance, and all that is required to use Gunzen with one equipment or another is the changing of a single chip which takes only a few seconds. Gunzen has already replaced FACE within 7 RHA who use their 105 mm Light Guns to support 5 Airborne Brigade and it seems likely that 29 Commando Regiment, RA, will also make the changeover.

Artillery Meteorological System (AMETS)

Until comparatively recently the art and science of artillery had little need to take the state of the weather into account, other than sometimes noticing the wind strengths in the immediate vicinity of a firing point. As artillery improved in range and power it was gradually noticed that weather phenomena could cause projectiles to deviate from their planned trajectories and the observation of meteorological factors became an important section of artillery studies. By the end of the Second World War the use of balloons and the consulting of meteorological instruments was commonplace and well-established, but the methods employed were often slow and cumbersome. With the advent of the fire control computer in the shape of FACE it became possible to take into account a whole range of factors that were up till then only theoretical niceties. Humidity, air density, air temperatures at the altitudes modern projectiles could achieve, and many other meteorological measurements could be readily assimilated and calculated by a FACE computer, but the problem was how could this information be gathered and distributed in time to be useful to the accuracy of the guns?

The answer was to utilise modern data collecting and process techniques in the shape of data processors, radar, transmitting sensor carriers (or radiosondes), all combined in a new system. The United Kingdom Meteorological Office, Plessey and Marconi Space and Defence Systems Limited combined their resources to develop and produce the Artillery Meteorological System, or AMETS. AMETS has now been in Army service for some years but it is still far in advance of any similar weather data information gathering system in use by any other field army.

AMETS consists of several inter-related components. The heart of the system is contained in a Command Post Vehicle (or CPV) which contains the main data processor. This is the Marconi-Elliott 920B computer as used with FACE. Along with the other CPV equipment the computer is housed in a container body mounted on a 4-tonne truck (the truck also tows the main power generator for the system). Another vehicle tows a trailer carrying the tracking radar—the radar itself is a military version of a civil model known as WF3M. The other component is a specially-designed balloon-borne radiosonde which weighs 0.75 kg.

In action, the AMETS troop is usually situated near the front line and in the centre of the formation (usually a division) it is supplying with information. Every four hours (and sometimes more frequently), a radiosonde and balloon are prepared and launched. As they rise they are optically monitored until the radar picks them up, after which the tracking is automatic. As the radiosonde rises, the wind strengths and direction are automatically computed, and at fixed intervals, temperature and other readings are transmitted and automatically processed. In the CPV all this information is produced by the computer in paper tape form, fed into a teleprinter and transmitted to the customer FACE teleprinter terminals. From them, the information is fed into the FACE processors themselves. In the CPV a printed feed-out may also be used. Although a full radiosonde mission is released every four hours, updates of wind situations are made every hour by balloon tracking alone.

AMETS troops consist of about 20 men, and are part of the Locating Regiment under Corps HQ control. In action they are usually distributed one troop to a division and each troop is equipped to supply meteorological information to all the batteries and other customer units in that division.

The system has been designed to operate over a wide range of climatic conditions, and can be used in temperatures from -32 to + 52°C. The radiosondes can supply data from up to 20,000 metres. AMETS is very mobile and easily serviced, and as all its components are well-tried and generally available, its reliability level is high. At present, AMETS is used to feed its data directly into battery FACE terminals. With the advent of BATES other forms of input at different command levels will become necessary, but it does not seem likely that the overall system will need to be altered to any great extent.

Position and Azimuth Determining System (PADS)

In modern warfare, the accuracy of weapon delivery systems is such that it becomes essential to know exactly where a potential target is situated. Just as important is to know exactly where the delivery system itself is located. Consequently there are several different systems currently employed to determine the exact location of a potential firing point, ranging from the time-honoured system of a finger on a map right up to the sophisticated systems associated with space satellites. The latter are very accurate position indicators in themselves (and are likely to be much used by future location-assessing systems) but at present they are very expensive, and the necessary ground equipment is bulky and too costly to issue on a large scale. As a result the British Army has invested in a self-contained system known as PADS, or the Position and Azimuth Determining System.

PADS is a self-contained unit carried on vehicles or helicopters which is capable of determining the exact location of the vehicle relative to a fixed point. To use PADS the vehicle is positioned on or near an accurately-determined survey point. The co-ordinates are entered into the PADS panel and the vehicle can then move off. As the vehicle moves, the exact amount of movement and bearing shifts from the survey point are registered automatically by the

Setting-up a PADS installed in a Bv202 (Ferranti).

PADS inertial navigation platform. The whole PADS system is self-contained and highly accurate. Up to an hour after the initial input of the survey point data, the PADS system can give the carrying vehicle position with an accuracy of about ten metres for both Eastings and Northings, and to an accuracy of less than one mil in azimuth. The data can then be used for navigation or for entry into FACE or any similar system. The data can also be used to locate minefields accurately, update maps, and for artillery survey.

The Army has invested heavily in PADS and consequently it is an important part of their inventory in the 1980s. Produced by Ferranti, the PADS system is housed in a single container weighing 35 kg. The dimensions of the container are 0.46 × 0.45 × 0.25 metres and the system runs off a single 28 volt DC power supply.

BATES

BATES is the acronym for Battlefield Artillery Target Engagement System which in its turn describes a semi-automatic data-processing and fire control system now in the final stages of development for the Army. The system has been developed to overcome the fact that in any future European conflict the NATO artillery, and the British artillery in particular, will be heavily outnumbered by their Warsaw Pact counterparts and in order to make the best use of whatever weapons are to hand a much better overall control system has had to have been evolved. The present artillery target and fire control data systems are perfectly efficient but they would lack the speed of response and command presentation that will be required.

BATES started as a definite project during 1976 but the need for some form of system like this had been forecast as early as 1970. Several nations have already made large investments in computerised fire control and data systems but, since they make a great deal of use of fully-automated computer systems, it was felt that in most of them the artillery commander had little personal say—BATES enables the commander to make his own decisions. In very simple terms BATES allows all forms of target data to be accepted by the system for presentation to artillery commanders. Target data from observers, radars, sound ranging, remotely-controlled drones and other sensors can be displayed to the commanders. The displays use rugged flat-screen liquid crystal displays under computer control and it is possible to call upon data banks to compare data or consult previous target records. The processing of all the data is automatic but the target selection and method of engagement will still be left to the commander. Target information fed down the command chain will be clearly displayed at all stages, right to the guns in some cases, and along the chain the system will replace FACE and some other equipments such as AWDATS and possibly some elements of AMETS.

BATES will considerably increase the speed at which engagements can be made but it will cause a considerable upheaval of existing artillery control methods. For this reason it is being carefully phased into service following the gradual spread of the Ptarmigan communications network, upon which BATES will depend, throughout BAOR. The first stages of introduction are already being made and it is expected that BATES will be fully operational within 1 (BR) Corps by 1987 or 1988.

According to some artillery officers the introduction will provide the Artillery with its biggest firepower multiplier for many generations, enabling their commanders to carry out their task with far greater flexibility, response and impact than has hitherto been even remotely possible.

The main contractor involved in BATES has been Marconi Command and Control Systems of Camberley, Surrey, but the full programme involves many other concerns.

The Corps of Royal Engineers & The Queen's Gurkha Engineers

The Royal Engineers have one main task—they provide military engineering support to the Defence Services. As far as the Army alone is concerned this means that they help the Army to fight, to live and to move, while at the same time denying the same functions to an enemy.

The main component of the Royal Engineers is the combat engineer. The modern combat engineer is a capable and skilled tradesman and technician and in a way he epitomises the wide variations in role and versatility that are typical of the Royal Engineers themselves. The combat engineer is first and foremost a trained soldier and well schooled in the basic Infantry and soldiering skills. He is also a trained combat engineer with all the specialist education that such a role involves, but in addition to the two above attributes every member of the Engineers can add a third function, for each man is also an artisan capable of turning his hand to a wide variety of tasks.

These tasks can involve a wide variety of military duties ranging from building a road through virgin country in all parts of the world to painting a sign to hang outside a building. The building itself may well have been built by the Engineers as well, for the Royal Engineers contain within their ranks some of the most widely diversified artisan skills that are to be found in any civil concern concerned in major civil engineering. But where the Royal Engineers differ from the civil concerns is in the fact that they also have to turn their hands to the military engineering tasks of bridging, road building and mending, battlefield constructions, life support constructions such as water supply and shelters and various other fieldworks. They are also concerned in such military functions as mine warfare, anti-tank obstacles and even such relatively peaceful duties as postal services, surveying and diving. Another Royal Engineer role that has both

Below A Light Tracked Tractor (LTT) complete with loading bucket and backhoe as used by 33 Engineer Regiment (EOD). The LTT is an International Harvester 100B. Bottom A Medium Tracked Tractor (MTT), a Caterpillar D6D, at work on the Chattenden Ponderosa training area.

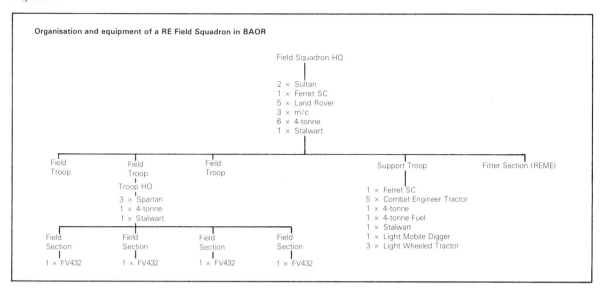

Organisation and equipment of a RE Field Squadron in BAOR

Field Squadron HQ

2 × Sultan
1 × Ferret SC
5 × Land Rover
3 × m/c
6 × 4-tonne
1 × Stalwart

Field Troop | Field Troop | Field Troop | Support Troop | Fitter Section (REME)

Troop HQ
3 × Spartan
1 × 4-tonne
1 × Stalwart

Field Section | Field Section | Field Section | Field Section
1 × FV432 | 1 × FV432 | 1 × FV432 | 1 × FV432

Support Troop
1 × Ferret SC
5 × Combat Engineer Tractor
1 × 4-tonne
1 × 4-tonne Fuel
1 × Stalwart
1 × Light Mobile Digger
3 × Light Wheeled Tractor

peacetime and wartime functions is bomb disposal.

In times of war, the combat engineer has to carry out a number of tasks and for this purpose they are organised into engineer regiments. In BAOR there are three types of engineer regiment, the armoured division Engineer Regiment, the Armoured Engineer Regiment and the Amphibious Engineer Regiment. The regiments based in the United Kingdom are known as Field Engineer Regiments. Of these regiments the armoured division Engineer Regiment will be considered first.

Each regiment is made up of a regimental headquarters and three field squadrons, and each is completely self-contained and can move and survive completely under its own resources. Once in action, the regiment has two prime functions. In defence, it has a responsibility to reduce the mobility of an enemy and protect friendly formations. In attack the engineer regiments have to remove obstacles and keep up the momentum of an advance.

The defensive role involves the engineer regiments in a number of tasks, as there are many different ways of placing obstacles in the path of an advancing force. One is mine laying and for this task the Royal Engineers use two main types of mine—the Bar Mine for use against tanks and the Ranger mine system for use against personnel. Other mines in use are the Horizontal Action anti-tank mine and the older Mine Mark 7. Since it is anticipated that any enemy advance would be based on large numbers of tanks and other types of AFV, the Engineers

Right *Royal Engineers at work on a radar site in the Falklands* (MoD).

employ other obstacles against tanks, one of which is the time-honoured anti-tank ditch. Despite the simplicity of the ditch, it is still a very effective obstacle which can be crossed only by the use of specialised filling or crossing equipment which has to be employed under fire and with a subsequent loss of time and momentum. Other obstacles can be created by the use of explosives to produce craters and the demolition of bridges or structures to hinder the movement of mobile forces. Defensive positions and fire positions can also be dug, often at short notice. All these measures are carried out by the engineer regiments.

In the attack, the combat engineers have to keep the advance moving and this involves the removal or neutralising of obstacles. Mines can be cleared by the use of such devices as Giant Viper or mine detecting equipment. Ditches and wet gaps can be crossed by bridging equipment, both mobile and constructed, and physical obstacles can be cleared by the use of engineering plant and machinery.

From the precis of the role of the combat engineer given above it can be seen that the role of the armoured division engineer regiment is a very varied one. It will also be seen that the skills and equipment involved are complex too, and the combat engineer is not only trained to carry out all the many jobs involved but he also has to master the many types of equipment issued to the engineer regiments.

Each of the three field squadrons in an armoured division engineer regiment can turn its hand to any of the above-mentioned tasks. To enable this to be achieved the three field squadrons are organised into a squadron headquarters and three field troops (see table). There is also a support troop at squadron level which holds the bulk of the specialised plant other than that held by the troops themselves, and another support squadron at regimental level holds the really heavy plant and such specialised equipment as bridging components. The field support squadron has three troops—a plant troop, a resources troop (which holds the bulk of the regimental stores) and a bridging troop.

As the name implies, the armoured division engineer regiments are based on the armoured

Top left *The Light Mobile Digger (LMD) is based on a Thornycroft Nubian 4 × 4 chassis and is used for trench digging.* **Above left** *The Light Wheeled Tractor (LWT) is one of the Royal Engineer's most versatile pieces of equipment and can be fitted with digging or loading buckets, a backhoe or fork lift. The LWT is the Muir-Hill A5000.* **Left** *The massive Heavy Wheeled Tractor (HWT), the Michigan 275B, is used only by ADR squadrons. It has a 5 cubic metre bucket and can carry a complete crater repair mat.*

FV432s and FV103 Spartans but of necessity they have to include a large wheeled transport element. Some of the plant is armoured, including the CET.

Within 1 (BR) Corps there are two further specialist engineer regiments. One is 32 Armoured Engineer Regiment under the control of HQ 1 (BR) Corps. This unit has the mobile bridging role and also operates the Centurion AVREs. The mobile bridges involved are carried by the FV4205 AVLBs based on the Chieftain chassis. 32 Armoured Engineer Regiment has a regimental HQ and three armoured engineer squadrons. Each squadron has its own squadron HQ troop and three armoured engineer troops.

The other specialist engineer unit is 28 Amphibious Engineer Regiment, also under the direct control of HQ 1 (BR) Corps. This formation is equipped with the M2 bridging and ferrying vehicle, and has a regimental HQ and two amphibious engineer squadrons. Each squadron has two troops. A third squadron is a training squadron.

To provide support for the Royal Engineer regiments in West Germany are a number of other Sapper regiments. The three divisional Engineer Regiments are 21, 35 and 26 Engineer Regiments and within 1 (BR) Corps they are provided with further support from 23 and 25 Engineer Regiments (the latter with only two field squadrons) which are under Corps control. The support does not stop there for another unit exists known as 65 Corps Support Squadron. This acts as a form of 'holding' unit for all manner of Sapper materials and equipment ranging from explosives to bridging equipment, much of which is held in Engineer Parks.

Further support will be provided for 1 (BR) Corps by TA Engineer Regiments moving to Germany from the United Kingdom, and elements from some Regular units in the UK. There are no fewer than seven TA Engineer Regiments, not all of them destined for service outside the home base, and most of them dependent on wheels rather than tracks for their transport—all of the TA Engineer Regiments have Field Squadrons with only three Field Sections in place of the four within BAOR. The United Kingdom would also provide a general equipment and resources back-up for units in BAOR.

At this point it must be mentioned that the Royal Engineers also provide a great deal of support for the

Top right *A Royal Engineer mine clearance team in action.*
Above right *A CET in action on a range in West Germany.*
Right *Loading a TEREX TS-8 Medium Scraper on to a Craven Task 37-tonne RE Plant semi-trailer. This special semi-trailer has a detachable goose neck to assist loading and unloading (Craven Tasker).*

Royal Air Force, both in West Germany and the United Kingdom. For RAF Germany the Royal Engineers provide much of the field site construction and support required by the two Harrier squadrons based at RAF Gutersloh. When they move out into the field the Royal Engineers construct their field sites, landing pads and taxi-ways. Support for the RAF does not end there, for the Royal Engineers are now heavily involved in the task of Airfield Damage Repair, or ADR. This includes not only the clearing of bomb craters so that runways and taxi-ways are made usable after an attack, but also the repair and maintenance of airfield services such as water supply, fuel pipeline and storage repair, electrical supply system repairs and other services. The unit mainly concerned with ADR is 39 Engineer Regiment which is based in the UK but in an emergency would take its four Field Squadrons (Construction) (48, 50, 52 and 53) to the four 'Clutch' airfields of RAF Germany where plant and other equipment is stockpiled ready for use. Airfields in the United Kingdom are the responsibility of 12 Engineer Brigade (ADR) which at present has four Field Squadrons (ADR) (V) although in time it is hoped to expand their number to eight (the present squadrons, all TA, are 216, 218, 219 and 277). These TA squadrons are smaller than their Regular equivalents for within the United Kingdom their responsibilities are confined to rapid runway repair (or repair of aircraft operating surfaces—RAOS).

In addition to all the above formations the Royal Engineers also provide two further specialist combat engineer units. These are 9 Parachute Squadron, RE, based at Aldershot and earmarked to provide Sapper support for 5 Airborne Brigade; and 59 Independent Commando Squadron, RE, based at Plymouth to provide engineer support for the Royal Marines of 3 Commando Brigade. All the Sappers in these two squadrons have to pass all the selection and training requirements of their 'user' forces and competition to join them is keen.

In recent years the public have had several reminders of one specialised function of the Royal Engineers—explosive ordnance disposal or EOD. In theory the Royal Engineers have a precisely prescribed responsibility in this area for they are responsible for aerially delivered devices such as aircraft bombs above the high water mark. (The RAOC deals with the terrorist-type device and ammunition, the Royal Air Force with devices on their own property and likewise the Royal Navy, who also deal with devices below the high water mark.) In practice this dividing line is not always adhered to for many reasons, but the main EOD unit within the Sappers is 33 Engineer Regiment (EOD) headquartered at Chattenden in Kent. It has two EOD squadrons, 49

and 58, and the Regimental Headquarters incorporates its own Training Wing. 49 EOD Squadron is rather unusual in that it has two Troops manned by civilians working under Royal Engineer officers and NCOs. 1 Troop, based at Felixstowe, is still partially manned by Ukrainians who have for years been moving around the United Kingdom to clear away the explosive debris of two World Wars. 2 Troop is based at Farnborough and has a similar role. The other two Troops, 3 and 4, are all-military. 58 EOD Squadron has a more conventional organisation with three Troops and a Support Troop. These two squadrons would operate in time of war in sections of eight to ten men. They would be led by a Bomb Disposal Officer (BDO) and at least one Senior NCO who would normally deal with a device while the rest of the section would be there to provide excavation and operate the specialist equipment. 39 Engineer Regiment (EOD) also has four TA squadrons. They are 579 EOD Squadron (V) at Dartford, 583 EOD Squadron (V) at Brighton, 590 EOD Squadron (V) at Rochester and 591 EOD Squadron (V) at Dartford. From time to time 33 Engineer Regiment (EOD) becomes concerned with terrorist-type devices but recently their role in the Falklands has been much more demanding of their time and efforts. The aftermath of the 1982 Falkland Islands' campaign left a considerable residue of hidden land mines and unexploded bombs all over the battlefields, some of which are by now so dangerous that many will have to remain where they are for years to come unless new clearance techniques can be devised.

Then comes military survey. The Royal Engineers have had a hand in survey and map-making for many, many years and the current Director of Military Survey is still a Royal Engineers' senior officer. Under him the Royal Engineers are responsible not just for map production for the Army but for all three Services (although the Royal Navy understandably still produces its own hydrographic charts). In fact, the Director's brief is 'to provide the Armed Services with geographic support and related materials required for military operations, on, over and in the vicinity of the land surface'.

The Royal Engineers' involvement within this responsibility is considerable. The main formation involved is 42 Survey Engineer Group headquartered at Hermitage, near Newbury, also the location of the School of Military Survey which is part of the Group. Two of the units involved within the Group are 13 Map Production Squadron, RE, and 19 Topographic Squadron, RE, both at Barton Stacey, north of Winchester. Another unit is 8 Map & Air Chart Depot at Guildford. These units make up the bulk of the United Kingdom strength of the Directorate but there is also 135 Field Survey Squadron, RE (V), at

Above *One of the Royal Engineers' more unusual pieces of kit, a Magirus-Deutz 6 × 6 chassis carrying a mobile well-drilling rig and used by 521 STRE (Well Drilling), part of the MWF.*
Above right *A Coles Model 335M Dynamic Compactor, one of the specialised pieces of plant used by the ADR squadrons; the Compactor is used to tamp down the infill used to repair a runway bomb crater prior to covering it with a repair mat (Coles Cranes).*

Ewell in Surrey. An Air Survey Liaison Section is maintained at RAF Wyton to work with the Royal Air Force photo-reconnaissance unit. Based at Feltham is the Mapping and Charting Establishment, RE, an all-civilian unit which concerns itself with all aspects of map making from basic library support to the use of advanced computers in every process involved in producing military maps. Overseas the Royal Engineers have a considerable survey showing with a unit at HQ BAOR overseeing a presence with 1 (BR) Corps, 14 Topographic Squadron, RE, at Ratingen and the Survey Production Centre, RE, at Rheindahlen. There are also survey teams in Hong Kong, Washington (where 512 STRE works with the Americans in the use of space satellites for survey and other purposes), and there are more survey staffs in the Falklands, Cyprus, Belize and Northern Ireland. These units produce not just maps alone, although the maps and charts they do produce are first class.

They can also overprint existing maps with tactical or other symbols (using a process known as TACI-PRINT), churn out maps on all manner of materials from transparencies (for use in the 'moving map' displays used in many Royal Air Force cockpits) to special papers and even textiles. Their work involves the frequent use of many of the latest computer and other techniques and in many ways the Royal Engineer involvement in military survey is way ahead of work carried out elsewhere.

If all the above was not enough for the Royal Engineers to encompass, there then comes the Postal and Courier Service, or PCS. In its full entirety the present title is the Defence Postal and Courier Services for not only does the PCS handle mail but also a courier service which operates throughout the United Kingdom and all over the world on behalf of the Ministry of Defence and various Government agencies. However, the PCS's main responsibility is the handling of the postal services for all the armed forces. The Depot for the PCS is at Mill Hill in North London, which is also the location of the sorting office through which all mail for the British Forces Post Offices (BFPO) passes for processing and forwarding. The Depot is only the tip of the iceberg for the PCS activities are carried out in all parts of the world. One of the main locations is, of course, BAOR which is the responsibility of 1 Postal and Courier Regi-

A pair of Medium Wheeled Tractors (MWT) or TEREX 72-51s, fitted with loading buckets.

ment, RE, based in Hannover with squadrons all over West Germany. To deal with NATO units outside BAOR there are more PCS units in locations such as Belgium, Norway, Italy and Portugal under the command of 40 (NATO) Postal and Courier Unit, RE, (ACE). However, this spread becomes small when one considers the activities of 2 Postal and Courier Regiment, RE. This regiment has its headquarters at South Cerney but its sub-units are spread wherever there is some form of British military presence—and that spreads from Korea to the Sinai. The list of these locations is seemingly endless and includes some rather exotic names such as Bangkok and Zimbabwe, but wherever they may be the PCS handles the mail and provides courier support when called upon.

To add to all these Royal Engineer PCS units there are no less than four TA PCS regiments, some of them earmarked for BAOR and others for use in the United Kingdom only. The PCS Royal Engineer staffs are assisted by a number of WRACs working at the Depot and elsewhere, while a number of Royal Navy personnel are also based there to deal with some of the mail for Royal Navy ships. There is, in addition, a sizeable civilian staff at Mill Hill.

Dotted around are still a number of Royal Engineer units to account for. There is a small Corps Lighting Troop within 1 (BR) Corps and one TA unit with a similar function, which is to provide lighting for various headquarters and searchlights to give 'artificial moonlight' or other lighting for some types of night operation. Then there are the 'special' units

such as 1 Fortress STRE at Gibraltar which runs many of the utility services on the Rock. Mention must also be made of the Queen's Gurkha Engineers. They are based in Hong Kong and consist of 67 Gurkha Field Squadron, 68 Gurkha Field Squadron and 70 Gurkha Support Squadron. They carry out all the usual combat engineer duties for the Brigade of Gurkhas. Not to be confused with them is 69 Gurkha Independent Field Squadron at Chatham, which operates within UKLF as part of 2 Infantry Brigade.

To back up all of these many Royal Engineer functions are a number of large stores depots and equipment parks in the United Kingdom. One of the largest of these is at Long Marston, near Stratford, the cost of which can be measured in millions of pounds. This wide array of functions and talents is kept constantly hard at work even when the usual round of training and other duties are completed. Royal Engineer units often find themselves in some odd parts of the world carrying out all manner of unusual tasks that might range from removing an old coast defence gun from the top of Gibraltar's Rock to building a road bridge in a remote corner of Canada. Such tasks call for more than the usual run of military talents, and here the Royal Engineers are well qualified for they have artisan skills in addition to their normal combat roles. It might well be that a CET driver is also a trained electrician, an AVRE gunner might well be a trained signwriter, and so on. There are even some really specialised skills within the Royal Engineers for the Sappers also provide the Army's divers for all manner of military purposes that might range from clearing underwater obstacles to the reconnaissance of river crossings. The divers are trained at a Combined Services establishment at HMS *Vernon*, Portsmouth, and there is a continuation school at Kiel in Germany.

All basic Royal Engineer recruit training is carried out by 1 Training Regiment, RE, at Hawley, near Cove in Hampshire. At the same location combat engineer training is carried out by 3 Training Regiment, RE, (there is another Combat Engineer Training Centre in Hameln). Advanced engineer studies are carried out at the Royal School of Military Engineering located mainly at Chattenden, near Chatham. This School is a sizeable establishment with a number of Wings. One is the Field Engineering Wing and another the Tactics Wing. Then there are the Signals Wing, the Plant Roads and Airfields Wing, an Electrical and Mechanical Wing and a Civil Engineering Wing. Outposts are maintained at locations such as Bovington to deal with armoured engineer matters and the Royal Engineers' Diving Establishment at HMS *Vernon* is part of the School. The Junior Leaders' Regiment, RE, is at Dover while the Army Apprentices' College is at Chepstow—plans are afoot to move the Junior Leaders to Chepstow as well. These two establishments train the future NCOs and perhaps some of the future officers of the Royal Engineers. Between them they provide nearly half the adult intake for the Sappers.

There is still one Royal Engineers' formation to be mentioned. This has been described as one that does good almost by stealth for few outside the Royal Engineers appear to have heard of it or its activities. It is the Military Works Force, an organisation formed to provide an engineering consultancy to all three of Her Majesty's Forces in the field. Under normal circumstances this role is carried out by the civilian Property Services Agency (PSA—the modern equivalent of the old 'Works and Bricks'), but there are times when the PSA cannot operate, ie, in war or during other military operations. The Military Works Force, or MWF, has several other roles, one of which is to provide technical support for various Royal Engineer activities around the world or when they are on military or disaster relief operations. These activities cover a wide scope of operations and the MWF is a very versatile and accomplished organisation.

The MWF is headquartered at Barton Stacey but its members seldom seem to be there. Headquarters MWF has all the usual administrative functions but in addition there are a number of sections which provide support services for the two main MWF units.

These are 62 CRE (Works) and 64 CRE (Works). The term CRE stands for Commander Royal Engineers which is fairly meaningless but it is retained as part of tradition in the same manner that each of the sub-units within a CRE are known as STREs, or Specialist Teams Royal Engineers. These STREs are the working units and consist of a number of Design Teams who provide general advice, reconnaissance and management for whatever

Below *The Volvo BM 4400, the Royal Engineers' new Medium Wheeled Loader* (Volvo UK). **Bottom** *A Royal Engineers search team, complete with search dog, on a road in County Antrim* (Army Information Service, Northern Ireland).

project they have in hand at the time. These projects can be both large and small but they nearly all seem to be far-ranging, and include drainage schemes in Hong Kong, building a school of infantry in Kenya, building bridges in Canada or simply constructing a small-arms range in the United Kingdom. In all such projects the MWF provides the overall expertise and guidance required while much of the work is carried out by Field Squadrons assigned to the task. It is not always as simple as that. The MWF did a great deal of unsung work during and after the Falkland Islands' campaign with some of it still continuing—for instance, they were responsible for much of the initial site reconnaissance for the airfield on Mount Pleasant.

There are two highly specialised STREs within the MWF. One is 521 STRE (Well Drilling) and the other 516 STRE (Bulk Petroleum)—their suffixes explain their roles. However, the MWF also has under its wing a number of TA STREs which have within their ranks some highly qualified civilian personnel who in an emergency would don their uniforms and continue under the auspices of the MWF. These STREs, ten in all, are mainly Works STREs but there are also three Bulk Petroleum STREs, a Railway Construction STRE and a Well Drilling STRE.

Much of the work of the MWF goes unnoticed by the general public but in many parts of the world they act as quiet ambassadors. They include some of the more highly qualified officers within the Royal Engineers, although even outside the MWF the Royal Engineers contain some unusually able officers and men. It is not uncommon for an officer to move outside the Army between postings and gain some form of civilian experience, such as helping to manage the building of an oil refinery, before returning to military duties. The NCOs in the Royal Engineers are all very able artisans as well as military leaders and their range of skills and abilities seems to be endless. When looking at their duties within the Royal Engineers one can understand why.

The Army Air Corps

The Army Air Corps (AAC) is one of the more recent additions to the corps and regiments of the British Army, despite the fact that the Army has long been involved in aviation (the Royal Engineers had a balloon section as early as 1873). The AAC was formed in September 1957 by amalgamating the old Glider Pilot Regiment with the Royal Air Force Air Observation Post squadrons—the latter being manned by Royal Artillery pilots—but the links with the RAF remain in the squadron designations, all of which begin with '6'.

The AAC has five main roles. Top of the list comes what is known as 'armed action'. In practice this usually means using helicopters in the missile-armed anti-tank role. Then comes observation and reconnaissance, followed by the direction of fire, usually artillery fire. There is also a command and control role and last comes a limited lift or movement of men and material, including casualty evacuation (casevac).

The AAC is an almost entirely helicopter-orientated corps—only a handful of their aircraft today are fixed-wing. The home of the AAC is Middle Wallop in Wiltshire, and the same location is also the main training base and home for some of the AAC's supporting arms. The three largest of these are the Aircraft Engineering Training Wing, REME, 70 (Aircraft) Workshop, REME, and 1 Aircraft Support Unit, RAOC. Middle Wallop also houses the Depot AAC and the headquarters of the Director Army Air Corps (DAAC).

The main strength of the AAC is based in Germany. Here there are three AAC regiments, each formed from three squadrons. These squadrons are equipped with either the TOW-armed Lynx or the Gazelle. They are as follows: 1 Regiment AAC: 651, 652 and 661 Squadrons; 3 Regiment AAC: 653, 662 and 663 Squadrons; 4 Regiment AAC: 654, 659 and 669 Squadrons.

As will be appreciated, one regiment is assigned to each of the three armoured divisions so 1 and 4 Regiments, being assigned to the two forward armoured divisions, have a preponderance of Lynx helicopters (armed squadrons have a 65- prefix, reconnaissance squadrons have 66-). Each of these squadrons has 12 helicopters and each squadron has its own particular role. The Lynx squadrons are used primarily for the missile-armed anti-tank role while the Gazelle squadrons are tasked principally with observation and reconnaissance. Each regiment has its own REME Light Aid Detachment (LAD) with more REME support not too far away.

Also in BAOR are a few further AAC units. HQ 1 (BR) Corps has its own Gazelle-equipped 664 Squadron and HQ BAOR has 12 Flight equipped with Gazelles at RAF Wildenrath. In Berlin, support is provided for the Berlin Brigade by 7 Flight. Apart from these two locations the main bases for the AAC in BAOR are Hildesheim, Detmold, Soest and Minden.

In the UK there is one AAC Regiment, 7 Regiment, AAC, based at Netheravon, whose main function is to support UKLF. The squadrons based in the UK are 658, equipped with a mix of Scout and Gazelle, 656 and 657 with a mix of Lynx and Gazelle (658 Squadron's Scouts are the last to be still equipped for the missile role). Within 7 Regiment, AAC, is 7 Flight HQ which maintains an Augusta-Bell A109A captured during the Falkland Islands' campaign. AAC bases away from Netheravon are Topcliffe for the support of units in the York area and Oakington for units based in East Anglia. There is also a regiment-sized formation known as AAC Northern Ireland (AAC NI). This is based at Aldergrove and Ballykelly. There are three units within AAC NI, 655 Squadron equipped with Gazelles and unarmed Lynx and the Beaver Flight which is self-explanatory. There is also a roulement squadron from BAOR at any one time with its base at Aldergrove.

Away to the south, the AAC has a presence in the Falkland Islands where the corps maintains the Garrison Air Squadron. This is manned by a roulement squadron from BAOR and once in the Islands they fly Scouts and Gazelles. Away in the Far East, Sek Kong is the home of 660 Squadron, still equipped with the Scout and with one Flight always detached in Brunei. Almost as far-flung is the AAC Detachment at BATUS in Alberta, Canada. This detachment has solitary examples of a Scout, a Gazelle and a Beaver—a Lynx may join them some time during the next few years. Somewhat closer to home is 16 Flight, the last unit still equipped with the Alouette 11, whose attentions are divided between the units in the Sovereign Base Areas of Cyprus with one base at Dekhelia and another in support of UNFICYP at Nicosia.

Closely associated with the AAC is 3 Commando Brigade Air Squadron (3 CBAS), a Royal Marine unit. One of the responsibilities of the DAAC is the recruiting and selection of personnel for this unit as well as for the AAC, and co-operation between the AAC and Royal Marines is so close that on occasion Royal Marine pilots fly AAC helicopters in Northern Ireland. 3 CBAS is based at RNAS Yeovilton and is equipped with the Gazelle and Lynx; it will be used to support 3 Commando Brigade in an emergency. Training for the aircrew is carried out by the AAC at Middle Wallop.

Training occupies a great deal of time and attention within the AAC. There are several career paths within the corps and a good place to start is that of a typical AAC soldier. The new recruit to the AAC carries out his basic military training with the RAC at Catterick and then proceeds to driver training with the RCT. From there he moves to the AAC Centre at Middle Wallop for groundcrewman training. This involves basic signalling and the aircraft training. He is then assigned to a squadron. After a minimum of two years he can apply to become an aircrewman. If he passes the selection process the potential aircrewman will return to Middle Wallop for a ten-week course covering such items as map reading, air OP

(the direction of artillery fire), flight servicing, basic tactics and other such skills. He will also be given some very basic flying training so that he will be able to land a helicopter in an emergency. From this course the aircrewman will be sent to a Gazelle squadron but a further course is necessary to convert him into an Air Gunner to fire TOW missiles from the Lynx.

The aircrewman will then spend at least two years with a squadron before he can apply to become a pilot. Subject to his CO's recommendation, he will be sent to the Aircrew Selection Centre at RAF Biggin Hill to assess his basic aptitudes for the task. If he passes the Biggin Hill requirements he will then journey to Middle Wallop to go before the AAC Pilot Selection Board to discover whether or not he is really suitable for the role of an AAC pilot. If he manages to impress the Board sufficiently he can then proceed to his pilot training proper.

Before the flying training commences, all students are given a five-week pre-flying training course with the real flying only then starting with the Basic Squadron. The Basic Squadron is equipped with the fixed-wing Chipmunk T 10 and all flying instruction at this stage is given by civilian instructors. The basic instruction period involves 60 flying hours which takes about 12 weeks, and is provided on the premise that to become a helicopter pilot one has first to master the basics of fixed-wing flying. Once qualified as a fixed-wing pilot, the trainee then passes on to the Basic Helicopter Flight. This unit is an all-civilian run establishment equipped with civil Bell 47G-4s and this stage of the training lasts a further 60 flying hours over a period of ten weeks. Then comes a one-week course away from Middle Wallop for aero-medical training including ditching drills and other such procedures. Then it is back to Wiltshire again for a period with the Advanced Rotary-Wing Squadron and conversion to the Gazelle. This is the longest part of the course and occupies 115 flying hours spread over 16 weeks. From this point the pilot can be assigned to a squadron. It is still not usual for a newly trained pilot to convert directly to the Lynx without a minimum of one year with a squadron. When the time does come to convert the course lasts 40 flying hours.

As can be seen from this very brief outline, becoming an AAC pilot is no easy matter and the corps does accept trainee pilots from all branches of the Army. Volunteers have to undergo the same selection procedure as the AAC personnel but once trained they stay with the AAC for a three-year tour. After that the officers and NCOs are given the opportunity of staying with the AAC (subject to there being places for them in the AAC) or returning to their parent regiments or corps. Officers with a career path to follow often return to their original units and may return to the AAC later in their careers, but some do stay. NCOs usually opt to remain with the AAC.

There is one further path into the ranks of AAC pilots and that is by way of a direct entry. Few are selected for this as AAC pilots are expected to have a considerable amount of Army experience to enable them to carry out their specialised role to the full—the normal AAC path ensures that a potential pilot has at least five years of Army experience, and secondment and transfer from other branches ensures that trained personnel only are chosen. Therefore the direct entry method is little used and is usually limited to a handful of hopefuls every year. If the potential direct entry pilots manage to negotiate all the normal selection processes they are sent first to Sandhurst for the normal period of training and then they have to spend six months with an Infantry unit before they can even commence their AAC training.

As well as training AAC personnel, the AAC Centre at Middle Wallop is responsible for training Royal Marine aircrew, and also the REME technicians who look after the AAC aircraft. Middle Wallop also houses WRAC and other personnel who assist in the handling of the resident aircraft. They, like all the other arms and services not part of the AAC but who are involved with AAC units, wear the distinctive light blue beret with their own parent cap badge.

In April 1986 No 666 Squadron AAC (V) was formed at Netheravon as part of 7 Regiment AAC. Equipped with 12 Scouts, it supports UKLF for Home Defence duties. It is the first TA AAC Squadron.

The Special Air Service Regiment

Despite the attention directed towards the Special Air Service Regiment by the various forms of the media in recent years, very little can be written regarding this most unusual formation as it does not welcome publicity and, indeed, at the time of writing it is still an offence to even take a photograph of a member of the regiment. Much has been written about the SAS, much of it sheer twaddle, for the regiment by its very nature attracts the romantically minded or the scrutiny of the very people the SAS is currently employed to combat. But despite all this attention it is still difficult to write anything really definite regarding the SAS.

There is only one Regular Special Air Service formation, namely the 22nd SAS, based at Hereford. Formed in 1950, the SAS is the modern equivalent to the various deep penetration and disruption units that sprang up during the Second World War in all theatres and caused so much havoc to their enemies by their unconventional methods and tactics. In time of war the SAS would retain the same role, namely that of penetrating the rear echelons of the enemy and disrupting communications, while at the same time carrying out reconnaissance of rear areas and targets. Exactly how the SAS would go about this operational task it is not possible to mention, or even discover, but the SAS is committed to the Strategic Reserve of the Supreme Allied Commander Europe (SACEUR).

Although the SAS has this war commitment, it has become better known in the public eye for its counter-insurgency role in Northern Ireland and elsewhere. This task was first carried out during the Malayan emergency and has continued ever since—the Ulster campaign is just another job to be carried out for the SAS and is, for them, nothing special. Again, exactly how the SAS conducts its role in Northern Ireland is very difficult to discover, but it has been involved in ambushes, the surveillance of suspected terrorist caches and arms dumps, the establishment of hidden sentry posts in rural and town areas, and the general infiltration of organisations known or suspected of being involved in revolutionary activities. All these tasks have to be carried out in a clandestine manner and as a result the SAS has gained for itself a notoriety out of all proportion to its involvement for even at the busiest periods of the Ulster situation it is doubtful if there are ever more than about 160 SAS members in the province. But the general 'success' rate has been high, even if many of the results of SAS activities seldom become known to the general public. The assault on the Iranian Embassy in London is, of course, an exception to this 'rule'.

From the above, it will become obvious that nothing definite can be written on the organisation of the 22nd Special Air Service Regiment. It is known that the three Regular SAS squadrons are committed to SACEUR in time of war, and that the squadrons (known as 'Sabre' squadrons—SAS members are 'Troopers') are broken down operationally to what are virtually individual teams which vary in size but are usually limited to four men. Each unit member has a particular specialised skill, and a typical team would consist of a signaller, a weapon specialist, a medical specialist and a linguist. All these skills are supposed to be interchangeable but exactly how they are imparted has not been made public. The size of the team will vary according to the specific task and the theatre of operations, but each member is trained to act independently and consequently each SAS trooper

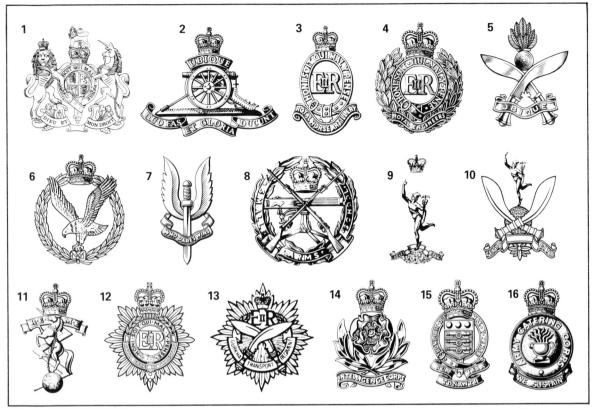

Corps badges. 1 *General Service Corps.* **2** *The Royal Regiment of Artillery.* **3** *The Royal Horse Artillery.* **4** *The Royal Engineers Regiment.* **5** *The Queen's Gurkha Engineers.* **6** *The Army Air Corps.* **7** *The Special Air Service Regiment.* **8** *The Small Arms School Corps.* **9** *The Royal Corps of Signals.* **10** *The Gurkha Signals.* **11** *The Royal Electrical and Mechanical Engineers.* **12** *The Royal Corps of Transport.* **13** *The Gurkha Transport Regiment.* **14** *The Intelligence Corps.* **15** *The Royal Army Ordnance Corps.* **16** *The Army Catering Corps.*

may be given responsibilities out of all proportion to his rank or position when related to other arms of the Forces. The equipment of the SAS is also a matter of conjecture, but it is known that SAS members often have their own choice of individual weapons. It can only be assumed that the operational equipment chosen will suit the role being carried out, but it has been noticeable that the Land Rovers once often seen at various Army displays on SAS display stands, and which were liberally covered in machine-guns redolent of the 'Popski's Private Army' era, are now conspicuous by their absence.

The SAS is now the only unit within the Army which does not recruit direct from the general public. SAS members are all trained soldiers who have spent some time in the Army, and are all volunteers. Admission to the SAS is no easy course of action, for all potential recruits have to undergo a four-week selection course which is held twice a year. The course is a strenuous one involving not

only tests of physical stamina (which sometimes hit the headlines when a course member becomes a casualty as a result) but tests of mental ability and determination to carry out assigned tasks with no imposed stimulii. Once past this exacting selection process the SAS member has to undergo what must be very involved training programmes before the operational roles can even be attempted (one important item of note regarding the training is that the SAS Trooper is trained as an individual and is personally responsible for his own follow-on training instigation and implementation), and it must be tempting to think of the SAS troopers as being very much members of an elite formation. The truth is that they do not regard themselves as such. They are selected from what are already regarded as elite formations (most SAS personnel seem to come from either the Guards Division, the Household Cavalry or the Parachute Regiment), and to them the SAS is just a unit with a role to play, albeit an unusual and flexible one. But the SAS does have its own particular distinctions.

For a start, the SAS is not part of the Infantry or indeed of any other branch of the Army, and it has its own Directorate. Individual members, both troopers and officers, cannot be named or identified publicly, which to the general public would seem to bestow a 'cloak and dagger' image, but such a policy is essential in view of the SAS's operational and peacetime roles. The number of soldiers within the SAS is never disclosed, nor is their participation in any particular campaign, although their involvement in Northern Ireland was announced as the result of a political decision. Another 'distinction' is that the SAS uniform or badge is seldom seen worn in public, for very often SAS members assume the uniforms or badges of other regiments, especially during counter-insurgency operations.

From all the above, it will be seen that the SAS is very much an undercover unit with an operational role in peace and war that will seldom gain much public recognition. To many the very nature, or indeed the existence of the SAS, may seem to be at variance with the generally established form of modern society, but such are the enemies who are set against the way we live that it is inevitable that corresponding measures have to be taken. The SAS has assumed some of those measures and its operational role has evolved from them—those who decry the activities and existence of the SAS would do well to remember why it is necessary.

The Small Arms School Corps

The Small Arms School Corps is a relatively small but important adjunct to the School of Infantry,

Corps Badges. 1 *The Royal Pioneer Corps.* **2** *The Royal Army Education Corps.* **3** *The Royal Army Medical Corps.* **4** *The Royal Army Dental Corps.* **5** *Queen Alexandra's Royal Army Nursing Corps.* **6** *The Royal Army Veterinary Corps.* **7** *The Army Physical Training Corps.* **8** *The Corps of Royal Military Police.* **9** *The Military Provost Staff Corps.* **10** *The Ulster Defence Regiment.* **11** *The Royal Army Chaplains' Department.* **12** *The Gibraltar Regiment.* **13** *The Royal Army Pay Corps.* **14** *The Women's Royal Army Corps.* **15** *The Royal Military Academy Sandhurst.* **16** *The Royal Military School of Music.*

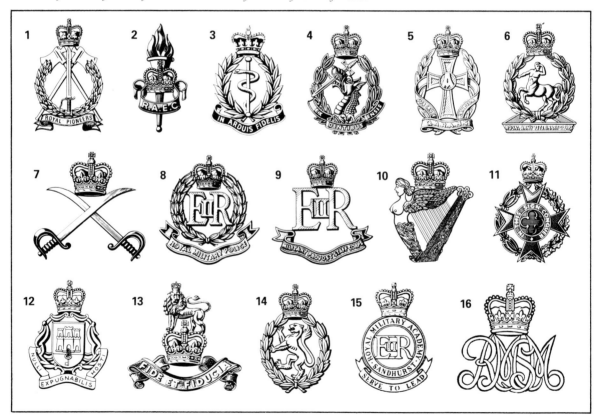

SASC marksman using the 7.62 mm L42A1 sniper's rifle.

based at Warminster. Stated briefly, its role is to maintain a high level of small arms skill and impart the same skills to the Army as a whole and the Infantry in particular. The SASC tends to regard itself as rather an Infantry elite, which indeed it is, for its role has an impact out of all proportion to numbers.

The SASC makes up the staff of the Small Arms Wing of the School of Infantry. This is divided between Warminster, which primarily caters for the man-carried weapons, and the Support Weapons Wing situated at nearby Netheravon. At both establishments, and the various depots and training establishments where SASC instructors spread their message, the SASC is concerned with the expertise necessary to use and maintain Infantry weapons in the field, and apart from the mere mechanics concerned, the corps has established an enviable reputation for marksmanship, a cachet borne out by the high number of Bisley prizes won by the SASC and the degree of expertise gained by the snipers trained by the corps. Perhaps one of the most important present-day influences of the SASC can be seen in the firepower philosophy of the Army. Prompted in no small way by the tactical situations prevalent in Northern Ireland, the accent on marksmanship imparted by the SASC has meant that the modern Army is now almost alone in devoting so much effort and training to the skill. Many other armies have now adopted the 'area fire' method of spraying areas with barrages of automatic fire to saturate any possible target. While this may be argued as effective, it is very wasteful in ammunition and manpower, and these are two

assets the British Army does not possess. Consequently the British soldier is trained to make every shot tell, to conserve ammunition and to maintain a high degree of fire discipline.

Apart from maintaining a pool of highly skilled weapons technicians, the SASC also has a trials and development function based at Warminster. It is thus involved with the current trials being carried out with the 5.56 mm Individual and Light Support Weapons.

The Royal Corps of Signals & Gurkha Signals

The role of the Royal Corps of Signals within the modern Army is much the same as it has been ever since the corps was first formed in 1920. Its role is to provide and maintain rapid, accurate and reliable communication systems for the Army, both when it is at peace or when it is engaged in a war. While the role may not have changed, the importance of effective communications certainly has, for a modern army cannot fight, move, feed, be maintained or be supplied without vast networks of inter-connecting communications of every conceivable kind. It might even be stated that modern warfare as it is now envisaged quite simply cannot take place outside the umbrella of costly and sophisticated command communication networks. With this in mind it can be seen that the task of the Royal Signals is thus essential to the smooth-running fighting effectiveness of the Army in times of war, and in peacetime it is no less essential for the day-to-day running and routine.

The importance of signals to the Army can be seen in that at any time 8.8 per cent of the soldier establishment is made up of Royal Signals personnel. Among officers the percentage is around seven per cent. As with all the other regiments and corps of the Army, all members of the Royal Signals are fully trained soldiers capable of carrying out all the many duties of fighting troops. What separates them from the rest of the Army is the involved and intensive technical training that enables them to use some of the most modern and effective communications equipment in operational use anywhere in the world. The varied and complicated signals equipment issued to the Army is equal or superior to any comparable equivalent anywhere, and the Royal Corps of Signals is more than equal to its task and provides a service to the Army that is capable of meeting any challenge. From telephones to communication satellites, the corps has a role and a task, and wherever the Army is stationed, there you will find the Royal Signals.

In addition to its communications functions, the Royal Signals now has an extra role, that of Electronic Warfare, or EW. EW is a complex branch of warfare that encompasses listening in to enemy radio transmissions and locating their source, jamming enemy radio transmissions, deceiving the enemy by electronic interference and generally disrupting enemy combat radio communications. In return the EW operator has to ensure that the enemy does not do the same in return. EW is a wide-ranging form of combat and is beset with ploys and counter-ploys, but one thing is certain and that is that in any future conflict EW will play an important part. The communications nets of modern armies are far flung and complex and that makes them vulnerable to all manner of interference from simple noise introduction to destruction of a transmitting point or piece of equipment, and the Royal Signals are now well equipped and trained to wage EW.

Signals in BAOR

Within 1 (BR) Corps each of the three armoured divisions has an armoured division Signals regiment at headquarters level—indeed, the regiment also supplies the main establishment of the armoured division headquarters, which gives an indication of the importance of the Signals role to the modern Army. Each of these regiments has an establishment of about 800 officers and men divided among three Brigade Signals Squadrons. In each armoured division the Royal Signals provide and maintain telecommunications down to task force level, not forgetting the links to the rear. Below task force level each individual unit is responsible for its own particular communications equipment but the Royal Signals also provide partial repair facilities for front-line sets by supplying repair units at battalion and other levels. These units are concerned only with front line repairs. Apart from this repair role, the Royal Signals are usually available to advise on communications matters at all levels.

The Armoured Brigade Signals Squadrons and Armoured Division Signals Regiments provide the central command and communications systems for 1 (BR) Corps using both Clansman and Ptarmigan. Above them in the command chain are two Corps Signals Regiments, one for communication from the Corps HQ to the forward combat units and the other for communications to the rear. Again, Ptarmigan is involved along with Clansman and line systems where possible (1 (BR) Corps also makes as much use of line systems as possible). Above Corps level the Royal Signals has one Army Group Signals Regiment and one Army Group Signals Squadron providing the command and communications for HQ NORTHAG. The equipment for these units is NATO-funded.

There is one Signals Regiment involved with HQ BAOR which also provides the static communications throughout BAOR in time of peace. This function is controlled by a small Signals HQ, HQ 4 Signals Group. On general mobilisation this regiment would be reinforced by a number of TA regiments from the United Kingdom who would then be responsible for providing a full communications system from the rear of 1 (BR) Corps back to the Channel Ports.

There are a number of specialist Signals regiments in Germany, including the EW specialists. There is one Air Support Regiment that provides ground and some ground-to-air command and control communications systems for the RAF Germany Harrier force. This regiment provides static airfield communications and also the mobile secure communications systems required by the Harriers and their support helicopter squadrons. One further Signals Squadron provides command and control communications for HQ AFCENT, and a further four Signals Troops provide specialist support to British and NATO Army elements in Germany and Holland.

Signals in the United Kingdom

Whereas the main function of the Royal Signals in Germany is a straightforward one of being prepared for a possible conflict, the function of the Corps in the United Kingdom is rather more complicated. The Royal Signals not only retain their normal duties of providing communications for the Army (and partially for the other Armed Forces and NATO), but also provide a back-up force for BAOR and at the same time have to stand ready for possible use anywhere in the world.

To achieve this the Royal Signals have four Signals Brigades in the United Kingdom, two Regular and two TA. The two Regular Signals Brigades are 1 Signals Group headquartered at Salisbury and 2 Signals Brigade at Aldershot. In a nutshell, 1 Signals Group is responsible for possible operations outside the United Kingdom and 2 Signals Brigade within it. The two TA brigades are 12 Signals Brigade (TA) headquartered at Chelsea and 11 Signals Brigade (TA) headquartered in Liverpool. 11 Signals Brigade is responsible for TA Signals units under NATO command and 12 Signals Brigade is responsible for communications in the 1 (BR) Corps rear area.

The number of units under the command of 1 Signals Group are legion. There is one Brigade Signals Squadron supporting UKMF(L) that normally operates on the NATO flanks. An Airborne Brigade Signals Squadron, based near Aldershot, provides support for 5 Airborne Brigade and all members of this squadron are parachute-trained. There is also a Special Air Service Signals Squadron (264), backed up by a TA squadron.

AMF(L) is afforded the support of a Signals Squadron and has the distinction of having its equipment NATO-funded. This squadron is frequently deployed abroad for exercises, usually on the NATO flanks. Another 'mobile' unit is the single Air Support Signals Squadron that provides the command and control communications to RAF strike aircraft and helicopters deployed in support of the AMF(L) and UKMF(L), and also 5 Airborne Brigade. Some members of this squadron are parachute-trained.

There is another Signals Regiment that might be regarded as a contingency unit. It provides the communication support for any unit that might be deployed from the United Kingdom for operational or training reasons. This is 30 Signals Regiment, the regiment that was so heavily involved during the Falkland Islands' campaign. This regiment always has a detachment on 24 hours' notice to move anywhere in the world.

In addition to all the above, 1 Signals Group commands the Infantry Divisional Signals Regiment and the Infantry Brigade Signals Squadrons that would move with 2 Infantry Division to join 1 (BR) Corps in an emergency.

On a more domestic note, one Signals Regiment looks after the United Kingdom's static command and control systems. Here, we are in 2 Signals Brigade territory and in use is a wide variety of equipment ranging from line systems to MOULD, a UHF command net system that operates automatically within each Military District. MOULD is meant to be an operational system since, for more day-to-day use, there are the usual British Telecom land-lines or BOXER micro-wave links. At present the Army has some dedicated land line systems using mechanical switching—these are to be converted to electronic switching with the FASTNET system. In the main, three Signals Squadrons look after these United Kingdom-based systems and their duties range from rigging up the wiring for the Trooping the Colour communications to supporting training units in their training areas. Finally, two further Signals Troops must be mentioned, one of them based in the Hebrides, which provide specialist support to the Armed Forces in the United Kingdom.

Signals elsewhere

One of the main responsibilities of the Royal Signals which has to be dealt with separately is their presence in Northern Ireland. There, the Royal Signals have a far greater responsibility than elsewhere for operational communication for their involvement reaches down to a much lower command level. The main reason for this is that Signals are used right down to patrol level and the Royal Signals are currently establishing a completely new radio network based on the use of Racal Cougar sets that can be carried in a pocket. Using a repeater system, the Cougar network will eventually cover the entire Province and enable patrols to report back to high command levels if necessary. There are three Signals squadrons in Northern Ireland, 233 Signals Squadron (NI) which acts as the communications branch of HQ Northern Ireland at Lisburn, and two Infantry Brigade HQ and Signals Squadrons at the two Brigade HQs at Londonderry and (again) Lisburn. Much use is made in Northern Ireland of land lines and the current system will convert to the new electronic FASTNET switching system. The current sytem is known as the PONI network (Post Office Northern Ireland) and teleprinters are widely used for message passing. As a back-up to the existing systems, a military radio relay system using standard BRUIN equipment is maintained.

Further afield, in Cyprus one Signals Regiment and two Signals Squadrons support British forces in the Sovereign Base Areas while a further Signals Squadron supports UNFICYP. Both EW and command and control systems are involved. In Hong Kong the Gurkha Signals Regiment prevails with one Gurkha Signals Squadron supporting the Gurkha

A Triffid radio relay installation mounted on a 4-tonne truck (School of Signals).

Field Force, two Gurkha Signals Squadrons providing trunk communications throughout Hong Kong Island, Kowloon and the New Territories, while one Gurkha Signals Troop is in Brunei.

In the Falklands, 266 Signals Squadron (BFFI) looks after all the communications covering the islands and uses a system known as FITS (Falkland Islands Trunk System). This was installed in the aftermath of the 1982 campaign and consists of a microwave system with 11 telephone exchanges and a number of underground cable systems. The network uses electronic switching throughout and is powered by generators that require refuelling only every three months or so. FITS has to interface with a Cable and Wireless INTELSTAT station and many other systems used by the Armed Forces. The Royal Signals look after all this and also provide EW support.

Apart from the locations already mentioned, there are Royal Signals Troops on Ascension Island, in Belize and on the Rock of Gibraltar. The Royal Signals serve wherever the British Army goes.

Signals training

The 'home' of the Royal Corps of Signals is now Blandford in Dorset, despite the fact that many serving officers and signallers were initially trained to regard Catterick in Yorkshire as their base. The Royal Signals Headquarters Mess moved from Catterick to Blandford in 1967 and it is there that the School of Signals is situated today. The school provides both officers' and NCOs' training courses in all aspects of military signalling and the associated technologies involved, but it has other roles. These include the development of new Signals equipment, the running of the various trials involved in such a task, and even at times the very manufacture and testing of the 'one-off' or specialised pieces of equipment.

Catterick still remains the main training base for the Royal Signals as it is the home of the Training Group Royal Signals. This group has three main elements. The first is 11 Signals Regiment, based at Catterick itself. This regiment is entrusted with basic recruit training and also concerns itself with the Junior Signallers Wing at Harrogate. The largest of all the Royal Signals regiments is 8 Signals Regiment, also at Catterick, which usually has around 1,000 men under trade training at any one time. The third of the training group elements is the Army Apprentice College at Harrogate, which is now concerned only with the training of junior technicians for the Royal Signals. All three of these elements are commanded by the Training Group Headquarters.

Mention must also be made of the Signals Training Centre in Scarborough which acts as a training centre and base for Royal Signals TA units. Some regular refresher training also takes place at Scarborough.

Signallers have a choice of five different types of trade grouping within the Royal Signals (not including bandsmen). These are electronics, telegraphy, combat, administrative and supervisory. (Electronic warfare [EW] specialists are mainly contained in the telegraphy group.)

It would not be possible to mention the Royal Corps of Signals without making some mention of its display team, the White Helmets. This motor cycle display team is now world-famous, and anyone who has witnessed its high-speed routines can be excused from forgetting that the motor cycle is now no longer used operationally by the Royal Signals, which puts the White Helmets into the same bracket as the King's Troop, RHA.

NATO communications

As will be already evident, the Royal Signals are involved not only with British Army communications

Containerised Royal Signals installation on a 4-tonne truck and using an air-actuated telescopic mast with dish aerial (MoD).

The interior of a Ptarmigan Trunk Switch (Plessey).

systems but with NATO ones as well. NATO communication systems have grown with the Alliance and were originally based on existing post office national systems, some of which are still widely used, but it was decided that militarily provided and manned communication systems were needed and so the Royal Signals became directly involved.

The first modern military communications capability was established in the 1960s when SHAPE installed the ACE HIGH tropospheric-scatter system. ACE HIGH is the name given to a complex network which supports the NATO radar early warning system and provides command channels for NATO's air response. High capacity microwave voice and telegraph circuits exist throughout the Allied Command Europe (ACE) area from northern Norway to Turkey. Royal Signals tradesmen, after qualifying at the NATO Communications School at Latina in Italy, are responsible for running the eight ACE HIGH stations in the United Kingdom as well as several stations abroad. Member countries provide the equipment for each station.

In the late 1960s two further steps were taken to improve NATO communications capability. The first was the establishment of a network for political consultation, for the exchange of intelligence and other data and to speed up decision-making, especially regarding the possible use of nuclear weapons.

This was called the 'NATO-Wide Communications Network', and it now provides direct and dedicated telegraph links between NATO HQs, capitals and Command HQs.

The second step in capability was the introduction of space satellites. In 1970 the first of the 12 satellite ground terminals of Phase 2 of the NATO Satellite Communications (SATCOM) Programme was brought into service. This system now covers the entire NATO area and all members have a ground station (except France and Luxembourg). This system will be improved further by the planned Phase 3 which will form part of the new NATO Integrated Communications System, or NICS.

NICS will provide a modern, automatically switched, common-user telephone and telegraph network covering the whole of the NATO area. Communications 'nodal' points and message distribution centres are to be established in the various NATO countries which will enable messages and telephone calls to be switched rapidly and automatically from one point in the system to another. The NATO Phase 3 SATCOM system, as well as the ACE HIGH and NATO-wide networks will form integral parts of NICS. The NICS plan will be implemented on an incremental basis throughout the 1980s and the

Royal Signals have an important part in its implementation.

To effectively plan and implement NICS, a communications agency known as the NICS Management Agency (NICSMA) has been established in Brussels. The operational management of the system has been given to the NICS Central Operating Authority (NICSCOA) based at Mons.

Ptarmigan

Modern armies depend to a far greater extent on their communications than they have ever done before in the history of warfare. Today, mobile forces can only move, fight and even exist within the framework of commands, information and all the mundane day-to-day routine provided by the links of their communication systems. Thus, in the modern British Army the provision of reliable and secure communications is as important as the provision of modern weapons. By the time these words are published the Army will be using some of the most advanced communication equipment in service anywhere in the world in the shape of Ptarmigan.

Ptarmigan provides the main information links which route all the Army's routine and tactical information from corps HQ down to the front line units. It is a mobile, automatically switched and secure area communication system designed to provide a very high measure of reliability and traffic capacity. It is also compatible with existing NATO systems.

Like so many programmes of a similar nature, Ptarmigan development has a fairly long history. The British Army was for years after the war searching for the answer to the secure area communications problem to replace the rather cumbersome systems built up during the war years and retained only because there were no funds to replace them. One of these early development projects was 'Project Hobart' which had to be abandoned due to the high costs that would ultimately have been involved. Then came 'Project Mallard', an international project involving the United Kingdom, Australia, Canada and the USA. The project began in 1967 but ended in 1969 when the US withdrew as the result of a political decision. But Project Mallard had shown the needs and the basic outlines of what any new system would require. Already the basic outlines were approaching the hardware stage as the 1 (BR) Corps in Germany began to be issued with the interim Bruin communication system, in the hopes that Project Mallard would eventually replace it. With the demise of Project Mallard, Bruin was improved somewhat and its expected service life was extended.

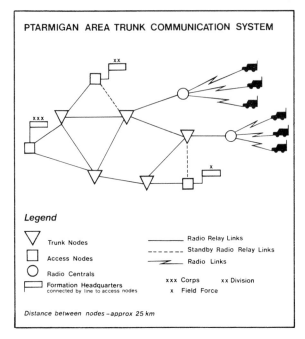

PTARMIGAN AREA TRUNK COMMUNICATION SYSTEM

Legend

▽ Trunk Nodes

□ Access Nodes

○ Radio Centrals

⊏ Formation Headquarters connected by line to access nodes

———— Radio Relay Links

- - - - - Standby Radio Relay Links

⌇ Radio Links

xxx Corps   xx Division

x Field Force

Distance between nodes – approx 25 km

Bruin is still a unique communication system in that it employs a secure system of links using a digital-based switching system. Despite its advanced nature and widespread use it does have several disadvantages which the Army wishes to have eliminated. One of these is that there is a distinct limitation to the amount of traffic it can handle, and there are restrictions on its operational flexibility. On the technical side, much of the equipment used was obtained from existing commercial sources and consequently some items lack the capabilities required. For example, most of the switching is carried out by electro-magnetic gear with all their attendant maintenance and reliability problems. Another difficulty is that, although messages are transmitted in pulsed (digital) form, they have to be converted to and from conventional electrical waveforms (analogue) before transmission and after reception—this adds to the reliability and maintenance workload.

Despite its present problems, Bruin provides 1 (BR) Corps with the outlines and experience of the next generation of communication systems. The British Army decided to adopt their new system, soon known as Ptarmigan, in 1973, and at the time of writing development is almost complete with a date into service stated to be in the early 1980s. From the outset, experience gained with Project Mallard was used but even so, a large number of agencies were involved. The British communications industry was deeply involved from the start and Plessey were appointed prime contractor in 1973. The Ministry of Defence, the Royal Signals and Radar Establishment (RSRE) and the Army School of Signals were also involved in the resultant series of studies and trials. Production of the actual hardware began during 1979 with a large number of firms involved, still under the overall direction of Plessey.

Ptarmigan uses thoroughly up-to-date technology to the extent that it is digital throughout. This means that switching and all the various message routing can be carried out swiftly and reliably using well-proven solid-state techniques. Very basically the Ptarmigan system is not unlike a modern telephone subscriber system in that each 'customer' unit has its own unique 'identify' number. If any unit wishes to contact any other unit the identify number is transmitted over a radio frequency. The code is picked up at one of what may be several switching stations, or nodes, in the area and directed along a selected radio path to its destination. All the switching involved is done automatically and electronically. There are three different types of switching node, each with its own particular task, but they all have basically the same function. For instance, the Headquarters/Access nodes are an integral part of all divisional and other formation

headquarters and can receive and transmit information not only to units under their control but also to other units in the general corps area.

One great advantage which the Ptarmigan system shares with Bruin is that it can deal not only with conventional voice traffic but also with the traffic associated with data links such as Wavell, teleprinter traffic, facsimile transmission and even pulsed video signals. The basic heart of the system lies in the switching nodes themselves which are usually contained in mobile container bodies carried by 4-tonne trucks. In a normal corps area there are about 20 of these nodes which intercommunicate with each other by UHF radio links involving a Ptarmigan sub-system which rejoices in the code name of Triffid. (This sub-system is provided by Marconi Communications Limited and the Triffid designation has been given purely to identify the components involved from the rest of the Ptarmigan system.) The various nodes are constantly in touch with at least three (and usually more) other nodes to provide a constant and flexible routing network for traffic. If any one node goes out of action, either for repair, maintenance, enemy inflicted damage or the need to move to a new location, traffic is automatically switched to its destination along other links. The link with the front-line battlefield radio

Interior of a Ptarmigan radio relay installation (School of Signals).

Ptarmigan Trunk Switch installation on a FV439 and with aerial elevated.

nets is via Radio Central switching stations which can thus link the front-line units direct into the complete network. No matter in which form a message enters the system, it is converted into a standard pulsed (digital) form which it retains until it is decoded by the receiver station.

For extra information, each of the switching nodes can be up to about 25 kilometres apart, although this can vary according to local conditions. Each radio link can have either 16 or 32 channels, two of which are permanently occupied for technical purposes leaving the rest for the actual communication network. Using a digital system, each message can be transmitted at a very rapid rate (a normal signal can be transmitted in a time scale measured in milliseconds). Apart from the usual message transmissions the whole network can be used for broadcast messages and, at the other end of the scale, secure and 'hot line' channels can be provided. Full cryptographical coverage of all messages is provided. As mentioned elsewhere, Ptarmigan is used for BATES and Wavell, but it also has many technical facilities which it is not possible to describe in a general work of this nature.

Ptarmigan is now being issued to the troops in Germany. Starting with the two 'forward' armoured divisions (1 and 4), Ptarmigan will be gradually issued to 3rd Armoured Division, then throughout BAOR and back to the Channel Ports. The re-equipment programme should be complete by 1988.

Clansman

Clansman is the cover designation given to a range of battlefield telecommunications equipments which together provide an integrated and compatible system for use by front-line formations and their vehicles. The Clansman designation covers seven different types of set—originally there were five but two have optional 'add-on' units and a further two have been added to the range. However, the Clansman compatability extends not only to the sets but to the wiring harnesses involved, their aerials, and also to the test and repair equipment involved. In addition, the British communications industry manufactures many other equipments built to the same exacting standards as Clansman which are compatible with the Service equipments.

When Clansman was first introduced, the British Army had more than 20 different types of radio equipment in service and general use. The bulk of these belonged to the Larkspur range, many of which are still in use, both in the front lines and

Clansman equipment	Frequency (MHz)	RF power	Range (approx) (Km)	Weight (Kg)
Manpacks				
UK/PRC-344	225-399.95	2.5W	10	7.6
UK/PRC-349	37-46.975	0.5W	2	1.5
UK/PRC-350	36-56.975	2W	5	3.6
UK/PRC-351	30-75.975	4W	8	6.3
UK/PRC-352	30-75.975	20W	16	9.1
UK/PRC-320	2-30	30W	50	10.8
Vehicle equipments				
UK/VRC-353	30-75.975	0.1-50W	30	22
UK/VRC-321	1.5-30	40W	60	23
UK/VRC-322	1.5-30	300W	80	52

elsewhere. The Larkspur range is a legacy of the days when the Army had a full global role, but once that had gone, many of the Larkspur sets were no longer really suitable for the European theatre (mainly for various technical reasons). Also the number of types of set was too many for logistic comfort. The decision was thus taken to introduce an entire new family of equipments embodying as many proven technical innovations as possible. The new Clansman sets were thus to be smaller, lighter and more reliable than Larkspur. After the usual issue of specifications, production of Clansman began during 1976 so that by the end of 1978 some front-line units had been issued and trained with the new sets. But by late 1981 Larkspur had still not been entirely replaced and even after it has passed from front-line use it will no doubt continue to be used by the TA and other formations.

Apart from their overall reliability, Clansman equipments are built to very tight and rugged specifications. Almost every set uses voice as a general medium but most can be converted for morse, facsimile transmission and data transmission, and all are compatible with Bruin and Ptarmigan. By the use of various 'add-on' units nearly every set can have its frequency range or combat range extended, and adaptors have been produced to enable hand sets to be able to feed direct into the Wavell system, or into other NATO networks. Most sets also have such refinements as microphone amplifiers for 'whisper' voice inputs, and every set has automatic aerial tuning when frequencies are changed. Vehicle sets can also have cryptographic devices attached.

Considering the number of different types of component involved in the Clansman system, it is not surprising to learn that nearly every manufacturer involved in the British telecommunications industry has become enmeshed in Clansman production. For overall production of the manpack sets, Racal have been involved, but Plessey are responsible for one set. Marconi and MEL produce

the vehicle range, but many other companies produce such items as test equipment, aerial tuners, wire harness switch boxes and all the many other similar essential items.

This book is not the place for a complete rundown of all the technical detail of the Clansman range, but the following table provides a general appreciation of the salient points. The outlines are only basic and do not provide for the fact that many of the sets can be altered and improved by the use of 'add-on' units. At the time of writing many Clansman improvement packages are in the pipeline or under trial, so the list may be yet extended.

Wavell

Wavell is a mobile, computer-based information system designed for service within 1 (BR) Corps, and using modern automated data processing equipment (ADP) converted to serve the needs of the modern Army. The need for some form of ADP system has long been painfully evident to higher command echelons, for the scale and demands of mobile warfare have grown to the stage where the passing and sifting of routine combat information and intelligence can submerge the command function. The introduction of Wavell is intended to place this flow of information under the control of an ADP system so that the command levels can deal with the command process alone, and the everyday routine of the task is reduced to a minimum.

Wavell has been under development by Plessey ever since the first ADP design contracts were issued during 1976. The introduction of Wavell into service has not proved easy as for some time after 1976 the system parameters were so undefined that it proved almost impossible to move into the hardware stage. But by the end of 1979 the first phase of its introduction had been completed. This involved HQ 1 (BR) Corps and only one division (2nd Armoured Division), while the actual hardware was confined to nine processing centres. The cost was some £6 million, but the results have been so encouraging that the second phase has now been given the go-ahead at a further cost of £31 million. The final number of centres will be 33 and they should be in service by the early 1980s.

The overall system can be roughly outlined as follows. At Corps HQ there will be a main Wavell terminal consisting of a central computer data bank using both floppy disc and bubble data storage. Included will be a paper ('hard') print-out for any required data, and a visual display unit (VDU) along with racked ADP modules, communications equipment and switching gear. All this is contained in a special air-conditioned container body carried on a 4-tonne truck. The central system is switched into either the Bruin trunk system or eventually Ptarmigan—Bruin has two channels reserved for Wavell use only, and Ptarmigan will also devote two channels to the system. Divisional HQs will also have a Wavell terminal which will be the same as that used at Corps HQ, but in most circumstances there will be an alternative installation in another location, also switched into the Wavell network. Below divisional level there will be at least two further Wavell installations in FV432s, but these will be employed at task force level and will have only input and output terminals. During the Phase One trials a number of hard-topped Land Rovers were used both as switching vehicles and as forward terminals.

The whole purpose of Wavell, for all its seeming complexity, is to act as a data switching system from corps HQ down to the task forces and back again. Data inserted into the system at task force level can be examined and acted upon at corps and divisional level, and as command HQs move from location to location, Wavell is carried with them ready to be switched into the network for almost immediate use. The information can be read out on a VDU or it can be printed out on to a 'hard' paper copy. Each formation can build up its own particular data bank, but this can be switched into any other formation's data bank, or the central HQ bank, at any time.

The introduction of ADP into the Army command structure has not been without its difficulties and prior to the first phase of introduction there were several problems that had to be ironed out. One was the possible amalgamation of Wavell and BATES, but for several reasons this was not proceeded with, although there will have to be interface communications between the two systems. There will also have to be interface with other NATO command systems such as the West German HEROS and the US Army TOS (Tactical Operations System).

The Phase One Wavell system was mostly adapted from commercial equipment and was based on the PDP 11/35 central processor. This uses a tape and disc memory, but the Phase Two installations will be based on a military computer, the GEC 4080M. The Phase One VDUs were commercial Cossor DID400 units adapted to military needs but with Phase Two they will be replaced by more compact units.

There are doubtless many more problems left to be solved before Wavell is in full-scale service but the Phase One installations proved to be so successful that they are to be retained until the Phase Two equipments are ready. With the old 2nd Armoured Division the use of Wavell was extended to include Artillery, Engineer and logistic functions and doubtless other uses for the system will be found. But already some questions are being asked. It is noticeable that the downward chain of information and input ends at the task force level while it is foreseen that battle groups may well be useful input and output customers. Another age-old problem is that when the data is finally put into use at any level it still has to be converted into visual form on the familiar perspex-faced map by hand. Input into Wavell will remain via a VDU keyboard for some appreciable while, but future developments may include the direct keying into the system via miniature keyboards plugged into radio equipments in the front line.

When Wavell is in full service it will conserve valuable manpower and time that is at present employed in sending, switching and receiving routine data and reports. Wavell will also act as a data sorting and storage bank that can be consulted at will, providing the information that commanders need, when they need it, and in a manner that all levels can assimilate and understand. The importance of Wavell to the Army of the future can be seen in the fact that the 1980 Defence White Paper estimates that it will cost £55 million to implement.

STARRNET

Keeping troops in Germany is not a cheap exercise and the Army is at all times watching out for methods and means of keeping down the overheads inherent in carrying out its European role. Wherever possible, any means of reducing costs is examined and many savings have been made in the day-to-day running of the Army in Germany, even if the initial capital costs may at first sight seem rather daunting. Typical of the cost-cutting exercises carried out in the past has been the reduction of the everyday telephone communication expenses that are inevitable if links between garrisons in Germany and the United Kingdom are to be maintained and the numerous message-

Off to the next job—a REME FV434.

passing admin tasks are to be continued. After 1945 and up to 1964 the vast bulk of the Army's day to day telephone costs had to be paid to the Deutches Bundespost, and the outlay was at times heavy. To make some savings the Army decided to set up its own secure microwave telecommunication links between the various garrisons. The result is known as STARRNET.

STARRNET is the acronym for Static Radio Relay Network, which works on the line-of-sight microwave principle. There are 300 channels available for telephone, telegraph and data transmission circuits, and it is possible to link STARRNET with both the United Kingdom and the Berlin Garrison, not by line of sight transmission but by tropospheric scatter—this consists of 'bouncing' a microwave beam off one of the various layers in the troposphere. The system was commissioned in 1964 and ever since then it has paid for itself over and over again—it had virtually saved its initial costs within four years. The system is run by the Technical Control Centre at JHQ Rheindahlen. In operation it has proved to be so reliable that the Rheindahlen centre is the only one that is permanently manned. Each station has a 'hot standby' facility in that if one main set should produce a fault

it automatically switches to a standby set.

The Rheindahlen station is controlled by 4 Signals Group which is thus responsible for the overall command of STARRNET within Germany. The United Kingdom link is at Dover. At the time of writing STARRNET is still being modified to extend its coverage and capabilities.

The Royal Electrical and Mechanical Engineers

The Royal Electrical and Mechanical Engineers, or the REME to give its more usual name, is a branch of the Army with a well-defined role—it is to keep the Army's wide range of equipment fit and ready for operational use. By the Army's standards the REME is still a relatively young formation since it was only raised in 1942, but ever since then it has established itself as probably the Army's most technical and versatile grouping of specialists. The REME provides the tradesmen for all branches of the Army, and where you find the British soldier, the REME tradesman is not very far away.

If it were possible to reduce the tasks of the REME from their wide-ranging complexities to a basic statement, it would be apposite to state that the REME is the Army's repair branch, but needless to say it is much more than that. It does have a repair task but it has many others as well, not the least of which is that of equipment recovery for re-use. Throughout this book it will become obvious that modern warfare is a frighteningly expensive business and any recovery or economics produced by the turnround or repair of damaged or worn items is an essential part of the Army's battle readiness. At the 'teeth' end, the battlefield recovery of damaged or broken-down tanks or other vehicle casualties could be essential, while further to the rear the repair of weapons and other equipment enables logistic and manpower loads to be diverted to supply other needs. In the front line and in the rear areas, the REME has an essential role to play in keeping the Army ready for battle, and in both sectors it is organised accordingly.

The importance of the REME to the modern Army can be seen in the way that the REME is incorporated into every strata of the Army's organisation. Two examples of this will suffice to illustrate the point. At the United Kingdom-based Infantry battalion level are between 11 and 28 REME tradesmen who are tasked with keeping the equipment and weapons of that battalion ready for use. In Germany, each armoured division established is sized to match their equipment. In between these two extremes there are many other levels of organisation and manning, but throughout all REME establishments the underlying theme is one of organisation and equipment designed to suit the particular needs of the types of unit they serve.

The composition of each of these particular types of REME establishment can be seen in the tables that accompany these words. From these it will be seen that most BAOR formations have workshops—the Infantry and Cavalry units have light aid detachments, or LADs. The role of the LAD is to accompany its particular units into battle and provide running repairs and recovery as and when they are needed. These repairs are very much first line—any major tasks are carried out by the rear echelons. The field workshops supplying the needs of the support arms are usually situated further to the rear of the main battle lines and do not need this forward element, although they often have

Types of REME organisation within BAOR

The vehicles mentioned include only 'A' and specialised vehicles.

1 Armoured Regiment LAD. Manpower: 2 officers + 91 soldiers. Vehicles: 5 FV434s, 4 FV432s, 5 Chieftain ARVs, 1 Samson and 1 Recovery Vehicle Heavy. Outline: regimental HQ and HQ squadron with 1 FV434 and 1 Recovery Vehicle Heavy; four sections, each with 1 FV434, 1 FV432 and 1 Chieftain ARV.

2 Mechanised Infantry Battalion LAD. Manpower: 1 officer + 66 soldiers. Vehicles: 5 FV434s, 5 FV432s, 1 Samson and 1 Recovery Vehicle Medium. Outline: LAD HQ and battalion HG fitter section with 1 Recovery Vehicle Medium; HQ company fitter section with 1 FV434 and 1 FV432; four mechanised fitter sections, each with 1 FV434 and 1 FV432.

3 Armoured Division Engineer Regiment Workshop. Manpower: 2 officers + 58 soldiers. Vehicles: 3 Samsons, 3 FV434s, 3 FV432s and 1 Recovery Vehicle Heavy. Outline: HQ and maintenance section with 1 Recovery Vehicle Heavy; field support squadron section and three field squadron sections, each with 1 Samson, 1 FV434 and 1 FV432.

4 Armoured Reconnaissance Regiment LAD. Manpower: 1 officer + 62 soldiers. Vehicles: 1 Ferret SC, 4 Spartans, 5 Samsons and 2 Recovery Vehicles Medium. Outline: HQ and HQ fitter section with 1 Ferret SC, 1 Samson and 2 Recovery Vehicles Medium; four recce squadron fitter sections, each with 1 Spartan and 1 Samson.

5 Armoured Division Transport Regiment Workshop. Manpower: 1 officer + 54 soldiers. Vehicles: 2 Recovery Vehicles Medium. Outline: workshop HQ and main repair section with 2 Recovery Vehicles Medium plus two squadron sections, each with 16 soldiers.

6 Field Regiment (Abbot) LAD. Manpower: 1 officer + 58 soldiers. Vehicles: 1 Recovery Vehicle Heavy, 3 FV434s, 3 FV432s. Outline: workshop HQ and HQ battery section with 1 Recovery Vehicle Heavy; three FV433 Abbot battery sections, each with 1 FV434 and 1 FV432.

7 Field Regiment (M109) Workshop. Manpower: 1 officer + approx 60 soldiers. Vehicles: 3 FV434s, 3 M578 ARVs, 1 Samson and 1 Recovery Vehicle Heavy. Outline: HQ and HQ battery section with 1 Recovery Vehicle Heavy; three FV433 Abbot battery sections, each with 1 FV434 and 1 M578 ARV.

8 Armoured Workshop (Large). Manpower: 16 officers and 350 soldiers (plus RAOC stores platoon). Vehicles: 12 FV434s, 12 Centurion ARVs, 2 Recovery Vehicles Medium, 10 Recovery Vehicles Heavy. Outline: each armoured workshop organisation is decided by each CO armoured workshop. Operationally each large armoured workshop will be divided into two FRGs and two MRGs.

one. All the BAOR-based REME formations are equipped with tracked vehicles, where possible. United Kingdom-based formations use wheeled vehicles, with only a relatively few tracked types. Like the BAOR REME units, each particular unit has its REME component tailored to suit its individual requirement.

To return to the BAOR organisation, each armoured division has two armoured workshops which are REME-manned units (plus some personnel from other arms) and which are completely mobile. Each individual armoured workshop has its own individual internal arrangements to suit the particular tasks and scope of its operations but in battle it is usually split into four sections. Two of these sections are the forward repair groups, the FRGs, and the other two are the main repair groups, or MRGs. The FRGs operate within a task force area (the LADS will be in the battle group areas), and they operate as far forward behind the battle lines as possible. Their task is to carry out the repair and recovery tasks the LADs cannot handle. These will include such major operations as engine

pack changes and weapon replacements. The MRGs are usually further to the rear and carry out those jobs that involve specialised repair or test equipment and bench work. To illustrate the differences between the types of armoured workshop unit, the FRG will change an engine pack but the MRG will replace a component of that engine pack.

As well as their battle roles, the armoured workshops also have peacetime functions. In addition to the day-to-day repair and maintenance functions, the workshops look after garrison vehicles and equipment and operate limited production and re-furbishing tasks. In peacetime, civilians are used to augment manpower levels.

Above divisional level come the Corps echelons which consist of a Mobile Corps Workshop, a Special Electronic Workshop (also mobile), and Aircraft Workshops, which are not fully mobile but are at least portable.

Backing up the corps REME units in BAOR are two large Base Workshops. These are run by REME personnel but are almost entirely manned by civilians. The biggest unit is 23 Base Workshop which deals with AFV major repairs and overhauls. It is much the larger of the two as 37 (Rhine) Workshop

A Chieftain ARV moves off to its next task.

deals with instruments, electronic equipment and all the many other specialised forms of Army equipment. Further support is given to BAOR by the four Base Workshops based in the United Kingdom. These are run along factory lines with planned workloads, schedules and many other disciplines normally associated with commercial concerns. They are almost entirely civilian-manned but are run by the REME. They consist of 18 Base Workshop which, like its BAOR equivalent (23 Base Workshop), deals with AFVs and is established at Bovington. The other base workshops are 35 at Old Dalby which handles electrical and electronic equipment, 34 at Donnington, dealing with gun systems, small-arms and other weapons equipment, and 32 at Bicester which also deals mainly with 'A' vehicles and their associated assemblies. In addition to their routine work, the Base Workshops are capable of producing various types of specialised equipment and major semi-production tasks such as the retrofitting of extra armour and accessories to vehicles used in Northern Ireland. Other production examples are machine-gun mountings and specialised internal security equipment.

Overseas there are REME workshops in Hong Kong, Cyprus and at Suffield in Canada. Northern Ireland has its own REME establishment, and there are similar bases in Belize and Gibraltar. As mentioned above, wherever the Army goes, the REME goes with it.

The home of the REME is Arborfield, the location of the REME Training Centre, the REME Officers' School, the Princess Marina College for REME apprentices and the School of Electronic Engineering. The School of Electrical and Mechanical Engineering is at Bordon.

Offering as it does such a wide range of trades and skills, recruiting is seldom a problem for the REME and the annual intake of around 1,200 entrants is usually over-subscribed. Once taken into the REME the recruit is offered an enormous range of possible trades, all of which can lead to the highly skilled level of artificer or specialised technician. There are many different types of trade which fall into six main groupings. They are electronic, aircraft, vehicles, weapons, driving and administrative. In each group there may be several sub-divisions: for example, in the vehicle group there are mechanics 'A' and 'B' and electricians, while in the aircraft group there are technicians aircraft and technicians avionics.

With the advent of more and more complex electronic and optical equipment, the importance of the REME within the Army is bound to increase, and with this has come a novel and significant role. All new military equipment is now scrutinised by REME personnel at almost every stage of its design and development, not only with a view to ensuring that it lives up to its performance specifications, but also to ensure that it has as much built-in reliability as possible and that it can be maintained with the minimum of cost, time and specialised back-up. The REME is not the only branch of the Service involved in this detailed assessment, but it is one of the more important. The new role is carried out by Maintenance Advisory Groups, or MAGs, and the REME personnel are usually officers with specialised knowledge of their particular field. The MAGs are controlled by their respective parent units which are Vehicles and Weapons Branch REME, Aircraft Branch REME, Workshop Technology Branch REME and Electronics Branch REME.

The Royal Corps of Transport & The Gurkha Transport Regiment

The Royal Corps of Transport (RCT) Year Book for 1977 opens with these words: 'The chief responsibility of the Royal Corps of Transport is to organise and operate the means of transport which support the British Army in war and peace. In addition, the corps executes the movement of men and material worldwide, operates ports and performs certain functions in connection with air movement and air logistic support.'

It would be difficult to find a more succinct statement of the role of the RCT, but to assess that role is a complex task. To simply state that the RCT deals with transport hardly deals fairly with all its varied operations, for the corps transports the Army not only on land (by road and rail), but also helps to move it by air and even carries some of the Army's loads by sea.

The Depot for the RCT is at Buller Baracks, Aldershot, but the Corps is based wherever the Army goes. It is to Buller Barracks that the new recruit is sent for his basic Army training and while there he is also given his Army driver training course. More advanced driving instruction is given at Leconfield in Humberside, and from there the qualified drivers go to their respective units for further instruction and duties.

Drivers can be assigned to a number of specialist units but the basic RCT formation is the Transport Squadron which forms part of an RCT Transport Regiment. Each squadron is made up of two or three troops with about 20 trucks apiece, and each troop is usually equipped with only one type of truck, either 4- or 10-tonne. Each 1 (BR) Corps armoured division has its own transport regiment. These transport units are the main carrying components of nearly all the Army's long- and short-haul operations, ferrying stores, fuel, ammunition, food and all the other items needed to keep the Army functioning.

Apart from the transport squadrons, the RCT also mans the Ambulance Squadrons and drives the ambulances for the RAMC, both tracked and wheeled versions. There are also Car Squadrons which operate staff cars at all levels from Land Rovers to six-seater saloons. At the top end of the scale are the Tank Transporter Squadrons which have the most highly qualified and experienced of all RCT drivers, namely the driver specialists. Perhaps the most prestigious unit in the RCT is 20 Squadron, which operates the six vehicles used to carry the Queen's Baggage Train.

There are several other driving skill trades open to soldiers in the RCT. The top driver is the Master Driver, a highly competent and experienced Warrant Officer who has the task of advising all other branches of the Army with reference to driving skills. Another specialist is the Driver Radio Operator who has a variety of communication roles.

The Army has its own railway specialists who operate the Army's own diesel railway based on Detmold. The function of this is not only to carry stores, but also to act as the training location for the Army's railway staff who can become qualified as shunters, guards, signalmen, yardmasters and controllers. All of these personnel would take over some civilian railways in an emergency. The unit that operates the Detmold complex is 79 Railway Squadron, which is backed up by 275 Railway Squadron (V), a part-time unit largely drawn from British Rail staff.

Perhaps the greatest surprise to many scholars of the Army comes when they learn that the Army has its own maritime detachment, with its own military port at Marchwood, on Southampton Water. Marchwood Military Port is operated by 17 Maritime and Port Regiment RCT (which also maintains troops in Cyprus and Hong Kong), but the majority of the maritime trade training is carried out at nearby Gosport (apart from the trade of Port Controller). These maritime trades include seaman, marine engineer, navigator and navigator ocean watchkeeper. All these naval-sounding trades are carried out by soldiers, and the RCT also has its own divers for various duties.

The shipping of the RCT is largely operated by 20 Maritime Regiment RCT. Pride of the Army's fleet are two Landing Craft Logistics (LCL) named HMAV *Ardennes* and *Arakan*. Both are used on the Marchwood to Antwerp run to supply BAOR, but they are also used to carry supplies to Northern Ireland and the various Army outposts and ranges in the Hebrides and other Scottish islands. A variety of smaller craft is operated by the RCT, some in association with the Royal Navy. The great bulk of the Army's wartime supplies would be carried on the Landing Ship Logistics (LSL) fleet of about 12 vessels operated by the Royal Fleet Auxiliary.

Supplies dropped by aircraft of the Royal Air Force to Army units in the field are the responsibility of another RCT unit, namely 47 Air Despatch Squadron. This squadron packs Army supplies, loads them into the aircraft and is also responsible for dropping them from the aircraft in flight. The RCT members of the unit are known as Air Despatchers, and the squadron is mainly based at RAF Lyneham in Wiltshire, but they travel with the aircraft (now nearly all C-130 Hercules) wherever they are needed as part of the aircraft's crew. The squadron also carries out some air despatch tasks for the Royal Navy and the Royal Marines, and deals with RAF Wessex, Chinook and Puma helicopters.

The moving of any number of soldiers and their families involves the RCT in yet another of its functions, this time movement control. The RCT has a specialised and far-flung formation known as 29 Movement Control which has a large and varied number of movement control detachments operating everywhere the Army is likely to travel to and from. These detachments carry out the essential tasks of administering and supervising all aspects of the Army on the move and they operate at ports, railway stations, airports and road locations.

An important part of the RCT's functions are centred on the AMF(L) Squadron, RCT, which is the central part of the AMF(L)'s Logistic Support Battalion. This squadron is a versatile and adaptable one for not only does it deal with wheeled transport but it also handles the support and despatching of the various types of helicopter likely to be used by the AMF(L) nations.

The Intelligence Corps

The Intelligence Corps, or Int Corps as it is often referred to, is one of the Army's newer formations, having been formed as recently as 1940 in the aftermath of the Battle of France. The precise duties of the Int Corps are not easy to put into a few words, but it is a body with a myriad of functions and tasks which fall into two main categories: security and combat intelligence.

There is often a considerable overlap between these. For instance, a security operative in Germany may have to be fully conversant in a language other than the usual English and German while at the same time having a considerable insight into the working methods and procedures of his possible opposite number on the enemy side. Combat intelligence operatives also have to have a good grasp of basic and battlefield security methods, with all that that entails. From this simple pair of examples it will readily be realised that the work of the Int Corps can be very varied and often extremely involved.

Soldiers joining the Int Corps are trained in both branches of their particular skill after going through the same basic training that all new Army recruits have to experience. Specialisation commences after the basic intelligence courses have been completed but there are several possible paths open to anyone joining the corps. The task of the security operatives is fairly straightforward in intention, as it is to deny access to any of the Army's premises, equipment, documents and personnel by a potential enemy. The task involves many specialised skills from knowledge of a language through to photography, co-operation with civilian police and other organisations, a good grounding in locks, and many other similar areas of knowledge.

Combat intelligence covers another wide area. Put once again into a very basic form, it is to supply to a commander all the whats, whys, wheres and whens of an enemy's intentions. This once again involves many skills from the rapid identification of items of enemy equipment through to the interpretation of aerial photographs. Language knowledge is an obvious asset in this field as the intercep-

tion and analysis of enemy signal traffic is often involved.

In both branches of Int Corps skills, co-operation and liaison are necessary with virtually all the other arms of the Services, and at all levels. Members of the Int Corps, at both commissioned and NCO level (soldiers joining the Int Corps usually assume junior NCO rank soon after their basic training) have to be able to express themselves in clear and organised terms, both verbally and in writing, and have to be able to pass their information to all levels of command. This latter requirement alone is what often limits the entry level into the corps, but at both commissioned and NCO level what is required is a well-organised and systematic mind with the ability to absorb information, the ability to adapt to new situations and the ability to learn. Life in the Int Corps is seldom dull, for when not on fully active duty the job's basic knowledge is always being updated and improved. Language tuition is seemingly always under way with courses being run at the Army School of Languages, situated at Beaconsfield. The corps depot is at Ashford in Kent, and it is there that the intelligence skills are given. Considering the requirements of the Int Corps it should come as no surprise to learn that the chances of gaining a commission from the ranks are thought to be higher than in any other branch of the Army. Many serving members transfer from other branches of the Army and once in, very few seem to transfer out.

The Royal Army Ordnance Corps

The usual image that comes to mind when the Royal Army Ordnance Corps is mentioned is that of a storeman working away amid piles of racking and odd-shaped cardboard boxes. The RAOC does indeed have such a stores function but it has many other roles as well. Basically the RAOC provides a fast and efficient supply service for the Army, but in these days of mobile warfare with all its attendant complexities, supply is no longer just a matter of stores. It is a complex and highly technical affair and thus the RAOC is one of the most technically diverse and specialised of all the support functions of the Army.

The RAOC has many bases but one of the main centres is at Deepcut where there is a sizeable training establishment at which recruits are given basic training in the 15 nominal trades open to RAOC recruits. These range from that of storeman to such specialities as ammunition technician or

A Coles Crane on a AEC 10-tonne chassis, typical of the handling devices used at the many depots and stores run by the RAOC.

photographer. Once past this training the RAOC technician or officer can find himself posted throughout the Army for the RAOC is a widespread and highly-involved corps.

Every fighting formation has an RAOC component somewhere in its organisation ready to supply whatever the soldier in the field needs. The armoured divisions in 1 (BR) Corps each have an ordnance company under the control of their division HQ. The role of the ordnance company is direct supply support of the troops in the field so each of these companies is mobile. The strength is about 100 men and the company carries around 10,000 different items with it on its own transport, ready for direct issue to the combat arms. They in their turn are backed up by combat supply battalions which contain nearly all the various tradesmen maintained by the RAOC. These two RAOC combat formations supply just about everything the troops need, from food to fuel and from transport vehicles to ammunition.

Further back are many more RAOC units that range from store and vehicle depots to bakeries and salvage platoons. Their role is to supply the needs of the forward RAOC units and they in turn are supplied by the large static depots with their huge parks of vehicles and warehouses full of spares, uniforms, ammunition and all the many other items the modern Army needs to function.

To service this massive organisation the RAOC has a pool of skilled tradesmen, many of whom are retrained for their roles within the RAOC itself, ie,

they have to serve within the RAOC for a period before they receive their retraining. This can be seen in the stores function itself for there RAOC personnel (assisted by some WRACs) have to master all the technicalities of stock control using ADP and computers, handling techniques, accounting and many other such skills. RAOC stores have to handle well over 500,000 separate items. These all have to be kept in serviceable condition, have to be readily available and have to be taken to where they are needed with the minimum of delay. This is particularly true where vehicles are concerned so the RAOC has its own vehicle specialists who are trained to maintain and drive all the many vehicles the Army has on its inventory—ranging from Chieftain tanks to Engineer equipment.

One of the most important functions is that of fuel supply. Fuel is perhaps the most important single item needed to keep present-day forces in the field and a correspondingly large proportion of RAOC effort is devoted to keeping the Army supplied with the vital POLs (Petrol, Oil and Lubricants). Today, the accent regarding fuel supplies is on bulk transport methods in which the jerricans of the 1939-45 war are replaced by bulk storage and supply using modern technology. BAOR is a case in point. The normal routine peace-time fuel supplies for BAOR are met by the huge petro-chemical complex situated around Hamburg and other such commercial concerns, but such plants cannot supply all the specialised needs of the Army. Some of them still have to come from the United Kingdom and a fair proportion pass along the NATO Central European Pipeline System (CEPS) which covers four nations and is run by a joint NATO staff based at Versailles (this is the Central European Operating Agency, or CEOA). Most of the fuel destined for BAOR travels from Antwerp or Rotterdam but some also comes from Marseilles and other ports. At each of these ports is a pumping station which transfers the fuels from their bulk transit carriers, which could be either fuel tankers or, in forward areas, dracones, which are huge rubber containers towed behind tugs. There are no restrictions between the different types of fuel that flow down the pipes. Petrol can be followed by kerosene along the same pipeline as the buried pipes would be too expensive to duplicate. When two differing fuels have to follow each other along the pipeline they are separated by huge steel spheres known as 'pigs'. On each side of the 'pig' there is a section which consists of a mixture of both fuels and the system is so arranged that these mixed sections are 'cut out' at the receiving station and passed into prepared slop tanks. At the receiving station the fuel is then passed into tanks ready to be further transferred into bulk carriers or more dracones which may be either simply laid on the ground surface or buried beneath ground. From there the fuels go to the units. The CEPS is a complex affair with 105 pumping stations and 53 storage depots. If one pipeline is put out of action, the fuel can be switched to another line, and in some areas of potential damage risk the pipelines are duplicated.

The RAOC is mainly responsible for the British Army side of the fuel operation although there is considerable RE and RCT involvement as well. To give an idea of the many types of POL the RAOC has to handle and supply there is a list of the main British POLs at the end of this section. Not all of these are handled in bulk. Some of the really specialist items are issued only in small containers or tubes, while others are issued in amounts that vary from a few litres up to thousands of litres—it all adds to the complexity of the RAOC supply function.

Stores sections are a vital part of many of the Army's support functions, and the RAOC provides a service to many other corps. There is an RAOC supply section at each REME workshop at all levels and there are similar supply sections serving with the Royal Artillery, the Royal Engineers and the AAC, as well as several other arms. The RAOC has a supply function for the Royal Navy and the RAF as well.

After fuel, perhaps the next most important supply item for the Army is ammunition. The RAOC not only stores and supplies ammunition but is also responsible for its maintenance and repair. This responsibility ranges from guided missiles to 7.62 mm ammunition and it is carried out not only in base depots but in field locations. An off-shoot of the ammunition technician branch is Explosive Ordnance Disposal, more popularly known as bomb disposal. The RAOC is the corps responsible for the safe disposal of the types of explosive device used by terrorist or criminal organisations, but they are also used to dispose of unwanted or time-expended explosives. The RAOC EOD role in Northern Ireland is now well known. The EOD role is shared with the Royal Engineers but the Engineers deal mainly with bombs and other devices dropped from aircraft and the like—the RAOC deal with the rest.

The RAOC trains and provides the Army's photographers and deals with the bulk of the Army's printing requirements. The RAOC also supplies clerks, but here there are two categories. The RAOC technical clerks are used only within the RAOC, mainly as inventory specialists. The other category is the staff clerk, a rather more attractive employment for they are employed as clerks at British Embassies all over the world. They are also used at NATO Headquarters and other similar locations.

Food is another prime RAOC function and the corps trains and mans the staff used in field bakeries and butcheries. These units are usually mobile and are backed up by RAOC cold stores at base depots.

There are many other RAOC functions as corps personnel are trained as crane operators, laundry operators, textile refitters and military programmers. RAOC officers are educated in a variety of management skills and are often on hand at all levels of Army command to advise on supply matters.

The RAOC is a diverse operation. In terms of the amount of capital the RAOC 'manages' and controls it must rank among the largest of all British business concerns, and its manpower and resources are among the most cost-effective in the nation.

RAOC-supplied POLs

Listed below are the different types of POL supplied by or through the RAOC. The designations given are British ones but where an asterisk (*) is used, the substance has an equivalent common to all NATO forces.

Fuels: AVGAS 100LL*, AVCAT*, AVCAT/FS11*, AVTAG/FS11*, AVTUR/FS11*, CIVGAS*, COMBATGAS*; Regular 47/0 DIESO*, General Purpose UK DIESO, General Purpose UK(MT) DIESO, DIESO F-76*, 3/50 FFO, 36/50 FFO, 125/50 FFO, 370/50 FFO, KERO/A, KERO/B*.

Oils: OC-65, OC-160*, OC-600, OEP-38*, OEP-70*, OEP-71*, OEP-215, OEP-220*, OEP-740, OM-1*, OM-11*, OM-13*, OM-15*, OM-16*, OM-17, OM-18*, OM-21, OM-33*, OM-58, OM-70*, OM-71*, OM-100*, OM-160, OM-750*, OM-1300*; OMD-30*, OMD-40*, OMD-45, OMD-60*, OMD-75*, OMD-113*, OMD-160*, OMD-250*, OMD-330*, OMD-370*; OX-7, OX-8*, OX-10, OX-14*, OX-18*, OX-26*, OX-38*, OX-165, OX-300, OX-320*.

Greases: XG-220, XG-235*, XG-250*, XG-264*, XG-271*, XG-276*, XG-279*, XG-284*, XG-285*, XG-293*, XG-300*, XG-315*.

Specials: ZX-1*, ZX-2, ZX-6*, ZX-8*, ZX-13*, ZX-16, ZX-20*, ZX-30, ZX-33, ZX-34*, ZX-38*; PX-3*, PX-4, PX-6, PX-7*, PX-10, PX-11*, PX-15, PX-19, PX-24*, PX-25, PX-26*, PX-28, PX-29, PX-30, PX-31; AL-11*, AL-14*, AL-34, AL-36, AL-38, AL-39, AL-40.

The Army Catering Corps

While the Royal Navy have their 'Fly Navy' recruiting slogan, the Army have their own counter —'Eat Army'. To clarify what I mean, the Army is fed by the Army Catering Corps, or ACC, an establishment which has still to overcome the image inherited from its often untrained predecessors, for it was only established in 1941 and by the time it had become fully operational and working properly the Citizens' Armies of 1939-1945 had already formed their uncomplimentary opinions. Since 1945, however, the standards of Army catering have improved out of all recognition, and the modern soldier is well fed and usually has a wide choice of types of meal on most occasions.

The Depot and Training Centre of the ACC is at Aldershot where a large and modern training establishment has been set up to teach cooking and catering at all levels of expertise. The new recruit to the ACC undergoes the usual basic soldiering skills course and then is taken through an Army catering course. This provides for all the essentials of modern catering from basic cooking techniques up to menu planning, food budgeting and food preparation and care. The course lasts 21 weeks during which the trainees often leave the kitchen behind to carry out practical cooking in the field under full operational conditions, which includes camouflage and self-defence of the area.

From the Training Centre the ACC cook is posted to a unit. This could be almost anywhere in the Army, ranging from a large garrison to an operational unit in Germany. On a large base the ACC also has to provide for special diets for sports or medical purposes, while the ACC cooks on large RAMC establishments often have to work very closely with RAMC personnel to provide special medical foods and diets.

The ACC cook with a field unit frequently has to provide a wide range of meals at what can be very short notice. When in the field or on exercise, the units themselves often provide their own catering facilities, based on the various forms of 'Compo' ration pack. These mostly utilise tinned foods which require a minimum of preparation other than heating and opening, and are issued on the basis of one pack being adequate for so many men for so many days—the types of pack vary. They provide an adequate diet, and even include such luxuries as sweets and chocolate (not forgetting such essentials as tin openers and toilet paper!) but they are meant to be supplemented by fresh vegetables and fruit when available, and after even a few days on compo rations the diet tends to become rather dull. This is where the ACC becomes such a morale booster for, using the same basic compo rations, a trained cook can provide really good and adequate meals from his knowledge and the extras he carries. The ACC in the field uses 4-tonne trucks which carry tools, supplies and cooking ranges fitted to a special trailer towed by the truck. Water boilers are carried for the essential tea, and for utensil cleaning purposes. The trucks also carry tents and some tables and other basics. With such equipment the ACC can serve simple hot meals which can transform units from tired men into refreshed soldiers. The number of cooks assigned to a unit varies from place to place and according to the type of unit itself—for instance a BAOR armoured regiment has an ACC complement of 16 men.

Troops in garrisons and permanent bases are often fed to the point of distraction and to the extent that the 'Fit to Fight' campaign has to be really put into active use. A visitor to some garrison messes will be greeted by a lunch menu with a long list of hot courses, salads and the almost inevitable curry. Other meals are just as varied.

Away from the day-to-day catering, the ACC has the opportunity to further its more delicate skills in such fields as pastrywork, the preparation of seafood and meat and all the other more advanced cooking skills. To assist in these areas the ACC Centre has prepared all manner of food routines and menus to suit almost any occasion—even the cooks in the field are issued with detailed menus and cooking guides. As the ACC cook proceeds through his Army career he can try for any number of civilian catering qualifications which will stand him in good stead in civilian life, and many famous civilian chefs were taught their trade in the ACC.

Many WRAC members are also taught alongside ACC personnel, and carry out the same duties as the men apart from the fact that they are not usually assigned to field duties.

The Royal Pioneer Corps

If there is one word that sums up the role of the Royal Pioneer Corps today, it is versatility. The modern RPC is a very far cry from the days when its personnel were the Army's labourers. Today their presence is an essential one for the Army, but there is no single role. The RPC assists in moving stores, loading and unloading the thousand-and-one items the Army needs to move and function, and also provides dog handlers. But first and foremost the Pioneers are fighting soldiers and the task they carry out in Northern Ireland is one in line with that of the rest of the Army.

The main depot and training centre of the RPC is at Northampton, where recruits go to be trained as Infantrymen. Thereafter they are trained in what is their central role, namely that of materials and stores handling. To this end they have to master all the many forms of handling equipment the Army employs, from Eager Beavers to dock cranes. This role is carried out not only in stores and base depots but also in the field in direct support of forward units. At any one time at least 40 per cent of the RPC strength is serving with other arms of the Army such as the RE and the RAOC. With the RCT the Pioneers not only assist with the loading and unloading of the vehicles but also act as drivers and even help in the running of the RCT railways.

The RPC is also involved in man management. The bases in Germany employ a great deal of local labour for the hundreds of tasks needed to keep the garrisons and bases functioning. A large proportion of this local labour is recruited, administered and supervised by RPC officers and soldiers.

Selected RPC soldiers are trained to be dog handlers for various tasks. Most RPC handlers are used in security roles at ammunition and other sensitive stores depots, being trained for their role by the RAVC.

To top its versatility, the RPC is also used in an Infantry role on occasions and has frequently been used in this way in Northern Ireland. When the first RPC units were stationed there, either on roulement or as part of the Ulster garrison, they had to draw on their flexibility yet again for they often had to build their own billets and guard posts while at the same time carrying out their various security duties.

Despite all its many modern tasks, on occasion the RPC has to revert to its original pick and shovel role. This usually occurs when the corps is in support of the RE road and bridging units when permanent structures have to be built—but Pioneers are also involved in the combat roles of the RE as well.

Whenever the Army has some unusual task that cannot be met by any particular corps or regiment, the RPC usually finds itself given the job. Such rapid and varied roles call for a large measure of adaptability and problem approaches which are met by giving all members of the RPC a sound grounding in all manner of military skills ranging from driving to stores management and layout. Senior NCOs and officers are given considerable training in management skills and problem solving. To add to its all-round capabilities the RPC often works with the Royal Navy and the Royal Air Force.

The Royal Army Educational Corps

The Royal Army Educational Corps (RAEC) was granted its Royal Title in 1946 after having been founded in 1920, although its recorded origins can be traced back over some 300 years. Today the RAEC has a wide role in the education and training of the Army, particularly in the fields of education for promotion and in support of training. Unlike many large civilian organisations, the Army cannot 'buy in' ready-made leaders as senior officers or NCOs. It has to cultivate its own; the young men and women who are recruited in their late 'teens or early twenties have to provide the leaders of the future. Consequently there is a progressive educational and training process to prepare officers and soldiers to fill positions of increasing responsibility as their Service careers develop. In order to cope with the increasing complexity of their profession and with the maintenance and operation of technically sophisticated weaponry and other equipment, they need to be well educated and trained. They also need to have an understanding of the role of the Army.

One of the main functions of the RAEC is to meet these military needs, a duty which will assume an even greater importance over the next ten years as the manpower pool from which the Army draws its recruits is reduced. Thus the RAEC role in the education of the Junior Army makes an important contribution to the successful manning of the Army. Cost-effective and efficient training is essential to ensure that the best use is made of the scarce human and material resources. In the training field the RAEC plays a full part, both in the provision of courses at the Army School of Training Support and through the various Training Development Teams in the Arms and Services which include a RAEC officer as an adviser.

In addition to these tasks the RAEC provides a resettlement training and advice service to assist Service personnel on their return to civilian life. In BAOR German language courses are an important part of Service life as are the Army schools, the Army Education Centres with their wide range of evening activities, and libraries, all of which help to make life in what may seem a very foreign country that much easier to understand and accept.

The RAEC is a combatant Corps and its all-officer members undertake operational duties as necessary. The Corps also has a large component of WRAC officers who serve permanently with the RAEC and who make an important and significant contribution to its work.

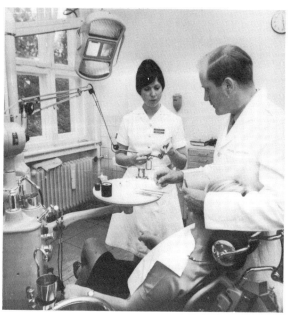

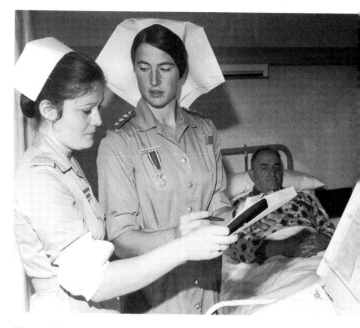

Above left RADC staff in action at the British Military Hospital, Rinteln (MoD). *Above QARANC staff on duty at the Duchess of Kent's Military Hospital at Catterick* (UKLF PR).

The Royal Army Medical Services

The Royal Army Medical Services are formed from three different corps, as follows: The Royal Army Medical Corps (RAMC), The Royal Army Dental Corps (RADC) and Queen Alexandra's Royal Army Nursing Corps (QARANC). Of these, the largest is the RAMC which has its main depot and training centre at Keogh Barracks at Ash Vale near Aldershot. Within the RAMC the differentiation between a war- and a peace-time footing is most marked, for in peace corps personnel are mainly based at the various Army hospitals but in war a large proportion of them will leave their bases to man forward field hospitals and other field force units. In both capacities the RAMC provides a complete medical service to the Army and the civilians attached to it as well. The duties of the RAMC include not only medical care, although that is one of their prime functions, but also general hygiene, the control of insects and other such pests, and the general supervision of food and water supplies. All RAMC doctors have commissions and are usually trained doctors or well through their medical courses when they apply to join, but there are also non-medical commissions in the RAMC such as technical, administrative and quartermaster officers in addition to nursing officers. Non-commissioned RAMC soldiers can be either laboratory technicians, physiotherapists, radio-

graphers, dispensers, operating theatre technicians, student nurses, clerks, environmental health assistants, medical assistants, storemen or pupil nurses. All these have their civilian equivalents.

Although the main body of the RAMC is based at the various hospitals, even in times of peace each battalion or regiment has its RAMC personnel for everyday routine medical duties. Each combat unit also has its own RAMC personnel and for example, each armoured regiment has one RAMC officer. But the main body of the RAMC remains in the base hospitals which are situated as follows: In the United Kingdom—Royal Victoria Hospital, Netley; Cambridge Military Hospital, Aldershot; The Duchess of Kent's Military Hospital, Catterick; Colchester Military Hospital; Military Wing, Musgrave Park Hospital, Belfast; Louise Margaret Maternity Hospital, Aldershot; and the Queen Elizabeth Military Hospital, Woolwich. In addition to these the RAMC has staffs in several civilian teaching and casualty hospitals—of the latter, perhaps the best-known being the Royal Victoria Hospital, Belfast. In Germany there are British military hospitals at Munster, Rinteln, Hannover, Iserlohn and Berlin, while further afield there are hospitals at Dhekelia, in Cyprus, at Hong Kong, and perhaps the most distant, the British Military Hospital at the Ghurkha base at Dharan in Nepal.

All these military hospitals are run very much on civilian lines and may have some civilians on their staffs. Their facilities and equipment rival any civilian hospital and their responsibilities to the large Army civilian population can be seen in the provision of the maternity hospital at Aldershot.

In times of conflict the RAMC assumes its war footing with the infusion of a large number of TA personnel and units. These would join the existing field units which consist of the two armoured field ambulances in every armoured division, field ambulances with other formations and field hospitals, each with between 50 to 200 beds. The latter are usually located in the Corps area and are fully equipped for treating medical and surgical cases in the combat zone. The armoured field ambulances are usually equipped with FV432 ambulances. The TA contribution to these regular units is considerable for they would form ten general hospitals, two field hospitals and 11 field ambulances. All the latter are formed by independent units or sponsored units and there are a further two general hospitals, one field ambulance and 50 various other medical units.

The RADC is the dental equivalent of the RAMC and has its main depot and training centre at Aldershot with more facilities at nearby Blackdown. Like the RAMC, RADC personnel are stationed wherever there are British soldiers and the standards they work to are as high, if not higher,

than those available to the average civilian. Normally, RADC officers and soldiers are stationed mainly in the base hospitals but there are some field units which take their skills directly to the soldier who is unable to reach the RADC base facilities.

The RAMC provides some male nursing staff but the main nursing unit for the Army is the QARANC which numbers about 1,500 personnel, of whom about 500 are officers. The women of the QARANC can be either State Registered Nurses or State Enrolled Nurses, or they can join the QARANC and obtain their qualifications in the service. Their main training centre and depot is at Aldershot but much of the training is carried out in the main base hospitals and at the RAMC centre at Keogh Barracks. Some members of the QARANC also serve as dental technicians, clerks and hygienists with the RADC.

The Royal Army Veterinary Corps

In a world where armies travel on tracks or wheels propelled by the internal combustion engine, it comes as rather a surprise to learn that the British Army still keeps a considerable number of animals for all manner of purposes. The Army's long association with the horse has still not come to an

Left *The RAMC in action in Northern Ireland* (MoD). **Right** *The training of the explosive-sniffing dogs used in Northern Ireland and elsewhere is carried out by the RAVC* (MoD).

end, and horses are still 'kept on the books' with duties ranging from the ceremonial to the recreational. The horses are joined by dogs that are used in a number of military roles, but the poor old mule is no longer a British Army animal—the last of them went some years ago. To add to the list, many regiments still possess mascots ranging from ponies to goats, and most garrisons have cats in one form or another. In fact the Army still has so many animals that it needs a corps to look after them— this is the Royal Army Veterinary Corps, or RAVC.

The Directorate of the RAVC is at Droitwich, but the main RAVC training centre is at Melton Mowbray. There are other RAVC centres at Aldershot and in some of the German garrisons, such as Sennelager. RAVC officers are all fully qualified veterinarians but the non-commissioned ranks of the corps contain farriers and other such qualified specialists. The Army's horses are all looked after by RAVC specialists, although the various units themselves care for their own animals on a day-to-day basis. But the RAVC does provide horse clinics and hospitals, and its vets run highly organised diagnostic laboratories. The main centres of 'horse activity' in the Army are at Knightsbridge Barracks in London (for the Household Cavalry), St Johns Wood (for the King's Troop, RHA), and Aldershot (where there are several horse establishments including the RMP Mounted Troop).

Today, the Army horse is now outnumbered by the Army dog which is used in a number of roles. Dogs are used by the RMP in a police dog role, by the RPC in a general security role, and by various units where they are used as 'war dogs' in a tracking role. There are even dogs used to 'sniff out' explosives. All these animals are trained, along with their handlers, by the RAVC at Melton Mowbray. The police dogs are employed much as their 'civilian' counterparts, and can be used to discover drugs and explosives. The security dogs are trained to be used mainly in a guard role, although they too are often called upon to carry out other duties. Usually the police and security dogs are Alsatians but the dogs used to discover explosives, as they have been for some years in Northern Ireland, are often Labradors. Labradors are frequently preferred for this dangerous role in Ulster as their normally gentle disposition makes them much more amenable to the variations in general routine and transport methods. Early experience with Alsatians in the sniffing role soon showed that they did not take kindly to the interiors of helicopters which circumstances frequently dictate as their mode of transport, while Labradors took such noisy things in their tolerant stride. The explosive-sniffer dogs and

their handlers (who are volunteers from all branches of the Army) undergo a basic three-month course before they can be assigned to their area, and even there training continues. In Ulster the dogs have proved to be very successful in finding explosives, and as their training teaches them to indicate anything unusual, they have often been instrumental in arms and ammunition finds. There have been casualties among the Ulster dogs, although not many, but a dog's service life is relatively short and the Army generally needs a turnover of about 350 a year to keep up the numbers. To obtain this operational number the Army has to find some 700 or so dogs as the course failure rate is about 50 per cent.

Tracker dogs are also used for search purposes, but as their name implies they are mainly used to track suspects or escaped prisoners. Any item left at the scene of a terrorist crime will often provide a useful scent and many arrests have been the result of tracker dog activity. Both Alsatians and Labradors are employed in this role. Although tracker dogs have been mainly used in Ulster, they are also trained for use in Germany for a variety of roles, often connected with discovering infiltrators and behind-the-lines agents.

The RAVC staff are frequently assisted by members of the WRAC assigned to them in a number of capacities ranging from laboratory technicians to kennelmaids.

The Army Physical Training Corps

The popular image of the APTC is one of early morning physical jerks on a freezing cold parade ground or in a draughty gymnasium, and to be strictly accurate there still is some small measure of truth in this image. However, these days the role of the APTC is the little-mentioned but important one of keeping the Army fit. Only over the last few years has it become painfully obvious that modern warfare will be even more exacting an experience for the soldier in the field than any previous conflict. Any future war will involve troops having to remain at their combat posts for days at a stretch and rest or sleep will be almost impossible. Physical fitness and stamina therefore become just as essential to the soldier as his weapons and equipment, and this is where the APTC takes on its important role.

Over the last few years the physical fitness of the Army has been improved beyond all recognition by the imposition of a new physical training routine far removed from the PT exercises of old. Today the soldier has to reach a fixed standard of fitness which is shown by his ability to cover a fixed distance in a prescribed time. At one time it was 1½ miles in 11 minutes, with a further 1½ miles within a further period. If any soldier could not achieve this, he was immediately placed on a course of dietary and physical exercise until he could. The programme was launched as the 'Fight the Flab' campaign and was so successful that it even had its effects on civilian life. The programme still continues and as a result the British Army is one of the fittest in Europe, a status rather improved by the extra toning-up programmes entered into before 'Operation Banner' tours in Northern Ireland. The body responsible for the overseeing and implementation of the fitness campaign is the APTC.

Based at Aldershot, the APTC is one corps that rarely recruits direct from 'civvie street' as most of the NCOs in the corps are recruited from within the Army itself, and even then not until at least one year has been served by any prospective member. After the usual specialist training courses at Aldershot the APTC NCOs are drafted throughout the Army, usually at the rate of one NCO to every battalion or regiment, although in some formations there may be more. Once with their unit they are responsible for its fitness and carry out physical training programmes, run combat obstacle courses, organise route marches and provide any specialist training that might be needed for unit sports teams. Needless to say they are also actively involved in all the many and varied Army sports activities which range from cricket to skiing. The Army's involvement in sport of all kinds is usually carried out under individual unit auspices, but the APTC is involved when the sport expertise reaches a higher level such as national and Olympic levels. The APTC is a corps that rarely hits the headlines but it is one that is essential to the combat efficiency of the modern Army.

Corps of Royal Military Police & Military Provost Staff Corps

The men of the Royal Military Police are among the most widely known of all the soldiers of the Army for their very appearance marks them as being soldiers of note. Their red caps have given them their nickname, and their duties have often bought them into direct contact with many members of the general public, sometimes in odd circumstances. Within the Army, though, they have a definite function which is simply to serve and assist the rest of the Army to carry out its duties. The old days of the Redcaps seeking out off-duty soldiers in order to

give them a dressing down and subsequent punishments have long since departed. The modern military policeman is a very different character, in himself a model soldier and an example to all.

In practical terms this means that the Royal Military Police have two roles. In time of peace the MP carries out all the normal everyday policing of the Army. As with his civilian counterpart, this includes everything from traffic control to all the normal powers of arrest. In time of war the MP's main role is traffic control, mainly getting the right traffic to the right places at the right time.

The men of the Royal Military Police are formed into two main branches. The largest is the General Police Duties Branch, or GPD. All members of the RMP pass through this branch after their initial training which is given at the RMP training centre at Chichester. In the GPD branch all the basic policing skills are taught with the addition of such military extras as the use of the 9 mm pistol, the sub-machine-gun and the L4A4. Training is given in first aid, photography, military law, traffic control, driving (both vehicles and motor cycles) and signals. Once trained the soldiers of the GPD branch are then assigned to the Provost companies.

The basis of all the Provost companies is the platoon, but the Provost platoon bears no resemblance to any other Army platoon. Each is commanded by a Staff Sergeant. Together with a driver and a cook he forms a small platoon headquarters overseeing two sections with a Sergeant and six Corporals in each. The number of platoons within a Provost company varies widely but within BAOR most companies have six platoons. The platoons within 1 (BR) Corps all come under Corps control but are assigned specific roles. Each of the divisions has its own Provost company. All Provost companies are fully mobile and use Land Rovers and motor cycles. Also under the control of 1 (BR) Corps are a further two Provost companies for control of the Corps Rear Area, each with six platoons and a further company to control the large Rear Combat Zone. In war, the latter would be reinforced by a further Regular company and three Territorial Army companies.

In time of conflict these Provost companies would be kept very active controlling traffic, routing and maintaining route signs, redirecting and re-routing stragglers and lost units, NBC monitoring and providing NBC tactical information. The RMP are constantly kept in training for these roles but they also have an important peace-time role which keeps them fully occupied. The Army in Germany maintains large garrison and base areas and the GPD branch of the RMP has the unenviable task of policing these against all the normal day-to-day occurrences that are likely to arise. Thus the RMPs are kept constantly busy with patrols, traffic control, road safety, the checking of premises and the general overseeing of the conduct of both the soldiery and the civilian elements who live and work in the British areas. To carry out these many duties there are only the wartime establishments available. Also in Germany there is 2 RMP as part of the Berlin Garrison with six platoons. A platoon from 2 RMP forms the Autobahn Control Detachment based at Helmstedt.

In the United Kingdom there are eight Provost companies. Normally they are stationed wherever there are sizeable concentrations of troops in locations such as Aldershot, Catterick, Edinburgh, Donnington, Bulford, Tidworth, Colchester and the London District. In an emergency one of these companies would reinforce the companies in Germany and one of them, 158 Provost Company at Bulford, forms a nucleus for the British military police contingent assigned to the ACE Mobile Force (Land). 160 Provost Company based at Aldershot provides support for 5 Airborne Brigade. The London District Provost Company has a home defence role, as have the remaining elements of the other United Kingdom-based companies. All the home-based and BAOR units would be reinforced in an emergency by members of the Royal Military Police Volunteers from the eight Territorial Army military police units and individual RMP reservists.

Northern Ireland is at present absorbing a considerable amount of RMP effort for it is the working area for three Provost companies. A company is assigned to each of the two Northern Ireland brigades where they are employed and based according to the local situation; the other company is responsible for all investigations within the Province.

Provost companies are also stationed in Cyprus and Hong Kong while at BATUS in Canada a single RMP keeps local order. There is also a six-man RMP unit in Gibraltar and a platoon in Belize. In the Falkland Islands the garrison is policed on a joint Service basis. This unit is commanded by an RMP officer and the majority of the policemen are RMPs.

A separate and less well-publicised task is that of Close Protection. This involves small numbers of specially selected and highly trained GPD NCOs who operate in teams looking after high risk military VIPs.

All the above units are part of the GPD branch. The other RMP branch is the Special Investigation Branch, or SIB, which is charged with the prevention of crime within the Army and the subsequent apprehension of offenders. It is the military equivalent of the civilian CID and operates along much the same lines. All members of the SIB are carefully selected from within the GPD branch and have to complete a six-month probationary period

Bombardier motor cycles used by the Royal Military Police.

with the SIB before they are even trained. Basic training for the SIB is carried out within the RMP but further training is often carried out at civil police establishments.

There is one further RMP establishment to mention, the Mounted Troop based at Aldershot. Competition to join the Mounted Troop is very keen as it has only 20 horses, and a potential recruit has to have at least two years' service before he can even apply to join. Once in the troop any RMP member will find himself kept busy. The horses are used mainly for the patrolling of the ranges and open areas around Aldershot, but they also have some ceremonial and display duties.

As is normal with civilian police forces, the RMP do not have a detention role. If a soldier commits a crime that merits imprisonment he is sent to a civilian prison, but if a soldier's conduct warrants a period of detention he is sent to the Army's only remaining detention centre at Colchester. There the offender will be placed under the control of the Military Provost Staff Corps, the military equivalent of the civil Prison Service. Once inside the Colchester establishment the MPSC has the task of turning a bad soldier into a good one. The regime is onerous but not over-rigorous. If any indication of the conduct of the modern Army was needed it is the fact that there is now only one Army detention centre—not so many years ago there were many,

many more, and all of them were kept busy. It is a measure of the standard of education and general behaviour of the modern soldier that the number of centres remains at but one.

But to return to the RMP: any recruit for the ranks of the corps must meet certain physical standards. He must be at least 1.7 metres tall (5 feet 7 inches) and fulfil weight, fitness and eyesight standards. He must also have a clean record. Once trained, the Military Policeman is segregated from the rest of the Army and messes separately. He has his own particular uniform distinctions of the red-topped service cap or the red beret. On duty he wears a red armband and a whistle and chain. At all times he has to maintain an example to all, and his conduct, bearing and appearance must be beyond reproach.

In the words of the Provost Marshal, the officer responsible for both the RMP and the MPSC, (incidentally the title of Provost Marshal is one of the oldest military titles still in use as it dates back to the time of William the Conqueror, and maybe before then), 'The Royal Military Police provide only two per cent of the Army, but they like to think they give ten per cent in value.'

The Ulster Defence Regiment

The Ulster Defence Regiment (UDR) has to be dealt with separately from the other branches of the British Army for several reasons. One is that it is the largest single regiment in the Army, being around 6,500-strong. Another is that it is the only regiment that recruits women as well as men. It is also the youngest of the Army's regiments, being formed as recently as April 1 1970. Another distinction is that the UDR is the only regiment in the Army which is continually in the 'front line', for it was formed for service only in Northern Ireland in order to combat the form of political terrorism that is prevalent there.

The UDR was created to replace partially the Reserve elements of the Royal Ulster Constabulary (RUC) that were disbanded for political reasons in 1970. The UDR's duties are straightforward enough, for it exists to provide assistance and aid to the RUC in its task of safeguarding lives and property against the extremists who have found Ulster such a fruitful ground for their destructive activities.

There are four categories of soldier in the UDR, Regular, Permanent Cadre (PC), Part Time (PT) and Greenfinches (the women soldiers), the breakdown being 100 Regular, 2,500 PC, 3,250 PT and 650 Greenfinches. The UDR is tasked with the pro-

vision of complete military support to the RUC over 85 per cent of the Province. The PC element, generally speaking, is on duty all the time, with the PT element taking over as much as possible at weekends and from 21:00 to 05:00 during the week.

When they are off-duty the PC return to their homes, the PT resume their everyday civilian tasks and activities and each carry on their normal lives in the community—for them there is no chance of relaxing in well-guarded barracks. Consequently the UDR is constantly in the front line. On uniformed duty its men and women are always possible targets for terrorist action. Off duty they have, in the past, been singled out for all manner of terrorist activity which has ranged from intimidation and local unpleasantness to the extremes of the bullet and the bomb—in the first 15 years of the Regiment 45 men and four Greenfinches were murdered. In spite of this the spirit of the UDR is amazingly high and recruiting is never a problem. If there is one continuing area of concern regarding recruitment to the UDR it is that the religious breakdown of Northern Ireland's population is not reflected in the ranks—only about three per cent are Roman Catholics. This is regretted within the UDR and those who have withstood the intimidation and violence of the terrorists and their sympathisers and who continue to serve are held in very high esteem. Despite this fact, the UDR acts without fear or favour in whatever duties it is tasked.

In its continuing fight against terrorism the UDR has several routine tasks. The patrolling of both built-up and rural areas is perhaps the most obvious activity, but there are others. UDR units also set up and man road blocks that are such a feature of anti-terrorist measures, but perhaps the most important contribution to the Army's activities comes from the UDR soldiers themselves. They are all very much a part of the local community, they know intimately the area they are patrolling and serving in, and they usually know the populace as well. Consequently they are well able to sense the times when something suspicious or out of the ordinary has occurred, or when someone or something unfamiliar is in the area. Such local knowledge is invaluable in anti-terrorist operations and the UDR uses this valuable attribute to the full in arms searches and the supply of tactical intelligence.

Patrolling is the usual form of active duty (apart from the guarding of essential services and locations) and the patrols can be by foot, vehicle or helicopter. Some battalions have boat sections for patrolling Ulster's numerous loughs and waterways, and nearly all companies have a dog section for guard and explosive search purposes. The UDR does not patrol the sensitive areas of West Belfast, Londonderry or the 'bandit country' along the South Armargh and

Fermanagh borders, nor does it participate in crowd or riot control duties.

The UDR has proved time and again that it is a very professional and effective force. It often serves alongside Regular Army units and Regular units frequently come under the command of UDR officers when on duty. This efficiency is the result of the years of experience since 1970 when some of the early efforts of the UDR were open to criticism, mainly as a result of equipment and training deficiencies. Those early days are now well past and any new recruit to the Regiment is soon made very aware of the dedication which the UDR applies to its often thankless tasks. New recruits are always put through a screening process to prevent some of the more undesirable elements of Northern Irish society from gaining admission to the ranks, not only from a security point of view (to prevent the infiltration of UDR activities by terrorist sympathisers) but also to prevent UDR weapons, equipment and training from being misused. Unfortunately this screening has not always been effective enough, as the political enemies of the UDR have often been quick to point out, but by and large the members of the Regiment have proved themselves to be more than worthy of the UDR's philosophy which is to be non-sectarian, impartial, courteous and fair. In the troubled nature of the Northern Irish situation such a philosophy would try the patience of angels but the UDR manages somehow. Under such circumstances it is no wonder that the UDR sometimes attracts criticism, usually from the very people who are disposed towards the forces the Regiment was formed to combat. To counter this the UDR has also attracted the praise and thanks of many more by far.

Once accepted by the UDR a PC soldier is given a nine-week course at the Regimental Depot in Ballykinler. In this he is trained to Regular Army standards in the Internal Security role. The PT soldier is given a one-week course in his own battalion and then further training in the evenings and at weekends. In all he must complete 22 training days in the year. If the occasion demands, the PT soldiers may be 'called out' for full-time duty alongside PC elements. Most PT soldiers devote at least two evenings per week and at least two weekends per month to UDR duties.

The women soldiers of the Regiment deserve their own special mention. Known throughout Ulster (and elsewhere) as 'Greenfinches', they carry out numerous duties. They are trained to administer first aid, act as mobile communications operators or telephonists, assist at check points or road blocks for search purposes, and also act as clerks, storewomen and cooks.

The equipment used by the UDR is similar to that used by other Infantry battalions. The basic weapon is the L1A1 rifle, along with the L2A3 sub-machine-

A unit made up of UDR soldiers and Greenfinches on board a Wessex helicopter (AIS NI).

gun and the L4A4 (Bren) machine-gun. UDR soldiers whose normal civilian activities present them as potential terrorist targets are sometimes issued with personal XLA47E1 Walther and L9A1 Browning pistols. On patrol the UDR uses the ubiquitous Land Rover fitted with armour and other fittings to suit the anti-terrorist role.

The UDR is organised into nine battalions. Each has the usual headquarters unit which administers the companies under its command, the smallest with three rifle companies and the largest with eight. Battalions each have a Regular Commanding Officer, Training Major, Quartermaster, Regimental Sergeant Major and seven senior ranks. The administration of the UDR is centred at Regimental Headquarters in Lisburn and operationally the battalions are tasked by 39 Brigade in the east and 8 Brigade in the west. The various battalion headquarters are situated as follows: 1st/9th (County Antrim) Battalion, UDR—Antrim; 2nd (County Armagh) Battalion, UDR—Armagh, Co Armagh; 3rd (County Down) Battalion, UDR—Ballykinler, Co Down; 4th (County Fermanagh) Battalion, UDR—Enniskillen, Co Fermanagh; 5th (County Londonderry) Battalion, UDR—Ballykelly, Co Londonderry; 6th (County Tyrone) Battalion, UDR—Omagh, Co Tyrone; 7th/10th (City of Belfast) Battalion, UDR—Belfast; 8th (County Tyrone) Battalion, UDR—Dungannon, Co Tyrone; 11th

A joint UDR/RUC police patrol on duty in County Antrim (AIS NI).

(Craigavon) Battalion, UDR—Portadown, Co Armagh.

There is no doubt that the UDR is a unique formation but in its relatively short life has proved to be as willing, efficient and operationally effective as any Regular unit based in Northern Ireland. A small measure of this effectiveness can be seen in the attention it has drawn from the security forces of many nations who have expressed keen interest in its organisation and methods, often with a view to instituting similar formations in their own potential trouble areas. But without a doubt, the UDR would not have proved to be the successful counter-terrorist Regiment it has become without the dedication, hard work and application of the ordinary men and women of Ulster who have joined its ranks. Their decision to counter and fight the political terrorist is the factor that motivates the UDR, and it is they who put meaning into the regimental byword—'Peace through Strength'.

The Royal Army Chaplains' Department

In the same way that any society depends not only on material things but on some other spiritual or moral guidance or order, the Army has its own department for its continuing religious ministrations. In an age where it might seem that the soldier has become a mere functional cog in a huge fighting machine, it is still apparent that the Christian faith has a place in the Army. Within this structure the Royal Army Chaplains' Department (RAChD) carries out the spiritual guidance of the Army and its associated communities. It has five Churches represented within its numbers, those of England and of Scotland together with the Methodist, Roman Catholic and United Board (Baptist and United Reform)

RAChD field communion set carried by Army chaplains.

Churches. There is also a Senior Jewish Chaplain to the Forces—he is a member of the Territorial Army.

Chaplains who administer any of these religions and who wish to minister to the Army have to undergo their normal religious instruction at civilian establishments. All Army chaplains undergo, after joining, a further period at the Training Centre at Bagshot Park and the RMA Sandhurst. From there they join a regiment or the equivalent and, as their career in the Department progresses, they may be assigned to a garrison or Junior Leaders' Regiment. Wherever they go they will minister not only to officers and soldiers but to their families and all the other personnel attached to the establishment.

The Army chaplain is given a commissioned rank but his role is to guide all ranks. While doing this he shares the hardships, upheavals and discomforts of the men and women under his guidance and is expected to take part in their activities. The RAChD is the only section of the Army where the personnel do not undergo weapon training or carry weapons. This does not mean that they do not assimilate military skills, for the chaplain has to be able to conduct himself sensibly under battle conditions to preserve life and limb, and he must be able to appreciate the operational tasks of the units he is assigned to. Perhaps the most extreme example of this can be seen with the chaplains assigned to the Parachute Regiment, who have to go through the full parachute training course and 'jump' with their units into whatever operational situations the regiment might find itself.

One unexpected result of Exercise Lean Look is that some large garrisons will in future be ministered to by civilian chaplains.

The General Service Corps

The General Service Corps is a rather odd formation with no real existence at the present time other than as a tiny cadre for possible administrative purposes. It remains in existence purely for convenience as it provides a ready holding unit to enable the Army to place specially recruited or short-service civilian specialists within its 'ranks' for a short period. It also provides a 'home' for any specialists who are assigned to the Army to carry out any function that does not enable them to be readily assigned to any other regiment or corps. But for most of the time, the General Service Corps is a 'paper' formation.

The Gibraltar Regiment

At one time, wherever the Army became established it raised formations of local inhabitants as adjuncts to the local garrisons. In time many of these levies grew into magnificent armies, of which the largest and finest was perhaps the old Indian Army. More modest establishments flourished elsewhere, many of them romantic like the various Arab State units, the others who provided sound functional formations such as the Royal Malta Regiment, the Cyprus Regiment, the King's African Rifles, and many, many more. With the withdrawal from Empire, most of these have been incorporated into their national forces and today, only one remains under British guidance (apart from the Gurkhas, who are really in a different category) and that is the Gibraltar Regiment.

Formed in 1939 as the Gibraltar Defence Force and renamed in 1958, the Gibraltar Regiment has as its primary task the defence of Gibraltar. For this it is divided into three main units. There is a Headquarters unit that administers and controls the two main units, an infantry company and an artillery battery. The Regiment is 256 strong of whom 45 are regular soldiers, and the Regiment takes its duties very seriously. Their training sessions are always fully attended, there is a thriving social side, and the Regiment even has its own 19-strong Corps of Drums (all volunteers). Apart from its purely defensive role the Regiment has several other tasks to perform, among these being the maintenance of some of the relics of the past that still exist on the Rock.

Pride of place must go to the splendid 9.2-in coastal defence guns of O'Hara's and Lord Airey's batteries. These magnificent guns are situated on some of the highest points of the Rock and command views that have to be seen to be believed. As the guns are now the property of the people of Gibraltar, the Gibraltar Regiment is charged with their upkeep and presentation, and present them they do. The guns are kept in fully working order and from time to time they are shown off complete with all the correct gun drill of their period, which lasted until the 1960s. Other artillery relics kept in shape by the Regiment include the massive 17.72-in calibre 100-ton rifled muzzle-loading gun at Rosia Bay, and the sealed-off 5.25-in anti-aircraft guns of the 1950s Princess Anne's battery. One unique duty carried out by a full-time Sergeant and Private of the Regiment is the care and general welfare of the Rock's apes. The Regiment also participates in many of the ceremonials carried out in Gibraltar, including the Ceremony of the Keys, a movable feast that takes place three to four times a year.

The Infantry Company has three platoons and a Company HQ. They are equipped with the normal infantry weapons but the heaviest they use is the GPMG. Every year they travel to the United

Kingdom to undergo training that cannot be carried out locally due to the rather obvious space restriction. Both sections provide their own independent signals.

The Artillery Battery has two sections, a Field Troop and an Air Defence Troop. The Field Troop is equipped with the 105 mm Light Gun and the Air Defence Troop uses Blowpipe. As with the Infantry Company, both Troops travel to the United Kingdom for range training, the Field Troop to Larkhill and the Air Defence Troop to Manorbier. On the Rock, both Troops fire salutes from the four 25 prs at Devil's Gap. Both Troops and the Infantry platoons carry out the same training requirements as any UK-based Territorial Army unit, apart from the fact that their enthusiasm is almost overwhelming. From time to time range practice is carried out on sea targets but space precludes many training activities that would otherwise be necessary. Thus the annual camps in the United Kingdom become even more important to a unit that is still little known away from the Rock.

The Royal Army Pay Corps

The men of the Royal Army Pay Corps are the Army's accountants, looking after all the many aspects of finances and associated tasks. Every unit in the Army has a member of the RAPC attached to administer its monetary affairs, either in the shape of RAPC unit paymasters or RAPC clerks.

The basic matter of pay for the Army is no longer carried out by the time-honoured and time-wasting procedure of pay parades (except where local conditions make them necessary) but via a computer-based system located at the RAPC's home at Worthy Down. The computer there is the central segment of the Army's pay and salary system and funds are assigned from it into individual bank accounts. The computer also deals to a large degree with the many and various allowances, allotments to families, and even with pensions. Worthy Down is also the home of the RAPC Training Centre.

Although every Army unit has its own RAPC personnel, the 'teeth' units of the corps are the field cash offices assigned to the four divisions of BAOR. The field cash offices are kept in being and train constantly but are normally only put into the field in an emergency or on exercises. The sums of money handled by these offices can be quite considerable, but the role of the RAPC extends down to such transactions as hire purchase advice for individual soldiers and the running of tote offices for regimental point-to-point meetings. All ranks of the RAPC are,

however, still fighting soldiers and they are all trained in essential combat skills.

The field cash offices are usually formed of an RAPC officer, two or three senior RAPC NCOs and a number of Corporals employed in a clerical capacity. Other RAPC personnel act as drivers and general administration staff. The office is fully mobile, usually using Land Rovers carrying accommodation, safes and the inevitable desks and furniture. The offices go wherever they are needed and administer not only pay and allowances to troops in the field but also unit funds for such purposes as local purchases, currency exchange and general finances.

The Women's Royal Army Corps

The Women's Royal Army Corps (WRAC) was established as a Regular corps in 1949 from the old Auxiliary Territorial Service, the formation that established the role of women in the Army. Today the WRAC consists of approximately 4,500 women who serve in a wide variety of jobs throughout the Army. They are a part of the same structure as their male colleagues and share in all aspects of Army life.

WRAC Servicewomen carry out their basic military training at the WRAC Centre at Guildford in Surrey. Following this they receive their employment training alongside their male counterparts. For example, WRAC drivers are trained by the RCT at Leconfield, and Signals personnel are trained at 8 Signal Regiment at Catterick. Once qualified they are posted to Army units where they live in self-contained accommodation.

In many of their employments the WRAC Servicewomen compete on equal terms with the men for promotion and jobs. However, there are some restrictions on their area of deployment. Women may not be used in direct combat and may only be armed for self-defence. Therefore they cannot serve in any peacetime post which will be filled by a man in war. In practice this does not significantly reduce their opportunities for postings and members of the WRAC serve in most areas where the Army operates. For instance, there are members of the WRAC posted to the Falklands and they also serve in Northern Ireland, BAOR, Cyprus and Hong Kong.

WRAC Servicewomen can be selected for a wide range of employments. The list includes Analyst (Special Intelligence), Linguist (Special Intelligence), Bandswoman, Cook, Range Assistant, Kennelmaid/Rider Groom, Medical Assistant, Military Policewoman, Military Accountant,

Members of the WRAC displaying the types of uniform worn on duty (UKLF).

Operator Intelligence and Security, Physical Training Instructor, Postal and Courier Operator, Supply Controller, Supply Specialist, Stewardess, Administrative Assistant, Army Welfare Assistant, Clerk, Data Telegraphist, Driver, Recruiter, Switchboard Operator and Terminal Equipment Technician.

WRAC officers are trained at the Royal Military Academy Sandhurst (RMAS), having undergone the same selection procedures as the men at the Regular Commissions Board (RCB) Westbury. WRAC officers can have a full career within the WRAC, being employed in a wide range of jobs throughout the Army. They compete for selection and training as staff officers including the technical appointments staff. Some WRAC officers elect for a permanent career with one of a number of the Arms or Services. These include the RE, R Signals, RCT, RAOC, RMP, RAPC, AAC and RAEC. When they leave Sandhurst these officers attend the same specialist courses as their male colleagues, for example WRAC officers who are permanently employed by the REME are trained at Arborfield. All WRAC officers come under the same employment restrictions as those mentioned above for Servicewomen, but again these restrictions do not prevent any WRAC member from enjoying a rewarding Service career or from reaching high rank. In March 1985 the Army had 1,009 WRAC officers.

The Royal Military Academy Sandhurst

The purpose of the Royal Military Academy Sandhurst is well set out in its Charter which states the following aims: To give the officer cadet a broad view of his profession as a whole and his responsibilities as a servant of the Crown; to develop the essential characteristics of leadership and man management, sense of discipline and sense of duty; and to develop his physical fitness.

All officers who are given the Queen's Commission have to pass through the RMAS at some stage or other of their military careers, usually at the beginning, and many return there either for further training or to become part of the instructional staff. Thus the RMAS is as important a part of the modern Army as it has been since the twin academies of Woolwich and Sandhurst were established during the 18th century. Now only the RMAS remains.

There are several different types of commission but all involve a period of training spent at the RMAS. For the direct entrant there is the Standard Military Course lasting about six months. Both short-term and career cadets take this course together, but the long-term cadets then go on to take a further six-month curriculum known as the Regular Career Course. In addition to these two basic courses there are more specialised ones run for entrants who will be going on to university, and for TA officer cadets.

Since the Standard Military Course is the one that most officers encounter it will be dealt with in some detail. It is an involved and exacting course involving all aspects of the future officer's work. As with other basic forms of military training the initial emphasis is on drill (in all its forms), weapon training and essential tactical skills. Where the RMAS differs from the rest of the Army is in the degree of expertise the officer cadet is expected to achieve—he must excel. Further basic military skills are imparted, not only in the Infantry role but in all the other arms of the Army as well. This intensive education is interspersed with lectures and practical training on the administration and organisation of the Army, leadership, military history, physical training, adventure training and sport. Sport plays an important part in the Sandhurst timetable and the facilities available range from the usual athletic pursuits to the almost inevitable horsemanship, and even flying.

Apart from the sporting aspects, the facilities at Sandhurst are first class in every respect while the instructional staff are drawn from well-qualified civilians and the military alike. The RMAS is set in several hundred acres of pleasant country near Camberley in Surrey and contained in its grounds are ranges, tactical training areas and all the accommodation needed for the cadets. The RMAS itself is divided into three colleges, 'Mons' (the Mons Officer Cadet School was joined on to the RMAS in 1972), 'Old' and 'Victory'.

The largest of these is Mons as this college is the one that caters for the Standard Military Course. It has two Wings, each divided into three companies as follows: Wing 1—Alamein, Burma and Normandy Companies; Wing 2—Arnhem, Rhine and Salerno Companies.

The officer cadets who will be going on to the Regular Career Course pass on to the Old College where they will be assigned to one of four companies, namely Blenheim, Dettingen, Waterloo or Inkerman. The third college is Victory, which caters for the university graduates and the like. It has three companies, Salamanca, Amiens and Gaza.

The RMAS also has five departments— Mathematics, Science, Political and Social Studies, War Studies and Languages. Each department is involved in all stages and forms of officer cadet training, but they are especially involved in the Regular Career Course where they combine to provide an extensive and comprehensive military education that will form the basis of the officer cadets' eventual career outlooks. The course lasts 21 weeks and covers such items as contemporary affairs, military technology in all its many aspects from basics to computers, ADP and electronics, further war studies and the essential techniques of instruction. The training is first-class and, although involved, is backed up by modern facilities and extensive libraries.

The RMAS education can also lead to further education at university level, either at the civilian universities or the Royal Military College of Science at Shrivenham. Further education comes from the officer cadets themselves, who now come from all walks of life, rather than the rather narrow band of the more privileged classes as of yore, and also from overseas. The overseas cadets usually come from the old colonies and British-influenced states, and on their return many have, in the past, gained high positions in their own armed forces or governments. This social aspect of the RMAS is one that is discreetly encouraged for the formation of character and leadership is just as important to the graduate officer as the technicalities of his calling.

The RMAS has over the years provided its own particular traditions, some of which have been passed down from previous academies such as that

as Woolwich. Perhaps the most widely known oddity that the RMAS brings to mind is that of the Adjutant riding his horse through the Grand Entrance at the end of the Sovereign's Parade, but there are others. The RMAS is the last home of traditional body armour in the British Army for the cadets still retain the gorgette as part of their parade dress. Numerous trophies are competed for every year—the best known being the Sword of Honour.

The Bands

Military bands have always been part of British Army life and they continue to be part and parcel of the modern Army in the missile age. Whether playing their music for parades or for entertaining the public, the bands act as a constant attraction and keep the Army in the public eye—their participation in the ceremonial life of the nation is an established fact. Every battalion of the Infantry has its own band of musicians and most of the regiments and corps have their own as well, although recent defence spending cuts have done away with some of them (for instance, both the Royal Artillery and the Royal Engineers lost a complete band apiece) and the remainder have had their numbers attenuated.

Bandsmen in the Army are not just musicians. They always have a secondary duty and tradition has it that they are stretcher bearers. In most regiments and corps they still are stretcher bearers or medical attendants while in others they are heavy truck drivers, as in the Royal Artillery.

At the time of writing the home of British Army military music was still the Royal Military School of Music at Kneller Hall near Twickenham, but its exact future is in doubt. Again, the defence spending re-arrangements have led to a re-appraisal of musical training for all the armed Services and it seems very likely that in future an inter-Service training establishment will be set up at Deal in Kent, leading to the closure of Kneller Hall.

The Territorial Army

The modern Territorial Army has a long history stretching back over several centuries to the era when every able-bodied man had to practice weekly with his longbow, but as the years went by its many forms gradually emerged as local militia units raised to be called upon in times of national emergency. Where the present-day Territorial Army (the TA) differs from its forebears is that it is no longer an armed force separate from the rest of the Army. Today the TA is an integral part of the Army's structure and its manpower and units form a large part of the Army's fighting strength.

The main strength of the modern TA lies within its 38 Infantry battalions. In addition to this total there are another 17 fighting units ranging from Gunner and Engineer formations to the two Yeomanry armoured reconnaissance regiments. But this is not all the TA can provide for, in addition to the major units, there are another 250 or so minor ones that vary from map-making squadrons to specialised Signal units. There are even two TA SAS units and three battalions of TA Parachute Regiment troops (described elsewhere).

The TA is made up mainly of part-time soldiers drawn from all walks of civilian life. Reservists and ex-Army soldiers who wish to retain some measure of the social and regimental spirit that the Regular Army provides add a valuable contribution to the technical skills needed by the modern TA, but the main training and administrative cadres are formed by Regular soldiers and officers. All arms of the modern Army are represented in the TA. Every unit is in some manner affiliated to a Regular formation and wears that regiment's badge. Their 'parent' formation usually provides some training facilities and other support and in time of emergency would become fully responsible for its mobilisation and deployment. However, many TA units have already been assigned their wartime roles. About 50 per cent of all TA units are intended for use in West Germany in an emergency. Some of these will be necessary to make 1 (BR) Corps up to its full numerical complement, but the majority of them will be combined with Regular units to form part of 1 and 19 Infantry Brigades. Those TA units remaining in the UK, apart from a few specialist formations, will form part of 5 Infantry Brigade for home defence. In this role they will be assigned to the various Military Districts and will be commanded by the local District Commanders. Regular units, along with troops raised from the various base and training establishments in the United Kingdom, will also be assigned to 5 Infantry Brigade.

As the modern TA is such an integral part of the Modern Army, its equipment is in most cases exactly the same as that of the front line units. However, especially with units intended for 5 Infantry Brigade, the accent is on wheeled rather than tracked vehicles. This has the combined attraction of lower costs coupled with less demanding maintenancing and training requirements. Thus an Infantry support weapons company would carry its Wombats and 81 mm mortars in Land Rovers rather than FV432s. Apart from this stricture the weapons involved are the same. Recently, some TA units have been issued with new equipment in advance of Regular units, but here and there some of the recently replaced front-line equipment takes on a new lease of life with the TA. An example of this can be seen in the adoption of Larkspur signal equipment by some home-based TA Signal units after they have been replaced by their Clansman counterparts. But generally speaking the TA units train with the same weapons and equipment as the Regular Army. Of course, there are some exceptions to this.

The present strength of the TA is around 55,000 men. To this may be added nearly 4,000 women who belong to WRAC TA units. As mentioned above, members of the TA come from all walks of life and by joining they take on various training and attendance committments. Each member of the TA has to attend at least 44 training days a year, of which 15 are spent full-time at a training camp or establishment. Many TA members exceed this total by a considerable margin. In return they are paid by a system of Regular pay scale rates and bounties. The minimum period of engagement is three years.

Despite the fact that some TA units are not up to full strength, the general standard of training is very high for the simple reason that members are all volunteers and do not join unless they wish to. The training is often hard, for some weekend training sessions take place in the field under all manner of conditions. TA soldiers often have to leave work on a Friday evening, travel straight to their training areas and commence their training exercises immediately. To make maximum use of the limited time available the exercises often carry on throughout the weekend without a break so that the soldier returns to work on the Monday morning after only a limited amount of rest. But they still turn out for the next weekend.

The annual training camp is a full-time affair and in many cases takes place in other locations than the United Kingdom. Units assigned to the 6th and 7th Field Forces often travel to West Germany, and small numbers of TA personnel have even made the long journey to Suffield in Canada. During the annual camp period, the TA units are treated exactly the same as their Regular counterparts but usually, such is their spirit and morale, they often try to outdo their colleagues in efficiency and expertise. To this extent there is a considerable degree of inter-unit competition between the TA units and other formations with trophies being awarded for specific tasks and competitions. Added to this is the considerable kudos that a TA soldier can obtain from being associated with such elite formations as the Parachute Regiment, while some TA units also have considerable social sway. Typical of the latter category is the Honorable Artillery Company based in London. As well as providing an Artillery regiment for ceremonial and field duties, the HAC also has a position of some social prominence in London life. It also provides another of the Army's structural anomalies. By tradition it is an Artillery unit but it is not part of the Royal Regiment of Artillery—in practice it is associated with the Gunners but it's constitution makes it a separate body.

Finally, mention must be made of the two basic types of TA unit—these are the Independent and the Sponsored unit. The Independent unit is what it says it is—it is one which can be formed with its own resources alone, and has its own centre. By contrast the Sponsored unit does not have its own centre and is dependent on a Central Volunteer Establishment of their own corps or regiment. The bulk of TA units (82 per cent) are Independent. Nearly all the Sponsored units are highly specialised and as a result have different training commitments.

Listing of the major TA units

The following list is provisional as TA units have been known to be rather prone to short-notice and short-term amalgamations or title changes. The list contains only those units of regimental size or status—there are many more units of smaller size. The units are not presented in order of precedence.
The Royal Yeomanry
The Queen's Own Yeomanry
The Wessex Yeomanry
The Mercian Yeomanry
The Duke of Lancaster's Own Yeomanry
The Honorable Artillery Company
1st Battalion, 52nd Lowland Volunteers
2nd Battalion, 52nd Lowland Volunteers
1st Battalion, 51st Highland Volunteers
2nd Battalion, 51st Highland Volunteers
3rd Battalion, 51st Highland Volunteers
5th (Volunteer) Battalion, The Queen's Regiment
6th/7th (Volunteer) Battalion, The Queen's Regiment
5th (Volunteer) Battalion, The Royal Regiment of Fusiliers
6th (Volunteer) Battalion, The Royal Regiment of Fusiliers
5th (Volunteer) Battalion, The Royal Anglian Regiment
6th (Volunteer) Battalion, The Royal Anglian Regiment
7th (Volunteer) Battalion, The Royal Anglian Regiment
4th (Volunteer) Battalion, The Queen's Lancashire Regiment.
5th/8th (Volunteer) Battalion, The King's Regiment (Manchester and Liverpool)
1st Battalion, The Yorkshire Volunteers
2nd Battalion, The Yorkshire Volunteers

3rd Battalion, The Yorkshire Volunteers
4th (Volunteer) Battalion, The Royal Irish Rangers
5th (Volunteer) Battalion, The Royal Irish Rangers
1st Battalion, The Wessex Regiment (Rifle Volunteers)
2nd Battalion, The Wessex Regiment
1st Battalion, The Mercian Volunteers
2nd Battalion, The Mercian Volunteers
3rd (Volunteer) Battalion, The Royal Welch Fusiliers
3rd (Volunteer) Battalion, The Royal Regiment of Wales (24th/41st Foot)
4th (Volunteer) Battalion, The Royal Regiment of Wales (24th/41st Foot)
3rd (Volunteer) Battalion, The Worcestershire and Sherwood Foresters Regiment (29th/45th Foot)
5th (Volunteer) Battalion, The Light Infantry
6th (Volunteer) Battalion, The Light Infantry
7th (Volunteer) Battalion, The Light Infantry
4th (Volunteer) Battalion, The Royal Green Jackets
4th (Volunteer) Battalion, The Parachute Regiment
10th (Volunteer) Battalion, The Parachute Regiment—London
15th (Volunteer) Battalion, The Parachute Regiment
21 Special Air Service Regiment (Artists) (Volunteers)
23 Special Air Service Regiment (Volunteers)
31 (Greater London) Signal Regiment (Volunteers)—Hammersmith
32 (Scottish) Signal Regiment (Volunteers)—Glasgow
33 (Lancashire and Cheshire) Signal Regiment (Volunteers)—Liverpool
34 (Northern) Signal Regiment (Volunteers)—Middlesborough
35 (South Midland) Signal Regiment (Volunteers)—Birmingham
36 (Eastern) Signal Regiment (Volunteers)—Wanstead
37 (Wessex and Welsh) Signal Regiment (Volunteers)—Bristol
38 Signal Regiment (Volunteers)—Sheffield
39 (City of London) Signal Regiment (Volunteers)—London
40 (Ulster) Signal Regiment (Volunteers)—Belfast
71 Signal Regiment (Volunteers)—Bromley
Royal Monmouthshire Royal Engineers (Militia)
71 (Scottish) Engineer Regiment (Volunteers)
72 Engineer Regiment (Tyne Electrical Engineers) (Volunteers)
73 Engineer Regiment (Volunteers)
74 (Antrim Artillery) Engineer Regiment (Volunteers)
75 Engineer Regiment (Volunteers)

111 Engineer Regiment (Volunteers)
100th (Yeomanry) Field Regiment Royal Artillery (Volunteers)
101st (Northumbrian) Field Regiment Royal Artillery (Volunteers)
102nd (Ulster and Scottish) Air Defence Regiment Royal Artillery (Volunteers)
103rd Lancashire Artillery (Volunteers) Air Defence Regiment Royal Artillery (Volunteers)
104th Air Defence Regiment Royal Artillery (Volunteers)

In 1984 plans to expand the strength of the Territorial Army were announced and these are being implemented over the period 1985-1987. These expansion plans cover all Arms and Services of the Army and are headed by the formation of three new light reconnaissance regiments to be manned by Yeomanry battalions. The plans even envisage a single AAC squadron flying Scout helicopters. The Royal Engineers will use volunteers to man four new Airfield Damage Repair (ADR) squadrons for use on airfields within the United Kingdom and the Royal Engineers have already formed a new explosive ordnance disposal (EOD) squadron.

These expansion plans will bring the manpower strength of the TA to 86,000 by 1990. The bulk of the manpower increase will come from the formation of six new TA infantry battalions that will commence formation during 1986. These six new battalions are as follows: 1st Battalion The Yorkshire and Cleveland Volunteers (York); 8th Battalion The Light Infantry (Volunteers) (Wakefield); 3rd Battalion The Devon and Cornwall Rifle Volunteers (Plymouth); 3rd (Volunteer) Battalion The Cheshire Regiment (initially Northwich, later Runcorn); 5th (Volunteer) Battalion The Royal Green Jackets (Oxford); and 8th (Volunteer) Battalion The Queen's Fusiliers (City of London) (London).

The Home Service Force

The Home Service Force (HSF) is an integral part of the Territorial Army and its role is to defend certain important installations in the United Kingdom, thereby freeing Regular and some TA units for other duties. The HSF is currently undergoing a period of expansion to a total of 47 companies with a manpower of 5,000. Most of these companies are attached to existing TA units but a few (five) will be attached to Regular Army units. Training will be based at TA drill halls.

Enlistment into the HSF will be restricted to trained male officers and other ranks who have either served with Regular or TA units, both full time and reserve, or who have reached high standards in Cadet units. Ministry of Defence Policemen are also eligible. It is expected that many ex-TA members who have left the TA for one reason or another will be attracted to the HSF by the less exacting training requirements. The minimum age for enlistment is 20 years and the normal maximum age 50 years. The maximum retention age is 60 years. The duties of the HSF will be mainly static guard duties and they will be armed with SLRs and some other light infantry weapons.

When complete the location of the 47 companies will be as follows:
Scotland (7): Elgin, Aberdeen, Perth, Dunfermline, Ayr, Dumfries and Edinburgh;
South-east (4): Canterbury, Horsham, Reading and Oxford;
North-east (7): Huddersfield, Scarborough, Newcastle, Bishop Auckland, Hull, Catterick and Leconfield;
East (7): Bedford, Norwich, Peterborough, Chelmsford, Worksop, Derby and Leicester;
London (5): Finsbury (two companies), Chelsea, Hammersmith and Kensington;
South-west (5): Truro, Plymouth, South Cerney, Bath and Salisbury;
Wales (3): Cardiff, Swansea and Wrexham;
West (4): Walsall, Worcester, Kidderminster and Donnington;
North-west (5): Lancaster, Chorley, Liverpool, Warrington and Runcorn.

The first four 'pilot' companies were those at Perth, Norwich, Reading and Worcester. The five HSF companies hosted by Regular Army units are those at Donnington, Salisbury, South Cerney, Catterick and Leconfield.

The Army in Northern Ireland

As these words are written, the present troubles in Northern Ireland have been extended over a period of more than 15 years. That period has seen the Army always in the thick of whatever unpleasantries the inhabitants of Ulster have chosen to inflict upon one another, and they have always borne the brunt of the open aggression so freely doled out by all the many sides in the multi-faceted social and political circumstances that continue to bedevil the Six Counties. During the past decade, the Army has come in for more than its share of 'blame' for events in Northern Ireland, but it has been called upon to carry out a thankless task that any other Army would have turned into something approaching a bloodbath, and it has to be stated as a fact that if the Army was not present in Ulster as it now is, ie, in strength and well-trained, life in Ulster would be a good deal worse than it is already.

A foot patrol, or 'brick' of the 1st Battalion The Cheshire Regiment (AIS NI).

The Army is no stranger to Northern Ireland. For many hundreds of years the Army has been a well-established part of the social and political landscape. Ever since William of Orange took over the sovereignty of the Province, and long before that, the people of Ulster have had soldiers of the Crown in their midst. The soldiers manned the garrison towns in the Province and raised many famous regiments that served the Crown well in numerous conflicts, and some of these regiments survive to this day. After 1922 the Province continued to supply men for the Services, and it should be remembered that between 1939 and 1945, Northern Ireland was excluded from the various Conscription Acts for the reason that so many Irishmen were crossing the Border to sign on for the British forces that conscription was never necessary.

When the present troubles 'began' in 1969 the Army was already present as part of the normal peace-time garrison. Within a very short time the prevalent social and political unrest erupted into open insurrection and rioting to the extent that the local civil and police authorities were completely unable to contain the violence and uproar that broke out in nearly all the major urban centres of Ulster. The Army was called in by the local government authorities to assist the Royal Ulster Constabulary to maintain order, but the strength of the local Army units was insufficient to take on such a task. Troops were brought into the Province from

the United Kingdom to swell the available numbers and they have never been able to return.

The Army in Northern Ireland is engaged in that most unloved form of military duty, 'action in support of a civil power'. This point has to be stressed for it is not widely understood that the Army by itself does not possess autonomous powers of action. In Northern Ireland the Army comes firmly under the control of the local civic authorities and their various offices. In Ulster that means the Army comes under the direction of the Royal Ulster Constabulary which in its turn takes its references from the United Kingdom Home Office, via an appointed Crown Minister. Acting under such a control the Army often finds itself in some very tricky legal circumstances. The Army does not have an automatic right to search or arrest. If soldiers are attacked or fired on, their powers to retaliate are carefully and rigidly proscribed. Such restrictions of the Army's activities are very necessary if our carefully preserved liberties are to be retained, but the restrictions often hamper the Army in their task of apprehending suspects and generally keeping the peace. All too often the Army has had to place itself and its members in positions of extreme risk with all too often no chance to effect redress or carry out any counter-activity.

As these words are being written for the third edition, the overall security situation in Northern Ireland has settled down to a level far below that of the excesses of the early 1970s. Bombings, shootings and violence are still no strangers to the Province but over the last few years the Security Forces (the RUC, the Army and the UDR—not forgetting the fact that the UDR is part of the Army) have gradually gained the upper hand to the extent that there are now large tracts of the Province where relative normality prevails and where no terrorists acts have taken place for years. To counter this it must be stated that there are other places where peace has not been restored to anything other than a nominal degree. These include parts of Londonderry and Belfast and the 'bandit country' along the borders of South Armagh and Fermanagh. Even in the cities, however, the crowd troubles so prevalent only a few years ago are now rare and seem to happen only when some 'anniversary' comes around. Even the security barriers in the centre of Belfast have been dismantled.

Of course, the terrorists of both sides of the Irish divide can still inflict casualties, destroy property and carry out their ruthless intimidations, for they will always have the initiative in such matters. Deaths are still inflicted and property is still wrecked but the degree of such actions has reached the point where the terrorists are now unable to raise the level of their activities above a certain point and the Security

Forces are equally unable to reduce those same activities below a certain rate. It would seem that some form of impasse has been reached, an impasse that would have seemed impossible when the first edition of this book was written. This has been the result of a great deal of hard work by the Security Forces and especially by the Army. Operating under the control of the RUC, the Army has gradually raised its counter-insurgency and internal security skills to the point where it is now probably the best-trained force of its type anywhere in the world. The terrorists from both sides now do their best to keep out of the Army's way and no longer attempt to carry out the random gun and bomb ambushes that were once too common. Today, the terrorists go for soft targets such as off-duty UDR personnel and only attempt to take on the Army when they think they can gain an advantage—and that happens infrequently.

The total number of soldiers in Northern Ireland at the time of writing is about 9,000 plus a further 6,500 from the UDR. They are organised into two brigades under HQ Northern Ireland at Lisburn. 8 Infantry Brigade is to the west at Londonderry and 39 Infantry Brigade to the east at Lisburn. Between them these two brigades command eight infantry battalions, six resident in North Ireland and two roulement on 4½-month tours. Between them these eight battalions are grouped to maintain security in the main trouble areas of the two cities and the border counties. To do this they are allocated Tactical Areas of Responsibility, or TAORs, which are located throughout the Province to roughly coincide with the RUC areas. In only three TAORs are resident Army battalions established and in two there are roulement battalions. The rest of the TAORs are manned by the UDR who alone provide support for the RUC in those TAORs, and that means well over 85 per cent of the Province.

No 8 Infantry brigade has four resident battalions in Londonderry, Ballykelly, Omagh and Aldergrove. 39 Infantry Brigade has two resident battalions at Holywood and Ballykinler with the two roulement battalions at Armagh and in a RUC station on the Springfield Road in Belfast. (There is also another small roulement unit known as the Prison Guard Force (PGF) that looks after the security of the exterior of the Maze Prison and is found from Gunner or RAC regiments, a battery or a squadron at a time.) One of the roulement battalions comes from the United Kingdom and one from BAOR.

Within each TAOR the Security Forces work in close co-operation with the RUC in charge. Co-operation between the Army and the UDR is particularly close, so close that at times the UDR takes control of operations. The 'regular' Army have long conceded that for many types of operation the UDR, and in particular the PC companies, are far better at

their job than they could ever be. The tasks carried out by the Security Forces include the inevitable patrolling, manning of vehicle check points (VCPs) and general searches. To these overt activities can be added the covert tasks of surveillance, infiltration and other such 'underground' ploys. The overt activities such as patrolling by foot, vehicle and helicopter go on around the clock. These patrols reassure the law-abiding populace, keep the terrorists off-balance by appearing in odd places at odd times, and they sometimes take a toll of terrorist equipment, arms and personnel. The covert activities are less easy to describe but include area or point surveillance, making use of night vision equipment and other such kit. Some of these surveillance operations last weeks, both in urban and rural areas.

For the average soldier in Northern Ireland the main activities are patrolling and VCPs, usually in company with the RUC. In the more extreme areas such as West Belfast, much of this patrolling has to be carried out using Pigs but elsewhere the usual vehicle is the ubiquitous Land Rover, usually protected by a layer of Macralon armour. The once-familiar Saracens have now been withdrawn. Helicopters are often used to carry patrols to remote areas and establish VCPs on country roads.

The long and winding border with Eire seems to have been established to invite infiltration from the south so the border areas are now the main centres of Army activity as they are for the terrorist. In the border areas all manner of overt and covert Army activities continue and UDR PC companies are stationed there from some of the larger battalions to the north. The border areas are now the main localities where terrorist weapons such as the culvert bomb or the home-made mortar are most likely to be encountered and it is here that the Army EOD teams often have to operate. Bombing still occurs in the towns but there the main terrorist target is the destruction of property—in the rural areas the targets are the Security Forces.

The Army no longer has to spend much of its time training for an 'Operation Banner' tour or winding down from one before normal training activities can resume. With only two roulement battalions involved at any one time, the upheavals are minor compared to what they once used to be. At one point in the 1970s there were over 22,000 soldiers in Northern Ireland with a further 8,000 members of the UDR—now the figures are much less with only the six Infantry battalions resident. Other troops are involved in roulement operations. An AAC squadron is always present in addition to the resident AAC Squadron (655) at Aldergrove and at any given time elements from REME workshops are on roulement tours. There is also a large Royal Military Police presence in the Province and all the usual support troops are present. To offset this it should be remembered that the TA is very active in Northern Ireland, supplying reserve units for BAOR and elsewhere, and the Province continues to supply recruits for units throughout the Army. In connection with the latter, units formed from within Northern Ireland (the Royal Irish Rangers, the Irish Guards, the Queen's Royal Irish Hussars and the 5th Royal Inniskilling Guards) do not serve in the Province, although it has happened.

Thus the current situation in Northern Ireland is relatively encouraging compared to the days when the first edition of this book was being prepared. But there has been a price to pay. At the time of writing Northern Ireland had cost in deaths alone the following: Army 381, UDR 149, RUC 212 and civilians 2,332. To add to these must be many more wounded and maimed and as many again mentally scarred. Yet there seems no end to the current Troubles. Terrorists can still operate and they still find support among a sizeable proportion of the resident population. There is also another chilling factor to bear in mind. Although the number of terrorists operating in Northern Ireland has been much reduced, those who survive are a very hard and dedicated core. Any operation they now undertake is far more likely to result in casualties to the Security Forces and population than hitherto, for they now operate only when they have some definite destructive objective to fulfil.

A soldier of The Duke of Edinburgh's Royal Regiment covering a joint RUC/Army patrol in South Armagh (AIS NI).

So although the Army, the UDR and the RUC are now on top, ahead still looms the prospect of continuing anti-terrorist commitments in Northern Ireland. The RUC will have to continue to call on the Army and UDR to provide support in keeping the peace and for years ahead it seems that the patrolling, the check points and the tensions will continue. Set against that is the realisation that over much of Northern Ireland one can travel for days without even seeing a soldier or indeed, any sight of anything connected with terrorism.

NBC

The abbreviation NBC stands for Nuclear, Biological and Chemical warfare which combine to form one of the most unpleasant and horrific facets of modern warfare. All three aspects of this nasty form of conflict produce their own particular hazards and combat risks but their effects can all be minimised by much the same form of defence, namely protection, and NBC defence is one area where the British Army is well provided for, to the envy of many Western armed forces.

Nuclear warfare is now seen as an almost unavoidable feature of any future conflict so protection against it has to be provided for by any armed force. For the soldier in the field Nuclear warfare means the battlefield use of tactical nuclear weapons delivered by a number of means. These are weapons that are relatively small in the nuclear sense and will thus be of the power of around 10-20 kilotons of TNT. Such weapons produce three main hazards—heat, blast and radiation, with the latter being both immediate and residual ('Fall-out'). While defence against nuclear devices is a complex and involved study, the main protection can be simply stated as the provision of adequate shelter. The immediate effects of a nuclear explosion can be considerably reduced by the use of even quite simple shelter but the long-term effects of nuclear radiation involve forms of filtering radioactive particles from the atmosphere. Thus simple digging can provide rudimentary defences for soldiers in the open but in the long term some forms of filtering and other measures must be taken.

Armoured vehicles can provide a great deal of their own protection and all British armoured and other vehicles have integral air-cleaning systems as part of their normal equipment. In a radioactive environment foot soldiers can still gain a measure of protection by the use of specialised clothing but generally speaking they cannot function or survive long so they have to go underground. The Army has a considerable number of mobile shelters known as the Field Shelter Mark 2, or Mexeshelter, which can

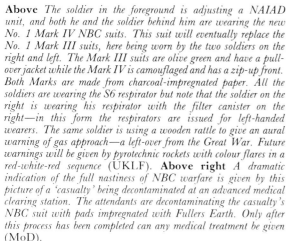

Above *The soldier in the foreground is adjusting a NAIAD unit, and both he and the soldier behind him are wearing the new No. 1 Mark IV NBC suits. This suit will eventually replace the No. 1 Mark III suits, here being worn by the two soldiers on the right and left. The Mark III suits are olive green and have a pull-over jacket while the Mark IV is camouflaged and has a zip-up front. Both Marks are made from charcoal-impregnated paper. All the soldiers are wearing the S6 respirator but note that the soldier on the right is wearing his respirator with the filter canister on the right—in this form the respirators are issued for left-handed wearers. The same soldier is using a wooden rattle to give an aural warning of gas approach—a left-over from the Great War. Future warnings will be given by pyrotechnic rockets with colour flares in a red-white-red sequence (UKLF).* **Above right** *A dramatic indication of the full nastiness of NBC warfare is given by this picture of a 'casualty' being decontaminated at an advanced medical clearing station. The attendants are decontaminating the casualty's NBC suit with pads impregnated with Fullers Earth. Only after this process has been completed can any medical treatment be given* (MoD).

be fairly rapidly constructed by digging trenches, erecting the shelter frame and its flexible walls and roofing, and filling in the sides and top with earth. This shelter, with its built-in air-filtering system, can also be used as a defence against chemical and biological attack.

Chemical warfare involves the use of various war gases which can range from the well-tried blister and choking gases through to the modern 'nerve' gases and other horrors which are as yet unrevealed. They are usually dispensed in cloud or aerosol forms by a number of methods which can range from ground-mounted cylinders to airborne dispensers. Of these thoroughly unpleasant forms of attack, the modern nerve gases are among the most

lethal. There are several different forms, eg, Tabun, the V-agents, GB, etc, but they all interfere with some aspect or another of the human body's basic functions and even small amounts can produce an unpleasant death. The only protection against such agents is to completely cover the body with a layer of impervious material, and the use of respirators to filter the air the soldiers breathe. The same measures can be taken against biologial warfare, which can be loosely regarded as an adjunct to chemical warfare except that the agents involved are intended to inflict a range of lethal or incapacitating diseases ranging from anthrax to 'artificial' diseases produced in laboratories.

In the British Army, the protection measures against chemical and biological warfare consists of the Mark III NBC Suit and the S6 respirator (see the uniform section for further details and illustrations). Wearing the Mark III, or 'Noddy' Suit, is not a pleasant experience and a soldier's fighting capabilities can be somewhat reduced by even a relatively short period encased in its total envelopment. The British suit does, however, at least provide some measures that enable some air circulation around the body, a feature not shared by many similar suits in service elsewhere. Wounded soldiers can be protected by being enclosed inside an all-enveloping Casualty Bag, and walking wounded can be covered by a bag which extends over the head (a vision panel is provided) and is secured at the waist. There are various decontamination measures available from simple water sprays to remove agents from vehicles and weapons through to special cleansing kits for personal decontamination.

But all the protective measure can be to no avail if there is insufficient warning or time to take them. Here the British Army is well in advance of many others with the provision of various forms of detection equipment. These can vary from simple treated papers up to one of the most advanced chemical detectors in service anywhere. Although it is still undergoing the final stages of development, the new detector, known as NAIAD, will become one of the most important defences against Chemical Warfare for it is a 'Black Box' that can synthesise the natural chemistry of the human body and thereby detect any agent that might prove harmful. NAIAD has two units. One is the detector and the other a remote alarm unit that can be placed up to 500 metres away from the detector. Thus a unit in the field can be given some measure of warning of the approach of harmful agents. The complete NAIAD system weighs 14 kg.

One other protection against the nerve gases is the use of small automatic hypodermic injectors which can inject the chemical atropine through the soldier's clothing into the body. Atropine has the property of reducing or minimising the effects of some nerve gases on the human body but it must be used quickly, hence the designation of Autoject No 2 Mark 1. Each soldier in the field is issued with at least one of these along with his other NBC first aid and decontamination kit. Other protective measures are still the subject of considerable research and development at a number of establishments. One of the most widely known is the civilian establishment at Porton, but the Army has its own Defence NBC Centre at Winterbourne Gunner. A great deal of the development work involving protective clothing is carried out by the Stores and Clothing Research and Development Establishment (SCRDE) at Colchester.

The Army and the Royal Air Force

The modern Army and the Royal Air Force (RAF) are today more interdependent than they have ever been. The Army relies on the RAF for much of its long-range and close-support weapons delivery, to say nothing of the tactical reconnaissance it provides and the degree to which 6 Airmobile Brigade may depend upon RAF helicopter support to make its important anti-tank missile role possible. In return the RAF relies upon the Army for the overall defence of its bases and also for a large proportion of its logistic support and supplies generally. Thus a full account of the modern Army cannot be complete without some

explanation of the RAF's role in Germany.

The RAF units based in Germany come under the command of RAF Germany, or RAFG. In its turn RAFG is under NATO command as part of the Second Tactical Air Force, or 2 ATAF, but only in time of war—at all other times it remains under national control. RAFG now has 13 squadrons based on four airfields, three of them grouped in an area close to the Dutch border and known as the 'Clutch' airfields. These squadrons have four main roles carried out in support of the Army: close air support, interdiction, tactical reconnaissance and battlefield supply and movements.

Close air support is the direct involvement of the RAF in the Army's land battle. In effect it replaces the tactical role played in the past by heavy artillery but today's air support is much more flexible. For the Army the main aircraft involved is the versatile Harrier GR 3 or T 4, to be replaced in the near future by the Harrier GR 5. The two squadrons involved will operate away from their home base of RAF

RAF squadrons in Germany

Unit	Aircraft type	Role	Base
2 Squadron	Jaguar GR 1/T 2*	Tactical recce	RAF Laarbruch
3 Squadron	Harrier GR 3/T 4†	Close air support	RAF Gutersloh
4 Squadron	Harrier GR 3/T 4†	Close air support	RAF Gutersloh
14 Squadron	Tornado GR 1	Tactical strike/interdiction	RAF Bruggen
15 Squadron	Tornado GR 1	Tactical strike/interdiction	RAF Laarbruch
16 Squadron	Tornado GR 1	Tactical strike/interdiction	RAF Laarbruch
17 Squadron	Tornado GR 1	Tactical strike/interdiction	RAF Bruggen
18 Squadron	Chinook HC 1	Transport support	RAF Gutersloh
19 Squadron	Phantom FGR 2	Air defence	RAF Wildenrath
20 Squadron	Tornado GR 1	Tactical strike/interdiction	RAF Bruggen
31 Squadron	Tornado GR 1	Tactical strike/interdiction	RAF Bruggen
92 Squadron	Phantom FGR 2	Air defence	RAF Wildenrath
230 Squadron	Puma HC 1	Transport support	RAF Gutersloh

*To convert to Tornado. †To convert to Harrier GR 5.

Gutersloh from 'hides' hidden in the country from where their remarkable vertical or short take-off and landing characteristics can be used to the full. The Harriers can carry bombs, rockets or 30 mm cannon. They may be supported by Tornados.

Interdiction is the penetration of the enemy's rear areas to attack, disrupt and generally harass supply columns and depots, break up enemy formations preparing to act as 'second wave' attackers, and disrupt communications. The aircraft involved here is the powerful (and expensive) Tornado GR 1 which has now become the main aircraft type within RAFG, replacing the earlier Buccaneers and the Jaguars. At the time of writing only two Jaguar squadrons remained in RAFG, both of them due to be re-equipped with Tornados, the last of them being 2 Squadron which is used for tactical reconnaissance. Some tactical reconnaissance missions may also be undertaken by the Harrier squadrons.

Battlefield lift and movement is provided by two RAFG squadrons, both of them helicopter-equipped. One is 18 Squadron equipped with the large Chinook and the other 230 Squadron equipped with the Puma. They provide general battlefield lift support for the Army and are involved with 6 Airmobile Brigade for their experimental anti-tank missile lift role.

RAFG also encompasses a number of RAF Regiment units including Rapier airfield air defence squadrons and light armoured squadrons for perimeter defence. Only one of these light armoured squadrons is normally based in Germany and the rest would arrive during the build-up period to an emergency. They are equipped with FV 107 Scorpions and FV103 Spartans and would be deployed for the defence of their base airfields or the Harrier hides.

Left A Chinook HC 1 of No 18 Squadron carrying out a heavy lift in a forward area (MoD). ***Below*** *RAF groundcrew servicing a Harrier GR 3 of No 3 Squadron in its field hide* (MoD).

The Rapiers would be used only for airfield defence.

In return for all this support, the Army provides most of the supplies the RAFG units need, from fuel to food. In particular the Harrier squadrons receive a great deal of in-field support from the Royal Engineers. 38 Engineer Regiment and 10 Field Squadron would be responsible for establishing and maintaining the Harrier operating pads and taxiways together with the communications and so forth that the sites would need. RCT and RAOC units would keep the supplies moving to the hides and it is possible that some local defence would be provided by Infantry units. Back on the RAFG airfields, runway and taxi-way damage would be repaired by the four field squadrons of 39 Engineer Regiment who would also be responsible for repairing any other airfield damage to keep the bases operational.

Mention must be made of the two Phantom FGR 2 squadrons at RAF Wildenrath. Their primary role is the defence of the airfields and this will normally be carried out far from the land battle. From time to time they might be called upon to carry out tactical reconnaissance missions. Mention must also be made of other squadrons operating under 2 ATAF but from other nations. To the British Army the most familiar of these are likely to be the A-10 Thunderbolts of the American 81st Tactical Fighter Wing based at RAF Bentwaters and Woodbridge in England but operating from forward bases in Germany. These low-level anti-tank strike aircraft will be operating at low altitude over the 1 (BR) Corps area, often in close co-operation with the TOW-armed Lynx squadrons of the AAC.

Away from the confines of RAFG the Army is still likely to be operating with the RAF close to hand. Within the RAF's United Kingdom command establishment is Strike Command, one part of which is 38 Group. No 38 Group would come under NATO command in time of war and would then supply a number of squadrons for use as and where required. This would involve Harrier, Jaguar, Puma and Hercules squadrons, along with Chinooks and Wessex squadrons.

For full details of RAF organisation and equipment refer to the companion *Encyclopaedia of the Modern Royal Air Force,* by the same author.

Weapons and equipment

The section devoted to the modern Army's weapons and equipment has been compiled from as many sources as has been found possible while at the same time having regard to security restrictions. I have attempted to make this section as comprehensive and up-to-date as possible but inevitably the scale of the modern Army's equipment is so vast that not every item can be included. Some of these items are still 'under wraps', while others are in use in such small numbers that they can be omitted, despite their relative importance to the units that use them. In this latter category come some rather odd and long-in-the-tooth items such as the FV13203 Commer Q4 trucks still used by some REME units based in Germany. Other elderly trucks still survive in some TA units and their omission has had to be decided upon for the simple reason that to include them all would make this book so large it would be unmanageable. However, in some cases the older equipments do rate a mention, if only to give a general idea of the gradual development of the modern Army's weapons and equipment.

Equipment designation system

The British Services have adopted a system for identifying and labelling all the equipment used by them that enables each item to be clearly differentiated from all the other items in use. At first sight, the system appears complex and not very clear but it is actually straightforward once the following guidelines have been understood.

Each item of equipment has a designation in a set sequence. The first part of the sequence describes exactly what the item of equipment is, eg, Gun, Howitzer, Rifle, Carriage, etc.

This is followed, where applicable, by the essential characteristics of the particular item. For instance, the term Rifle is followed by its calibre of 7.62 mm in the form Rifle, 7.62 mm. A howitzer is described as Howitzer, 8 inch.

Then comes the model number, which in the Army is usually prefixed by the letter 'L'. In this context the L stands for 'Land Service'. If an item starts with a prefix L it is usually an approved and in-service item. If it is itself prefixed by an 'X', it denotes it is still in the development or experimental stage, and in some cases the same letter is used to indicate a limited procurement item. Returning to the rifle example we thus have Rifle, 7.62 mm, L1A1.

To explain the further import of the 1A1 after the L in the last example, the 1 refers to the model number, ie, Rifle, calibre 7.62 mm, Land Service Model 1. The A1 part of the quoted example refers to the modification state of the model, ie, it is still unchanged from its state when it was introduced into service. In the unlikely event of the standard rifle being extensively modified for some reason it would become the L1A2. X prefixes use E numbers in this context, eg, Pistol, Automatic Walther Type PP XL47E1. Note that this example amplified its essential characteristic identification by the addition of a commercial name.

At this point it must be mentioned that a designation is not necessarily peculiar to one particular item. To quote an extreme example it is possible to have a Pistol L1A1 and a Gun Carriage L1A1—the L1A1 must be prefixed by the basic name of the item concerned.

Needless to say there are some variations to this system, usually when American designations are carried into British use. The American system is similar to the British one in many ways but each item model number is prefixed by the letter 'M'. In many cases the American designation is used in place of the British one, eg, Anti-personnel Mine M18A1.

Another anomaly arises with the use of the old designation system in use until just after the end of the Second World War. This involved the use of numbers of each item of equipment and Mark numbers. In many cases to avoid the duplication of a great deal of paperwork on items that were expected to go out of service in time anyway, the old system was retained. But in some cases the old items are still in use and some anomalies remain with them. An example is the Trailer, Tank Transporter, No 1 Mark 3. (Asterisks (*) were added to Mark numbers to denote substantial alterations to the state of the Mark that did not warrant a new Mark number.) The old system was dropped mainly because, although it seems fairly straightforward, in practice it became very complex and cumbersome. The present L system is more versatile, shorter in use, and more in line with similar systems used by other Allied nations.

FV designations will be found wherever they can be accurately attributed throughout this book. It is applied to all wheeled or tracked vehicles, whether powered or not. The letters FV refer to 'Field Vehicle'.

Infantry weapons

9 mm Pistol Automatic L9A1
Calibre 9 mm; **Length** 0.196 m; **Length of barrel** 0.112 m; **Weight empty** 0.88 kg; **Weight loaded** 1.01 kg; **Muzzle velocity** 354 m/s; **Magazine capacity** 13 rounds; **Rate of fire** Single-shot; **Maximum effective range** 40-50 m.

The design of the Browning pistol was finalised in 1925 but it was not until 1935 that production commenced at Herstal in Belgium. During World War 2 production continued in Belgium for the German forces but drawings shipped to Canada

enabled the firm of John Inglis, situated in Toronto, to manufacture slightly modified pistols for issue to the Allied armies. In February 1943 drawings were finalised for a version known originally as the Pistol, Browning, F.N. 9 mm H.P., No. 2 Mark 1*, and soon afterwards this version was issued to various special-purpose formations such as Commandos and airborne forces. Thereafter the use of the 9 mm automatic gradually spread throughout the forces, at first supplementing and finally replacing the existing .38 revolvers in service. The pistol finally gained the seal of approval by being termed as available for issue in February 1961 by which time there were few .38 revolvers left. Now designated the L9A1, the pistol is the general service issue pistol for all branches of the Service.

The L9A1 is an unusual pistol in that its magazine holds 13 rounds. Not only can this be a valuable asset in combat but the oversize grip provides a good hold for above-average shooting, even by relatively untrained personnel. Normally the L9A1 is carried in a webbing belt holster, but it has on occasion been issued with a shoulder holster for plain-clothes undercover missions.

7.65 mm Pistol Automatic Walther Type PP XL47E1
Calibre 7.65 mm; **Length** 0.173 m; **Length of barrel** 0.099 m; **Weight empty** 0.68 kg; **Weight loaded** 1.00 kg; **Muzzle velocity** 290 m/s; **Magazine capacity** 8 rounds; **Rate of fire** Single-shot; **Maximum effective range** 40 m.

Left *A Sapper firing a 9 mm L9A1 pistol.* **Right** *The PP XL47E1 Pistol.*

Relatively few of these pistols are in use as they are normally issued only to those who carry out what are categorised as 'special duties'. This usually entails undercover and plain-clothes tasks. The pistol is a German commerical model designed for easy concealment, has been widely used by many police forces ever since it was first introduced in 1929 and is still in production. Designed and made mainly by the German Walther concern, its commercial designation is Model PP (PP—Police Pistol). Recently this design has rather fallen from favour with many civilian police forces as it was the model involved in the now-infamous attempted kidnapping of Princess Anne in The Mall in 1974, when a police example failed to fire. However, it must be stated that when correctly maintained the PP is an excellent pistol for its role.

Sub-Machine Gun 9 mm L2A3

Calibre 9 mm; **Length (butt folded)** 0.482 m; **Length (butt extended)** 0.69 m; **Length of barrel** 0.198 m; **Weight empty** 2.7 kg; **Weight loaded** 3.5 kg; **Muzzle velocity** 390 m/s; **Magazine capacity** 34 rounds; **Rate of fire (cyclic)** 550 rpm; **Rate of fire (practical)** 102 rpm; **Rate of fire (single-shot)** 40 rpm; **Maximum effective range** 200 m.

Known unofficially as the 'Sterling', the L2A3 had a rather protracted development timespan as the original version, then known as the Patchett, was used for troop trials in action in 1945. It was not until 1951 that the first service model (the L2A1) was produced, followed in 1953 by the L2A2. In 1954 the type was adopted as the standard British sub-machine-gun as the L2A3, after which it gradually replaced the well-tried Sten. Since 1954 the L2A3 has undergone some slight changes but it is still in production at the Sterling Armament Company Limited at Dagenham, and is in use by well over 80 police and military formations.

Construction of the L2A3 is extremely robust and its blow-back mechanism has proved to be reliable under a wide range of conditions. The side-mounted magazine is designed to hold 34 rounds but in practical service two or three rounds less than this number are loaded. The breech block has inclined splines which effectively clear any debris which enters the receiver and reduces the likelihood of jamming. A small bayonet can be fitted to the muzzle. The main users of the L2A3 in the British Army are tank crewmen, Engineers, the Artillery and second-line support services.

Sub-Machine-Gun 9 mm L34A1

Calibre 9 mm; **Length (butt folded)** 0.654 m; **Length (butt extended)** 0.857 m; **Length of barrel**

On the ranges with an L2A3.

0.198 m; **Weight empty** 3.54 kg; **Weight loaded** 4.25 kg; **Muzzle velocity** 308 m/s; **Magazine capacity** 34 rounds; **Rate of fire (cyclic)** 515-565 rpm; **Rate of fire (practical)** 102 rpm; **Rate of fire (single-shot)** 40-45 rpm; **Maximum effective range** 150 m.

The L34A1 is the service version of the Sterling Patchett Mark 5 which was produced in 1964 as the result of a General Staff request for a silent weapon. It was adopted in small numbers and is usually issued to special-duties formations only. The L34A1 is basically the same weapon as the L2A3 but the barrel housing is longer and has a number of holes along its length which vent off the propellant gases, produced after firing, through a wire mesh sleeve into a diffuser tube. These gases are then passed through a spiral diffuser so that by the time they vent around the muzzle they are virtually noiseless. Also, by the time the bullet leaves the muzzle its velocity has become sub-sonic and the overall effect is that the

Above *The L34A1 silenced sub-machine-gun—this particular example is a commercial model with a special plated finish but is exactly the same as the Army version.* Below *A L1A1 fitted with the 30-round magazine from the L4A4 machine-gun.* Above right *An L1A1 (SLR) at the ready.* Below right *A TA para with his L1A1 Rifle—which is fitted with the L1A2 blank-firing attachment over the muzzle.*

L34A1 is an effective soundless weapon. Normally the L34A1 would be fired single-shot with the fully automatic feature being used only under special circumstances. Although the firing mehanism is similar to that of the L2A3 a lighter bolt and less powerful return spring are needed. For use at night a Scotos night sight can be fitted.

Rifle 7.62 mm L1A1

Calibre 7.62 mm; **Length overall** 1.143 m; **Length of barrel** 0.5334 m; **Weight empty** 4.337 kg; **Weight loaded (20-round magazine)** 5.074 kg; **Muzzle velocity** 838 m/s; **Magazine capacity** 20 or 30 rounds; **Rate of fire** 40 rpm; **Maximum effective range** 600 m plus.

The L1A1 is the British version of the Belgian FN FAL (Fabrique Nationale—Fusil Automatique Leger) which was selected for service after trials with two versions of the original Belgian model that commenced during 1955. Modifications were made to the basic design, not the least of which was the removal of the fully automatic fire mode of the FAL, and the L1A1 thereafter replaced the Rifle No. 4 Mark 1 as the British Army's standard service rifle. Production was carried out at the Royal Ordnance Factory at Fazackerley, and the Royal Small Arms Factory at Enfield Lock. The early production versions were fitted with wooden furniture but this was later changed to black nylonite.

The L1A1 Self-Loading Rifle (SLR) uses a gas-operated mechanism that is robust and dependable. Field stripping is straightforward and easily carried out. The basic sights consist of the normal 'iron' variety with a sight radius of 553.7 mm, but the SUIT (Sight Unit Infantry Trilux) L1A1 or L1A2 is now a virtual standard combat fixture adding a further 0.435 kg to the loaded weight. The Infantry Weapon Sight (IWS) L1A2 is another sighting fixture. Other combat accessories include a bayonet (L1A3 or L1A4), and a grenade launcher (L1A2). For training purposes a blank firing attachment can be fitted over the muzzle—this is the L6A1 or L1A2. When indoor or small rifle ranges have to be used the .22-in Conversion Set L12A1 can be employed—this is produced by the West German Heckler and Koch concern.

The rounds fired by the L1A1 are 7.62 mm in calibre and the cartridge cases are 51 mm long—hence 7.62 × 51 mm. There is a wide range of types of ammunition produced in NATO 7.62 mm, not all of which is fired by the L1A1 (for instance, tracer is rarely fired from rifles but is in common use with machine-guns). The more common types in Army use are the Round 7.62 mm Ball L2A2 (standard ball round); the Round 7.62 mm Ball Target L2A2 (selected 'Green Spot' round for target use); the Round 7.62 mm Ball L11A1 (NATO round produced by Raufoss in Norway);

Round 7.62 mm Tracer L5A3 (red tip to bullet); the Round 7.62 mm Short Range L14A1 (training round with plastic bullet—little used); the Round 7.62 mm Blank L13A1 (crimped green case nose); the Round 7.62 mm Drill L1A2 (inert round with red grooved case); the Round 7.62 mm Inspection L3A1 (inert round for armourers' use—silver case);

and the Cartridge 7.62 mm Rifle Grenade L1A2 (for firing Energa grenade—now little used). With the Ball L2A2 and L11A1 the bullet weighs 9.33 grams and is projected by a charge of 2.85 grams.

Rifle 7.62 mm L39A1

Calibre 7.62 mm; **Length** 1.18 m; **Length of barrel** 0.7 m; **Weight empty** 4.42 kg; **Weight loaded** ?   kg; **Muzzle velocity** 841 m/s; **Magazine capacity** 10 rounds; **Rate of fire** Single-shot only; **Maximum effective range** 1,000 m plus.

The Rifle L1A1 is a good combat rifle but does not have the inherent accuracy that is necessary in the exacting sphere of competition rifle shooting. As always the Army is very involved in this field and to keep up its showing at such places as Bisley the Army has to have a viable competitive rifle. NRA rules dictate a non-repeating weapon for all its major contests so the Army decided to convert its old surplus No. 4 Mark 1 and 2 .303-in rifles for competition work. The old Mark 1 rifles proved unsuitable for the role but numerous Mark 1/2 and 2 rifles were selected for conversion which involved replacing the barrel with a new heavier item in 7.62 mm calibre and changing much of the furniture—the basic Lee-Enfield bolt action was retained. The conversions were carried out at the Royal Small Arms Factory at Enfield Lock and the

final product is an excellent target rifle which is good enough to be produced commercially as the 'Envoy'. The L39A1 is usually delivered without sights to enable each individual or unit to fit their own choice and the maximum effective range quoted in the table is dependent upon individual skill and choice of ammunition batch. The round most commonly used in competitions is the Round 7.62 mm Ball Target L2A2 ('Green Spot') ammunition produced at the Royal Ordnance Factory, Radway Green.

Rifle 7.62 mm L42A1

Calibre 7.62 mm; **Length** 1.181 m; **Length of barrel** 0.699 m; **Weight empty** 4.43 kg; **Weight loaded** ?   kg; **Muzzle velocity** 838 m/s; **Magazine capacity** 10 rounds; **Rate of fire** Single-shot only; **Maximum effective range** 1,000 m plus.

The L42A1 is a sniper's rifle and is a conversion of the .303-in Rifle No. 4 Mark 1(T) to the 7.62 mm NATO calibre. As with the earlier rifle the standard Lee-Enfield bolt action and trigger mechanism have been altered in various ways to ensure better accuracy and the butt has been altered to accommodate a cheek rest. Although normal 'iron' sights are fitted the L42A1 is usually used with the Sighting Telescope L1A1. A special sling with alternative sling swivels on the rifle is another

Below *The L39A1 competition rifle.* **Bottom** *The L42A1 sniper's rifle.*

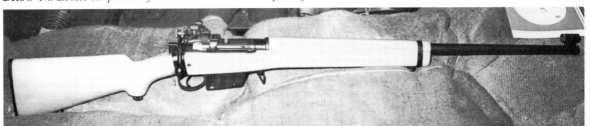

'extra'. The maximum effective range of this weapon depends greatly on conditions and the skill of the individual sniper, and for the sniping role special ammunition batches are selected.

Good as the L42A1 is, it was recently decided that a new 7.62 mm sniper rifle would be procured to take advantage of the many overall improvements made possible by recent advances in small-arms design. Three models of modern sniper rifle underwent trials at the School of Infantry, Warminster, under the aegis of the Small Arms School during late 1984 and early 1985. The model finally selected was one produced by Accuracy International and is a futuristic-looking weapon fitted with nylonite furniture and a Schmidt & Bender telescopic sight. This model had already been selected by the SAS for their own use which no doubt assisted in its final selection.

The Accuracy International bolt-action rifle is the Model PM in a special Infantry version using a 6 × 42 scope. It also has 'iron' sights that are effective up to 900 m. A heavy stainless steel floating barrel is used and there is an integral ten-round magazine. An initial order for 1,212 has been placed.

Training rifles

The Rifle No. 8 Mark 1 was first issued in September 1950 and ever since then its role has been the same, namely that of providing low cost target practice on small or indoor ranges. Over the years it has been issued to virtually every arm of the Service but its use is now largely confined to Army Cadet and Combined Cadet units. Designed and made by the Royal Small Arms Factory at Fazakerley, some were made by BSA at Shirley. The Rifle No. 8 has proved itself to be an excellent training rifle but it has never equalled the standards of accuracy achieved by many commercial target rifles. Numbers are now appearing on the commercial market for disposal to rifle clubs.

Some .22 training is carried out using the semi-automatic Rifle, .22, Sportco, L29A2, which has been purchased from the Australian concern Sporting Arms Limited of New South Wales. This blow-back operated rifle has a ten-round magazine, and weighs 2.61 kg.

With the introduction of the SA 80 family of small arms it has been decided that a new training rifle for use by Army Cadets would be an advantage and one adjunct of the SA 80 has been introduced as the Ensign. This is a simplified version of the L85 Individual Weapon (IW) without the full gas-operated mechanism which is replaced by a self-loading single shot mechanism. The muzzle does not have the grenade launching attachment and 'iron' sights only are fitted. The Ensign may be supplied in

Above *The Accuracy International Model PM 7.62 mm sniper's rifle, the next sniper equipment for the British Army.* **Below** *The Royal Ordnance Ensign training rifle (Royal Ordnance).*

either 5.56 mm (but capable of firing a special low power round) or 0.22—the latter seems more likely for Cadet applications. During 1986 it was announced that the Ensign would be procured for use by ACF and CCF units. Production will be carried out at the Royal Ordnance Small Arms Division at Enfield Lock.

Cadet Training Rifle L81A1

Calibre 7.62 mm; **Length** min 1.162 m, max 1.213 m; **Length of barrel** 0.66 m; **Weight (complete with sights)** 4.98 kg; **Muzzle velocity** Approx 838 m/s; **Magazine capacity** Single-shot; **Rate of fire** Single-shot; **Maximum effective range** According to user skills.

The Cadet Training Rifle L81A1 has a distinguished pedigree for it has been developed from the Parker Hale PH 1200TX target rifle and the Parker Hale Model 82 sniper rifle. The base model of the L81A1 is the Parker Hale Model 83 target rifle which uses a Mauser-type bolt action but it is single-shot only—there is no magazine. The L81A1 is used for training on the more advanced marksmanship skills imparted by the various ACF and CCF units and it is an extremely accurate weapon. For maximum firer comfort and efficiency the butt length is adjustable from 0.305 to 0.365 m by the insertion of various sizes of butt stock pads which affect the overall length of the rifle.

A very similar rifle to the L81A1 but fitted with a five-round magazine and some other refinements was entered by Parker Hale for the recent new sniper rifle 'contest'. This was the Model 85 which was approved for service but the contract was actually awarded to the Accuracy International entry.

Rifle 5.56 mm M16

Calibre 5.56 mm; **Length** 0.99 m; **Length of barrel** 0.508 m; **Weight (gun alone)** 3.1 kg; **Weight loaded (20-round magazine)** 3.68 kg; **Weight loaded (30-round magazine)** 3.82 kg; **Muzzle velocity** 1,000 m/s; **Magazine capacity** 20 or 30 rounds; **Rate of fire (cyclic)** 700-950 rpm; **Rate of fire (practical)** 40-60 rpm; **Maximum effective range** 400 m.

The British Army was one of the very first customers for Eugene Stoner's Armalite AR-15 automatic rifle, and it actually took delivery of its first examples before the US Army, which then went on to become the largest users of this rather controversial weapon. The choice of a miniature rifle calibre has long been a feature of British small-arms development but with the arrival of the 5.56 × 45 mm cartridge it became possible to fully

Soldier of The Duke of Edinburgh's Royal Regiment carrying an M16 rifle in Northern Ireland (AIS NI).

evaluate its worth without the political and economic restrictions imposed by membership of NATO or the threat of imminent large-scale conflict, both of which have intervened to curtail earlier British projects. Apart from this evaluation, the introduction of the M16, or AR-15, was considered as a method of providing light automatic rifles for jungle warfare in the Far East. Since the first purchase in 1961 the M16 has been in action on numerous occasions in that theatre. Although it cannot be confirmed, it would appear that about 10,000 M16s were obtained and most of these are now used by Gurkha regiments based in Brunei and Hong Kong. Units in the United Kingdom use them for training and familiarisation. Most of the AR-15s used by the Army are of the M16 pattern and lack the external bolt plunger fitted to the later M16A1 which is the American Army general issue pattern.

The M16 was manufactured by Colt Firearms at Hartford, Connecticut. It is a gas-operated weapon that uses the rotary locking mechanism that is now almost universally adopted for this kind of firearm, and which has been selected for the new British 4.85 mm Individual Weapon. The construction of the M16 has been carefully designed for ease of mass production, but for all that it is remarkably well-finished and can operate well under a variety of conditions. The 5.56 mm cartridge used by the M16 has for long been the subject of much controversy but its eventual success can be measured by its adoption by many nations and gun designers, and it will doubtless emerge, in a modified form, as the future standard NATO calibre. The 5.56 mm cartridge produces low recoil forces which make the M16 easy to aim and fire and the bullet possesses sufficient striking power to disable an opponent at most combat ranges.

In recent years the Army has obtained a number of M203 40 mm grenade launchers direct from Colt in the USA. These grenade launchers are mounted under the barrel of the M16 rifle and can fire a 40 mm grenade (the same as that fired from the M79 grenade launcher (qv)) to a range of about 80 m. Most of these launchers are used for training in such locations as Hong Kong and Belize.

5.56 mm Individual Weapon L85 (Endeavour)

Calibre 5.56 mm; **Length overall** 0.785 m; **Weight (complete with optical sight and loaded magazine)** 4.98 kg; **Muzzle velocity** 940 m/s; **Magazine capacity** 30 rounds; **Rate of fire (cyclic)** 650-800 rpm; **Combat range** Up to 400 m.

Ever since the First World War the British Army has been trying to produce a new small calibre rifle for front-line troops but many reasons, varying from political uncertainties and wrangling to the intervention of war, have prevented anything in the hardware line ever reaching the troops. A move to a

new small calibre cartridge was quashed during the early 1950s by the political imposition of the American .30/7.62 mm (7.62 mm × 51) cartridge that became the NATO standard. By the 1970s it was widely acknowledged that this was an unwise choice, and even the Americans, who had been instrumental in the adoption of the 7.62 mm NATO cartridge, had adopted the 5.56 mm M193 cartridge as their standard ammunition during the 1960s. Thus the British Army found itself saddled with a cartridge that was too powerful and bulky for much of their current infantry requirements, along with most of the other NATO armed forces.

The British Army had long anticipated the move to smaller rifle calibres and during the 1970s began the design and development of its own new small calibre weapons and ammunition. After much investigation into an 'optimum' 6.25 mm × 43 cartridge a decision was made to adopt a new 4.85 mm × 49 cartridge and a new weapon, the Individual Weapon XL65E5 or XL68E2, was developed to fire this. The 4.85 mm cartridge was an excellent performer and was based on the dimensions of the American 5.56 mm cartridge but necked down to the smaller calibre. As far as the rest of NATO was concerned, however, 4.85 mm was definitely non-standard, even though some other countries were busy developing their own national calibres and ammunition types. The result of these varying proposals was a protracted series of international weapon and ammunition trials carried out over a period of years by all the interested nations and manufacturers. The British 4.85 mm cartridge and the XL65E5 took part and performed well but both were competing against a well-entrenched preference for some form of 5.56 mm cartridge, a choice virtually dictated by the existing availability of manufacturing facilities and weapon types already in production to follow the American 5.56 mm lead.

The overall 'winner' of the NATO trials was the

The XL70E3 Individual Weapon (IW) that acted as the pre-production model for the L85—it differs only in small detail.

Guard Sergeants from the Guards Drill Demonstration Squad presenting arms with the IW. The short length of the IW has meant that a new form of arms drill has had to be devised.

Belgian SS109 that fires a 3.95 g streamlined bullet using a steel core. This cartridge has a more powerful propellant load than the M193 cartridge and requires a different rifling to that in most existing 5.56 mm weapons to obtain optimum results. A complete SS109 cartridge weighs 12 g. There was no overall weapon design 'winner' as it had become obvious that each competitor nation would produce its own weapon designs, whatever the competition outcome. Thus the XL65ES was re-chambered and re-barrelled to accommodate the SS109 cartridge and became the interim XL70E3. The degree of re-engineering was not too great as the 4.85 mm cartridge was originally based on the 5.56 mm cartridge dimensions but the XL70E3 appeared to be a very different weapon from the earlier XL65E5.

The main reasons for the change in appearance are due to production engineering and some alterations made as a result of experience during the NATO

trials. This experience plus more troop trials have resulted in the L85 which is the full production model of what is now known as the Enfield Weapon System or Small Arms 80 (SA 80) or Endeavour. The L85 is also known as the Individual Weapon, or IW, and it will be the standard Service rifle of the British Army for years to come. Troop trials with the L85 have resulted in some internal design changes and an overall 'beefing up' of the construction to the extent that the IW is now somewhat heavier than had originally been intended, but it is still an extremely compact weapon that balances and handles well. It uses what is known as a 'bullpup' layout where the trigger group is forward of the magazine instead of the more conventional opposite layout. This will make the IW much easier to stow and handle in the close confines of helicopters and APCs where the modern soldier has to spend much of his time. The mechanism is gas-operated and uses the rotary bolt-head locking system that is now a virtual standard choice for all comparable weapons. Both single and fully automatic fire can be selected. After some trials with a 20-round and a 30-round box magazine, the 30-round magazine has been selected. This is based on the universal design of the American M16 magazine but the Enfield magazine is constructed from light alloy. This magazine may be loaded using ten-round charger clips but it is anticipated that the front-line soldier will be issued with ready-loaded magazines to take into action—combat experience in the Falklands demonstrated only too well that there is little chance to re-load magazines once in action.

The IW muzzle is fitted with a rifle grenade launcher despite the fact that there are no rifle grenades in British Army service at present. The muzzle fitting can also accommodate a socket bayonet that is a little marvel of design engineering in itself. The bayonet has been designed to act as a fighting knife and general purpose tool as well. In conjunction with the bayonet scabbard it can be used as a wire cutter and the scabbard incorporates a saw blade and a bottle opener. A sharpening stone for the bayonet is included with the scabbard.

Two types of sighting system are to be used with the IW. One is an optical sight known as the Sight Unit Small Arms Trilux, or SUSAT, which provides the user with a × 4 image to enable him to engage targets accurately under poor lighting conditions. The SUSAT is mounted over the top of the weapon on a small table that allows accurate calibration of the sight but permits easy removal for any reason. Despite the many advantages of using the SUSAT sight, it is a rather expensive component and so not all Army units will be issued with it, only the front-line combat troops. Other troops will be issued with the second type of sight that uses orthodox iron sights. Due to the in-line design of the IW these iron sights have to be raised above the overall weapon level so the rear sights are incorporated into a carrying handle. A raised foresight is also provided. A Pilkington night sight has been selected for use with the IW.

The IW will be issued with various accessories. A sling will be provided along with a cleaning kit and a multi-purpose tool for maintenance. Other items include a blank firing attachment to fit over the muzzle and a plastic cap that also fits over the muzzle to keep out dirt. A .22 chamber adaptor can be fitted to keep down ammunition costs during training. The IW is in production at Royal Ordnance Small Arms Division (formerly the Royal Small Arms Factory) at Enfield Lock, Middlesex. Much of the production is carried out using robotic handling devices and automatic machine tools. The barrel is cold-forged and is chrome-plated to reduce wear.

The 5.56 mm ammunition for the IW is manufactured at the Royal Ordnance facility at Radway Green in Cheshire. Types already in production include ball, tracer, blank and drill. The ball cartridge weighs 12 g, tracer 12.25 g (marked with a red tip on the bullet nose) and blank 7.87 g. These rounds will be issued packed into 150-round light canvas bandoliers and it is anticipated that magazines will be loaded before the soldiers go into action and carried in special webbing pouches. Consideration is being given to supplying ready-loaded magazines direct from the factory.

5.56 mm Light Support Weapon L86 (Engager)

Calibre 5.56 mm; **Length overall** 0.9 m; **Weight (complete with sight and loaded magazine)** 6.88 kg; **Muzzle velocity** 970 m/s; **Magazine capacity** 30 rounds; **Rate of fire (cyclic)** 700-850 rpm; **Combat range** Up to 1,000 m (unconfirmed).

The Light Support Weapon L86 was designed in conjunction with the Individual Weapon L85 and forms part of the Enfield Weapon system, or SA 80. Usually referred to as the LSW, the L86 may be regarded as the squad support weapon equivalent of the IW and the two weapons share 80 per cent component commonality. Where the LSW differs is in having a longer and heavier barrel, a mechanism that fires from an open or closed bolt, and the fitting of a bipod for firing stability. Originally the LSW was known as the XL65E4, calibered in 4.85 mm as part of the original NATO rifle calibre competition, but with the adoption of the Belgian SS109 cartridge the re-chambered LSW became the XL73E2. This acted as the trials and pre-production version for the L86 which is the full production version that will be manufactured at Enfield Lock alongside the IW. There are some noticeable differences between the XL73E2 and the L86, the most immediately apparent being the long extension under the barrel

The L86 Engager Light Support Weapon in use in the field (Royal Ordnance).

Above *L4A4 machine-gun.* **Below** *A L7A2 GPMG on a DISA mount aboard a Saxon APC.* **Bottom** *The L7A2 GPMG on the L4A1 Buffered Tripod.* **Bottom right** *The L8A1 Chieftain co-axial machine-gun.*

that is used to secure the bipod. This extension became necessary following firing trials when it became apparent that the XL73E2 was unstable when firing bursts. The use of the bipod extension plus the addition of a rear hand-grip behind the magazine have now eradicated this firing instability.

On the LSW the SUSAT sight will be fitted as standard. The same 30-round magazine of the IW will be used on the LSW and it is anticipated that the rate of issue of the LSW will be two to every infantry section. It is not expected that the LSW will be fitted with a bayonet.

Some degree of uncertainty exists as to exactly what form of weapon category the L86 falls into. Some references describe it as a light machine-gun but it does not have a rapid barrel change (in fact the barrel cannot be removed for cooling) and the magazine capacity is limited. Other references describe it as a machine rifle and perhaps this is a more accurate description. It is certainly a very accurate weapon for the heavy barrel and bipod combine to make a good and stable aiming system. It has even been suggested that the LSW would form the basis of an excellent sniper rifle system but that application is still a long way off, if it ever materialises at all.

7.62 mm Machine-gun L4A4

Calibre 7.62 mm; **Length** 1.133 m; **Length of barrel** 0.536 m; **Weight empty** 9.96 kg; **Weight loaded** 10.68 kg; **Muzzle velocity** 869 m/s; **Magazine capacity** 30 rounds*; **Rate of fire (cyclic)** 500-575 rpm; **Rate of fire (practical)** 120 rpm; **Rate of fire (single-shot)** 40 rpm; **Maximum effective range** 800 m.

*In an emergency the 20-round magazine of the L1A1 Rifle can be used.

The L4A4 is the 'modern' version of the well-known and well-tried Bren Gun which was introduced into British Army service prior to World War 2. Originally chambered for the .303-in cartridge, the adoption of the NATO 7.62 × 51 mm round prompted a revision of the Bren Gun to accommodate the new calibre. The changes involved a new chromium-plated barrel which enabled barrel wear to be reduced to the extent that barrel changes in combat could be virtually ignored. Other alterations were to the breech block and the magazine. Originally the L4A4 was the basic infantry squad weapon, but it was gradually replaced by the GPMG, and it is now used mainly for local and anti-aircraft defence of vehicles belonging to the Royal Artillery, the Royal Engineers and other such units. It is also used by TA units intended for Home Defence only, and by the Ulster Defence Regiment.

7.62 mm General Purpose Machine-Gun L7A2

Calibre 7.62 mm; **Length as LMG** 1.232 m; **Length as HMG** 1.049 m; **Length of barrel** 0.629 m; **Weight empty (LMG role)** 10.9 kg; **Weight loaded (LMG role)** 13.85 kg; **Weight of tripod** 13.64 kg; **Muzzle velocity** 838 m/s; **Type of feed** 100-round belt; **Rate of fire (cyclic)** 625-750 rpm; **Rate of fire in LMG role** 100 rpm; **Rate of fire in HMG role** 200 rpm; **Maximum effective range (LMG)** 800 m; **Maximum effective range (HMG)** 1,800 m.

The General Purpose Machine-Gun (GPMG) concept was a German innovation that came into being during the Second World War, in that the old machine-gun divisions into light and heavy types were resolved into one design that could fulfil both roles. After 1945 there were numerous new designs along the same lines and in 1957 a series of trials were held to determine the future machine-gun for British service. The result was announced in June 1958 when the Belgian FN MAG was selected but further development was needed before British production began in 1963. The first production model was the L7A1 but further modifications resulted in the L7A2 which is the current version.

The L7A2 is a very well-made weapon that in many ways reverts to the old 'solid metal' designs of pre-1939. It cannot be said that it is a popular machine-gun for in its light role (with a bipod) it is really too heavy and awkward a load while in the heavy, or sustained fire role, it lacks the high fire volume that is often needed as the barrel tends to overheat too quickly. In the latter role the standard tripod is the Mounting Tripod L4A1 and in this configuration an indirect fire sight, the Sight Unit Trilux C2, can be fitted (this sight is the same as that used with the 81 mm mortar). Nevertheless, for all its unpopularity, the GPMG is the standard British machine-gun and is used not only as a squad weapon but also for anti-aircraft defence (on a variety of mountings), as a vehicle defence weapon, and for the sustained fire role. There are also a number of special purpose variants which are mentioned below.

L8A1: The Chieftain tank uses a special conversion of the L7A2 known as the L8A1 which has numerous design changes to suit its role in the confines of an AFV interior. It can be modified for normal ground use.

The L8A2 is a version produced for installation in the FV4030/4 Challenger.

L20A1: This variant features a solenoid-operated trigger as it is used in helicopter and aircraft pods, and is produced in right- and left-hand feed versions (the L7A2 uses a left-hand feed only).

L37A1: Machine-gun fire from APCs and other light armoured vehicles often involves the use of extra tracer rounds for sighting as direct vision of a target is not always possible. Thus a special barrel is fitted and the L37A1 is made up of a mixture of L7A2 and L8A1 components. Like the L8A1 it can be converted for the normal ground role.

The L37A2 is a version produced for installation on the cupola of the FV4030/4 Challenger.

L41A1: This is a drill or training version of the L8A1 and cannot be fired.

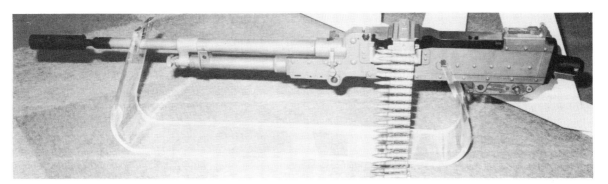

Left *The L37A1 machine-gun.*

Below *The L43A1 ranging machine-gun for the FV101 Scorpion.*

Bottom *A demonstration version of the EX-24 Chain Gun.*

Bottom right *L3A3 machine-gun on an AVRE 165.*

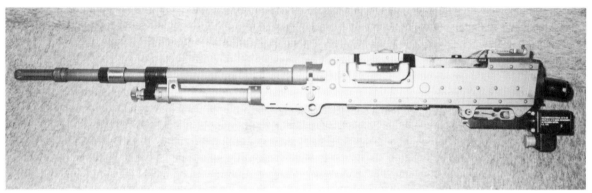

L43A1: The L43A1 is fitted as the ranging machine-gun for the Scorpion's 76 mm main armament, but is has a secondary role as a co-axial machine-gun.

L46A1: Another drill or training version, this is an inactive L7A2. It cannot be fired.

EX-34 Chain Gun
Calibre 7.62 mm; **Length** 1.25 m; **Length of barrel** 0.703 m; **Weight unloaded** 17.858 kg; **Muzzle** velocity 862 m/s; **Type of feed** Metal link belt; **Rate of fire (cyclic)** 570 rpm; **Maximum effective range** 600 m (est).

The EX-34 Chain Gun is an American machine-gun produced by Hughes Helicopters Inc, of Culver City California, but built under licence by the Royal Ordnance Small Arms Division at Enfield Lock. It is a 7.62 mm weapon that has all its various moving components powered by an internal chain powered by an electric motor to ensure a smooth and reliable action. The EX-34 has a compact main body that

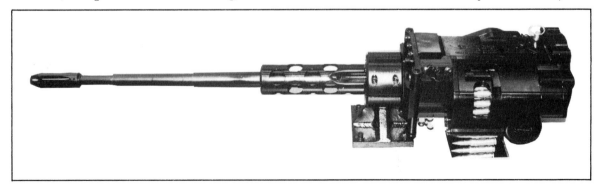

makes it ideal for use as a co-axial weapon or for use in confined spaces. It will be used as the co-axial weapon on the section commander's version of the MCV-80 (the one with the Rarden turret) and trials are being conducted to mount the Chain Gun in the Saxon wheeled APC. It is possible that the Chain Gun will be used as the co-axial weapon on late production versions of the Challenger MBT. The version shown in the photograph lacks the usual barrel tube usually fitted to co-axial versions of this weapon.

.30 Machine-Gun L3A3 and L3A4

Calibre 7.62 mm/.30 in; **Length** 1.044 m; **Length of barrel** 0.61 m; **Weight of gun** 14.1 kg; **Weight of tripod** 6.36 kg; **Muzzle velocity** 860 m/s; **Type of feed** 250-round belt; **Rate of fire (cyclic)** 400-550 rpm; **Rate of fire (practical)** 120 rpm; **Maximum effective range** 1,000 m.

Although the L3A3 and L3A4 are obsolescent it would be futile to suggest that they have yet to pass from British Army service. The two sub-variants are both based on the same American Browning design, the Model 1919A4 which first entered American service soon after the end of the Great War. In British service the L3A3 is a fixed vehicle version (and the most common) while the L3A4 is the same weapon mounted on a normal ground tripod. The L3A3 version is still used on such 'last generation' vehicles as the Saladin and the Saracen.

Machine Gun 12.7 mm L1A1

Calibre 0.50 in/12.7 mm; **Length** 1.653 m; **Length of barrel** 1.143 m; **Weight of gun** 39.1 kg; **Muzzle velocity** 858 m/s; **Type of feed** Metal link belt; **Rate of fire (cyclic)** 450-600 rpm; **Maximum effective range** Over 1,000 m.

This heavy machine-gun is none other than the famous .50 calibre Browning M2, a weapon that had its origins as far back as 1921. Ever since then it has been rated as one of the best heavy machine-guns ever produced for its combination of cartridge and weapon have made it a superlative weapon for use against all manner of targets from personnel to light armour. Many of these machine-guns were used by the British Army during the Second World War but in the years after they were gradually withdrawn from service and the weapon even went out of production for a while. But if the fashion for heavy machine-guns changed the tactical applications for them did not and after a period of some years, years in which a large number of manufacturers all over the world found it very worth while to manufacture spares and ammunition for the M2, the Browning M2 was placed back in production. At least three concerns found it profitable to manufacture the M2, FN in Belgium and two concerns in the United States, Ramo Inc and the Saco Defense Systems Division of the Maremont Corporation.

During the 1970s the British Army decided to purchase a quantity of M2s from an American

A 12.7 mm L1A1 machine-gun on a M63 anti-aircraft mounting (Ramo Inc).

source. At that time the M2s were fitted with British-made barrels and were placed in a warehouse ready for use. That use came in 1982 during the Falklands War when 24 M2s were taken south along with a number of M63 anti-aircraft mountings. Once in the Falklands, the M2s were deployed for air defence of the San Carlos area. After the Falklands the L1A1 underwent a period of appraisal and is now being issued to some Infantry battalion support companies. The main drawback at present to a more general issue is that the British stockpiles contain a number of models and barrel lengths. Once this is sorted out the L1A1 may become a more generally used weapon.

The M2 can fire a wide range of ammunition from ball to armour-piercing. Tracer elements may be added to each projectile. One of the most commonly used rounds in service within NATO is the Norwegian Raufoss NM 140 which is described as a multi-purpose projectile. The NM 140 is able to penetrate light armour and once through the armour the projectile will detonate to produce a number of harmful fragments. It is not certain if this cartridge is used by the British Army but it is in use with many other nations, including the United States.

The Machine-Gun 12.7 mm L2A1 is a drill version of the L1A1; another training version is known as the L30A1.

.50 Machine-Gun L40A1

Calibre 12.7 mm/.50 in; **Length** 1.094 m; **Length of barrel** 0.813 m; **Weight empty** 11.3 kg; **Weight loaded (approx)** 13.5 kg; **Muzzle velocity** 536 m/s; **Magazine capacity** 10 rounds; **Rate of fire** Single-shot; **Maximum effective range** 1,100 m.

Although it is classed as a machine-gun the L40A1 could perhaps be better classified as a spotting rifle for it is used in that role for the Wombat 120 mm anti-tank gun. L40A1 is the British designation for the American Rifle, Spotting Cal. .50 M8 and it is mounted over the barrel of the Wombat. When fired its projectile shows its path by tracer and if it hits its target it emits a small smoke marker. As the barrel of the Wombat is aligned with that of the L40A1 (their ballistics are very similar) it is then accurately aimed and can be fired.

Shotgun, Automatic, 12 Bore, L32A1

Calibre 12 bore/20.2 mm; **Length** 1.247 m; **Length of barrel** 0.752 m; **Weight** 3.83 kg; **Magazine capacity** 5 rounds.

During the 1960s the Army had a requirement for fighting shotguns for specialised jungle and close-quarter warfare. Before that time shotguns had been 'unofficially' obtained from local sources but this led to a variety of types in use until the L32A1 was standardised in 1965. The L32A1 is a virtually unmodified Browning automatic shotgun produced by Fabriques Nationale in Belgium and has few changes, if any, from the widely-used commercial model. In service some changes might be introduced locally, such as shortened barrels and matt metal finishes, but these changes are few.

Today, fighting shotguns are little used by the Army and consequently many are now in store, along with smaller numbers of Remington Model 870 Wingmaster pump-action repeating shotguns, another model obtained at about the same time as the L32A1. From time to time they are used on 'special missions' and for training purposes.

The ammunition used differs from commercial ammunition in having heavier loads. The Americans, who have long favoured the use of shotguns for short-range combats, use loads with only nine shot spheres or less (single ball loads have been reported but it is not known if these have ever been used by the British Army). The cartridge cases are usually plastic-coated, but all-brass cases are often used in combat.

40 mm Grenade Launcher M79

Calibre 40 mm; **Length** 0.737 m; **Length of barrel** 0.356 m; **Weight empty** 2.72 kg; **Weight loaded** 2.95 kg; **Muzzle velocity** 76 m/s; **Weight of grenade (HE M406)** 0.227 kg; **Magazine capacity**

Single-shot only; **Rate of fire** 6-10 rpm; **Maximum effective range (area targets)** 400 m; **Maximum effective range (individual targets)** 150 m.

The M79 grenade launcher is an American weapon that is used to fire a wide range of 40 mm grenades. At one time it was under serious consideration as an Infantry weapon but at that time problems arose as to long-term supplies and the idea was dropped. When the Northern Ireland Troubles began back in 1969 a number of M79s were obtained for possible use as point defence weapons for static locations and for possible crowd control firing CS or dye marker grenades. In the event they were never used for that purpose and with the gradual scaling-down of the Army's activities in Northern Ireland, the M79s have been taken to some of the Army's more outlying locations such as Hong Kong and Belize where they are used for training in jungle warfare, the purpose for which the M79 was originally developed.

The M79 resembles an oversize shotgun with a short barrel and it is 'broken' and loaded exactly like a shotgun. The 40 mm grenade fired by the M79 is contained in an aluminium cartridge case. When fired the grenade propellant gases expand in a small chamber at high pressure and only when a predetermined pressure has been reached will the main propelling body of gas escape into the main case chamber at a lower and more manageable pressure. Once in flight the grenade spins at a rate of over 600 revolutions per second to provide in-flight stabilisation for reasonably accurate aiming, and the high spin rate also arms the fuze. The type of grenade normally used is high explosive but many more types are available from smoke to special training rounds.

Right *The L40A1 spotting rifle mounted over a Wombat barrel but minus its magazines.*

Below *The 40 mm M79 grenade launcher, used in small numbers only.*

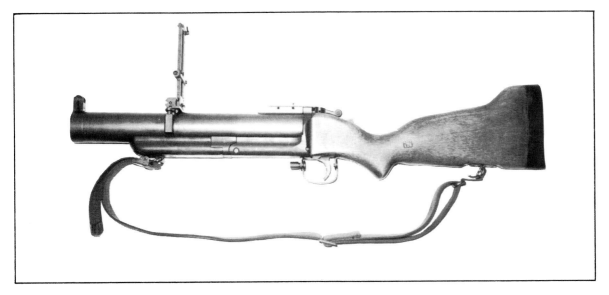

Grenade Discharger L1A1

Length 0.695 m; **Weight** 2.7 kg; **Weight of grenade (nominal)** 0.55 kg; **Maximum range** 100 m.

The L1A1 is mainly used to fire irritant CS grenades to break up rioting crowds or unlawful assemblies, but it can also fire smoke grenades for screening purposes. The discharger cup has an internal diameter of 66 mm and the power source for grenade propellant ignition consists of two U2 batteries housed in the section just forward of the padded butt. To fire the discharger the grenade is loaded from the muzzle. The cocking plunger just forward of the pistol grip is then pulled to the rear. The grenade is discharged by pulling the trigger at the same time as the safety button just behind the discharger cup is pressed. Thus both hands have to be used to fire the discharger which is a considerable safety factor in its favour. The grenades fired by the L1A1 discharger are as follows: Smoke Screening L5A1 and L5A2; Anti-riot Irritant L6; Smoke

The L1A1 at the ready.

Screening L7 Green; Anti-riot Irritant L9; Anti-riot Irritant (Long Range) L11; Practice Anti-riot (Long Range) L14; and Drill Grenade (Discharger) Smoke L1—drill only, not fired. The L1A1 is manufactured by the Royal Small Arms Factory at Enfield Lock.

High explosive grenades

Grenade, Hand-Rifle, Anti-Personnel L2: Now the standard British hand grenade, the design of the L2 series is based on that of the American M26 but differs in having a separate fuze assembly (the Fuze L25A6). Produced by The Royal Ordnance factory at Chorley, there are two versions, the L2A1 and L2A2, but they differ only in manufacturing expedients. The egg-shaped body is 84 mm long and has a filling of 170 g of RDX/TNT 55/45. Although it was originally intended that this grenade should be fired from a rifle as well as being thrown by hand, the rifle role no longer applies, and it is a hand grenade only. There are two practice grenades, both inert, the L3A1 and L4A1.

Grenade, Rifle M406: Fired from the 40 mm Grenade Launcher M79, this American grenade weighs 0.227 kg. It was employed only in Northern Ireland. At one time it was intended that the 40 mm grenades and their launcher would become a standard service issue for the Infantry, after trials held in 1972, but supply difficulties prevented this happening.

Smoke grenades

Grenade No. 80 WP: Although this grenade is scheduled to be replaced by the XL21E1, there are still considerable stocks available and they will continue to be used for some while yet. The design originated during World War 2 and as well as being thrown by hand, it was also intended to be fired from AFV smoke dischargers. Weight is approximately 0.55 kg.

Grenade, Hand No. 83 Smoke: Another World War 2 veteran, but still in production at the Royal Ordnance factory at Glascoed, the No. 83 can emit red, blue, green or yellow smoke for marking purposes. The grenade is 140 mm high and has a diameter of 63.5 mm. Weight is about 0.5 kg. It is scheduled for replacement by the XL6E1.

Smoke Grenade XL21E1: Originally known as the XL5E1, this grenade will in time replace the No. 80. It is filled with red phosphorous and weighs about 0.45 kg.

Grenade, Hand, Coloured Smoke Marking XL6E1: Very similar to the XL21E1, this grenade will eventually replace the No. 83. Like the latter it can be issued with smoke of several colours.

Smoke Screening Grenade L5: Fired from the Grenade Discharger L1A1, this grenade exists in two versions, the L5A1 and the L5A2, which differ only in the filling. Both are 178 mm long and 63.5 mm in diameter. They can discharge white smoke for about 30-50 seconds and can be fired to a range of about 60 metres.

Smoke Screening Green Grenade L7A1: This is similar in appearance and performance to the L5 but emits green smoke.

Smoke Screening Grenade L34A1: While the above-mentioned grenades are all products of the Royal Ordnance factory at Glascoed in Gwent, the L34A1 is a commercial product from Schermuly Limited of Salisbury. The L34A1 has a 'twist-and-pull' operated fuze, and weighs 0.308 kg. A hand-thrown grenade, it is 105 mm long and 55 mm in diameter. After a delay of 1-2 seconds it emits grey-white smoke for up to 45 seconds.

Smoke Screening Grenade L8A1: While the above grenades are all intended for use by Infantry, the L8 has been designed to be discharged from AFV and vehicle smoke dischargers. Electrically fired, the L8 is a cylindrical metal and rubber grenade filled with red phosphorous. When fired the casing breaks up and the smoke cloud then covers an area some 35 metres in diameter at a height of about six metres, and about 25 metres away from the vehicle. The 360 gram filling enables the cloud to last for about three minutes. The L8 weighs 0.68 kg, is 185 mm long and 66 mm in diameter.

Smoke Screening Grenade L27: The L27 grenade is the same size as the L8 but is lighter at 0.535 kg. It uses the 23-pellet system used by CS grenades but is intended to be fired from vehicle smoke dischargers. The grenade bursts about five metres from the ground and 25 metres from the vehicle, dispersing the 23 pellets which then produce green screening smoke. The smoke produced lasts for about 12 seconds before it breaks up, but this is usually sufficient for the firing vehicle to move to a fresh position, and the L27 has also been used for riot control. The area covered by the smoke cloud is about 20 metres in diameter.

Grenades, Hand, Signal Smoke: These grenades are a relatively new product from the Royal Ordnance factory, Glascoed, and there are four different types in the range. They differ only in the

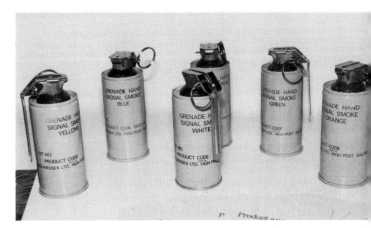

Top right *L2A2 anti-personnel grenades. Fully assembled examples are on the left, while those on the right await their fuze assemblies.* **Above right** *These smoke grenades are typical in shape and appearance to many types, including the various CS grenades.* **Right** *Fox firing L27 smoke screening grenades.*

colour of smoke they produce, and are the L46 (blue), L47 (green), L48 (red) and L49 (orange). These smoke grenades are used for a variety of purposes which include position indication, signals to aircraft or helicopters, target indication at short ranges, wind and speed indicators for helicopters and other aircraft and as a search and rescue marker. The grenades all have a prominent screw cap which, once removed, can be used to pull a lanyard to initiate the two- to four-second delay. Once the smoke is produced it lasts for at least 45 seconds. Each of these smoke grenades is 135 mm high, 55 mm in diameter, and the weight is 0.35 kg.

VIRSS: VIRSS stands for visual and infra-red screening smoke and has been introduced to counter the growing use of the thermal imager (TI) that can penetrate and 'see' through conventional smoke screens. What VIRSS does is introduce a screening element that will mask off TI vision in the most commonly used infra-red wavebands as well as providing visual screening smoke. VIRSS does this in a novel way for instead of producing the single smoke cloud of an orthodox system such as the L8, VIRSS is a re-generative system that continues to fire a number of small smoke grenades that cause air bursts in a rapid succession, blanking out any TI vision in the vicinity of the user vehicle and producing a cloud that can be produced irrespective of local wind directions.

A VIRSS munition consists of a mounting with 20 launch tubes arranged in four rows of five. An AFV can have a number of these munitions arranged on the turret (the Challenger can have 12, six each side)

A Challenger MBT fitted with VIRSS munitions on the turret (Royal Ordnance).

to provide an arc of fire. The munition fires sub-munitions to a range of approximately 25 m where they burst in the air to provide a 'hot spot' on any TI screen along with screening smoke. Each sub-munition is followed in quick succession by another to make the screen regenerative and provide visual and infra-red cover for up to one minute. Most of the smoke-producing material in each non-metallic sub-munition is used before the device reaches the ground.

A VIRSS munition weighs 1.2 kg and measures 160 × 135 × 130 mm. It is made of a strong plastic material and is disposable. The munition fits into a lightweight alloy unit frame mounted on a back plate. The overall design is modular and only the back plate needs to be particular to any one vehicle. Inside the user vehicle the existing L8 grenade launcher wiring harnesses can be retained but a new firing box is installed together with a pulse generator to actually fire the sub-munitions in sequence. VIRSS has been accepted for future use by the British Army.

Irritant grenades

CS is perhaps better described as a disabling agent rather than an irritant but its effect on concentrations of personnel has much the same result. The term CS is a manageable term for ortho-chloro-benzalmalono-nitrile which in its stable form is a solid substance. Exposure to the atmosphere produces a vapour (usually white or light grey) that causes the disabling effect by inducing choking, eye tearing and a general difficulty in breathing. High concentrations can cause nausea and vomiting. The effects are usually not totally disabling but can persist, especially if droplets of the vapour adhere to clothing. CS has a general odour of pepper. It was first used by the British Army in 1959 when it began to replace CN which is conventional tear gas (alpha-chloroaceto-phenone).

Grenade Hand No. 91: Although it was declared obsolete in 1958, this tear-gas grenade is still used for training purposes, usually in giving troops confidence in their protective equipment. It weighs about 0.45 kg.

Grenade, CS Anti-riot, Irritant, L1A1 and L2A1: These two CS-filled grenades are the same size, being 114 mm long and 57 mm in body diameter. They differ in their action as the L1A1 emits CS smoke from holes drilled in an internal sleeve. This has the disadvantage that it can be smothered or even thrown back by a determined rioter. The L2A1 overcame this problem by the use of a small internal gunpowder charge which scattered 400 smoke-producing pellets over a wide area, but *this* had the disadvantage that the CS cloud was sometimes of insufficient density to produce any lasting effects. Both types have now been replaced by the L13 but they are still likely to be encountered.

Grenade, Hand, Anti-riot Irritant, L13A1: Although similar in appearance to the L1A1 and L2A1, the L13A1 is slightly larger as it is 175 mm long and 66 mm in diameter. It weighs 0.55 kg and can be thrown to about 25 metres. Once thrown there is a delay of 2 to 2.4 seconds before an internal charge detonates scattering 23 CS aluminium-encased pellets over a radius of seven to eight metres. Each pellet emits CS smoke for about 12 seconds. The Grenade, Anti-riot, Practice L16 is used for training and operates in exactly the same manner as the L13A1, but the pellets produce only harmless smoke.

Grenade, Hand, Anti-riot Irritant, L1A3: While the grenades mentioned above are Royal Ordnance factory, Glascoed, products, the L1A3 is a Schermuly product. The L1A3 is 140 mm long, has a diameter of 64 mm, and weighs 0.454 kg. When thrown there is a delay of 1.5 seconds in order to enable the thrower to withdraw before the CS smoke cloud is emitted in such density that it cannot be thrown back without considerable risk to the would-be thrower. A training version producing orange smoke is available.

Grenade, Discharger, Anti-riot Irritant L6A1: Basically similar in appearance to the Smoke Screening Grenade L5, the L6A1 contains two pellets of irritating agent which are scattered by the detonation of a 2.6-gram charge of gunpowder. It is fired by the Grenade Discharger L1A1 to a range of about 60 metres. It has now been replaced by the L11 but may still be encountered.

Grenade, Discharger, Anti-riot Irritant L9A1: Designed to be fired from the Grenade Discharger L1A1, the L9A1 is now obsolescent and due to be replaced by the L11. In use the L9A1 scatters 400 CS pellets which, like the Hand Grenade L2A1, often proved unable to produce sufficient concentrations to disable determined rioters.

Grenade, Discharger, Anti-riot Irritant (Long Range) L11A1: This is now the 'standard' anti-riot grenade fired from the Grenade Discharger L1A1. It can be fired to a range of about 80 to 100 metres and when detonated, ideally about six metres above a rioting assembly, scatters 23 CS pellets over a 25-metre diameter circle. The L11A1 weighs about 0.56 kg and is 185 mm long with a diameter of 66 mm. Each CS pellet can emit gas for about 12 seconds. For training purposes, the Grenade, Discharger, Anti-riot Practice L14 operates in exactly the same way as the L11A1 but emits only harmless smoke.

Cartridge, 1.5-in, Anti-riot Irritant L3A1: Another Schermuly product, the L3A1 is fired from the various 1.5-in pistols and riot guns in service. It has replaced the earlier L2A2 cartridge which had a pressed-paper body, for the L3A1 has an aluminium case. Each cartridge is 120 mm long and weighs 0.2 kg, of which 0.098 kg is the CS element. Each CS filling can produce disabling smoke for up to 25 seconds, and can be fired up to 100 metres. The L4A1 is a practice version.

CS Hand Spray L1A1: Although it is not a grenade in any sense the CS Hand Spray L1A1 is included here as it does not fit readily into any other category. It is a small aerosol spray can intended for close-quarter use in order to disable or pacify an opponent at very short ranges (up to about one metre). It can thus be used in riot situations for self-protection or in arresting violent opponents. Each can, which resembles a conventional aerosol container apart from the markings, weighs only 0.12 kg and contains enough CS filling for 50 two-second bursts. The can is 123 mm long and 38.5 mm in diameter and can thus be easily concealed on the person. It is produced by Schermuly.

Baton rounds

Baton rounds were originally an American idea intended to assist in breaking up riotous assemblies. It had been discovered that conventional firearms were often worse than useless in some circumstances as they either produced only harmless noise when fired over heads, or deaths and serious injuries which provided not only political problems but often accentuated the situations, both long and short term, by producing martyrs. The baton round was introduced as it was designed to stun or disable rather than injure or maim. Properly handled, it could even be used to disable ringleaders or other individuals.

The first baton rounds were wood but they proved lethal under certain circumstances. They were replaced by the infamous 'rubber bullets', but experience and analysis in Northern Ireland indicated that rubber rounds still had a statistical risk of producing serious injury, even though no really serious wounds had been inflicted by their use. Thus the present baton round in British Army use is a blunt slug of PVC, which not only decreases the injury risk but is more accurate at ranges up to 30 metres. The PVC round in service is the Round, Anti-riot, 1.5-in Baton L5A1, and is fired from a variety of projectors. The complete round is 107 mm long with a diameter of 38 mm. Weight of the complete round is 0.199 kg of which the PVC projectile makes up 0.135 kg. The worst injury that the PVC baton round is expected to produce is severe bruising and the resultant shock.

While the L5A1 is produced by Royal Ordnance, the commercial concern of Schermuly also has two of its products in service as baton rounds. They are the L3A1 and the L5A2, both of which are slightly lighter than the L5A1 and can be fired to slightly longer ranges. The weight of both complete rounds is 0.17 kg and the baton component is 0.107 kg. The L3A1 has a longer range than the L5A2. Cartridges firing multiple baton projectiles are now coming into use.

51 mm Mortar L9A1

Calibre 51.25 mm; **Length overall** 0.75 m; **Length of barrel** 0.543 m; **Outside barrel diameter** 55 mm; **Weight complete (with sling)** 6.275 kg; **Weight of ancillaries wallet** 1.4 kg; **Weight of SRI** 0.25 kg; **Maximum range** 800 m; **Minimum range** 50 m; **Bomb weight (HE L1A1 fuzed L127)** 0.92 kg; **Bomb weight (smoke L2A1)** 0.9 kg; **Bomb weight (illuminating L3)** 0.8 kg; **Rate of fire (normal)** 3 bombs per min for 5 mins; **Rate of fire (rapid)** 8 bombs per min for 2 mins.

The 51 mm Mortar has had a very protracted development life ever since it was decided to introduce a lightweight weapon to replace the venerable 2-in mortar (which has now all but passed from use and is used only occasionally, if at all, as a flare or illuminating device launcher). To date the development period has extended to well over ten years. Much of the development work has been carried out by the Royal Armament Research and Development Establishment (RARDE) at Fort Halstead in Kent, and for much of its early life the 51 mm mortar featured a monopod leg which was a protracted source of design troubles, even though the Army had long since decided that such a nicety was not really required anyway. The ammunition was a further source of development delay for a while but by the late 1970s the 51 mm Mortar design was finally frozen and made ready for production. When production finally begins, it will be carried out at the Royal Ordnance factory at Nottingham.

The 51 mm Mortar at first sight appears to be a simple weapon as it is but a barrel placed on a spade-shaped breech-piece, a sight and a sling. In fact it is the result of a great deal of detail design work, and has been designed from the outset to be carried and used by one man, although in action the team would actually be two, with one carrying extra ammunition. In action the bombs are introduced into the barrel from the muzzle and fired by a waterproof trigger mechanism at the base of the barrel. The spade breech piece absorbs the recoil. To aim the mortar the firer uses a line painted along the barrel for direction and range is then read off the

Loading the 51 mm Mortar with a HE bomb; note the ammunition satchel (Royal Ordnance).

Trilux sight—the barrel is held steady using a webbing gaiter around the barrel. For short range use a special insert (SRI) is placed in the barrel. This insert restricts the depth to which a bomb can fall inside the barrel and the resultant propellant gases can expand further than usual, thus forcing the bomb to a shorter range than normal. This feature is especially useful in close-quarter combat.

The ammunition used with the 51 mm Mortar consists of HE, smoke and illuminating bombs, the latter being intended for use with close-range anti-tank weapons such as the LAW, or even Milan. The HE bomb has its case interior serrated so that when the charge detonates a large number of lethal steel segments are produced to enhance its effectiveness. The bombs are carried in a webbing satchel, each holding six in waterproof tubes. Practice bombs are available for drill and training purposes, and the 51 mm Mortar can also fire existing stocks of old 2-in Mortar bombs that remain.

Rocket 66 mm HEAT L1A1

Calibre 66 mm; **Length extended** 0.893 m; **Length closed** 0.655 m; **Length of rocket** 0.508 m; **Weight complete** 2.37 kg; **Weight of rocket** 1 kg; **Muzzle velocity** 145 m/s; **Maximum effective range** 300 m; **Armour penetration** Up to 300 mm steel plate.

The L1A1 is the British designation for the American M72A1 and M72A2 HEAT rocket (HEAT—High Explosive Anti-Tank). Designed originally as the successor to the large and cumbersome 3.5-in 'bazooka' rocket launchers, the L1A1 in some ways resembles the World War 2 German 'Panzerfaust' anti-tank weapon as it is intended to be a 'one-shot and throw away' device. Basically the L1A1 is a smoothbore tube containing the anti-tank rocket. In action the waterproof sealing caps on each end are removed and the tube is telescoped outwards to its full length. Simple sights are then raised and the rocket fired by percussion. Once fired a dangerous exhaust cone area extends to some 15 metres to the rear of the launcher tube and a further 25 metre 'caution zone' has to be left clear to avoid further hazards caused by the rocket exhaust. After firing the tube is discarded. The rocket has an armour penetration capability against most AFVs in service and the weapon is so light and handy that it can be carried by almost every member of an infantry squad. The L1A1 is American in origin but the British version is made under licence by Raufoss in Norway.

Below *The L1A1 ready for firing.* **Bottom** *Small Arms School officer demonstrating a rather battered Drill LAW 80.*

But for all its handiness and light weight, the L1A1 must now be regarded as, at the best, obsolescent. Its hollow-charge warhead is now too small to make any real effect on the armour protection of the latest Warsaw Pact MBTs and in future it will probably prove effective only on such MBTs as the T-54/55 and lighter tanks. It is for this reason that the Light Anti-armour weapon (LAW) has been developed.

LAW 80

Projectile calibre 94 mm; **Launcher length, extended** 1.5 m approx; **Launcher length, closed** 1 m approx; **Weight overall** 9.5 kg; **Weight of projectile** 4 kg; **Maximum range** 500 m; **Combat range** up to 300 m.

LAW 80 is the latest name for the British Army's new **L**ight **A**nti-armour **W**eapon. It has long been recognised that for the infantryman or front-line soldier to be able to tackle the increasing carapaces of armour that surround the modern and future main battle tanks, something better than the existing 66 mm L1A1 rocket and the 84 mm L14A1 gun was needed. The problem is that thick armour requires a large warhead to penetrate it, and that large warheads have required large launching systems, be they guns, rockets or whatever. For the average front-line soldier to be able to use such a large warhead, the launching system had to be portable and handy enough to be deployed efffectively without having manpower tied up with heavy weapon systems. The British Army answer is LAW 80.

LAW 80 is a rocket system that can be carried and used by one man. It is powerful enough for its rocket projectile to be able to have an armour penetration 'well in excess of that required to penetrate present and future MBT frontal armour'. Put into everyday terminology, that means armour well over 600 mm thick. To penetrate such an armour thickness the LAW 80 rocket projectile has a warhead diameter of 94 mm, but the warhead design is such that its performance produces results well in excess of what might be expected from a conventionally designed hollow-charge warhead. The internal features of the LAW 80 warhead are obviously very closely guarded secrets, but it is obvious that some form of anti-armour design breakthrough has been made.

The LAW 80 rocket has wrap-around folding fins to provide stability in flight and travels towards its target at a speed of nearly Mach 1. The LAW 80 launcher is a filament-wound Kevlar in epoxy resin tube which can be telescoped for storage and carrying. Just before it is required for action the tube is extended and the end covers removed. The launcher tube also carries the shoulder rest, firing grip and the x1 plastic optical sight. To back up the sight there is an integral aiming rifle under the launcher tube with its own six-round magazine. Once the target is in the sight the firer can select the aiming rifle to fire a spotting round. This not only accurately determines the aim but also the range. If the aiming round hits the target tank it produces an indicating flash, and the main projectile can then be selected and fired. If, for any reason, the main projectile is not fired, the tube can be once more telescoped for later re-use. The six aiming rounds are considered to be enough for two possible engagements. Once fired, the launcher tube is discarded.

LAW 80 can be handled and stored exactly as a conventional round of ammunition. The tube is weatherproof and has a shelf life of about ten years. Using the weapon in enclosed areas, however, produces its own hazards as the rocket uses a fair amount of propellant and an area to the rear of about 20 metres could be dangerous to personnel and equipment. Once fired, the rocket warhead will not be armed until it has travelled about 10 to 20 metres.

LAW 80 is still under development although troop trials are continuing. The production and general involvement of various concerns in the production programme is quite a list. The prime contractor, Hunting Engineering, is dealing with the launcher, sights and various types of training equipment. The Royal Ordnance Factory at Blackburn (among others) will produce the projectile, and the Royal Small Arms Division at Enfield Lock will produce the spotting rifle. Other Royal Ordnance Factories or facilities will produce the rocket motor and general technical advice and design detail. Miltrain Limited and Hendry Electronics will be involved in some quite involved indoor training systems, and EPS (Research and Development) Limited will be responsible for the important packaging. This list of companies involved is included to give some idea of the scope of manufacturing and other skills involved in a modern weapons programme, even one as compact as LAW 80.

The introduction into service of LAW 80 is expected to be some time in 1987. In the meantime considerable efforts are being made to interest other NATO nations in its potential. When it gets into service the front-line soldier will have the ability to destroy virtually any armour that is set against him. It will be issued widely, not only to the front-line but to troops on supply routes and in rear areas. In time it will no doubt be issued to soft-skin and armoured

vehicle crews as a standard issue item. It will be a formidable weapon.

Ordnance Muzzle-Loading 81 mm L16A2

Calibre 81 mm; **Length of barrel overall** 1.28 m; **Weight of barrel** 12.7 kg; **Weight of bipod mount** 12.3 kg; **Weight of sight unit** 1.25 kg; **Weight of base plate** 11.6 kg; **Weight complete in action** 37.94 kg; **Muzzle velocity max (L5 mounting)** 250 m/s; **Maximum range** 5,650 m; **Minimum range** 100 m; **Bomb weight HE L15A3** 4.47 kg; **HE L36A2** 4.2 kg; **Smoke L19A4** 4.5 kg; **Smoke L40** 4.2 kg; **Rate of fire** 15 bombs per min.

The 81 mm Mortar entered service in 1961 only four years after a design study was initiated at the then Royal Armament Research and Development Establishment at Fort Halstead in Kent. The Canadian equivalent establishment was also involved and produced two components of the overall equipment in the shape of the Sight Unit C2 and the base plate (this has a diameter of 0.546 m, can allow a full 360 degree traverse without re-bedding and can also accommodate the American M29 81 mm mortar barrel). The mounting used is the Mounting 81 mm Mortar L5A2 and is of a type known as a 'K' mount, an arrangement that enables levelling to be effected by using only one of the mounting legs. The latest mortar barrel is the L16A2 which has some improvements over the original L16A1 introduced as part of a programme to sell the 81 mm Mortar to the US Army (where it is now known as the M252). The barrel is made from high tensile alloy steel with fins around the bottom to partially dissipate the heat produced by firing. Detail design points are the provision of a slight muzzle taper internally to ease loading, and a removable breech plug for easy replacement of the fixed firing pin and to facilitate a variety of possible mountings.

The ammunition used with the 81 mm Mortar is of an advanced design and despite the recent introduction of some new models is still the subject of development. Three types of HE bomb are available, the L15A3, the L31E3 and the L36A2. All use the L127A2 nose fuze. Smoke bombs may be neither the L19A4 or the more recent L40. The Illuminating bomb is of French origin, being the Brandt M1 62, known in British service as the L20. A practice bomb with a range of only some 80 m (it is re-usable) is the L27A1. As the 81 mm calibre is a NATO standard, bombs produced in other NATO states can also be fired.

In BAOR the normal carrier for the 81 mm Mortar is an adapted FV 432 which has a 360 degree traverse mounting for the barrel fitted to the rear compartment floor with the barrel firing through the vehicle

Above *Ordnance Muzzle-Loading 81 mm L16* (Royal Ordnance). **Below** *The Morzen mortar fire control computer.*

roof hatch. In the mortar role the FV 432 can carry 160 bombs in ready-use racks. The other infantry carrier is the Land Rover in all its forms but for really basic use the 81 mm Mortar can be broken down into three man-pack loads of which the heaviest is 12.3 kg. It was in this man-pack form that the 81 mm Mortar was used during the Falkland Islands' campaign where it greatly impressed the unfortunate Argentinians by its rate of fire and its accuracy. So accurate was some of the fire that after-the-battle reports from Argentina stated that the 81 mm mortar bombs were fitted with heat-seeking warheads that could sense the presence of human targets! One innovation that the Falklands did produce, to prevent the baseplates sinking into soft ground, was packing a canvas bag full of earth or other soil and placing it under the baseplate.

Electronics have now been introduced to 81 mm Mortar fire control. Until recently the mortar teams had to rely upon time-honoured methods of range tables and plotting boards but that has now been replaced by a hand-held miniature fire control computer known as Morzen. Morzen can perform all necessary fire control tasks. Once data such as the location of the mortar, observation post and target have been inserted using a simple key board it will then provide firing data for the target and subsequent fall of shot corrections. Bearings, elevations, charges and time of flight are calculated and there are further facilities for counting down the time of flight, calculating fuze times for illuminating bombs and many other useful calculations which should make a mortar team commander's life much easier. The Morzen is easy to use once a simple sequence drill is mastered. There are even moves afoot to enable Morzen to provide a paper print-out using a small printer. Morzen is shock-proof and waterproof and is powered by small internal batteries.

Development of the 81 mm Mortar is far from over. Work is still in progress to produce a bomb with a possible range of over 6,000 m. As such bombs would need a powerful propellant charge, a special anti-blast muzzle attachment shaped like a cone may eventually be adopted for British Army use. This muzzle attachment was developed as part of the programme to sell the 81 mm Mortar to the US Army. An improved mounting is also scheduled.

Gun, 84 mm Infantry L14A1

Calibre 84 mm; **Length of barrel** 1.13 m; **Weight complete** 16 kg; **Muzzle velocity** 160 m/s; **Weight of HEAT round L40A4** 2.59 kg; **Weight of HEAT projectile** 1.7 kg; **Range, anti-tank (mobile)** 400 m; **Range, anti-tank (stationary)** 500 m; **Range, HE and smoke** 1,000 m; **Rate of fire** 6 rpm; **Armour penetration (HEAT at 60°)** 228 mm.

An 84 mm 'Carl Gustav' team wearing NBC kit (BAOR PR).

The usual name given to the L14A1 is 'Carl Gustav' as the origins of this shoulder-fired recoilless gun are Swedish. Designed and produced by the Förenade Fabrikswerken (FFV) at Eskilstuna, the Carl Gustav is now the usual squad anti-tank weapon although it can be used for other tasks. Although it can be loaded and fired by one man, two usually make up the gun team with one loading and the other aiming and firing. As with all recoilless weapons, a considerable amount of dangerous (and visible) back-blast is produced on firing, but this is more than made up for by the armour penetration capabilities of the large HEAT projectile which can penetrate up to 228 mm of armour. 84 mm rounds are manufactured in the United Kingdom, and HEAT practice and drill rounds are all produced by the Royal Ordnance Factories. High explosive and smoke rounds can also be fired from the Carl Gustav. For training on indoor ranges a 6.5 mm (L10A1) or .22 sub-calibre device (L1A2) can be fitted into a specially converted round which is then loaded into the barrel in the normal way. Although it is intended as a man-portable weapon, the Carl Gustav can be fired from open-topped vehicles, and the FV 432 can be fitted with a special resting bar across the top hatch.

Gun, 120 mm BAT L6 Wombat

Calibre 120 mm; **Length overall** 3.86 m; **Length of bore** 2.34 m; **Weight in action (approx)** 308 kg; **Traverse** 360°; **Elevation** −8° to +17°; **Muzzle** velocity 463 m/s; **Round weight** 27.3 kg; **Projectile weight (HESH)** 12.8 kg; **Maximum effective range** 1,100 m; **Rate of fire** 4 rpm.

The development of the Wombat can be traced back to the immediate post-war years when it was decided to produce a 120 mm recoilless gun to replace existing anti-tank guns. The first of these was the 120 mm BAT L1 (BAT—Battalion Anti-Tank gun) which was almost as heavy as the weapon it was supposed to replace, namely the well-tried 17 pr. The L1 did enter service but further development led to the lighter and handier 120 mm BAT L4, the Mobat. In time the L4 replaced the L1 in service but it was felt that there was room for improvement, both in weight and performance, so further development at the Royal Armament Research and Development Establishment at Fort Halstead produced the 120 mm BAT L6, soon named the Wombat. The Wombat is less than half the weight of its predecessor and also has a better range, mainly due to the use of a .50 Machine-Gun L40A1 for aiming purposes (the Mobat used a Bren Gun for the same purpose). There are several other improvements over the earlier gun, especially in the sighting unit which can accommodate both light intensifier and infra-red devices.

Normally the Wombat is served by two or three men, one of whom acts as loader and another as layer. Laying the Wombat involves the use of a rather complex sighting telescope which is first used to direct the single-round fire of the .50 spotting rifle. The round fired by the rifle emits a stream of tracer which clearly shows its trajectory, and if a hard target is hit a small burst of marker smoke is emitted. As the barrel of the rifle and the gun are aligned the main projectile can be fired—the trajec-

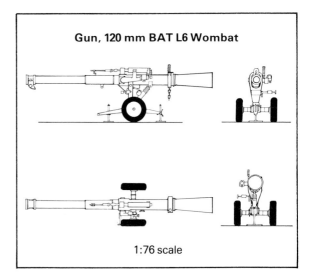

Gun, 120 mm BAT L6 Wombat

1:76 scale

tories of the .50 and 120 mm projectiles are ballistically matched out to about 1,100 m. The accurate laying of the main barrel is most important for firing the Wombat produces two unfortunate effects: not only an alarmingly loud report, but the considerable back-blast kicks up a very large cloud of dust and debris, both of which can combine to reveal the firing position. Not surprisingly, many soldiers refer to the Wombat as the 'VC Gun', but it has already been recognised as obsolescent and has been replaced by Milan. Nevertheless, it seems likely that the Wombat will remain in service for some years to come, especially with TA and other reserve units.

The round used with the Wombat is still that used on the very first BAT, namely the L1. The projec-

tile used against tanks has a HESH (High Explosive Squash Head) warhead, and is stated to be effective against any known AFV, but exact figures cannot be quoted.

Ordnance

Cannon, 30 mm Rarden L21

Calibre 30 mm; **Length overall** 2.96 m; **Length of barrel** 2.44 m; **Weight** 110 kg; **Round weight (HE L13, APSE L5, TP L7)** 904 g; **(APDS L14)** 770 g; **Projectile weight (HE L13, APSE L5, TP L7)** 357 g; **(APDS L14)** 235 g; **Muzzle velocity (HE, APSE)** 1,070 m/s, **(APDS)** 1,175 m/s; **Maximum effective**

Above *The L6 Wombat* (MoD).

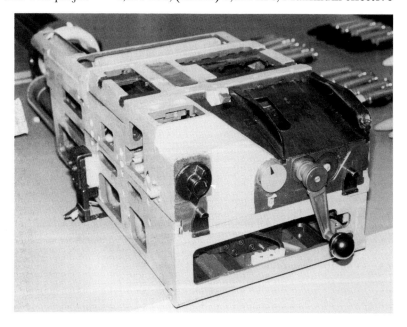

Right *The 30 mm Rarden Gun in cutaway. The handle at the breech is the charging/cocking handle.*

30 mm Rarden fitted to a FV107 Scimitar.

range 4,000 m plus; **Rate of fire (cyclic)** 80-90 rpm.

One of the more interesting aspects of the Rarden is its original design philosophy which was evolved during the early 1960s. At that time it was decided to produce a light AFV gun that could perforate the armour expected to be carried by a new generation of APCs, and which would be capable of this task at ranges of over 1,000 metres. It was envisaged that the new gun would be fitted into relatively light vehicles and thus the trunnion forces exerted had to be fairly light as well, while to add an extra stricture to the design specification the gun had to take up as little space as possible. Other requirements were a useful HE shell performance and the ability to be used against slow low-flying aircraft and helicopters. Of all these specifications the most restricting was the low trunnion loading but it could be met if a low rate of fire was accepted, and this was subsequently agreed. The end result was a 30 mm gun with a rate of fire of 80-90 rpm. The only design specification that was not met was the anti-aircraft and helicopter capability as such a low rate of fire would be fairly ineffective against such targets, but all the other requirements were achieved.

The design of the Rarden was a combined effort by the then Royal Armament Research and Development Establishment at Fort Halstead in Kent and the then Royal Small Arms Factory at Enfield Lock (now the Royal Ordnance Small Arms Division), hence the name 'Rarden'. Initially two types of ammunition were developed for the gun, one an armour-piercing shell with secondary effects (APSE—this type of projectile is designed to explode only after the target armour has been penetrated) and a high explosive shell (HE or HE-T with tracer). One

logistic advantage that was incorporated into the ammunition design was that the Rarden could also fire the existing and readily available Hispano-Suiza 831 L 30 mm rounds—the HE round is the UIAT and the AP the RINT. Considerable effort was invested to develop an armour-piercing/discarding sabot (APDS) round but the technical difficulties in producing this type of projectile in such a small calibre were such that at one point the project was dropped altogether. Eventually an APDS round, the L14, was jointly developed by Royal Ordnance in conjunction with Patec of California and it is now in production. This round uses a sabot that completely encloses the penetrator and is so arranged that seen head-on the sabot is divided into four sections that break up outwards once the projectile has left the barrel. The penetrator can go through 40 mm of armour set at an angle of 45 degrees at ranges in excess of 1,500 m.

The rounds are loaded into the Rarden in clips of three, and the gun can hold up to six rounds ready to fire. Only 0.43 metres of the gun's total length protrudes into a vehicle's turret, and the only external part of the gun mechanism handled by the crew is the cocking handle—the rest is sealed off and no fumes can escape into the turret itself. Two rather unusual features of the operation are that the Rarden uses the little-encountered 'long recoil' system of operation, and an automatic sliding breech block. The low rate of fire has the real advantage that it makes the Rarden very accurate; target groupings of one metre at 1,000 metres have been quoted.

The Rarden is fitted to two in-service vehicles, the FV107 Scimitar and the FV721 Fox, both of which are employed as light reconnaissance vehicles. They have essentially similar turrets but the Scimitar can carry 165 rounds and the Fox 99. A turret derived from that of the Fox was at one time intended for use on the FV 432 but that programme was terminated in 1976 after only 13 had been produced. These vehicles were all sent to service with the Berlin Brigade where they still remain. The Rarden will be fitted to some models of the MCV-80 Warrior.

Gun 76 mm L23A1

Calibre 76.2 mm; **Length overall** 2.156 m; **Weight complete** 150.59 kg; **Muzzle velocity (HESH)** 533 m/s; **Muzzle velocity (HE)** 514 m/s; **Muzzle velocity (smoke)** 290 m/s; **Round weight (HESH L29A3)** 7.4 kg; **Round weight (HE L24A4)** 7.33 kg; **Round weight (smoke L32A5)** 10.2 kg; **Shell weight (HESH L29A3)** 5.39 kg; **Shell weight (HE L24A4)** 5.36 kg; **Shell weight (smoke L32A5)** 8.51 kg; **Maximum direct range (HESH, HE)** 2,200 m; **Maximum indirect range (HESH, HE)** 5,000 m; **Maximum range (smoke)** 3,700 m.

Right *A 76 mm L23A1 gun just off the assembly line at the Royal Ordnance Factory, Nottingham* (Royal Ordnance).

Below *Ammunition for the 76 mm L23A1. From left to right: Drill; L29A3 HESH; Smoke (BE) L32A5; HE 24A4; HE/PRAC L25A4 and Canister L33A1.*

The L23A1 is a lightened version of the earlier L5A1 fitted to the FV601 Saladin, and uses much the same ammunition. To date, only one British Army vehicle is fitted with the L23A1 and that is the FV101 Scorpion which can carry 40 rounds. Rounds available which are not mentioned in the above table are SH/Prac L40A1 (Squash Head/ Practice), HE/Prac L25A4 (High Explosive/ Practice), Illuminating L32A5 and Canister L33A1. The latter is an anti-personnel round intended for use against infantry tank-hunter squads or massed infantry at ranges up to about 100 metres (it is also a reversion to an ancient artillery practice).

The Canister projectile is a thin-walled container packed with steel balls—the container breaks up as the projectile leaves the muzzle and the lethal balls are scattered in a wide cone. The weight of the L33A1 round is 7.76 kg.

The L23A1 is an entirely conventional gun using a falling-block breech. The recoil length is approximately 0.28 metres.

Ordnance, QF, 25 pr Marks 2/1, 3/1 and 4

Calibre 87.6 mm; **Length of bore** 2.346 m; **Length of rifling (Mark 3/1)** 1.877 m; **Length**

overall 4.65 m; **Width overall** 2.134 m; **Track width** 1.79 m; **Height travelling** 1.65 m; **Weight in action** 1,801 kg; **Traverse on carriage** 8°; **Traverse on platform** 360°; **Elevation** −5° to +40°; **Muzzle velocity (HE)** 518 m/s; **Shell weight (HE)** 11.34 kg; **Shell weight (smoke)** 9.93 kg; **Maximum range** 12,253 m; **Rate of fire** 10 rpm.

Although the 25 pr has long been out of service as a front-line artillery piece it is still in use today, although its duties are confined to saluting and ceremonial purposes. Some are also used by various Cadet units for training, while others continue firing for various trials and experiments.

The 25 pr has had a long and respected service life as it entered service in 1940 and was not withdrawn from front-line use until 1967 when the last example was ceremoniously retired by 14 Field Regiment RA. Even then it served on with the TA, and it still remains a front-line weapon with many other armies. One of the main reasons for this longevity is the robust and compact construction, but perhaps the real reason so many remain around is that the gun (actually a gun-howitzer) gained so many laurels in the years between 1940 and 1945. The full story of the 25 pr has no place here, but it was replaced by the 105 mm Pack Howitzer L5 which, in its turn, has been replaced by the 105 mm Light Gun L118. But still the 25 pr remains, and its future status seems to be that it will be around for a long while, even if its role is purely symbolic. The Royal Regiment of Artillery uses its guns as its colours, and this means that the present missile batteries are somewhat at a loss for colours when on ceremonial parades. Therefore it has been suggested that a 25 pr should be issued to each missile battery to fulfil this task, and this might well happen. In the meantime, 25 prs are used at many locations as 'clock' guns (as at Edinburgh Castle) and as saluting batteries (as at Gibraltar). Many more act as gate guardians. Some cadet units continue to fire live ammunition but this is now in short supply, and any future stocks will have to come from other nations such as India, where the 25 pr is still a front-line weapon. But the 25 pr is still used to at least partially equip a few TA batteries and it is used by at least five OTUs. The Honorable Artillery Company still uses a small number.

Gun 105 mm L7A2

Calibre 105 mm; **Length overall** 5.89 m; **Length of recoil** 0.29 m; **Weight** 1,300 kg; **Muzzle velocity (HESH)** 732 m/s; **Round weight (HESH L35)** 21.23 kg; **Projectile weight (HESH L35)** 11.26 kg; **Maximum effective range (HESH)** 4,000 m; **Rate of fire (normal)** 6 rpm; **(rapid)** 10 rpm.

The 105 mm L7A2 appeared in the first edition of this book but was removed for the second edition as it appeared that the Centurion MBT was finally removed from service. However, the Centurion is back again as the Royal Engineers' AVRE 105. These AVRE 105s were originally the Centurions used by Royal Artillery forward observers and when they were withdrawn from service some years back they underwent a conversion to AVRE standards but the 105 mm main gun was retained as the preferred 165 mm demolition gun for the AVRE is no longer in production. Thus the 105 mm L7A2 is no longer used

Below left *Men of the Gibraltar Regiment firing a salute from one of the 25 prs held at the Devil's Gap battery.* **Below right** *The 105 mm L7A2 tank gun, now used by the Army as a demolition weapon* (MoD).

by the Royal Engineers as an anti-armour weapon but as a form of demolition gun firing HESH projectiles only—it is not intended that the AVRE 105s will be used as gun tanks so no anti-armour projectiles such as APFSDS will be carried.

This is something of a change for the 105 mm L7A2 for it is one of the most widely used of all tank guns and is fitted to more types of tank than any other gun. As a demolition gun intended for the stand-off destruction of structures such as bridges the L7A2 lacks the power of the larger 165 mm demolition projectiles but it is still an effective weapon although sometimes two 105 mm HESH projectiles might be needed to complete a task that a single 165 mm projectile could accomplish. The accuracy of the L7A2 firing HESH is such that there is better than a 90 per cent hit probability against a 2.3 × 2.3 m target at a range of 1,500 m.

The HESH (high explosive squash head) round now in use is the L35 and a training practice round is the L38. It is possible that the guns mounted on the AVRE 105 might be called upon to fire the Smoke BE (BE—base ejection) L39. This has a round weight of 26.37 kg and produces a dense smoke cloud for 50 seconds.

Ordnance, BL, 105 mm Field L13A1

Calibre 105 mm; **Length of barrel** 3.25 m; **Muzzle velocity (maximum)** 708 m/s; **Shell weight (HE L31)** 15.1 kg; **Projectile weight (HESH L42)** 10.49 kg; **Shell weight (smoke L51)** 15.98 kg; **Shell weight (HE M1)** 14.9 kg; **Propellant weight (HE and smoke)** 2.4 kg; **Propellant weight (HESH)** 3.52 kg; **Maximum range** 17,200 m; **Maximum range (American M1)** 15,000 m; **Rate of fire** 12 rpm.

The 105 mm L13 gun is at present fitted to only one vehicle, namely the FV433 Abbot, and is thus the main armament of the Abbot field regiments based in Germany. It is yet another product of the Royal Armament Research and Development Establishment at Fort Halstead in Kent. It came into service in 1965 and from then onwards has been the main close-support weapon of the Royal Artillery. When it first came into service the Abbot with its L13 gun was a considerable advance on the 25 pr it was replacing, both in range and shell weight, but by the late 1970s it was seen to be approaching obsolescence as 105 mm fire has been proved to be incapable of inflicting sufficient damage on the massed AFV attacks expected in any future European conflict. However, it still has a considerable capability against 'softer' targets, and is expected to remain in service for many years yet.

The L13 gun has considerable range for its calibre, while the varieties of ammunition developed for it have many advantages in perfor-

Above *The breech of a 105 mm L13A1 gun. This photograph was taken inside one of the Value-engineered Abbots used at BATUS, Suffield, and thus it lacks the power rammer of the normal version.*

mance over the American 105 mm M1 types in use before the advent of L13. Unfortunately this has the logistic disadvantage within NATO that the British ammunition is non-standard with other 105 mm weapons. To some extent this incompatability can be reduced by the ability of the L13 to fire American projectiles with British charges, but the range is then reduced to 15,000 metres (this is still far greater than any other NATO 105 mm artillery piece can achieve). Another factor is that the ammunition is also used by the British L118 Light Gun. The main offensive projectile is the Shell, 105 mm, Field, High Explosive L31, but for anti-tank use a High Explosive Squash Head (HESH) round is available but no longer in production. Other projectiles in service include Illuminating L43. The basic smoke round is the L45 but there is a red (the L37) and an orange smoke round (the L38).

The L13A1 has a vertical sliding breech block,

Gun, 105 mm L118

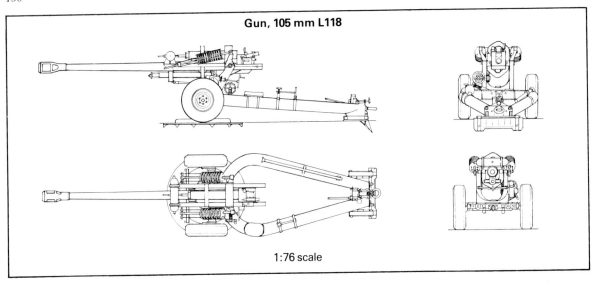

1:76 scale

Below left *A REME fitter carrying out adjustments to the breech of a 105 mm Light Gun.* **Below right** *The RAF's Chinook can carry two Light Guns plus some ammunition. The Puma can carry a single Light Gun slung under the fuselage while the Chinook can carry them either internally or underslung as here* (Royal Ordnance).

and the ammunition is loaded separately with brass cases holding the propellant charges. Up to eight separate charges can be selected. When using American M1 ammunition a shorter cartridge case is used. The gun has a prominent muzzle brake and a bore evacuator is fitted to eliminate propellant fumes in the Abbot turret. Barrel life is stated to be well over 10,000 rounds.

Gun, 105 mm Field L118

Calibre 105 mm; **Length of barrel** 3.17 m; **Length overall (firing at 0°)** 7.01 m; **Length overall (folded)** 4.8 m; **Width overall** 1.78 m; **Track width** 1.42 m; **Height travelling** 1.22 m; **Weight in action (approx)** 1,858 kg; **Traverse on carriage** 11°; **Traverse on platform** 360°; **Elevation** −5.5° to +70°; **Muzzle velocity (maximum)** 708 m/s; **Shell weight (HE L31)** 15.1 kg; **Shell weight (HESH L42)** 10.49 kg; **Shell weight (smoke L51)** 15.98 kg; **Maximum range (HE)** 17,200 m; **Minimum range (HE)** 2,500 m; **Maximum range against AFVs (HESH)** 800 m; **Rate of fire** 6 rpm.

Usually known as the Light Gun, the L118 is now the standard equipment of field regiments based in the United Kingdom, having replaced the last of the 105 mm Pack Howitzers L5 at the end of 1978. The Light Gun has had an extended development time scale as the first design studies were begun during the mid-1960s and the gun was accepted for service in 1971. Like so many other British weapons the Light Gun was a design product of the Royal Armament Research and Development Establishment at Fort Halstead but the production lines are at the Royal Ordnance Factory at Nottingham, from which the first production examples were delivered in 1974.

Designed from the outset to provide as much range as possible with a high degree of portability, the Light Gun fires the same ammunition as that used with the 105 mm gun fitted to the FV433 Abbot. With this ammunition it has a range of 17,200 metres which is well in excess of that of any comparable gun, but the price paid for this performance is that the gun is now heavier than earlier design estimates indicated. Nevertheless, it is light enough to be carried in a C-130 Hercules transport aircraft, and it can be carried into action slung beneath a helicopter. On the ground the normal towing vehicle is the 1-tonne Land Rover which carries the crew of six and a limited number of rounds, while a second 1-tonne Land Rover acts as a limber vehicle carrying 28 rounds. Normally the Light Gun is towed with its barrel turned through 180° and clamped over the curved tubular box trails. Getting the gun into action thus involves the removal and refitting of one of the wheels but this can be accomplished by a trained

crew within a very short time. This towing configuration is used because, with the gun in the normal 'action' position, the towed load is very long when compared with the tyre track, and the gun is then likely to turn over rather easily. Reversing the barrel over the trails lowers the centre of gravity considerably making it much more stable and capable of an excellent cross-country performance.

The ammunition used with the Light Gun is separate and there are seven propellant charges available. This number of charges along with a very wide elevation arc (−5.5° to +70°) makes the Light Gun an extremely flexible weapon, and to reduce the range down to 2,500 metres at high angles of elevation, spoiler rings can be added to the noses of the projectiles to degrade their performance. In addition to the Shell, 105 mm, Field, High Explosive L31, there are available smoke, High Explosive Squash Head, illuminating and various

Below A Light Gun in action in Norway (Royal Ordnance).
Bottom The 105 mm Light Gun fitted with the L119 barrel for firing American ammunition (Gunner Magazine).

practice rounds. But there are still considerable stocks of the American M1 105 mm ammunition on hand so in order to use these up for training purposes a separate gun barrel and breech can be fitted on to the Light Gun carriage. This new ordnance is designated L119 and is shorter and lighter than the L118, and with a different muzzle brake. The changeover takes about two hours, and the range is reduced to 11,400 metres.

The Light Gun has many modern features, not the least of which is the general method of construction in order to keep down weight, but it does have one rather obvious 'throw-back' to an earlier era. This is the 360° traverse platform which is normally carried over the trails. In action this is placed on the ground and the gun wheels are placed on it. One man can then make very rapid traverse changes using the trail handspike which can be a valuable asset when fighting tanks and other AFVs at short ranges. As it is expected that the Light Gun will encounter tanks in any future conflict the platform has been retained and the gun can thus fire HESH projectiles at combat ranges up to about 800 metres. HESH is now no longer in production.

The Light Gun proved its value in the Falklands where, during the final siege of Port Stanley, up to 400 rounds per gun per day were being fired.

The Light Gun is used by only two Regular Army Field Regiments, 7 RHA who provide the artillery support for 5 Airmobile Brigade and 29 Commando Regiment, RA, who provide artillery support for the Royal Marine Commando Brigade. There is also a single battery based at Larkhill and earmarked for service with AMF(L). There are also two TA regiments using the Light Gun, 100th (Yeomanry) Field Regiment, RA (V), and 101st (Northumbrian) Field Regiment, RA (V). All these batteries use six guns each.

With 7 RHA the use of the FACE fire control computer has already been phased out. Instead all 7 RHA batteries (F (Sphinx) Battery, G Battery (Mercer's Troop) and I Battery (Bull's Troop)) now use the hand-held Gunzen computer. Gunzen is a close relative of the Morzen mortar fire control computer (qv) and as well as being able to operate with the Light Gun it can also be used with any artillery equipment in Royal Artillery service, up to and including Lance. The only change required when a Gunzen computer is used with a different equipment is the alteration of a single microchip.

Ordnance, BL, 120 mm Tank L11A5

Calibre 120 mm; **Length of bore (approx)** 6.6 m; **Muzzle velocity (HESH L31A7)** 670 m/s; **Muzzle velocity (APDS L15A4)** 1,370 m/s; **Projectile weight (HESH L31A7)** 17.08 kg; **Projectile weight (APDS L15A4)** 10.36 kg; **Projectile weight (smoke L34A1)** 17.5 kg; **Propellant weight (HESH and smoke)** 3.03 kg; **Propellant weight (APDS)** 8.845 kg; **Maximum effective range (HESH)** 8,000 m; **Maximum effective range (APDS)** 3,000 m plus; **Rate of fire (normal)** 6 rpm.

The 120 mm tank gun fitted to the FV4201 Chieftain is regarded as one of the most powerful tank guns in service anywhere, and is capable of defeating any tank armour likely to be pitted against it—even the latest Soviet AFVs are regarded as being vulnerable at long ranges. There are several versions in service including the L11A3 and the L11A7 in addition to the L11A5, but all are basically similar. Where the L11 series differs from other contemporary tank guns is that it uses separate ammunition and the propellant is totally combustible when ignited. This bagged combustible propellant is stowed inside the tank in water-surrounded compartments, a system which has been chosen as not only does it save weight, but as there is no sizeable cartridge case to dispose of, there is a substantial saving in stowage space, and the risk of fumes within the turret is greatly reduced. The gun has a sliding breech block which also holds a ten-tube magazine holding the electrical vent firing tubes.

To ensure that accuracy is kept to a high order, the L11 series have an advanced form of fire control (IFCS), and one of the factors that this system has to compensate for is the degree of barrel warping induced by external heating effects. Even under moderate climatic conditions the barrel is so long that even a slight side breeze can induce warping due to a difference in temperature from one side of the barrel to another. These slight warpings can make a difference to long-range accuracy, so they are almost entirely eliminated by the use of insulating thermal sleeves wrapped around the whole length of the barrel. Another feature of the L11 barrel is the fitting of a fume evacuator half way along the bore to prevent propellant fumes from entering the turret.

The main offensive projectiles fired by the L11 series are HESH. Other projectiles used are smoke and illuminating, and special training projectiles (inert projectiles so designed that barrel wear is greatly reduced when compared to live projectiles) have been developed for HESH and APDS—they are SH/Prac L32A5 and DS/T L20A1 respectively.

The L1 guns remain very powerful weapons but within recent years a general 'upgunning' has been under way in some of the major NATO nations. Whereas the West Germans have seen fit to change

Above *A 120 mm L11A5 gun on a test stand at the Proof & Experimental Establishment at Shoeburyness.* **Below** *Ammunition for the 120 mm L11 tank gun. From left to right: Propelling charges; Smoke; DS/PRAC; APDS; PRAC/SH and HESH* (MoD).

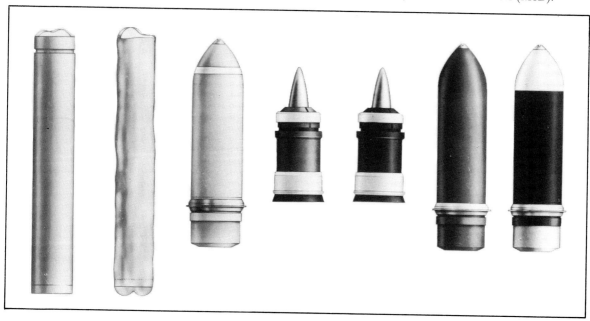

the main armament of new tanks such as the Leopard 2 and late production versions of the American M1 Abrams to a new smooth-bored Rheinmetall gun, the British Army will continue to use rifled guns. Thus the new Challengers at present in production retain the L1 gun but under development is a new 120 mm rifled gun that will be fitted to late production versions of the tank (known provisionally as Challenger II). This new gun will be known as the L30 and is the outcome of a series of new weapons known collectively as the 'Modern Technology' guns. Guns involved in the development of the L30 included weapons such as the EXP 14M1, M7 and M13A, followed by the EXP 28M1 (intended for use on the defunct MBT 80 project) and the forerunner to the L30, the EXP 32M1.

The L30 will use a monobloc barrel constructed using electro-slag refined (ESR) steel. It will not have a bore evacuator or a muzzle brake and, although the length of the barrel has not been announced, it will be shorter than the L11. The breech mechanism is of a type known as the 'split sliding block breech' in which the obturating (sealing) ring, made necessary by the combustible plastic propellant charges employed, is mounted on a split rising block. The rising block is held in place for firing and a second rising block falls to release the upper block after firing. The two blocks then fall together for reloading to take place. This system manages to combine strength with compactness, and the system can be made fully automatic or merely semi-automatic.

The L30 will probably use RDX stick propellant and a new family of 120 mm ammunition is currently under development. Already in service with the L1 gun and likely to be used in the L30 is the L23A APFSDS-T (armour-piercing fin stabilised discarding sabot—tracer) projectile, and it will be joined in time by product-improved HESH, HEAT, smoke and illuminating projectiles. There will also be an improved APDS-T.

Howitzer, 155 mm L121 (FH70)

Calibre 155 mm; **Length of bore** 6.037 m; **Length overall (firing)** 12.43 m; **Length overall (travelling)** 9.45 m; **Width over wheels** 2.58 m; **Height travelling** 2.64 m; **Weight in action (approx)** 9,144 kg; **Traverse** 52°; **Elevation** –5.5° to +70°; **Muzzle velocity (HE, max)** 827 m/s; **Shell weight (HE M107)** 43.5 kg; **Maximum range (HE normal)** 24,000 m; **Maximum range (rocket-assisted M549 (L15))** 30,000 m; **Rate of fire** 6 rpm.

FH70 is rather rare within NATO as it is an example of a completed collaborative project carried out by NATO members alone. The United

Kingdom was one of the two founder members of the FH70 project which began with an agreement between the United Kingdom and West Germany to develop and produce a new 155 mm towed howitzer. That agreement was signed in August 1968, and Italy became a participating member in 1970 (the USA were invited to take part but declined). All three interested states wanted the new 155 mm to replace existing field equipment. The United Kingdom needed it to replenish their medium field regiments which used the venerable 5.5-in gun-howitzers, not only on the grounds of age but as the result of collected battle evidence that the 155 mm calibre was the smallest-sized projectile capable of breaking up massed tank attacks while the tanks themselves were in the forming-up phase, and after.

The new howitzer was given the development designation FH70 and this has been continued. All three nations took over a part of the total design and development, and later, production. The British share was divided between the Royal Armament Research and Development Establishment (which was involved in the early design stages), Vickers-Armstrong (much of the carriage design and construction) and various Royal Ordnance factories which became involved with the ammunition. The West German firm of Rheinmetall carried out much of the work on the ordnance itself and got involved in such items as the sights the auxiliary power unit (APU), and also in ammunition design. Italy contributed by developing various cradle components and other sub-assemblies, and again were involved in ammunition design and development.

The first trials battery was a three-nation unit and had six guns. It was formed in 1975, in Germany, and was responsible for many of the early development trials. The first FH70s differed in several respects from the production models, the most noticeable of these features being the recuperator cylinder over the barrel—later models had this under the barrel. But the overall layout of FH70 was basically the same as it is today. The gun has a long barrel with a prominent muzzle brake which is reported to be 23 per cent efficient). The carriage has long split trails with large spades. Forward of the main cradle is an auxiliary power unit which is used to drive the FH70 over short distances; this is a Volkswagen 4-stroke petrol engine of 1,795 cc capacity which can deliver 76 bhp. The APU is necessary as the FH70 is a bulky and heavy artillery piece and man-handling, even over short distances, is a considerable task. Power is directed to both the main gun wheels and two dolly wheels can be unfolded from their position just forward of the trail spades.

In action the howitzer rests on a firing platform

Right *A FH70 moving under its own power.*

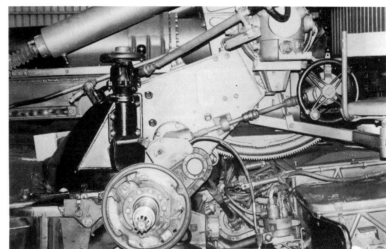

Right *A plumber's nightmare—some of the workings of the FH70 revealed during maintenance.*

Below *The FH70* (Vickers).

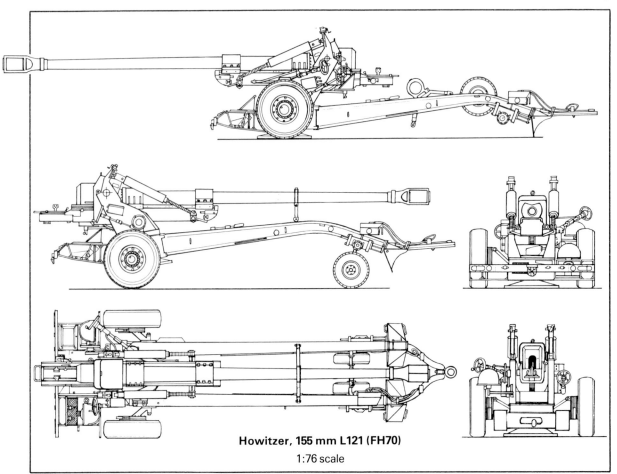

Howitzer, 155 mm L121 (FH70)

1:76 scale

under the main axle. The sighting mechanism is rather complex and is on the left of the cradle. While the barrel is a conventional monobloc component it incorporates modern metallurgical practices and is thus lighter than older designs of the same nature. The buffer and recuperator are situated below the barrel, and the breech block is similar in concept to that used on the Rheinmetall-designed 155 mm howitzer fitted to the American M109G self-propelled howitzer. Thus it has upward-opening, sliding breech block with the added feature of an automatic ignition tube loader holding 10 or 11 tubes.

Although trials and development of much of the ammunition intended for the FH70 continue, the first production examples of the gun came off the lines in early 1978—the main United Kingdom production centre is at the Vickers-Armstrong works at Barrow-in-Furness. The first Royal Artillery unit to receive FH70 was B Battery, 1 RHA, which was fully equipped by October 1978. Produc-

tion total for the United Kingdom is reported to be 71.

As stated above, the ammunition trials continue. FH70 can fire existing American 155 mm projectiles but all three user nations will use ammunition developed during the FH70 programme. Already available are HE and smoke shells, both of which can be fired to a range of 24,000 metres. Still under development is a rocket-assisted shell (the L15) which is reported to be capable of ranges up to about 30,000 metres, and sub-calibre projectiles are another longer-range alternative. Electronically set fuzes are on the way. Up to eight propellant charges can be selected. The FH70 ordnance is similar to that intended for use on the self-propelled SP70, and the ammunition fired is the same.

The tractor and limber vehicles selected for United Kingdom Army use are the Foden FH70 6x6 tractor and limber. Like the 105 mm Light Gun, the FH70 is towed with the barrel over the trails.

Cannon, 155 mm Howitzer M185; Mount, Howitzer, 155 mm M127

Calibre 155 mm; **Length of barrel** 6.045 m; **Weight (approx)** 1,700 kg; **Muzzle velocity (HE, smoke)** 684.3 m/s; **Shell weight (HE M107)** 42.91 kg; **Shell weight (smoke M116)** 42.22 kg; **Shell weight (illuminating M485)** 41.73 kg; **Maximum range (HE, smoke)** 18,000 m; **Rate of fire (rapid)** 3 rpm; **Rate of fire (normal)** 2 rpm.

The M185 is an American howitzer with a development history that can be traced back to 1952. In that year it was projected as a 156 mm howitzer intended for a self-propelled mounting, but in time the calibre reverted to the more conventional 155 mm as the T255E5. In 1961 this was standardised by the US Army as the M126 with an overall length of 4.598 metres (the barrel length was L/23.4) and a range of 14,700 metres. It was fitted to only one self-propelled mounting, the M109. In time the M126 was further developed and lengthened to L/39 which increased its range to over 18,000 metres. The new lengthened barrel became the M185 and vehicles fitted with the new barrel became the M109A1 or M109A2.

The M109, with the early M126 barrel, first entered British Army service in 1965 and from then onwards it became the standard equipment for the Royal Artillery's medium self-propelled batteries. It was intended that they would be replaced by the SP70, but this equipment has had such a prolonged development period that it was decided to retrofit the M185 into the existing M109s. With this in

The breech mechanism of a 155 mm M185.

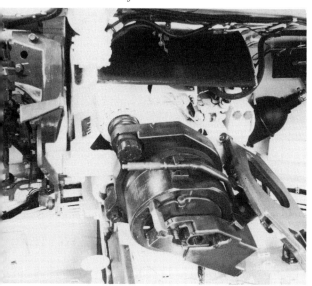

mind, two M109A1s were delivered to the Royal Artillery for trials that began in 1975. As a result of these, a major retrofitting programme was completed by late 1978. The first formation to receive their new howitzers was 39 Field Regiment, Royal Artillery, and they had the unusual experience of proof firing their new pieces themselves, on the artillery ranges near Munster, in West Germany.

The M185 is a rather complex piece of artillery with a very prominent muzzle brake and a bore evacuator. The breech mechanism is a large semi-automatic screw arrangement which tends to produce a rather slow rate of fire, even though a power rammer is fitted. Even with the rammer, the normal rate of fire is still only some two rounds per minute. Separate loading ammunition is used, and the same projectiles as those used with the M126 are fired. But the propellant charges have been increased in number and variety to make full use of the longer barrel with its advantages in projectile range. The number of propellant charge combinations gives the M185 a wide choice of elevation angles to suit particular fire tasks. To illustrate this, one of the Larkhill Open Day 'party pieces' is an M109A2 (and before it, an M109) firing its howitzer at maximum elevation and near minimum elevation—the two shells arrive on the same target simultaneously.

Cannon, 175 mm Gun M113; Mount, Gun-Howitzer M158

Calibre 175 mm; **Length overall** 10.87 m; **Length of barrel** 10.49 m; **Length of rifling** 8.87 m; **Weight** 6,259.5 kg; **Muzzle velocity** 914 m/s; **Shell weight (HE M437)** 66.78 kg; **Maximum range** 32,700 m; **Rate of fire (rapid)** 2 rpm; **Rate of fire (normal)** 1 rpm.

The development of this American long-range gun began at the Watervliet Arsenal, New York, during the late 1950s. It entered British Army service during 1965 and 1966, and ever since then has been the Army's 'long-range rifle'. The M113, originally known as the T256E3, is a very long-barrelled gun, but it does have an extremely long range to match, and it is thus used mainly in the long-range harassing and interdiction role. Only high explosive projectiles are fired. The use of such a long barrel does have the constraint that considerable internal pressures are reached and these have the effect of reducing the barrel life to about 1,200 rounds. The early guns had an even shorter life of some 400 rounds but the weapon was modified to the M113E1 standard and the expected life was trebled. The M113 will be replaced in its long-range role by the MLRS rocket system.

Above *The great length of the 175 mm Gun M113 can be seen from this side-on view.* **Right** *An MLRS rocket being launched from its tracked vehicle* (Vought).

Cannon, 8-in Howitzer M201; Mount, Gun-Howitzer M158

Calibre 203 mm/8 in; **Length overall** 7.85 m; **Weight (approx)** 6,400 kg; **Muzzle velocity (HE charge 8)** 711 m/s; **Shell weight (HE M106)** 92.53 kg; **Maximum range** 21,300 m; **Rate of fire (normal)** 1 round every 2 minutes.

The 8-in howitzer used by the Royal Artillery is an American piece with a British provenance. The US Army adopted the 8-in howitzer from the British in 1917 and ever since then they have retained the weapon in some form or another. The early British model was followed in 1940 by a updated and improved American version, the M1 which, in its turn, was replaced by the M2 in 1945. The M2 was a towed weapon which was redesignated the M115 in 1961, the same year in which it was decided to adapt the barrel for mounting on the new self-propelled carriage M110—the same as that used for the 175 mm Gun M113. The British Army used the self-propelled M2 for many years on the M110, but as always, the gunners called for more range and a longer version emerged.

The 8-in M201 is virtually a longer version of the earlier M2, and was originally produced for the US Army. The British Army decided to adapt their existing 8-in self-propelled carriages to take the new barrels and the changeover was made during 1981. The longer barrel enables a larger charge to be used and the increased muzzle velocity increases the range by a substantial margin.

In all its forms the 8-in howitzer has gained for itself an enviable reputation for accuracy, and the heavy shell has a devastating effect over its target. The usual conventional projectile is the American

HE M106 but in the British Army the M201 will fire nuclear shells. A nuclear shell has been under development for the 8-in howitzer for some years at the Atomic Weapons Establishment at Aldermaston, and is now probably ready for use, but there is an existing American nuclear shell, the M422, with the XM753 under development.

The M201 has a Welin-type breech mechanism little changed from the British original, although the whole piece has benefited from gradual metallurgical and other improvements over the years. The M201 can employ up to eight separate bag charges. It is expected that, as the 175 mm M107 guns and carriages are phased out in favour of MLRS during the late 1980s, the carriages will be converted to take new 8-in barrels and thus increase the nuclear potential of the Army.

Rockets and missiles
Multiple Launch Rocket System

Rocket body diameter 227 mm; **Rocket length** 3.96 m; **Rocket weight** 272 kg; **Rocket range** at least 30,000 m.

Vehicle: Crew 3 or 4; **Length (travelling)** 6.97 m; **Height (travelling)** 2.617 m; **Width (travelling)** 2.97 m; **Track width** 0.533 m; **Ground clearance** 0.43 m; **Maximum speed** 64 km/h; **Range** 483 km; **Engine type** Cummins VTA-903 turbocharged diesel; **Engine power** 500 hp at 2,400 rpm; **Fuel capacity** 617 litres.

In 1976 the US Army issued a requirement, and development contracts, for a long-range rocket system that was intended to provide some form of counter to the expected disparity between the

NATO armies and the Warsaw Pact forces in artillery strengths—on some European fronts this is expected to be of the order of at least 2.7 to 1 against NATO. The new system was expected to be both powerful and flexible, and was initially known as the General Support Rocket System (GSRS), but by 1978 the programme became an international one with the added involvement of the United Kingdom, France and West Germany. The programme then became known as the Multiple Launch Rocket System, or MLRS, with plans being made for production lines to be set up in both Europe and the USA. Italy has also joined the group.

There were two prime contractors bidding for the

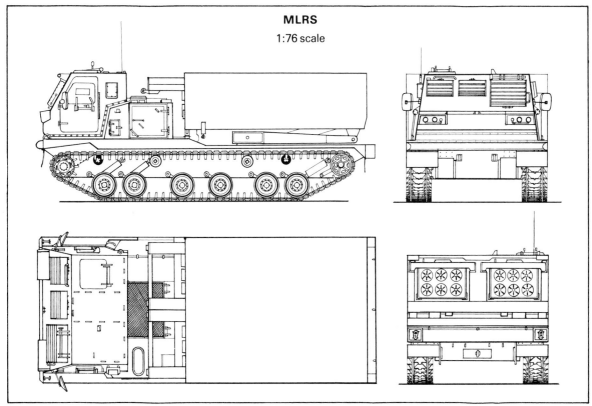

MLRS

1:76 scale

MLRS contract initially, Boeing and the Vought Corporation. Following an involved 'shoot-out' on the White Sands Missile Range, Vought was awarded the contract in May 1980.

The Vought MLRS system is based on a much-modified M2 Bradley Infantry Fighting Vehicle chassis and consists of an armoured crew cab forward with the launcher assembly to the rear. The long rockets are carried in pallets each taking six rockets, and the missiles are loaded into the vehicle launcher on their pallets. Once loaded the pallets act as the launcher frames. Each pallet weighs about 1,800 kg, and the loading sequence is mechanical from a power-assisted limber vehicle. Each loading sequence takes about five minutes. The launcher can be traversed and elevated from within the vehicle cab and laying is assisted by the vehicle's inertial navigation system.

The first batch of rockets will have a warhead payload consisting of over 600 M42 scatterable minelets, each weighing 0.23 kg and with a small hollow-charge warhead capable of penetrating up to 100 mm of armour. Later rockets will use the West German AT-2 anti-tank mines and future developments include binary chemical warheads and terminally-guided anti-armour submunitions.

MLRS has now become a truly international programme even in a production sense, for plans have been made to produce launch vehicles in Europe with a long-term possibility of rockets being produced as well. The latest purchaser has been the Netherlands but the British purchase has been delayed somewhat to at least 1988. The original plan appears to have been that the first regiment to receive MLRS would have been 32 Heavy Regiment at Dortmund with another regiment (5) being formed at the same location later. However, the delays may well have re-arranged things somewhat. In the interim the Royal Artillery has had selected personnel training in the United States for some time and for training four MLRS launchers and 108 practice rockets have been delivered.

Lance

Weight at launch 1,285.47 kg; **Length of rocket** 6.146 m; **Diameter of body** 557 mm; **Weight of warhead (M234)** 210.92 kg; **Maximum speed** Mach 3 plus; **Maximum altitude reached** 45,720 m; **Range limits** 4.8 to 121 km; **Maximum flight time** 200 seconds.

Lance is the main artillery 'punch' of the British Army as it is a ballistic artillery rocket fitted with a nuclear warhead. It is an American design produced by a bevy of contractors under the aegis of the LTV Aerospace Corporation, Michigan. Known originally as the Missile B, Lance eventually obtained the service designation of MGM-52C. The development of Lance started in 1962 and firing trials commenced during 1965 but it was not until 1971 that the first production examples were issued to the US Army. It was then offered to NATO nations and the United Kingdom was one customer, with the first equipments being issued for Army service during 1976, when they replaced the obsolete Honest John rockets then in use.

Lance is a free-flight missile, ie, it does not have any form of external guidance once it has been launched. This does not mean that Lance is unguided, for it is, but all the guidance is fed into the missile before launch. The Lance missiles are carried to the firing point in a tracked carrier known as the M752 Self-Propelled Launcher, or SPL. This carrier is used as the missile launcher and also carries the crew of six men—two in the driver's cab and four alongside the Lance missile. The M752 SPL is based on the suspension and power train of the American M113 APC, as is the other carrier associated with the Lance missile. This other vehicle is the Loader-Transporter, or LT, with the designation M688. The LT carries a crew of two men and two Lance missiles minus their fins which are stowed along the insides of the carrier. The LT also has a small crane to load the missiles on to the SPL. Both vehicles have the same dimensions but differ in their battle weights. The data for both vehicles is as follows. **Length** 6.568 m; **Width** 2.709 m; **Height to top of cab** 2.715 m; **Weight in action (SPL)** 9,075.02 kg; **Weight in action (LT)** 10,691.63 kg; **Engine type** GMC Model 6V53; **Engine power** 215 bhp; **Maximum speed (road)** 64 km/h.

The SPL carries the Lance missile and its launcher, and once in the firing position the missile is aligned to its target using normal artillery techniques. As this is being carried out the flight in-

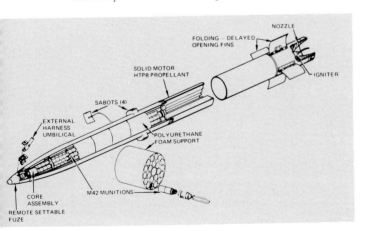

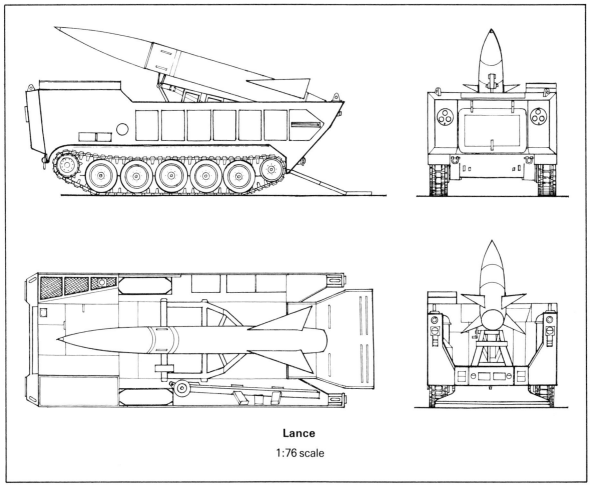

Lance

1:76 scale

Left *Cutaway drawing of a MLRS rocket* (Vought).

Right *A Lance missile ready for launch.*

Above Blowpipe *(Short Brothers and Harland).* **Below** *Cutaway example of a Blowpipe missile head in its launcher, showing the aiming unit and the missile guidance fins.*

formation is fed into the missile inertial guidance system from a solid state programmer (the AN/GJM-24(XO-2)) which then goes on to monitor and control the launch while also supplying all the necessary pre-flight electrical power supplies. On firing, a rocket boost motor provides the main launch power for a period of 1.5 to 6 seconds, depending on the range required, after which a smaller rocket motor takes over. Flight stabilisation is provided by the spin initiated by inclined jets tapped off from the main booster motor. The inertial guidance system, using the pre-programmed directions and data, determines when the motor should switch off, and Lance then completes its journey in free flight.

The British Army uses only nuclear warheads in its Lance missiles, taking the view that to launch and maintain such an expensive missile system is not worth the cost and effort involved if conventional warheads alone are involved. However, other NATO forces are equipped with conventional Lance warheads, usually the M188 with a weight of 453.59 kg, and some interchange of such warheads may take place.

At present, the Royal Artillery has only one Lance regiment in the shape of 50 Missile Regiment, Royal Artillery. It is under the direct control of HQ 1 (BR) Corps, and consists of the following four batteries; 15 Missile Battery, RA; 19 Missile Battery, RA; 36 Missile Battery, RA; and 51 Missile Battery, RA. Each battery has three launcher sections equipped with SPLs, two assembly sections equipped with LTs, and a single reconnaissance/survey section.

Blowpipe

Weight complete 19.39 kg; **Weight with IFF** 21.2 kg; **Length of missile** 1.349 m; **Body diameter** 76.2 mm; **Fin span** 0.274 m; **Maximum range** 3,000 m plus.

The Blowpipe ground-to-air missile was originally a private venture developed by Short Brothers and Harland of Belfast, who incorporated into the missile much of the know-how gleaned from their Seacat and Tigercat missile systems. The choice of the Short Brothers missile came from the results of a programme undertaken by the Royal Radar Establishment starting in 1966, which was meant to investigate the possibility of providing a one-man missile for defence against low-flying attack aircraft. Blowpipe was the missile chosen as a result of that study and it is now in service with the Royal Artillery Blowpipe batteries in 1 (BR) Corps, and three TA air defence regiments.

Blowpipe is a small light missile contained in a sealed canister which can be taken from store into the field without any prior preparation. In the field it is prepared for use by clipping-on the aiming unit, which takes only a few seconds. The system is then ready for use. Once a target is seen, if IFF (Identification Friend or Foe) is fitted the target is immediately challenged. If the result is hostile the missile can be fired. As the trigger is pulled a primary rocket motor propels the missile out of the canister. The secondary motor then cuts in and carries the missile towards its target. Using a monocular graticuled sight the firer can guide the missile with a small thumb-controlled joystick—to assist him the missile has small flares in its tail. When at its target the warhead is detonated by either an impact or a proximity fuze. If it misses it is automatically destroyed by a self-destruct mechanism. After firing, the aiming unit is removed from the empty canister and clipped on to a fresh round, ready for re-use. In use Blowpipe has proved to be a very accurate system, mainly due to the manoeuvreability which is made possible by the small canard wings around the warhead being able to swivel independent of the rest of the missile body. All guidance commands are transmitted by radio via the transmitting aerials in the canister walls.

Blowpipe is backed up by simple test equipment and for training a simulator mounted on a test stand is available. Also available are training rounds which use only the primary firing rocket and inert missiles. It is also possible to use the simulator against live targets without firing a missile.

Blowpipe is used by one air defence battery in each armoured division and the teams are normally carried in FV103 Spartan APCs. The three TA air defence regiments are 102 (Ulster and Scottish) Air Defence Regiment (V), 103 (Lancashire Artillery Volunteers) Air Defence Regiment (V) and 104 Air Defence Regiment (V). It is expected that Blowpipe will gradually be phased out of use over the next few years in favour of Javelin.

Javelin

Javelin may be regarded as an improved Blowpipe but the method of guidance differs in being of a type known as SACLOS (semi-automatic command to line of sight). On Blowpipe constant missile in-flight corrections have to be made using a rather fiddly little thumb-controlled joystick that takes a lot of getting used to. On Javelin this is done away with and all the firer has to do is keep the aiming mark on the target and a microprocessor keeps the target and missile aligned via a video system on the launcher. The Javelin missile is slightly longer than Blowpipe at 1.4 m and it also has a freely rotating nose section to improve manoeuvrability. The rocket motor has a new second stage and the warhead is also of a new type. Range is stated to be over 4,000 m.

The first operational Javelin was fired at Manorbier in South Wales during late 1984. The unit involved was 46 Air Defence Battery, 2 Field Regiment, RA.

Javelin is seen by some soldiers as only an interim weapon. What they are looking forward to is an entirely new high velocity missile (HVM) that will have a better range than existing weapons and will be able to use its extremely high speed to such effect that only limited in-flight guidance will be required. However, this missile is still a long way in the future and British Aerospace and Shorts are both undertaking project definition contracts that will last for some years to come. The full title for the new missile is Short Time of Flight Close Air Defence Weapon system. British Aerospace's submission is code-named Thunderbolt and the Shorts design is Starstreak. When, and if, the new missile enters service it will be used to equip an entirely new air defence regiment.

The Javelin launcher showing the revised tracking head for the new SACLOS guidance system (Shorts).

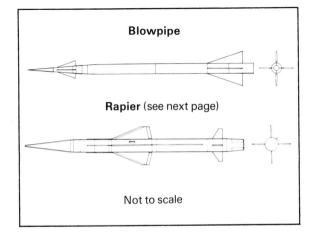

Blowpipe

Rapier (see next page)

Not to scale

Left *The Rapier Fire Unit.* **Right** *The DN181 'Blindfire' radar used with the Rapier system* (Marconi SDS).

Rapier

Weight at launch 42.6 kg; **Length of missile** 2.235 m; **Body diameter** 0.133 m; **Wing span** 0.381 m; **Maximum range** 6,800 m; **Maximum operational height** 3,000 m; **Maximum speed** Mach 2 plus; **Fire unit weight** 1,227 kg; **Fire unit length** 4.064 m; **Fire unit height** 2.134 m; **Fire unit width** 1.778 m; **Radar weight** 1,186 kg; **Radar length** 4.14 m; **Radar height (in action)** 3.378 m; **Radar height (travelling)** 2.032 m; **Radar width** 1.753 m; **Optical tracker weight** 119 kg; **Optical tracker height** 1.549 m; **Tripod diameter** 1.828 m; **Generator weight** 243 kg; **Generator length** 0.991 m; **Generator height** 0.914 m; **Generator width** 0.832 m.

The early development story of Rapier is a rather involved one which began in the early 1960s when it was decided to develop a point-defence anti-aircraft guided missile for Army use known as the PT 428. Early studies revealed that PT428 would be an expensive proposition so in 1962 it was decided to drop the project and adopt the American Mauler system. The choice was unfortunate for early tests of the Mauler soon showed that it would be even more expensive, and that the Army would be able to purchase only a small number of the units it felt it required. As a cheap back-up it was decided during 1963 that a new system, soon to be known as the ET.316, should be developed by the British Aircraft Corporation (now part of British Aerospace). BAC had already been working since 1961 on a private venture known as Sightline, and this formed the basis of the ET.316 which in time became known as Rapier. The first test firings were made during 1965 and in the same year the American Mauler programme was cancelled, so the Rapier system then stood alone.

Progress with Rapier was steady and generally successful. In 1968 a production contract was issued, and by 1971 the first units were being issued to the Army and the Royal Air Force Regiment.

In its basic form the Rapier system consists of three parts—the fire unit, the optical tracker, and the generator—but the addition of a 'Blindfire' (DN181) radar unit makes the Rapier system into an all-weather weapon. The complete system can be deployed in the field by seven men with no recourse to mechanical handling equipment. Once in position the complete system covers an area of about 30 metres in diameter. The fire unit is loaded with four missiles and then receives no further attention once the connections to the other units have been made. The time-into-action is usually about 15 minutes, but once ready the radar unit commences a constant 360° scan out to about 12 kilometres. Any aerial target approaching is automatically interrogated by an IFF query signal, and if the result is hostile the operator on the tracking unit is warned. The operator then searches for the target, as does the fire unit radar head. If both find the target the operator has a choice of either a visual or a radar engagement. If radar is selected the sequence is automatic. If a visual engagement is chosen, the operator uses the tracker head and a control joystick to guide the missile. The radar proved to have limitations during the Falklands fighting, possibly due to damage incurred during the long sea voyage.

When it is considered that each fire unit can cover an area of sky about 100 square kilometres in area up to a height of some 3,000 metres, the full defence capability of Rapier can be appreciated. One of the more important features of Rapier's performance is its reaction time. From acquiring a target to firing the missile the time lapse can be as little as six seconds, and the time to engage another target can be as little as a further three seconds. Once the fire unit has expended all four of its missiles, two men can reload in about 2½ minutes.

Rapier demonstrated its capabilities during the 1982 Falkland Islands campaign when out of 24 missiles fired 14 were 'kills' and six 'probables'. Rapiers are still deployed in the Falklands for local air defence and are manned on a roulement basis by Gunners from BAOR where there are now two Rapier air defence regiments. These two regiments are based at Dortmund and are currently undergoing a change from being all-towed Rapier units to being half towed Rapier and half Tracked Rapier with each regiment having two batteries of each type. These two regiments are 12 and 22 Air Defence Regiments, RA, with another regiment, 16 Air Defence Regiment, based in the United Kingdom at Kirton-on-Lindsay and likely to retain towed Rapier for the foreseeable future.

Each towed Rapier battery has three troops. Each troop has four fire units, each being towed by a 1-tonne Land Rover. A second 1-tonne Land Rover tows the radar unit. The fire unit carries the optical tracker and the three men on the vehicle can visually engage a target by themselves if the need arises. Two men and four missiles travel on the second 1-tonne Land Rover while a ¾-tonne Land Rover makes up

the rear with a further two men, all the remaining stores and a further nine missiles in a special trailer.

Swingfire

Weight of missile 37 kg; **Length** 1.067 m; **Maximum body diameter** 0.17 m; **Wing span** 0.373 m; **Maximum effective range** 4,000 m; **Minimum range** 150 m; **Arc of fire (traverse)** 90°; **Arc of fire (elevation)** ± 20°.

Swingfire is an anti-tank missile that can trace its origins back to the late 1950s and a Fairey missile venture code-named Orange William. When Fairey was taken under the umbrella of the British Aircraft Corporation, the design was taken over and developed to the stage where it became Swingfire and accepted for service by the British Army. That was during 1969 and once in service Swingfire replaced the large and cumbersome Malkara missile in the anti-tank role.

Swingfire derives its name from the fact that it can be launched at an angle from its target, ie, it can 'swing' round corners. The missile is wire-guided which produces the definite battlefield advantage that once launched, enemy electronic or other counter measures cannot affect its guidance. Due to its size and weight, Swingfire is carried into action on a vehicle, and two Army vehicles now in service have been adapted for this role. They are the FV438, an adaptation of the FV432 APC, and the FV102 Striker. (The earlier FV712 Ferret Mark 5 was an interim vehicle only, and was withdrawn by the end of 1978.) The FV438 has two missile launchers and

FV102 Striker with missile bins raised.

can be reloaded from inside the vehicle, while the FV102 Striker has five launchers but has to be reloaded from outside. Both these vehicles have the advantage that they need not launch missiles using the internal sighting and firing systems. If required, they can be hidden behind cover with the firing unit/sight remote from the vehicle and up to 100 metres away.

The missiles are delivered in sealed containers. As soon as it is launched the Swingfire missile is pre-programmed to fly into the centre of the line-of-sight of the sight in use. It can then be controlled by the operator's thumb joystick on the sight unit. On most occasions the guidance changes need only be minor for the angle of the sight from the angle of launch is computed constantly with corrections being passed along the guidance wires. In-flight corrections are usually allowances for side-winds and variations in wind strength. If it hits its target, the warhead is said to be capable of destroying or severely disabling any known MBT.

Swingfire control has now changed from the Royal Artillery to the Royal Armoured Corps. With the RAC, the Swingfires now operate as part of the armoured reconnaissance regiments within each of the three armoured divisions and as part of each armoured regiment, although it is possible that they may be specially organised to meet any particular threat. All Swingfire units are now equipped with the Swingfire Combined Sight which enables missile tracking to be undertaken at night or in poor visibility. This sight combines thermal imaging with the orthodox optical sight and uses passive infra-red sensing to detect a target in the first place.

Milan

Weight of missile 6.65 kg; **Weight of missile and container** 11.5 kg; **Weight of launch unit** 15.5 kg; **Length of missile** 0.769 m; **Body diameter (minimum)** 90 mm; **Wing span** 0.225 m; **Weight of warhead** 2.98 kg; **Weight of warhead charge** 1.45 kg; **Velocity** 75 to 200 m/s; **Maximum range** 2,000 m; **Minimum range** 25 m; **Rate of fire (maximum range)** 3-4 rpm; **Time of flight to 2,000 m** Up to 13 seconds; **Armour penetration** Up to 352 mm.

Milan is the acronym for 'Missile d'Infantrie Leger Anti-Char', and is a second generation wire-guided anti-tank missile which has been in production since 1972 from a French-West German consortium known as Euromissile (formed by Aerospatiale and Messerschmitt-Bölkow-Blohm). The first major production batches for French and West German Army service were made by 1975. In that same year the first contacts to negotiate the procurement of Milan for the British Army Infantry battalions were made, but the subsequent negotiations dragged on until 1978, and became the subject of considerable political acrimony within the United Kingdom. Some small trial batches were obtained before 1978 but in that year it was announced that Milan would be procured in quantity and would be in full-scale service by the early 1980s.

Milan is a one-man weapon, but in action it would be served by two or three men with the 'extras' carrying additional missiles. The missiles themselves are issued in sealed container tubes

Front view of a Milan firing post (MoD).

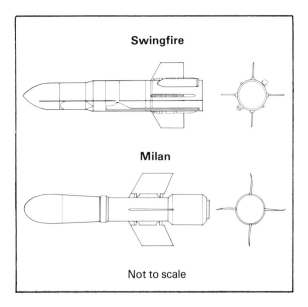

Swingfire

Milan

Not to scale

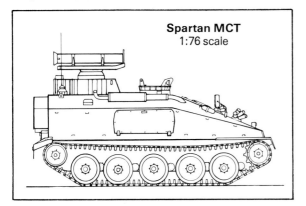

FV103 Spartan bearing a Milan Compact Turret (MCT)—this is an early development version.

which are clipped on to the launching unit. The launcher unit is fairly bulky and is either used on a low tripod mounting, mounted on to a monopod support, or mounted on a light vehicle. The firer/aimer uses a periscopic optical sight with the eyepiece behind the launcher front which also acts as a shield. When the missile is fired it is pushed forward out of the tube by a gas generator at the base of the container tube—the pressures involved also propel the empty tube to the rear about three metres to allow another container tube to be clipped on to the launcher. When the missile has 'coasted' far enough forward to prevent the rocket motor exhaust from harming the firer (and also preventing the launch position being given away by the exhaust 'signature'), the main motor ignites. Once in flight four fins spring outwards into position ready to provide flight stabilisation, and the guidance wire unwinds from a bobbin (the wire is less than 0.4 mm in diameter). Small flares around the missile tail enable the firer to track it towards its target, but the actual guidance is automatic once the firer has pinpointed the target using an illuminated graticule in the sight.

The Milans used by the British Army are licence-produced in the United Kingdom by the Dynamics Group of British Aerospace. Unfortunately, a Treasury 'leak' that emerged during early 1979 revealed that this arrangement cost the nation some £40 million more than if the missiles had been purchased direct, and not surprisingly this revelation added yet more acrimony to the existing political wrangles involving Milan. But the introduction of Milan into service has been much more smooth. The introductory training for the weapon is carried out at Netheravon and lasts five weeks.

Milan is now the Infantry's main anti-tank weapon. The mechanised battalions in BAOR each have a strength of 24 Milan firing posts and the Type A (Saxon-based) battalions also have 24 firing posts—the UK-based Type B battalions have only six Milan firing posts. It is possible that some battalions within 6 Airmobile Brigade may have their Milan strength doubled if current plans go ahead. They will then be able to act as a highly mobile (helicopter-portable) task force to be used to plug any enemy armoured breakthrough.

Each Milan section has two elements. The first is a two-man team in a Ferret scout car, one of whom is the section commander. They act as a small reconnaissance team for the rest of the section based in a FV 432. This FV432 carries four firing posts and their two-man teams plus a total of 48 missiles—there is also one extra firing post within the section. One of the sections in any BAOR anti-tank platoon is mobile. At present the mechanised sections use the FV103 Spartan with the teams leaving the vehicle for firing. There are now plans that these Spartans will be fitted with a small turret known as a Milan Compact Turret (MCT) which has two Milan launcher tubes, one either side of a traversing housing. It is possible to reload the launcher tubes from within the vehicle.

TOW

Weight of missile (approx) 24 kg; **Length of missile** 1.168 m; **Body diameter** 0.152 m; **Minimum range** 65 m; **Maximum range** 3,750 m; **Length of launch tube** 2.2 m; **Speed** 200 m/s plus; **Armour penetration (60°)** 408 mm.

The designation TOW is yet another acronym, this time an American one for Tube-launched, Optically-tracked, Wire-guided. During 1978 it was

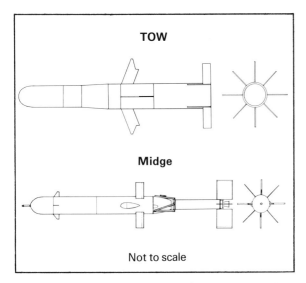

announced that the contest for the next generation of helicopter-launched anti-tank missiles was to be between the British Hawkswing (a variant of Swingfire), the Franco-German HOT and the American TOW. TOW emerged as the final choice and will enter service during the early 1980s as the main anti-tank armament of the Lynx.

TOW has been in service for some years with the American services (the first firing trials were made during 1965) and it has long been an American ground and helicopter-launched missile. The American design designation is BGM-71A, while the service designation is M151E2. Only the helicopter version will be obtained by the British Army. The usual launch configuration on American helicopters is four tubes on each side of the aircraft, but the Army Air Corps uses only three a side. As mentioned in the acronym, TOW is wire-guided and optically tracked, but where TOW scores over other systems is its relatively high missile velocity and the ease with which it can be guided. All the firer has to do is fire the missile and keep the optical sight graticules on the target—the rest is done automatically.

In the USA, TOW is produced by several concerns but the main contractor is the McDonnell Douglas Helicopter Company of Culver City, California.

Midge

Length with booster 3.73 m; **Length in flight** 2.6 m; **Wing span** 0.94 m; **Body diameter** 0.33 m; **Engine type** Williams WR2-6 single-stage turbo-jet; **Booster type** Bristol Aerojet Wagtail; **Operational speed (maximum)** 740 km/h; **Operational altitude** 300 to 1,200 m; **Range** 155 to 160 km.

Top *TOW launching tubes as fitted to Lynx helicopters.* **Above** *A Midge ready for launching.*

Midge is the general-use British Army term for the Canadair AN/USD-501 reconnaissance drone system. Based on what was originally a Canadian development known as the CL-89, the system is now an international one with Canada, West Germany and the United Kingdom all being involved.

Within the British Army, Midge is used by the Royal Artillery locating regiments, but they are under the control of divisional intelligence (G Int). When tasked for a mission the Midge drone is pre-programmed and zero-length launched from a specially equipped Bedford 4-tonne truck. Initial propulsion comes from a rocket booster motor which burns for two seconds after which a small jet engine takes over. The drone then follows its programmed course and fires its cameras or infra-red sensors at preset intervals. The cameras used are Zeiss stereoscopic tri-lens devices which can give overlapping negatives for eventual stereoscopic examination to show up detail. If fitted, the infra-red sensors produce a visual record on to film through mist, darkness and conventional camouflage of any heat-emitting objects. As an alternative for night photography, flares can be discharged from the drone tail to illuminate ground targets.

The flight path is usually a circular or elliptical one as the drone must end up somewhere near its launch site for rapid recovery (it is theoretically possible to preset a straight unit-to-unit course but for operational reasons this is rarely carried out). As the drone nears its launch site it is homed-in by radio beacons up to the point where the engine shuts down and parachutes open to lower the drone to the ground. Air bags in the nose are inflated to reduce the shock of landing. Once recovered, the camera or infra-red pack is removed and hurriedly taken for processing at a special high-speed processing station near the Midge command section. As a rough guide the time interval between a launch request and the examination of dried negatives is about one hour, although for night missions it is longer. As the Midge sections are rarely used in the forward battle areas this limits their operational ranges to about 55 kilometres for a there-and-back mission beyond the front line. Each drone can be re-used.

Phoenix

The Army has appreciated for some time that its existing Midge equipments are too slow, not only in performance but in the time it takes to get useful target information into the hands of the various 'users' after a flight. Over the years several attempts have been made to introduce replacement equipments, one of which was known as Supervisor, but all of them were eventually terminated for a number of reasons, not the least of which was cost. However, the need for a Midge replacement is now pressing and the decision has been made to procure a remotely-piloted surveillance system known as Phoenix.

Phoenix will be the Army's first fully equipped pilotless aircraft system for real time remote targeting and battlefield surveillance. It comprises a small aircraft with advanced avionics and an infra-red imaging system, an air-to-ground data link, a mobile ground station and logistics vehicles for launch and recovery. Several industrial concerns are involved in Phoenix but the prime contractor is GEC Avionics Ltd of Rochester, Kent. Also involved are Flight

Refuelling Ltd of Wimborne, Dorset. The air vehicle is based on experimental work carried out with a vehicle known as MACHAN, flight trials being conducted by the Royal Aircraft Establishment at Bedford. Phoenix uses components formed from sandwich composite construction and is a twin-boom aircraft with the main 'payload' pod slung under the high wing. It is powered by an air-cooled engine driving a propeller that provides the vehicle with a low sound signature.

The main advantage that Phoenix provides over existing in-service systems is that it can transmit its target data while it is still in flight. From the moment of launching the various sensors carried by Phoenix can transmit their data and the use of thermal imaging and infra-red sensors enables Phoenix to spot targets through fog, smoke and the general poor visibility factors present on a battlefield. In flight it has a low radar signature and is difficult to detect using infra-red imaging devices. No details have yet been made public regarding dimensions or weights for Phoenix is still in a relatively early state of development with an £80 million development and production contract having been placed with GEC Avionics at the beginning of 1985.

General layout of the Phoenix remotely piloted surveillance vehicle, showing the modular construction and some of the 'payload' sensors (GEC).

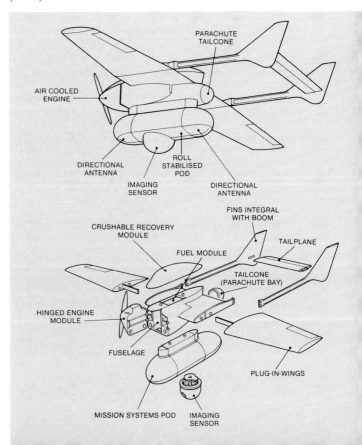

Special equipment

Heli-Telly & Nitesun

One of the off-shoots from the Army's enforced investment of resources in Northern Ireland has been the detailed operational experience gained from the use of airborne vision devices. There are several of these in use, of which only two have been revealed publicly—these are Heli-Telly and Nitesun. Of these, Heli-Telly has perhaps the greatest operational interest as it consists of an airborne television system with a role to play outside that which it has in Northern Ireland. The system, at present installed in Scout helicopters but likely to be used also by the Lynx, was developed by Marconi Elliott Avionics Systems.

The airborne component of Heli-Telly consists of a television camera weighing some 150 kg. In service with the British Army, an all-colour system is employed but monochrome can also be used. Once airborne the camera can give ground-based commanders an excellent idea of the ground to be covered in an operation and prevents them having to spend a portion of their valuable time in operational reconnaissance of specific areas. In the close confines of the type of operations carried out in Northern Ireland, Heli-Telly is invaluable. In town areas it enables commanders to see exactly what is happening in streets several blocks away, and in country areas a single Heli-Telly can be used to cover a wide area or several road blocks or other specific points. The camera itself can be focused into a 1° beam enabling the operator to pick out individuals at ranges of up to 1.5 kilometres. The signals picked up can be transmitted to mobile or temporary ground stations which in their turn can retransmit to permanent stations—a permanent ground station can receive signals from up to 40 kilometres away. As a general rule, all transmissions are video recorded. The mobile ground stations are housed in specially equipped Land Rovers.

The airborne equipment is mounted on a stabilised platform on the helicopter to ensure the transmitted pictures are as free from vibration blurs as is possible. The camera itself is operated by a joystick and can be pointed in almost any direction from the rear cabin out to one side. Image intensifiers may be fitted to the camera enabling Heli-Telly to be used under poor visibility or starlight conditions—the operational value of such a system can be readily imagined.

In contrast, Nitesun is a more specialised device with specific applications for the internal and security type of operation carried out in Northern Ireland. Nitesun consists of a small and powerful searchlight suspended under a helicopter. Its value lies in that the beam can be accurately concentrated to pin-point any particular area, so that a location such as a suspected ambush point can be suddenly illuminated. The beam is so powerful that the helicopter can fly above normal small-arms retaliatory fire and from a height it also has the advantage that the beam can be widened to sweep larger areas.

The searchlight itself weighs 11.34 kg and is usually used suspended from Scout helicopters. It is pointed by means of a small remote control unit (weighing 0.85 kg) carried within the cabin. Apart from the usual powerful light beam, an infra-red filter may be fitted for less obvious surveillance. In use as a conventional searchlight the beam can give an illumination intensity fifty times brighter than clear moonlight up to 1,000 metres away (with a beam some 100 metres in diameter). Nitesun is an American product and it was developed by the Spectrolab concern at Symlar in California. Their design designation was SX-16.

Night vision devices

Night vision devices fall into two main categories, infra-red (IR) and image intensifiers (II). Of the two, the image intensifiers are now the more widely used as the infra-red devices not only need large and bulky power supplies, but can be relatively easily detected on the battlefield. The image intensifiers have the advantage that they are 'passive' and emit no easily-detected radiation. They rely entirely on the amplification of available light, for even on the darkest night there is still sufficient light to be amplified electronically to make it visible to the human eye—some image intensifiers are capable of amplifications up to 50,000 times and more. Image intensifiers can also be relatively small and light as they are often powered by little more than torch batteries (some of the larger instruments do have larger power sources), and they can double as weapon sights or surveillance devices.

Some infra-red devices are still used by the Army, the main users now being Chieftain tank crews. Image intensifiers are now used by nearly every arm of the Services and a wide range of models and devices is now in use. The accompanying table shows only the main types at present in service or under development. Many trials have been made with various image intensifier devices from within the United Kingdom and elsewhere and some of these (such as the Scotos weapon night sights) may be encountered, but they have, to date, been obtained in small numbers only.

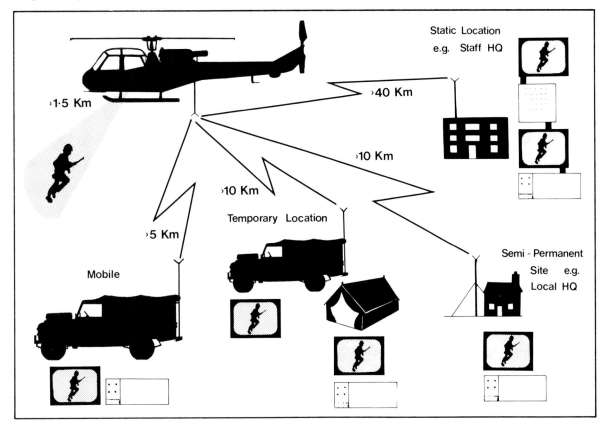

Static Location
e.g. Staff HQ

›40 Km

›1·5 Km

›10 Km

›10 Km

›5 Km

Temporary Location

Mobile

Semi - Permanent
Site e.g.
Local HQ

Infra-red devices	Magnification	Field of view (mils)	Weight (kg)
Commander's IR periscope	× 3	250	19
Gunner's IR sight	× 3	250	13

These are both fitted to the FV4201 Chieftain.

Yet another night vision system that is now coming into more general use is the thermal imager. This system uses infra-red, but in a passive form in that it converts infra-red sources into visible images.

Thus a vehicle or human form that is constantly emitting infra-red radiations in the form of heat can be rendered visible. The radiations can be detected and seen even when cover from vision or camouflage is used by the 'target'. Thermal imaging sights are now under development for a variety of weapons and vehicles, and one application being in area surveillance. Use of such a sight can enable troops to detect when an infra-red emitting source moves into a covered area, when a visual or aural signal can

Image Intensifiers

	Magnification	Field of view (mils)	Weight (kg)	Remarks
Pocketscope	× 1.15	711	0.9	Hand-held
Individual Weapon Sight (IWS)L1A2	× 3.75	180	2.78	SLR, Carl Gustav, etc
Telescope Straight II L1E1 (Twiggy)	× 5	129	11	Tripod-mounted
Crew Served Weapon Sight (CSWS)	× 5.7	108	8.54	Wombat
Night Observation Device	—	—	—	
Sight Unit II L3A1	× 1.4	380	5	Spartan Chieftain ARV
Night Sight L2E1	× 5.8 or × 1.6	142 or 498	59	Fox
Night Sight L2E1	× 5.8 or × 1.6	142 or 498	57	Scorpion, Scimitar
Driver's Periscope L4A1	× 1	890	10.34	Chieftain
Commander's II Sight	× 1	—	56	For Chieftain, still under development.

then be given. Known as the thermal pointer, one version is under development for the Chieftain commander's image intensifier periscope.

Two new pieces of equipment have now been added to the array of night vision devices used by the Army, both of them based on the thermal imaging principle. The largest of the two is known as OTIS

Right The Crew Served Weapon Sight fitted to a 'winterised' Wombat. **Below** *A Night Observation Device (NOD) with the lens cover fitted.* **Below right** *Head-on view of an OTIS with the MRTI on the right, with its large light-gathering lens, and the laser rangefinder on the left, both combined on the same angulation head.* **Bottom** *A Chieftain with its infra red/white light search-light switched on to indicate its position on a dusty road.*

(Observer Thermal Imaging Sight) which is a relatively large piece of kit normally mounted on a tripod. It is meant for use by forward observers of artillery and mortar units and consists of a thermal imager combined with a laser rangefinder on the same angulation head. If required the thermal imager can be used by itself when it is known as the MRTI (Multi-Role Thermal Imager) and trials have been conducted using this device mounted on a helicopter. OTIS and MRTI are both Thorn-EMI products as is a much smaller thermal imager device known as Spyglass or Hand-held Thermal Imager (HHTI). This weighs 5 kg complete compared to the 10.7 kg of the MRTI and has been ordered in large numbers for forward observers and reconnaissance troops.

The Army has made a considerable investment in thermal imagers and has even gone to the extent of procuring mobile workshops for their maintenance and repair. These are standard container/shelters

The Thorn-EMI hand-held thermal imager (HHTI).

carried on the backs of 4-tonne trucks containing all manner of specialist test and repair equipment.

Mines and mine detectors

Anti-Personnel Mine M18A1 (Claymore)
Weight 1.58 kg; **Length** 0.216 m; **Height** 0.083 m; **Width** 0.035 m; **Weight of charge** 0.68 kg.

The Claymore mine is an American anti-personnel device of undoubted lethality and unpleasantness. It is a small curved and innocuous box supported by four scissor-type metal legs which is set up, usually hidden in long grass or undergrowth, covering a path or route it is expected that an enemy will take. As the enemy approaches, the Claymore mine can be fired, either remotely or by a trip wire. As it fires the curved face of the mine faces towards the enemy and the main bursting charge (0.68 kg of C-4 plastic explosive) projects 700 small steel balls forward in a 60° arc. The arc ranges out to about 50 metres and upwards about one metre. Any personnel caught in this fan of steel projectiles cannot escape injury. In the mine the steel balls are held ready for firing in a plastic matrix. Not all of the blast is projected forwards for an area up to 16 metres to the rear of the mine is also a danger area.

The Claymore mine is carried in a bandolier which also holds the firing cap fitted to the mine, the firing device, and a small test set.

PADMINE
Weight 1.26 kg; **Height** 0.12 m; **Width** 0.205 m; **Range** Up to 160 m; **Number of steel projectiles** 650.

PADMINE was originally developed for use as a point defence weapon in Northern Ireland but it has now been developed to the stage where it will eventually replace the M18A1 Claymore mine in Army service. In many ways the PADMINE is similar to the M18A1 but it spreads its lethal steel projectiles in a much more clearly defined and aimable arc. Its arc is so accurate that it can be emplaced and aimed using a special Trilux optical sight that is fitted to the mine as it is emplaced and then removed for re-use with other PADMINES. As with the M18A1, PADMINE can be detonated by a tripwire but it can also be command-detonated using an exploder known as Shrike, a small hand-held device that is normally used for demolition work. Each Shrike exploder can be used to

Below left *A Claymore anti-personnel mine.* **Below right** *A PADMINE with its Trilux optical sight in place.*

detonate up to four PADMINEs. The PADMINE is an all-British product manufactured by Royal Ordnance.

Ranger mine system

Weight loaded 630 kg; **Weight of loaded magazine** 14 kg; **Tube capacity** 18 mines; **Height above platform** 1.295 m; **Width** 2.21 m; **Length** 1.473 m; **Range (approx)** 100 m; **Rate of fire** 1 tube (18 mines) per second; **Total capacity** 1,296 mines; **Elevation** +5° to +35°; **Traverse** 180°.

The Ranger anti-personnel system is a joint development by the Royal Armament Research and Development Establishment at Fort Halstead and EMI Electronics Limited of Hayes, Middlesex. It was developed specifically to meet the mine-laying needs of modern mobile warfare when anti-personnel minefields will have to be laid rapidly and with none of the careful planning and patterned layout of past conflicts. With Ranger, minefields can be laid as and when the situation demands. Existing anti-tank minefields can be sown with anti-personnel mines to delay clearing by the enemy, river crossing approaches can be sown from the other side of the river, tracks can be denied to enemy infantry, and so on.

The main reason for the rapid laying ability of the Ranger system is a multi-barreled projector which can be mounted on the back of a truck or on the roof of a mobile tracked vehicle—in the British Army the usual carrying vehicle is the FV432. The projector carries 72 disposable tubes, each of which contain 18 anti-personnel mines. The tubes are issued in magazines of four, so the total projector capacity is 18 magazines. In use the projector is loaded and the traverse and elevation are pre-set. As the carrying vehicle moves the projector is fired, one tube at a time at the rate of a tube every second. As each tube fires the 18 mines contained are distributed to a range of up to 100 metres. As they fly through the air they are dispersed in a random pattern, and 20 seconds after they are fired each mine becomes armed automatically. The dimensions of the mine are 34 mm deep with a diameter of 62 mm. Each mine, which is usually coloured green, contains a 10 gram charge of RDX/Wax which is pressure detonated. The charge is sufficient to inflict sufficient damage to disable, but not to inflict a fatal wound.

Once the projector is fired and empty, it can be reloaded by two men with fresh magazines in about six minutes. Normally, the Ranger system is used in conjunction with the Bar Mine Layer, so sizeable tracts of country can be rendered impassable to advancing forces in a very short space of time. In this

Top *Ranger anti-personnel mine. Left, the base of an unprimed mine; centre, the top; right, base of a primed mine.* **Above** *A fully loaded Ranger mine system fitted to a FV432.*

way, an enemy can be channelled to any direction that suits the defender, unless of course they are willing to give up the momentum of an advance and spend time in mine-clearing. Even here the Ranger mine does not lend itself to rapid clearing, for apart from landing in random patterns, the body is plastic and difficult to detect using conventional mine detectors.

Although the Ranger system is usually mounted on FV432s, other vehicles can be adapted to carry the projector. One vehicle that has been seen so adapted is the FV622 Stalwart. For training purposes special magazines are issued, each of which fires compressed peat 'mines' which do not require clearing after use, but inert plastic mines are also available.

C3A1 non-metallic anti-personnel mine (Elsie) (Canadian Arsenals).

C3A1 Non-metallic Anti-personnel Mine (Elsie)

Weight 57 g; **length** 75 mm; **Diameter** 50 mm; **Charge weight** 9.45 g.

Elsie is a small anti-personnel mine produced in Canada by Canadian Arsenals Ltd. It is used by the British Army as a hand-emplaced anti-personnel mine and its small size and lack of metal parts makes it difficult to detect. It is cone-shaped and driven into the ground by hand; detonation is caused by treading on the mine. The small charge contained within an Elsie mine is sufficient to disable only. The normal C3A1 Elsie mine is coloured olive drab but an inert drill version known as the C4A1 is coloured blue.

Bar Mine system

Mine layer weight 1,240 kg; **Length** 1.22 m; **Height** 0.84 m; **Width over wheel cages** 1.02 m; **Mine weight** 11 kg; **Length** 1.2 m; **Width** 0.108 m; **Depth** 0.081 m; **Weight of explosive** 8.4 kg.

The Bar Mine system was developed for the same reasons that gave rise to the Ranger anti-personnel mine system, and enables the Army to sow anti-tank minefields rapidly as and when they are required. As with so many other weapon systems, the Bar Mine and its layer are design products of the Royal Armament Research and Development Establishment at Fort Halstead in Kent. Production is carried out at Royal Ordnance factories, the mine itself at Chorley and the layer at Nottingham.

The Bar Mine itself is capable of disabling any tank by blowing off one or more of its tracks. To assist in the speed of the laying operation, the mine is issued with its fuze already installed, and for storage and transport the mines are packed in palletised loads of 72 ready for easy handling by mechanised means such as the Eager Beaver. The load weighs 855 kg and can be quickly unpacked for use. For use on a small scale, packs of four mines

are available. Once laid the Bar Mine is not easy to detect as it has few metal components.

The Bar Mine Layer is normally towed behind an FV432 although other vehicles can be used—the main advantage of the FV432 is that the crew can operate under cover. Vehicles that can be used include the various versions of the Land Rover, any 4-ton truck (including GMC trucks at the Suffield Training Ground in Canada), and the FV622 Stalwart. The layer is towed behind the vehicle with its conveyor projecting over the tailboard, or into the towing vehicle. As the layer progresses a plough blade cuts a furrow. The Bar Mines are then placed on the conveyor and as they pass through the layer body the fuze is activated automatically. Once the mine has been placed in the ploughed furrow, two disc wheels bury it and smooth down the earth surface. In a remarkably short time the furrow soon blends with the surrounding surface and the mines remain well hidden. Up to 600 or 700 mines can be sown in an hour using one vehicle and a three man crew, but logistic back-up is needed for this rate to be usefully maintained.

Normally the Bar Mines are laid in conjunction with the Ranger anti-personnel mines. A Bar Mine minefield, once laid, presents a formidable obstacle to attacking armour and unless time is spent clearing it, attacking forces can be usefully 'channelled' along the routes the defenders dictate. The shape of the Bar Mine also has the effect that fewer are needed to cover any given area than the conven-

Bar mine layer in use behind a FV432 (MoD).

tional dish mines, and as they are capable of being laid at greater speed as and when the tactical situation dictates, they are far more cost-effective than the older mine systems.

The Bar Mine system has one additional cost-effectiveness advantage. When the mines are newly sown the channel furrows are highly visible, but due to the random method used when laying the mines, crossing the channels is a risky business. As a result time-consuming clearing methods have to be employed, or a way round discovered. This gives rise to the possibility of laying 'false' minefields by simply ploughing tracts of ground, without sowing any mines at all.

In recent years the Bar Mine has been the subject of much development, mainly with regard to fuzes. The introduction of a new family of fuzes into service has led to the Bar Mine being re-named the Full Width Attack Mine (FWAM). The first of these new fuzes was a double-impulse fuze intended to defeat mine flails or rollers in which the first impulse (the rollers or flails) is ignored and the mine only detonates when the pusher tank rolls over the mine. The second new fuze uses a mast-operated sensor which causes the mine to detonate only when the target tank is fully over the mine (this fuze is the L127). There is also a L128 electronic fuze which operates only when a particular radiation signal is given out by a target tank as it rolls nearby. All three of these new fuzes are in service with the Army and all can be used with the Bar Mine Layer after a simple modification has been introduced. It is intended that these three types of FWAM fuze will be laid in a 'mix' in a minefield to hamper clearing.

Horizontal Action Anti-tank Mine
Weight 12 kg; **Length** 0.26 m; **Body diameter** 0.2 m.

The Horizontal Action Anti-tank Mine is a French device used to cover tracks and other likely points used by AFVs. The original French designation is MIACAH, or Mine Antichar à Action Horizontale, and consists of a drum-shaped charge mounted on a circular frame. In use it is placed close to the probable path of an AFV and a wire is stretched across the path. The front of the mine is pointed towards the wire and the mine itself is concealed or camouflaged. As an AFV crosses the wire the charge is detonated and the shaped charge forms a projectile which is fired against the side of the target. Depending on the angle of impact the mine can penetrate up to 70 mm of armour and as it is likely to be fired at the sides of AFVs this is often sufficient to cause extensive damage. The mine is effective up to about 80 metres. The mines in British Army use are filled in the United Kingdom.

A Horizontal Action Anti-tank Mine, also known as the Off-Route Mine.

LAWMINE
Few definite details have been released regarding LAWMINE other than that it has been developed to replace the existing Horizontal Action Anti-tank Mine and that its main offensive 'warhead' is a development of the LAW 80 rocket projector. LAWMINE will be used in very much the same manner as the existing off-route mine and will be mounted on a light adjustable tripod. It consists of

An emplaced LAWMINE showing the optical sight and with the launcher tube closest to the camera (Hunting Engineering).

two tubes, one containing the LAW 80 projectile and acting as the rocket launcher, the other being shorter and containing the sensor system that relies upon various electronic and other sensors to determine when a target tank is in range. If it is, the LAW 80 projectile is fired automatically. A simple optical sight is used to aim the LAWMINE along the line it will be used and the sensor is stated to operate at ranges in excess of 100 m and down to less than 10 m. LAWMINE will be issued as a ready-to-use expendable weapon for, once fired, the launcher is discarded.

LAWMINE has been developed by British Aerospace Dynamics Group at Bracknell and Hunting Engineering Ltd of Ampthill, Bedford.

Anti-Tank Mine Mark 7

Weight 13.6 kg; **Diameter** 0.325 m; **Depth** 0.13 m; **Weight of charge** 8.89 kg.

Although it is now being replaced by the Bar Mine system, the Mark 7 mine is still likely to be used in any future conflict, mainly because there are still large stocks to hand. As they are still sown by time-honoured manual methods, the Mark 7 minefields are more likely to be static and pre-planned affairs.

The Mark 7 mine is disc-shaped with the conventional domed top. The actuating pressure is 275 kg which means it can be crossed by walking infantry but will detonate when a vehicle passes over. Anti-handling devices can be fitted to slow down clearance.

In order to prolong the service life of the Mark 7 mine, a new tilt rod fuze kit known as the L93A1 has been introduced. This is used in place of the normal pressure fuze and consists of a number of frangible carbon rods of varying lengths (to suit local conditions) secured to the fuze socket. As a tank rolls over the mine it breaks the carbon rod to release a spring that initiates the mine detonation chain. The longest available carbon rod is 0.85 m long and detonates the mine 0.7 second after the rod has been broken. As the mine detonates it directs its blast against the relatively thin belly armour of a target tank and thus makes the Mark 7 mine a still-viable anti-tank weapon.

Giant Viper L3A1

Weight complete with trailer 4,483 kg; **Weight of Giant Viper complete** 2,880 kg; **Weight of hose** 2,136 kg; **Length of hose** 229 m; **Diameter of hose** 68 mm; **Trailer weight (unloaded)** 1,651 kg; **Trailer length** 5.867 m; **Trailer height** 1.829 m; **Trailer width** 2.489 m; **Wheel track** 2.159 m.

While the Giant Viper minefield clearing equipment is intended rapidly to clear all types of minefield, its prime function is the clearing of anti-tank minefields. The equipment is used by the Royal Engineers and consists of several parts, the main component of which is a 229 metre-long hose filled with plastic explosive. The hose is fired from a special carrying trailer towed behind an FV4003 Centurion AVRE, an FV180 CET or an FV432. To fire the hose a cluster of eight rockets is used, stabilised in flight by three parachutes. The sequence

Below left *Mark 7 anti-tank mine with tilt fuze fitted.* **Below right** *A Giant Viper (GV) on its FV3705 trailer.*

is as follows. Once the edge of the minefield has been located, the towing vehicle approaches within about 45 metres of its edge. The rockets are then aligned to the path required through the mine field and the rockets are fired from within the towing vehicle. When fired the rockets make a very impressive roar, and the hose unfurls from its special packing case as they progress. Once on the ground the plastic explosive contents are fired, again from the towing vehicle. The path cleared is up to 7.28 metres wide and up to 189 metres long. Up to 80 per cent of the mines along this strip will have been detonated, and often more.

The trailer used to carry the Giant Viper is a special one, the FV3705 Trailer, Mine Clearance Equipment Giant Viper, No. 2 Mark 3. Normally the Giant Viper parts are carried in a 4-tonne truck but only the hose box requires mechanical handling.

During 1979 the first examples of a new Giant Viper trailer were seen. They consist of converted Heavy Floating Bridge (now obsolete) trailers. The conversion work was carried out by the Royal Ordnance factories, and the idea seems to be to provide a cost-saving exercise in order to increase the number of Giant Vipers available for mine-clearing.

Mine Plough
Clearance width 3.787 m; **Uncleared centre lane width** 1 m **Number of tines** 14; **Weight** 2,300 kg; **Depth of tines** 0.23 m

The Army's current mine plough had rather an involved development history for it was originally designed and produced by T. B. Pearson and Sons Engineers Ltd of Newcastle-upon-Tyne for the Imperial Iranian Ground Forces. With the overthrow

of the Shah that contract came to an abrupt end but the British Army also had a requirement for some form of mine plough to be fitted to combat engineer tracked vehicles. Pearsons therefore developed and offered a model known to them as the Engineer Mine Plough (EMP) that used two plough shares, each with seven tines protruding from the bottom of each blade. These were used for BAOR trials during the early 1980s and in late 1982 the EMP was ordered into production.

The Army's mine plough is used to plough an area ahead of a forward-moving AVRE to lift any mines that might be in its path and move them to one side. The mine plough unit is a 'bolt on' unit that fits on to the carrier vehicle with an adaptor plate secured to the front hull. The plough shares are raised and lowered under hydraulic power and the depth of ploughing can be altered by the vehicle driver. Overload devices are incorporated into the system to prevent further progress if the plough shares or tines strike an immovable object such as a rock. The plough shares are made of high yield steel to withstand most mine blasts and spare tines can be carried to replace any that might get damaged in use. The unploughed area between the two plough shares is usually 'covered' by a chain and bobbin arrangement slung between them to trigger off any mast-sensored mines that might otherwise pass under the carrier tank.

The mine plough is at present used by only one unit in BAOR, 32 Armoured Engineer Regiment, Royal Engineers. Their first mine ploughs are fitted to the Centurion AVRE 105 although the AVRE 165 can also carry the device. It is also planned that mine ploughs will be fitted to Chieftain Bridgelayers to increase their tactical flexibility when not required for

Left *Centurion AVRE 105 fitted with a mine plough; this picture shows only one of the ploughshares with its seven tines.*

Above right *A Mine Detector Mark 4C in use* (United Service Instruments).

Right *A P6/2 'Sweep' in use with the probe head fitted* (Plessey Radar).

bridging. Pushing the mine plough ahead of a Centurion AVRE takes almost all the power the tank engine pack can muster. When using the plough the AVRE has to remain in bottom gear and thus progress is slow. However, the mine-clearing efficiency is high for the plough can clear virtually all mines from a defined path.

Mine Detector No. 4C

Weight in use 9.15 kg; **Weight in transit box** 14.4 kg; **Search head length** 0.286 m; **Search head height** 0.108 m; **Search head width** 0.184 m; **Amplifier depth** 0.216 m; **Amplifier height** 0.108 m; **Amplifier width** 0.108 m; **Handle extended** 0.127 m; **Handle collapsed** 0.38 m; **Detection depth (soil)** 0.51 m; **Detection depth (pavé)** 0.305 m.

The Mine Detector No. 4C is the standard metal mine detector in service with the British Army and has been in use since 1968. Developed from the earlier No. 4 and 4A, the No. 4C is produced by United Scientific Instruments Limited, based in London. It works on the principle that two wire coils produce a mutually balanced inductance. When a metal object comes within their electrical field an imbalance is caused which produces an amplified tone in the user's headset. In operation the search head can be used in two configurations. The more usual is with the handle extended and the search head parallel to the ground. In some exposed positions the prone configuration can be adopted where the handle is collapsed and the head is adjusted to lay along the ground. In either configuration there are two degrees of sensitivity that can be selected. The normal can detect metal objects up to 51 cm below the surface, but some soils contain ferrite particles and are known as pavé, so the second degree of sensitivity can be selected. This facility can also be used when the anti-sweep ploy of spreading minute steel needles or filings across minefields is encountered.

P6/2 Sweep Metal Detector

Weight complete 4.5 kg; **Length of long probe** 1.016 m; **Length of short probe** 0.4 m; **Length of open loop probe** 1.143 m; **Length of personnel probe** 0.4 m; **Dimensions of electronic unit** 0.25 × 0.08 × 0.25 m.

The P6/2 Sweep metal and mine detector has been in Army service since 1975 and is a militarised version of the Plessey P6 pulse induction metal detector. In Army use the Sweep is issued with four different probes which can be used to fulfil almost any mine or metal detection role from conventional mine detection to personnel body searches. The probes are an open loop probe for normal ground searches, a ferrite rod for searching foliage and water locations, a short probe and the personnel search probe. Using the ferrite probe an object the size of an automatic pistol can be detected up to 0.28 metres away. Any metal or mines detected indicate their presence by aural signals from a small loudspeaker or through headphones. The main electronic unit is carried in a shoulder-slung haversack. Needless to say the Sweep has been put to good use in Northern Ireland and has been instrumental in many weapon finds.

Wheelbarrow

Weight in action 195 kg; **Length** 1.22 m; **Height (minimum operational)** 0.82 m; **Width** 0.69 m; **Maximum speed** 33.5 m/min; **Range (standard)** 100 m; **Endurance (approx)** 2 hours.

Wheelbarrow is a remotely controlled EOD vehicle, specifically designed to meet the operational need which has arisen from the large scale escalation in terrorist and urban guerrilla activity over the last decade. The current version in service is the Mark 10, and the data above refers to this version.

The original Wheelbarrow was designed and produced in just over one month in early 1972 in response to an urgent request from the EOD personnel in Northern Ireland, and went into service immediately. The first version had three wheels and was in fact based on an electrically powered garden wheelbarrow—hence its name. The name has been retained ever since despite the adoption of tracks and numerous modifications to the extent that the present Mark 10 bears little resemblance to its precursor. Over the years the Wheelbarrows have been drastically improved both in performance and versatility until today they are very advanced devices, and have proved so successful in their dangerous role that they have joined the long list of British defence exports to all parts of the world. The Mark 10 Wheelbarrow is a remotely-operated device which can be used in a range of circumstances where the use of a human investigator would prove hazardous or lethal. In service a number have been destroyed in circumstances that would have caused death or serious injuries in conventional search and clearing operations.

Wheelbarrow is electrically driven by two battery-operated motors. Commands are made on a hand-held control box and transmitted through a 100 metre-long 18-core cable. The commands are given to a wide variety of fixtures on the Wheelbarrow vehicle, most of which are on a moving and extendible boom mounted over the vehicle itself. This boom can carry a variety of accessories but an almost universal fitting is a small television camera feeding a nine-inch monitor viewed by the operator. The boom also mounts a five-round automatic shotgun which can be fired to blast open

suspect packages or even force an entry into doors or vehicle windows, but for smashing open windows there is another special device available. Handling devices and grabs can also be fitted and there is even a device for placing a car-towing hook in position. To give an example of the degree of sophistication that has been reached by Wheelbarrow there is the now almost universal fitting of downward-firing nail guns that fire nails into the floor once a Wheelbarrow enters a doorway. The nails prevent the door closing and blocking the vital exit. Other and more recent attachments and weapons fitted to Wheelbarrow are still subject to security restrictions.

As the various forms of terrorist bomb and explosive devices proliferate, more and more experience is being gained in handling and neutralising them. Wheelbarrow has proved invaluable in this essential and unpleasant form of warfare and as the years go by the Wheelbarrow type of vehicle will become even more complex and sophisticated. Already Marauder has been developed and no doubt even more specialised variants will emerge in time. Many lives (and a great deal of property) have already been saved by their use and no doubt many more will be saved in the future, but Wheelbarrows and their ilk are relatively expensive items and should not be hazarded wantonly. Whenever possible they are withdrawn from disruptive or controlled explosions and are not used in such a fashion that they are liable to be blown up without good cause. If for no other reason than that their operators become quite attached to their own particular vehicles, Wheelbarrows are used carefully with as little risk as possible.

The Wheelbarrow Mark 10 is manufactured by Morfax Limited of Mitcham, Surrey. It and other EOD equipments utilised by British EOD teams are carried in specially modified and armoured Ford Transit vans.

Portable Explosives Detector

Weight 12.5 kg; **Height** 0.42 m; **Width** 0.43 m; **Depth** 0.195 m.

The Portable Explosives Detector is not really related to other mine warfare equipments but is best inserted here for the British Army has recently had too much experience of detecting explosives, often using large and static equipments that cannot be moved about easily. Thorn EMI SIMTEC have now developed a portable explosives detector that has been purchased by the Army for obvious applications in Northern Ireland and elsewhere. The equipment consists of a back-pack with an umbilical cord connected to a probe unit with a long sensor wand. The idea is that the wand is placed close to a point to be

Left *The Thorn-EMI SIMTEC Portable Explosives Detector in use with the wand being placed close to an air vent to detect the presence of any explosives inside the building* (Thorn-EMI SIMTEC). **Right** *The radar head of a ZB298 mounted on a tripod.*

sampled for explosives. Pressing a button takes a sample of air from the point and passes it along the umbilical cord into the back pack where it is electronically sampled and analysed. If any explosive material is present, even in minute quantities, the device will give an aural or a visual indication. The sensitivity of this equipment is extremely high and it can not only detect explosives in vehicles or buildings but, applied to a human being, will tell whether a person has been in contact with explosives.

Radar

Radar, GS No. 14 Mark 1 ZB298

Weight complete with tripod 40.16 kg; **Weight less tripod** 30.16 kg; **Head dimensions** 508 × 483 × 178 mm; **Minimum range** 50 m; **Maximum range** 10,000 m.

The Radar, GS No. 14 Mark 1 is often referred to by its commercial designation of ZB298. It is a Marconi-Elliott product that was developed to a Government contract issued in 1964—the first prototypes were completed in 1966. It is now the standard Infantry surveillance radar and is used mounted on a tripod for field use or on a vehicle such as the FV432 or FV103 Spartan—the FV701(H) Ferret Mark 2/3 was at one time a ZB298 vehicle.

The ZB298 operates on a slight modification of the Doppler effect in which moving objects appear to produce different frequencies as they move, with the differing frequencies being relative to a fixed position. With the ZB298 a fixed frequency beam is transmitted over a sector and any moving object is detected and displayed on a console as a series of blips, the size of the blips being used to determine the speed and range of the moving object. With the minimum of training an operator can determine the size and nature of the object so displayed. Men moving, whether they are running, walking or crawling, can be easily detected and the range from the radar head can be determined down to five metres. Vehicles produce their own pulse 'signature', as do such static objects as waving tree branches. An aural signal in headphones assists in the discrimination.

The primary role of the ZB298 is night surveillance but it can also be used in fog and other poor visibility conditions, or for artillery and mortar fire control.

Radar FA No. 15 (Cymbeline)

Weight of equipment 390 kg; **Weight of complete trailer** 980 kg; **Length of trailer** 1.5 m; **Height of trailer (in action)** 2.29 m; **Height of trailer (folded)** 1.07 m; **Width** 1.68 m; **Minimum range** 1,000 m; **Maximum displayed range** 20,000 m; **Scanned sector** 40°30'; **Elevation** −5° to +20°15'.

The mortar took such a toll of casualties during World War 2 that after 1945 a great deal of effort was expended in finding a method of locating mortars in the field. The method finally chosen has been used on several location radars and is still in use on the present locating radar, namely Cymbeline. Very simply, when a mortar is fired its bomb rises at a steep angle. If the bomb can be detected on a radar beam, the detecting radar can then be automatically switched to a higher angle when the bomb trajectory will be once more intercepted. Using a rapid calculator the path of the bomb can be quickly traced back to its firing point and counter-fire can be directed in a very short time.

The first mortar locating radar in Army service on a large scale was the Radar, FA No. 8, or Green Archer. It has now been replaced by the Radar FA No. 15 Marks 1 and 2, known as Cymbeline. Cymbeline is much smaller and lighter than its predecessor and much easier to use. A product of EMI Industries, the first examples were delivered to the Army in 1973. There are two marks, the Mark 1 being mounted on a towed trailer and the Mark 2 mounted on an FV432.

Both marks operate on the same principle which has been outlined above. Cymbeline does have one refinement in that its beam is switched electronically across its 40°30' sector 16 times a second—an alert beam angle can be selected if required so that the two detection beams can be used with great accuracy. The detection range will vary with the calibre of the mortar bomb being detected. An 81 mm bomb can be detected up to 10,000 metres away, while a 120 mm bomb can be detected at ranges of up to 14,000 metres—the maximum range of Cymbeline is 20,000 metres.

Cymbeline is self-contained and has its own power generator driven by a Wankel engine. On the Mark 2 version the radar aerial is levelled independently of the vehicle, but the Mark 1 trailer version is lifted off its trailer and then levelled—the aerial unit can be lifted by four men. With the Mark 1 the display unit is set up about 15 metres from the aerial—with the Mark 2 the unit is inside the FV432. The normal crew for a Cymbeline is four men, with another two in a forward area to give aural warning of mortars firing and in roughly what sector.

There are other roles that Cymbeline can fulfil apart from mortar detection. It can be used in a coastal or ground surveillance role, it can be used to control helicopters or light aircraft in its detection

Cymbeline aerial extended on a FV432.

area, it has a limited artillery control and survey capability, and as well as detecting mortar fire it can also detect rocket firing locations.

To back up the Cymbeline sets in the field a special field repair workshop container can be loaded on to a 4-tonne truck, which is also used to tow the workshop's power generator. A training simulator is also in service.

Each 105 mm field regiment in 1 (BR) Corps and elsewhere has a Cymbeline troop. Its make-up can vary but it usually comprises four tracked Cymbeline sets.

The trailer used to carry the Mark 1 Cymbeline is a rather complex one known as the FV2425 Trailer, 1-tonne, Lightweight Field Artillery Radar No. 2. Its dimensions are as follows: **Weight unladen** 447 kg; **Length** 3.353 m; **Height** 0.711 m; **Width** 1.778 m; **Wheel track** 1.499 m.

Radar No. 17 Mark 1

The Radar No.17 Mark 1 is the Army version of the widely-used Decca Marine Radar, but only a relative handful are in British Army service. The first examples were procured during 1971 and were sent to Gibraltar where they were used (and still are) by 8 Surveillance Troop, RA. Since then more have been obtained and they are currently in service in Belize and Northern Ireland, as well as being used for range safety in the Hebrides.

The Army version of the Decca Marine Radar is carried in a specially-equipped version of the Land Rover with the rotating aerial very prominent on the special body roof. In this form the radar is designated Radar No.17 Mark 1 (Mobile). As such the radar is completely self-contained and powered by a 24 volt generator towed by the vehicle. Each unit has a crew of six men who operate in three-man shifts.

The rotating aerial feeds signals into the equipment which has a visual PPI (Planned Position Indicator) display giving an indication of the position and range of any target relative to the radar. The maximum range of the equipment is some 24 nautical miles but boats about 50 metres long can be picked up out to a range of about 20,000 metres. At shorter ranges (the equipment has eight range 'bands') the radar can be quite discriminating as small 10-metre craft can be detected up to 5,000 metres away, and even swimmers can be detected up to 750 metres away. This discrimination is invaluable for coast or harbour surveillance and the Radar No.17 Mark 1 has many applications.

Radar, GS No. 18 Mark 1 (Prowler)

Weight of radar head 3.5 kg; **Weight of tripod** 3.5 kg; **Weight of battery** 3.5 or 1.1 kg; **Range (men)**

The Radar No. 17 Mark 1 (Mobile) used at Gibraltar by 8 Surveillance Troop RA.

900-1,500 m; **Range (vehicles)** 3,000 m; **Minimum range** 75 m.

Prowler is a product of Marconi Radar Systems Limited, and is intended for general battlefield surveillance at Infantry company level. It can be carried and operated by only one man, and its operation has designed to be as simple and rugged as possible (there are only four controls). Prowler is operated in two modes—Search and Range. In the Search mode the equipment acts as a conventional doppler radar, but in the Range mode the doppler pulses are generated to determine the range of any particular target using an LED display marked in 25 metre graticules. Two batteries can be used with Prowler and differ only in their operational life. A tripod can be used with Prowler for static 'sentry' duties. The radar head is 0.28 metres high, 0.3 metres wide and 0.095 metres deep.

Radar, GS No. 20 Mark 1 (Claribel)

It is not possible to quote very much data regarding Claribel as it has not long been in service. Developed to an Army requirement and using experience gained the hard way in Northern Ireland, Claribel is used to detect incoming sniper fire from hidden positions. In the past mobile patrols or fixed installations have been fired on but it has not often proved possible to gain an aural fix on the firing point. Very often follow-up search patrols have been misdirected or even random with no idea of the correct area to search. Claribel is a simple light radar system that can be mounted on the roof of a vehicle or a fixed installation to detect incoming fire and visually indicate the appropriate sector from which it came. When a round is fired at a vehicle it is immediately detected and an aural warning signal is given. At the same time the appropriate sector is visually displayed on a small indicator—up to two firing points can be detected at any one time.

The installation of Claribel takes up very little space and it can even be hidden in vehicle bodywork if so desired. The detector elements are four small box aerials, one at the front and rear and one on each side. They all feed into the main control box which then feeds the indicator and warning device. As mentioned above, not only vehicles are equipped for such locations as guard posts and the like are fitted with Claribel, and in some fixed installations remote display units are used. The aerials can detect incoming rounds of all calibres and velocities from 5.56 mm up to 120 mm, and even slow-moving projectiles such as rockets can be detected. Claribel is manufactured by Microwave and Electronic Systems Limited of Newbridge, Midlothian, now part of the Racal Group.

Armoured Fighting Vehicles

FV4201 Chieftain

Armament 1 × 120 mm L11A5 Gun, 1 × 7.62 mm L8A1 Machine-Gun, 1 × 7.62 mm L37A1 Machine-Gun and 2 × 6-barrel smoke dischargers; **Crew** 4; **Weight in action** 55,000 kg; **Length (gun forward)** 10.795 m; **Length (gun clamped)** 9.73 m; **Length of hull** 7.52 m; **Height (top of cupola)** 2.82 m; **Width (with searchlight)** 3.62 m; **Width (over skirts)** 3.504 m; **Width (over tracks)** 3.33 m; **Track width** 0.61 m; **Ground clearance** 0.508 m; **Maximum road speed** 48 km/h; **Range (roads)** 400-500 km; **Range (cross-country)** 200-300 km; **Engine type** L60 No. 4 Mark 8A; **Engine power** 750 bhp at 2,250 rpm; **Engine capacity** 19 litres; **Fuel capacity** 950 litres; **Ammunition capacity** 120 mm—64 rounds, 7.62 mm—6,000 rounds; **Main armament elevation** –10° to +20°; **Main armament traverse** 360°.

Chieftain is the Main Battle Tank (MBT) of the British Army and as such forms the central striking force of the armoured divisions of 1 (BR) Corps in West Germany. Despite the fact that it has been in front-line service since 1967, it is still widely regarded as one of the most powerful fighting tanks in the world, and progressive improvements and modifications to the basic design and equipment seem to ensure that it will remain so for many years.

The FV4201 Chieftain had its origins in the early 1950s. The basic design concept was born in an era when the General Staff was acutely aware that up to the advent of the Centurion, British tank designs were either under-armoured or under-gunned, and in many cases both criticisms applied. As the Centurion had amply proved its battle value during the Korean War it was decided to procure a follow-on design which was formulated under the general designation of Medium Gun Tank No. 2. Initial design studies envisaged a low hull, low-slung suspension and a 105 mm gun, but the design specifications were constantly being improved and upgraded so it was not until 1954 that the first 'paper' designs approached the stage where hardware could be considered. Even then there was a brief interlude of collaboration on various component interchanges between the United Kingdom and the USA, but that eventually came to naught and the General Staff specification was finally issued in August 1958. It called for an effective gun-to-armour combination, combined with agility and the ability to stay in action for prolonged periods. The main armament was to be capable of engaging armour at very long ranges, but the armour carapace had to be capable of withstanding enemy artillery fire from medium calibres.

Already the main engine had been selected, as had several of the new tank's design features. To save on the all-important height the driver was to be in a reclining position, which would greatly reduce the hull depth, and the main armament was to be mounted in a sloping turret front without a mantlet. Both these features, and several others, were tested in the experimental FV4202 during 1956. Leyland built the FV4202 and were also given the overall design leadership. They had already selected their L60 engine pack as the main power-plant, and if hindsight can be introduced to pinpoint the main weakness of the Chieftain design, it must be stated that this has not proved to be a happy choice.

The L60 was originally designed as one of the various multi-fuel engines sought after by the Army in the years following the 1939-1945 war. Time was to show that the multi-fuel concept was an engineering blind alley which left the L60 with several unfortunate shortfalls, not the least of which was that the early examples proved to be incapable of delivering more than 650 bhp instead of the required 700 bhp. While the output was later increased to the proper figure (and even beyond to 750 bhp), it proved to be of no avail for, by the time it was attained, Chieftain was overweight. Numerous teething troubles with the gearbox, suspension and engine cooling had all added their individual weight penalties to the extent that the

Above *An immaculate Chieftain on the Lulworth ranges, clearly showing the muzzle reference sight on the end of the 120 mm gun barrel.*
Below *A Chieftain in the process of being loaded on to an Antar trailer.*

suspension had to be strengthened, adding yet more weight. Consequently, Chieftain is still far less agile than many of its contemporaries, and the added load on the main engine (plus the unfortunate design faults) has generally rendered the L60 engine pack prone to constant troubles.

The first Chieftain prototype was ready in September 1959, and a series of six prototypes were delivered by the end of 1962. The resultant troop trials revealed the many problems mentioned above, but production finally got underway at two separate locations, the Vickers-Armstrong works at Elswick and the Royal Ordnance Factory at Leeds. The first examples were issued in May 1963 but it was not until early 1967 that the first full service versions were ready. To date there have been eight main marks and several sub-marks (and doubtless there are more to come), but the main versions are as follows: **Mark 1** 40 built with 585 bhp engines and used only for training and trials; **Mark 2** First service version with 650 bhp engine, issued in 1967; **Mark 3** Much revised Mark 2 with new cupola, new suspension and many other detail alterations, in service from 1969; **Mark 4** Development model only; **Mark 5** Revised Mark 3 with new engine and

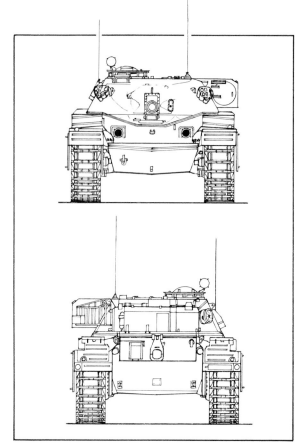

Below *A Warminster-based Chieftain fitted with a dozer blade and with the barrel disguised by camouflage.* **Below right** *D Squadron of The Queen's Own Hussars on parade in Berlin and displaying their 'rubic' camouflage scheme (Army PR, Berlin).*

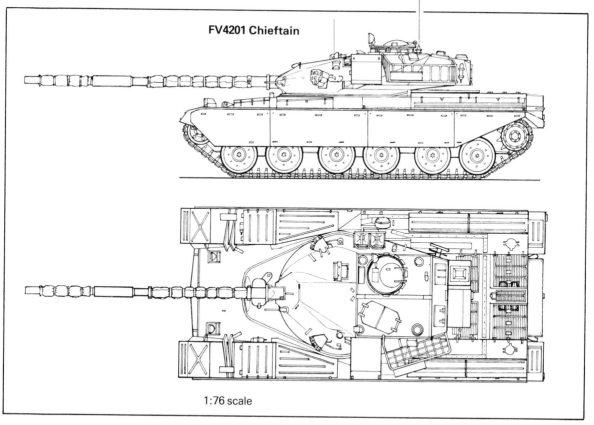

FV4201 Chieftain

1:76 scale

gearbox, improved ventilation and improved exhaust system; **Mark 6** Improved Mark 2; **Mark 7** Revised Mark 3 with engine improvements; and **Mark 8** Mark 3 with full complement of modifications. With the service introduction of IFCS, the Mark 9 is a Mark 6 with IFCS, the Mark 10 a Mark 7 with IFCS, the Mark 11 a Mark 8 with IFCS and the Mark 12 a Mark 5 with IFCS.

The above remarks give only a rough outline of the main versions, and in addition to them there are several sub-marks with varying modification states. It is quite possible that there will be more variants in the future as the Chieftain is still the subject of a considerable amount of development work covering all facets of tank technology and its associated equipment.

Chieftain production for the British Army ceased several years ago after some 700 to 800 examples had been delivered. Early versions, apart from the low-powered Mark 1, are all being gradually updated to late standards by the addition of several innovations. One of these is the Improved Fire Control System (IFCS). Prior to the introduction of this, the main 120 mm armament was aimed and ranged by the use of a .50-in spotting machine-gun (the L21A1) mounted co-axially above the main gun barrel. When fired the machine-gun emitted three-round bursts of tracer. Observing their trajectory through the main gun sight the gunner could correct his aim accordingly. While this method had the advantage of simplicity, the early Chieftains had their offensive range restricted by the limitations of the machine-gun which had a range of only some 1,500 metres, although with the Mark 3 this was considerably improved to around 2,500 metres. Even with this improvement it was felt that something better was needed and that came with IFCS. Very basically, IFCS uses a GEC-Marconi 12-12P computer which handles all the variables likely to affect the projectile of the gun once it is fired. The computer is coupled with the tank laser sight (of which there have been four marks to date), which incorporates a laser range-finder with an accuracy of ±10 metres out to a range of 10,000 metres. The gunner and the tank commander both have sighting telescopes which contain aiming marks, and the control of the IFCS and the gun are both achieved by employing a small joystick operated by the left hand. Aiming is carried out by placing one aiming graticule on to the selected target, and the computer automatically moves the main gun to the correct elevation and 'aim-off' to obtain a hit. This usually takes but a few seconds, even with moving targets. Just about every variable possible is taken into consideration by the IFCS. For example, if the target is moving the movement rate is at once calculated by

measuring the traverse rate of the Chieftain turret and the elevation movement of the gun barrel. Cross-winds and headwinds are taken into account by a roof-mounted sensor which also measures temperature. The angle of gun trunnion tilt is noted by another sensor. Thus with IFCS, Chieftain has a very good chance of obtaining that 'first round kill' that is so vital in tank warfare.

IFCS is now in full-scale service with early marks being updated to accommodate the new equipment. The old ranging machine-guns are now a thing of the past and have been replaced by barrel counter-weights to retain the correct trunnion balances. Development work is still being carried out to integrate IFCS with other new equipment such as a thermal imager to go with the gunner's and commander's vision equipment and sights. The commander is also being provided with a new type of cupola on some vehicles.

Both the gunner and commander can obtain target information, but the commander has a manual override control for target selection. The gunner has control of the co-axial L8A1 machine-gun, while the commander controls the L37A1 machine-gun mounted on his cupola. To provide some small measure of anti-aircraft defence this cupola machine-gun can be elevated and fired at angles up to 90° from within the turret. The interior of the Chieftain turret is crammed with all manner of gear apart from the IFCS and fire control apparatus. Apart from the commander and the gunner to the right of the gun, the loader on the left combines his task with that of radio operator, utilising two Clansman VRC 353 sets. Around the loader are the various ammunition stowage points and bins, and to the rear of the turret is the NBC ventilation equipment. On the early marks the NBC system was an over-pressure version, but eventually this will be replaced by the Mark 6 system which uses full filtration. At the front, the driver normally drives the tank with his front hatch open, but once in action the hatch is closed and the driver then assumes the fully reclining position using vision periscopes. Full night driving facilities are provided, and for night fighting a combined white light/infra-red searchlight is fitted to the left-hand side of the turret.

It has not proved possible to quote the armour thickness of the Chieftain but even a cursory glance will reveal the extra protection provided by the curved front glacis plate and the sloping turret. The side skirting plates provide some measure of protection against light hollow-charge missiles and also double as dust deflectors to keep the all-important vision devices and weapon sights clear.

The engine compartment at the rear is so

A Chieftain with the turret partially traversed and showing the driver's central position.

designed that the L60 engine pack can be removed in one piece in a relatively short time—which, in view of its general reliability record, is just as well. At one point the L60 reliability history came under Parliamentary scrutiny (1977) and as a result a series of trials, known under the code-name 'Sundance', was undertaken to improve matters. As a result of these the main sources of troubles were eliminated and steps taken to introduce modifications to retrofit to all L60 packs. The main improvements were made by fitting new piston liners, but many other changes were added. The end result should substantially improve the reliability of the L60 engine pack, and a slight increase of power from 750 to 800 bhp may be possible. Meanwhile, the transmission and many other automotive components continue to be the subjects of continued development. In parentheses it should be noted that the main engine compartment also houses a 37 bhp auxiliary engine which is used for various purposes, one of them being recharging the batteries situated in the driver's compartment.

Chieftain can wade through up to one metre of water—an early attempt to provide a method of sealing the hull and turret for really deep obstacles did not pass beyond the acceptance stage (a high schnorkel tower was a prominent feature of the kit). A more widely-issued 'bolt-on' kit consists of a dozer blade that can be fitted to the front of the tank in about six to nine hours. Once fitted, Chieftain can then be used to excavate firing positions or remove obstacles, and at least one vehicle per troop is usually so equipped. The blade, once fitted, is

hydraulically powered and controlled by the driver.

Major variants of the Chieftain are the FV4204 Armoured Recovery vehicle and the FV4205 Bridgelayer.

FV4030/4 Challenger

Armament 1 × 120 mm L11A5 gun, 1 × 7.62 mm L8A2 machine-gun, 1 × 7.62 mm L37A2 machine-gun, VIRSS smoke dischargers; **Crew** 4; **Weight in action** 62,000 kg; **Weight training** 60,900 kg; **Length (gun forward)** 11.56 m; **Length (gun to rear)** 9.8 m; **Length of hull** 8.327 m; **Height (top of commander's sight hood)** 2.95 m; **Height (turret roof)** 2.5 m; **Width overall** 3.51 m; **Width over tracks** 3.42 m; **Ground clearance** 0.5 m; **Maximum road speed** 56 km/h; **Vertical obstacle** 0.9 m; **Maximum gradient** 58% (30°); **Trench crossing** 2.8 m; **Fording** 1.07 m; **Engine type** Rolls-Royce CV12 TCA diesel; **Engine power** 1,200 bhp at 2,300 rpm; **Engine capacity** 26.11 litres; **Ammunition capacity** 120 mm—48 to 52 rounds according to mix; 7.62 mm—4,000 rounds.

While the FV4201 Chieftain is still one of the most powerful tanks in the world, development work on its successor began many years ago, as far back as the late 1960s. The story of its successor is a long and complicated one which at one time involved an international programme but eventually that period passed and work concentrated on a new project, the MBT-80. MBT-80 involved a considerable amount of time and resources during its early project definition period but as time went on it began to become apparent that not only would MBT-80 be a very expensive project but the time factor began to weigh against it as a replacement for Chieftain would be needed by the mid-1980s at the latest, and it was very possible that new and powerful Warsaw Pact tanks would be in service even before then. Something was needed quickly, and thus MBT-80 came to an abrupt end in the middle of 1980.

It was replaced in the planning sequence by a new vehicle, the FV4030/4 Challenger. Challenger is a development of the Chieftain line, a line that grew from the British Army's Chieftain design via a string of export and development models. The Chieftain was awarded several export contracts during its production life, many of which were able to benefit from the experience gained with Chieftain in British Army service. One of these export orders was made by the Shah of Iran who obtained large numbers of the Shir Iran 1, based on Chieftain but with an uprated engine. Then came the Shir Iran 2 with the new Chobham armour, an armour formed of layers of ceramics, aluminium and other, as yet, unannounced materials. But the Shah was toppled in the Iran Revolution leaving numbers of developed and completed Shir Iran 2s still on the production

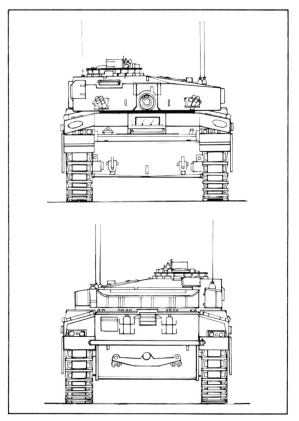

Below *A Challenger with the turret traversed to show the flat silhouette and considerable overhang.* **Below right** *Challenger at speed showing the crew cupolas and hatches open, providing a clear indication of the turret shape.*

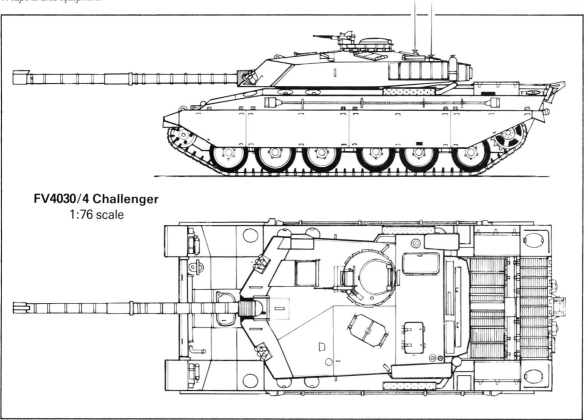

FV4030/4 Challenger
1:76 scale

lines of the Royal Ordnance factories, and with all manner of long-dated parts and equipment ordered and paid for. The Shir Iran series was designated FV4030 and by 1980 the FV4030/3 prototypes were running and on trials. From these the FV4030/4 was projected for British Army service, and the initial order was announced for 240 during July 1980. The cost was reported as some £300 million.

The first FV4030/4 examples were produced during late 1981 but their first public appearance did not take place until summer 1982, when the accompanying photograph was taken. The Challenger tank retains the main armament of the Chieftain in the shape of the 120 mm L11A5 rifled gun but it is expected that eventually some form of revised 120 mm rifled gun will be introduced. New and improved ammunition for the L11A5 will be used, including a new FSAPDS armour-penetrating shot. In time the Hughes Chain Gun might replace the L7A2 co-axial machine-gun but for the present the orthodox 7.62 mm machine-guns will be retained. The IFCS fire control system will also be

used in its fully developed form, and generally, the overall shape and feel of the Chieftain series will be retained.

The main changes come with the new engine and the armour. The new 1,200 hp engine is a Rolls-Royce Motors product contained in an engine pack weighing 5.49 tonnes. It will provide Challenger with a far more lively performance than the generally underpowered Chieftain. The main engine is backed up by a Coventry Climax auxiliary engine for general battery-charging and stand-by use for systems.

The armour is of the Chobham type but is of the latest version. One source states that it might consist of several layers of nylon micro-mesh bonded on both sides by sheets of titanium alloy, and this might well be in addition to layers of ceramics and other exotic armour. It is stated to be virtually immune to nearly all types of modern anti-armour projectiles, and it gives Challenger a slab-sided appearance with the armour being obviously very chunky and thick. The vehicle uses a bolt-on hydro-

A general shot of a Challenger of the 14th/20th King's Hussars in the wet on the Bovington training area, with the main armament at a high elevation to keep out the dirt.

pneumatic suspension system that can be easily replaced in the field. Clansman radio communications equipment will be used throughout. Thermal imaging sights will be provided as standard.

The FV4030/4 is now in production at the Royal Ordnance factory at Leeds. The first Challengers entered service in 1983 with the Royal Hussars (RH) being the first regiment to be fully equipped. 2 RTR received their first vehicles during 1984. The current order situation is that there will be enough Challengers to form as many as nine three-squadron regiments and it is hoped that follow-on orders will be made. Work is now well advanced on the updated L30 120 mm gun although no in-service date has yet been announced. In the meantime all manner of new equipment is under development including a new TN54 transmission and TOGS (Thermal Observation and Gunnery System), which will provide thermal-imaging generated sighting vision for the gunner and commander under night and low visibility conditions.

There will be at least one Challenger variant. This is an armoured repair and recovery vehicle (ARRV) that will be produced by Vickers Defence Systems (see following entry).

The Challenger is a spartan fighting vehicle with an excellent all-round performance but crew kit stowage is somewhat limited as Chobham armour cannot be easily drilled to provide the necessary racking. However, it is still popular with its crews who find it an excellent fighting machine.

FV4204 Armoured Recovery Vehicle

Armament 1 × 7.62 mm L37A1 Machine-Gun, 2 × 6-barrel smoke dischargers, 2 × 4-barrel smoke dischargers; **Crew** 4 + 1; **Weight in action (with crane)** 56,000 kg; **Length (travelling with blade)** 8.57 m; **Height** 2.79 m; **Width (over blade)** 3.53 m; **Width (over tracks)** 3.33 m; **Track width** 0.61 m; **Ground clearance (approx)** 0.5 m; **Maximum road speed** 42.4 km/h; **Range (roads)** 400-500 km; **Range (cross country)** 200-300 km; **Engine type** Leyland L60 No.4 Mark 8A; **Engine power** 750 bhp; **Engine capacity** 19 litres; **Ammunition capacity** 7.62 mm—1,600 rounds; Smoke grenades —20.

While the FV4006 Centurion Mark 2 ARV has given good service, the idea of using a new ARV compatible with the FV4201 Chieftain MBT has

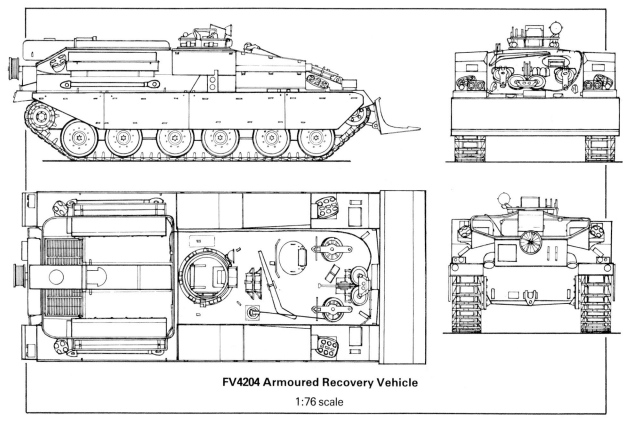

FV4204 Armoured Recovery Vehicle

1:76 scale

obvious attractions, so starting in 1964 the development began of a Chieftain ARV. The first prototypes were ready in 1971 and full production of the new vehicle began in 1974 at the Vickers Works at Elswick, Newcastle-upon-Tyne. It was not until 1976 that the first examples were issued for full service, when they were issued to REME recovery units.

The FV4204 ARV is based on the hull and suspension of the FV4201 Chieftain Mark 5. Numerous changes have been made to the Chieftain layout to enable it to carry out the ARV role. Starting at the front of the vehicle a large dozer blade has been fitted which is not intended primarily for the clearance of earth or obstacles (although it can be used for those purposes), but for stabilisation when the towing winches are in use. The driver's position has been shifted to the left to make room for the main winch. Behind him is the commander's hatch with a 360° swivelling cupola and a machine-gun and behind this is the main compartment with space for the other two or three crew members. The main winch has a pulling capacity of 30,000 kg, but with the dozer blade dug in this can be increased up to 90,000 kg—the dozer blade is operated by hydraulic rams. Inside the same compartment is a second, smaller winch with a towing capacity of 3,000 kg. The length of towing cable for this second winch is 259 metres, while the main winch is provided with 122 metres. Both winches are driven via a power take-off from the main engine, but the smaller winch is hydraulically driven and controlled, and has an infinitely variable speed control. The winch controls are in the main crew compartment. Scattered in various stowage points are

brackets, towing eyes, cables, special tools and all the varied paraphernalia required by the REME in the ARV role.

With the arrival of the Challenger MBT in service a situation arose where the existing FV 434 REME repair vehicles could not handle the 5.49-tonne weight of the Challenger engine pack. This led to the development of the Chieftain Armoured Repair and Recovery Vehicle (ARRV Mark 2), a development made considerably easier by the development of an essentially similar vehicle for the late Shah of Iran before his downfall. The Chieftain ARRV is a conversion of the existing ARV to accommodate an Atlas hydraulic crane on the left-hand side of the vehicle (looking forward) and an engine stand over the vehicle rear. The ARRV has limited repair capabilities as well as the usual recovery function but it will act only as an interim vehicle pending the arrival of the Challenger ARRV. Based on the Challenger, this new ARRV will be produced by Vickers Defence Systems and will have a crew of three (plus seating for four more). It will have a heavy winch, an Atlas crane, a bulldozer blade, and there will be provision for carrying a complete Challenger engine pack and transmission plus other spares and tools. The first production models are expected during 1988.

FV4205 Chieftain Bridgelayer
Armament 2 × 7.62 mm L7A2 Machine-Guns, 2 × 6-barrel smoke dischargers; **Crew** 3; **Weight in action** 53,300 kg; **Length with bridge** 13.741 m; **Length of hull** 7.52 m; **Height with bridge** 3.923 m; **Width (with bridge)** 4.165 m; **Width (over skirts)** 3.504 m; **Width (over tracks)** 3.33 m;

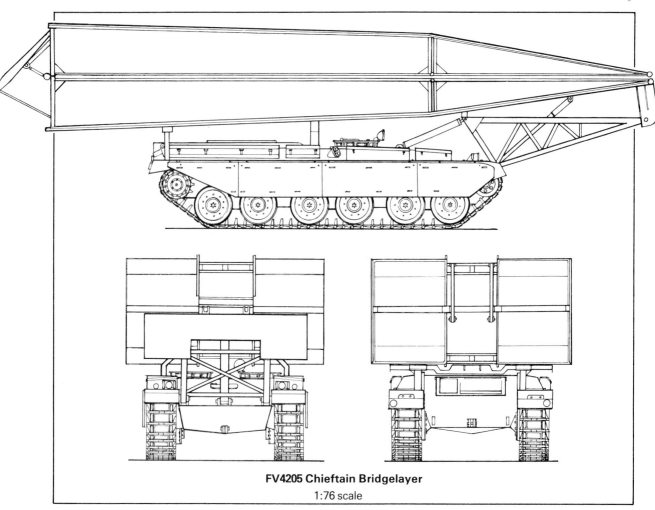

FV4205 Chieftain Bridgelayer

1:76 scale

A Chieftain bridgelayer, minus its usual side skirts, carrying a No 9 bridge.

A Chieftain Bridgelayer in the process of laying a No. 8 Bridge.

Track width 0.61 m; **Ground clearance** 0.5 m; **Maximum road speed** 43 km/h; **Range (roads)** 400 km; **Engine type** L60 No. 4 Mark 7A; **Engine power** 730 bhp; **Engine capacity** 19 litres; **Fuel capacity** 886 litres; **Ammunition capacity** 7.62 mm—3,200 rounds; **Bridge length (No. 8)** 24.384 m; **Bridge width (No. 8)** 4.165 m; **Bridge weight (No. 8)** 12,200 kg.

The Chieftain Bridgelayer, or FV4205 AVLB, was a joint effort with the design work being shared by the MVEE at Chobham, Tubes (Birmingham) and Lockheed Precision Products. The project was initiated in 1962 but requirement changes and the necessary re-designs delayed production until 1974 when the first examples were delivered to the Army. Once in service they soon replaced the earlier Centurion bridging variants, the FV4002 AVLB and FV4016 ARK. Stripped of their bridges, these two vehicles may still be encountered in use for driver training.

The Chieftain Bridgelayer can be used to lay two different bridges. The one usually carried is the No. 8 Tank Bridge which is folded into two halves over the vehicle. Once in the location that requires to be bridged the No. 8 bridge is laid in three stages. Power for the operation comes from a hydraulic pump located within the hull and driven by a take-off from the main engine. Five cylinders are driven by the pump for the actual bridging operation, two for each of the first two stages and one for the third and final stage. The complete launch operation usually lasts from three to five minutes. Once completed, the parent vehicle can disengage and either cross the bridge or withdraw to allow other vehicles to cross. If required, the bridgelayer can cross and recover the bridge ready for another crossing elsewhere—the recovery operation lasts about ten minutes. Once laid, the bridge has two trackways, each track with a width of 1.62 metres which enables small vehicles to cross on one track. The No. 8 bridge, like the No. 9 can be recovered from either end. Overall length is 24.4 metres and weight is some 12,700 kg.

The No. 9 Tank Bridge is part of the AVLB equipment and is usually carried on a semi-trailer. It is a one-piece bridge, 13.411 metres long and 4.165 metres wide. When in use with the Chieftain Bridgelayer it is operated in a straightforward up-

and-over sequence in from three to five minutes. Weight of the No. 9 bridge is 9,144 kg, and it is produced by Laird (Anglesey) Limited.

The widths that can be bridged by the two bridges are from 22.25 metres to 22.86 metres for the No. 8, dependent on the state of the banks, and 12.2 metres for the No. 9.

Production of the Chieftain Bridgelayer is carried out at the Royal Ordnance factory, Leeds, with final production taking place at Nottingham.

The Chieftain Bridgelayer is used by only one regiment in BAOR, namely 32 Armoured Engineer Regiment, Royal Engineers. Within each of the three squadrons of this Regiment the bridgelayers are organised as one of the sections of each Armoured Engineer Troop. Each section has three bridgelayers, each with a No 8 bridge, a No 9 bridge and a Scammell Tractor with a special semi-trailer carrying the spare bridge. 32 Armoured Engineer Regiment, RE, is currently undergoing a programme of expansion and re-organisation that has resulted in more bridgelayers being required. To meet the demand a number of early marks of Chieftain MBT are being converted by Vickers for the bridging role. These variants will be known as Mark 6 AVLBs and will be some 3,000 kg heavier than existing models as they will have a more powerful hydraulic system and other extras such as a new toe plate for fitting the mine plough and an intercom system built into the pick-up boom.

FV101 Scorpion

Armament 1 × 76 mm L23A1 Gun, 1 × 7.62 mm L43A1 Machine-Gun and 2 × 3- or 4-barrel smoke dischargers; **Crew** 3; **Weight in action** 7,938 kg; **Length overall** 4.788 m; **Length of hull** 4.572 m; **Height** 2.102 m; **Width (overall)** 2.235 m; **Width (over tracks)** 2.134 m; **Track width** 0.432 m; **Ground clearance (approx)** 0.356 m; **Maximum road speed** 80.5 km/h; **Range (roads)** 644 km; **Engine type** Jaguar J60 No. 1 Mark 100B; **Engine power** 190 bhp; **Engine capacity** 4.235 litres; **Fuel capacity** 423 litres; **Ammunition capacity** 76 mm —40 rounds, 7.62 mm—3,000 rounds; **Main armament elevation** −10° to +35°; **Main armament traverse** 360°.

By 1960 it was becoming apparent that the time was approaching when consideration would have to be given to replacing the then current family of reconnaissance vehicles which included the FV701 Ferret, FV601 Saladin and FV603 Saracen. As always, it was decided that the new vehicle was to be lighter, faster and air-portable. The early specification called for a weight limitation of 8,200 kg which made the new vehicle about one-third

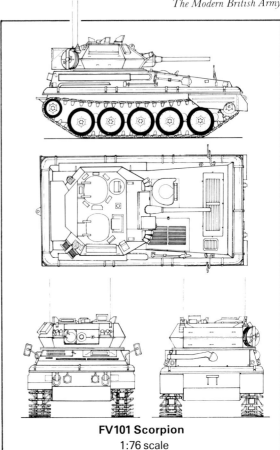

FV101 Scorpion
1:76 scale

lighter than any existing comparable type. To make the specification more difficult it was requested that the one vehicle should be capable of three major tasks—reconnaissance, fire support and anti-tank fire. Several design studies were made, one of which was the Armoured Vehicle Reconnaissance armed with a 76 mm or 105 mm gun. All these early studies had one major weakness in that they were too heavy. The end result was that it was decided to produce a family of tracked vehicles able to specialise in the various roles, since no one vehicle could combine all the requirements and still meet the air-portability strictures.

By 1963 the first hardware of the new project was produced as the TV15000 test vehicle. Much of the early work was carried out at the Fighting Vehicle Research and Development Establishment at Chobham in Surrey. The early results with the TV15000 led to the Mobile Test Rig which embodied nearly all the main motive and suspension details which were to become production features of what was by then known as the Combat Vehicle

Reconnaissance (Tracked), or CVR(T).

In September 1967, Alvis Limited of Coventry were awarded the initial contract for 17 prototypes of what was eventually labelled FV101 Scorpion. Alvis rolled out the first prototype in January 1969, and by just over one year later all the prototypes had been delivered. Following extensive trials in all variations of terrain and climate, Alvis were awarded the full production contract for over 2,000 vehicles for the British Army—that was in May 1970 and the first full production model was completed in early 1972.

FV101 Scorpion was able to meet its stringent weight limits by the lavish use of welded aluminium armour which resulted in a much lighter hull and turret than the conventional steel. The thickness of the aluminium plates involved also allowed the main construction to be accomplished without the use of internal frames and stringers which enabled the weight to be reduced still further. The early weight restrictions were based on the carrying capacity of the Hawker Siddeley HS681 military transport project but that aircraft was one of the many victims of Government defence spending cuts and was never built. The aircraft now most likely to carry the Scorpion is the C-130 Hercules which can take two vehicles at one loading.

The general layout of Scorpion places the engine forward and the turret at the rear. The power plant is a de-rated version of the famous Jaguar 4.2-litre engine, but even in this form it gives Scorpion a very high power-to-weight ratio with all its subsequent advantages in agility and cross-country performance, which can be said to be limited by what the crew can physically stand. The turret accommodates two of the three crew members—the commander is on the left with the gunner on the right. Forward of the turret, the driver sits on the left. All the crew members are furnished with vision devices, and night vision devices can be added for all positions. The gunner controls not only the 76 mm main gun but also the L43A1 Machine-Gun which doubles as a ranging device and co-axial weapon. Water obstacles present no problems for Scorpion, as it is able to ford about 1 metre without preparation. For deeper obstacles an integral wading screen can be raised by the crew in about five minutes, and the vehicle can then float using the tracks as the propulsion components, but a propeller kit has been developed which raises the water-crossing speed from 6.4 km/h to 9.65 km/h.

FV101 Scorpion is now used by the armoured reconnaissance regiments of 1 (BR) Corps in West Germany. It has also been a considerable export success and has been sold to many nations, but within NATO the most important of these is Belgium, who ordered some 700 examples of the Scorpion family in October 1970. In late 1979 it was reported that the cost of a fully-equipped Scorpion was then about £120,000.

While the Scorpion has emerged as a highly successful and useful reconnaissance vehicle it cannot be said to be capable of fulfilling all the roles required of it—for one thing its 76 mm gun, while useful as a support weapon and capable of defeating light armour, cannot deal with heavy main battle tanks. From this has grown the family of Scorpion variants which are described later.

During 1978 it was announced that the ranging machine-gun used with the Scorpion's 76 mm gun would be replaced by a laser rangefinder. The rangefinder involved is the LV10 produced by

A FV101 Scorpion fully closed-down.

United Scientific Instruments. The new rangefinder will eventually be only one part of a more general improvements package to be applied to all Scorpions and other vehicles in the CVR range. For the Scorpion the main changes will be a new thermal imager sight for the commander, an improved anti-aircraft gun sight, improved external stowage, and powered traverse for the turret (some of these improvements will also apply to the FV107 Scimitar and the FV721 Fox). Other alterations will be made to the suspension and track to increase the track life, and some modifications will be made to the engine exhaust and ventilation systems to reduce the vehicle's 'thermal signature' detectable by infra-red and thermal imaging devices. For the crew, some changes will be made to internal ventilation and various crew stations to make the interior more habitable when the vehicle has to operate closed down over extended periods. Well before the planned completion date the flotation screens will have been removed from the Scorpion range of vehicles as it has now been assumed that their use in Europe will be limited—this will apply only to CVR(T)s used by the armoured divisions, and similar vehicles used by other arms of the service may retain them.

FV102 Striker

Armament 10 × Swingfire missiles, 1 × 7.62 mm L37A1 Machine-Gun and 2 × 4-barrel smoke dischargers; **Crew** 3; **Weight in action** 8,346 kg; **Length overall** 4.826 m; **Height (overall)** 2.21 m; **Height (top of hull)** 1.727 m; **Width overall** 2.242 m; **Track width** 0.432 m; **Ground clearance (approx)** 0.356 m; **Maximum road speed** 80.5 km/h; **Range (roads)** 483 km; **Engine type** Jaguar J60 No. 1 Mark 100B; **Engine power** 190 bhp; **Engine capacity** 4.235 litres; **Fuel capacity** 350 litres; **Ammunition capacity** 10 × Swingfire missiles, 7.62 mm—3,000 rounds; **Main armament elevation** 35°; **Main armament traverse** 53° left, 55° right.

FV102 Striker entered service during 1978 and at present at least one troop of each reconnaissance regiment allotted to each armoured division in 1 (BR) Corps is equipped with this vehicle. Using the same suspension and automotive components as fitted to the FV101 Scorpion, Striker uses a hull similar in shape and outline to that of the FV103 Spartan but at the hull top rear are five racks for Swingfire anti-tank missiles, with capacity for a further five ready for loading inside the hull. The resemblance to Spartan is no accident or manufacturing expedient. Striker is designed to be a tank killer capable of destroying enemy tanks out to a range of 4,000 metres, but like all similar tank killers, it is the prime target not only of enemy tanks but also of missile-armed helicopters and ground attack aircraft. Normally, Striker is deployed with the five missile bins lowered—only when the missiles are due to be launched are the racks raised 35° to the firing position. With the racks lowered Striker is then almost indistinguishable from Spartan, and enemy attention is thus far

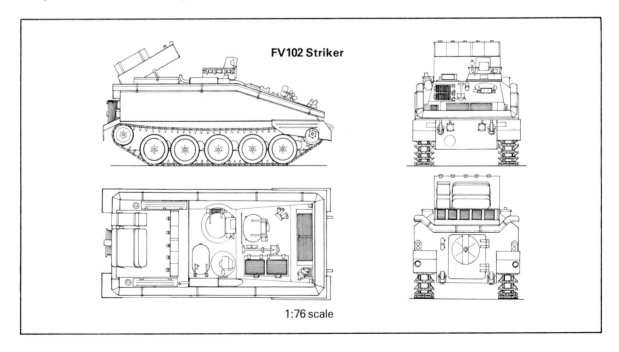

FV102 Striker

1:76 scale

Right *A FV102 Striker in the days before the Royal Artillery transferred Swingfire to the Royal Armoured Corps.*

Below *A FV103 Spartan.*

less likely to be attracted towards it, while other contemporary tank killers betray their role by the prominent missiles strewn over their hulls and turrets.

Striker is not just a Spartan with missile racks. It can be regarded as a weapon system with several unusual features. Like all Swingfire launchers, the firing can be controlled from inside the vehicle or remotely from outside it. Experience has shown that controlling the Swingfire missile in flight is no easy task, especially in a cross-wind, so the vehicle sight has the unusual extra of a flight simulator built

in. Operators can then gain valuable experience in using the sights and the missile controls, both in training and, if necessary, on the battlefield. This simulator is considered to be a valuable aid to combat efficiency and to date, Swingfire is the only known missile system with this facility.

For close-in defence a 7.62 mm GPMG is fitted to the commander's No. 26 cupola, and the usual smoke dischargers are fitted to the hull front. As with all the Scorpion variants, night-driving and night-fighting vision devices can be fitted and the wading screens are optional.

182

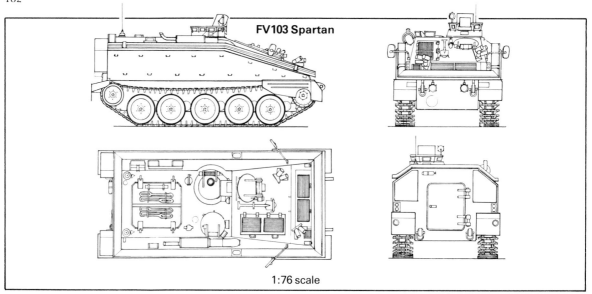

FV103 Spartan

1:76 scale

FV103 Spartan

Armament 1 × 7.62 mm L37A1 Machine-Gun, 2 × 4-barrel smoke dischargers; **Crew** 3 + 4; **Weight in action** 8,172 kg; **Length overall** 4.93 m; **Height** 2.26 m; **Width** 2.242 m; **Track width** 0.432 m; **Ground clearance (approx)** 0.356 m; **Maximum road speed** 80.5 km/h; **Range (roads)** 483 km; **Engine type** Jaguar J60 No. 1 Mark 100B; **Engine power** 190 bhp; **Engine capacity** 4.235 litres; **Fuel capacity** 386 litres; **Ammunition capacity** 7.62 mm—3,000 rounds.

FV103 Spartan is the armoured personnel carrier (APC) component of the Scorpion range, and as such it consists of a box-type aluminium armour body built on to the basic Scorpion hull and suspension. Inside the box is accommodation for the driver, commander and machine-gunner, plus four men with all their equipment. As these 'four men' are rather less than the conventional infantry squad or team, Spartan is used as a special purposes vehicle rather than a normal APC. Possible roles that Spartan will fit are Blowpipe anti-aircraft missile team carrier, assault pioneer team carrier, anti-ambush patrols in rear areas, and as a carrier for the No. 14 (ZB298) battlefield surveillance radar. The first Spartans were issued for service in 1976.

FV104 Samaritan

Armament 2 × 4-barrel smoke dischargers; **Crew** 2 or 3; **Weight in action** 8,664 kg; **Length overall** 5.067 m; **Height (overall)** 2.416 m; **Height (top of hull)** 2.016 m; **Width overall** 2.242 m; **Track width** 0.432 m; **Ground clearance (approx)** 0.356 m; **Maximum road speed** 72.5 km/h; **Range**

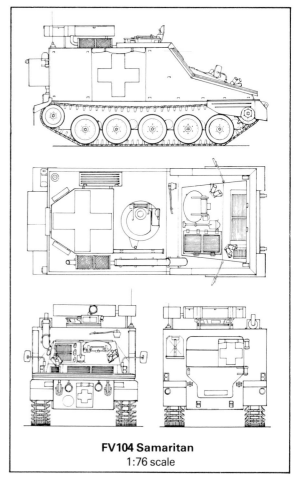

FV104 Samaritan
1:76 scale

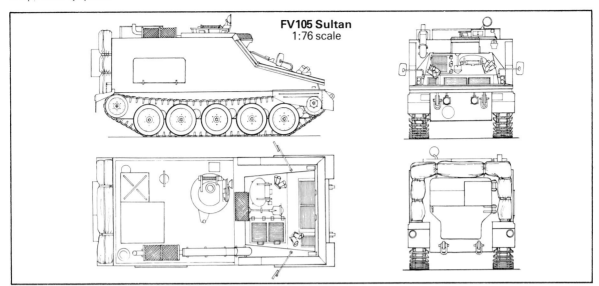

FV105 Sultan
1:76 scale

(roads) 483 km; **Engine type** Jaguar J60 No. 1 Mark 100B; **Engine power** 190 bhp; **Engine capacity** 4.235 litres; **Fuel capacity** 395 litres.

FV104 Samaritan is the armoured ambulance component of the Scorpion range of vehicles, and as such uses the Scorpion automotive components allied to a new armoured box hull. The roof of the Samaritan has been appreciably raised to make more room for the stowage of casualties, together with space for a medical orderly to administer medical care and attentions. The carrying capacity of Samaritan is flexible according to the situation. In peacetime the commander doubles as a medical orderly which gives room for four stretcher cases, or five sitting wounded—a mix of two stretcher cases plus three sitting is possible. In combat conditions it is intended that the crew will be augmented by a medical orderly, leaving the commander to look after the vehicle, but this extra crew member reduces the casualty capacity to only four stretcher cases or four sitting wounded. For a mixed situation two stretcher cases and two sitting can be carried. Other facilities to suit the medical role are improved ventilation and some consideration has been given to reducing internal noise levels. An extra large door is also fitted. The hull shape and configuration is shared by FV105 Sultan.

The first Samaritans entered service in 1978. Being an ambulance, Samaritan carries no defensive armament other than the two multi-barrel smoke dischargers on the hull front. Like most other Scorpion variants wading screens are fitted.

The FV104 Samaritan. Note that screens can be rolled down to obscure the Red Cross markings if necessary.

FV105 Sultan

Armament 1 × 7.62 mm L7A2 Machine-Gun, 2 × 4-barrel smoke dischargers; **Crew** 5 or 6; **Weight in action** 8,664 kg; **Length overall** 4.8 m; **Height overall** 2.559 m; **Height (top of hull)** 2.026 m; **Width (overall)** 2.242 m; **Width (over tracks)** 2.134 m; **Track width** 0.432 m; **Ground clearance (approx)** 0.356 m; **Penthouse length** 2.591 m; **Penthouse height** 2.235 m; **Penthouse width** 2.134 m; **Maximum road speed** 72.5 km/h; **Range (roads)** 483 km; **Engine type** Jaguar J60 No. 1 Mark 100B; **Engine power** 190 bhp; **Engine capacity** 4.235 litres; **Fuel capacity** 395 litres; **Ammunition capacity** 7.62 mm—2,000 rounds.

FV105 Sultan is the armoured command vehicle component of the Scorpion family, and as such uses a raised box hull to contain the radios, control equipment and mapboards, to say nothing of the extra men, that will be needed in this role. Command vehicles are subject to much coming and going and although the interior of the Sultan can accommodate its crew of five or six men, it cannot accommodate everyone who will require access to the information and communication equipment installed, so a collapsible 'penthouse' is fitted over the rear, ready for use as and when required. The exact 'fit' of the Sultan can be altered to suit the needs of any particular unit or type of unit, but mapboards, plastic screens and radios are standard, as is extra lighting. As with FV104 Samaritan, extra air conditioning is fitted in the roof (the hull shapes are the same), and the sloping front hull mounts a radio aerial which, like its supporting joists, is collapsible. The roof hatch is fitted with a pintle for an L7A2 GPMG which can be dismounted for local defence.

FV106 Samson

Armament 1 × 7.62 mm L7A2 Machine-Gun, 2 × 4-barrel smoke dischargers; **Crew** 3; **Weight in action** 8,738 kg; **Length overall** 5.004 m; **Length of vehicle** 4.788 m; **Height overall** 2.254 m; **Height (top of hull)** 1.718 m; **Width overall** 2.43 m; **Track width** 0.432 m; **Ground clearance (approx)** 0.356 m; **Maximum road speed** 72.5 km/h; **Range (roads)** 483 km; **Engine type** Jaguar J60 No. 1 Mark 100B; **Engine power** 190 bhp; **Engine capacity** 4.235 litres; **Fuel capacity** 404.5 litres; **Ammunition capacity** 7.62 mm—2,000 rounds.

Entering production during 1979, FV106 Sultan was the last of the Scorpion family to be produced. It is an armoured recovery vehicle using the basic box structure of the FV103 Spartan carrier, but many interior design changes have been made. For its main recovery role, Samson is fitted with an internally-mounted winch driven from the main engine. The winch can be driven at variable speeds up to a maximum of 122 metres a minute and the drum is fitted with 229 metres of wire rope. Using a standard 4:1 snatch block the winch can pull a load of up to 12 tons and is thus capable of pulling a load greater than the weight of the Samson itself. To

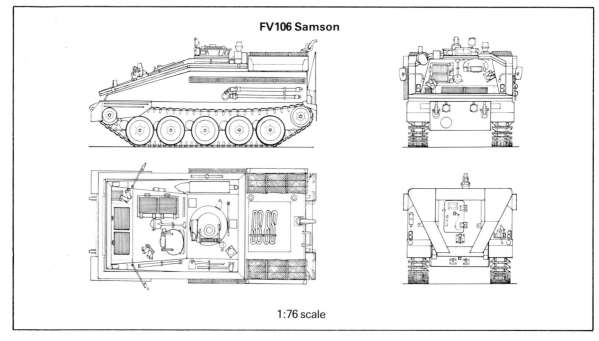

FV106 Samson

1:76 scale

assist the pulling of such heavy loads, Samson is fitted with a large and heavy pair of spades hinged on the rear bulkhead—in use these are swung downwards and the vehicle is reversed so that the spades dig into the ground and lift the vehicle rear upwards. In this manner the winch can pull heavy loads without moving the Samson itself, and vehicles the size of the FV432 can be pulled without too much difficulty. Other fitments that can assist in the recovery role are a small jib crane, also driven from the main engine, and a bench vice, along with other specialised equipment. Racks on the sides hold baulks of timber for a hundred-and-one purposes, and extra hand tools. The rear door is rather small and the interior rather cramped as the winch takes up most of the available space. A GPMG is fitted to the commander's hatch pintle, but this can easily be dismounted for local defence.

FV107 Scimitar

Armament 1 × 30 mm Rarden L21 Gun, 1 × 7.62 mm L37A1 Machine-Gun and 2 × 4-barrel smoke dischargers; **Crew** 3; **Weight in action** 7,750 kg; **Length overall** 4.985 m; **Length of hull** 4.572 m; **Height** 2.096 m; **Width (overall)** 2.242 m; **Width (over tracks)** 2.134 m; **Track width** 0.432 m; **Ground clearance (approx)** 0.356 m; **Maximum road speed** 80.5 km/h; **Range (roads)** 644 km; **Engine type** Jaguar J60 No. 1 Mark 100B; **Engine power** 190 bhp; **Engine capacity** 4.235 litres; **Fuel capacity** 423 litres; **Ammunition capacity** 30 mm—165 rounds, 7.62 mm—3,000 rounds; **Main armament elevation** −10° to +35°; **Main armament traverse** 360°.

Despite having the highest FV number in the Scorpion family, Scimitar was actually the second variant to go into production and service (the last was delivered during late 1978). Scimitar is basically the same vehicle as the FV101 but the turret does differ in some ways from that of the Scorpion, and is armed with a 30 mm Rarden gun. Otherwise the two vehicles differ but little, but tactically their roles are not interchangeable, or at least, not in BAOR. In the armoured reconnaissance regiments of 1 (BR) Corps, each regiment has one squadron equipped with Scimitar for the close reconnaissance role. As such it is assigned in independent troops at task force level. In a UK-based armoured reconnaissance regiment the medium reconnaissance troops use both Scimitar and Scorpion. In the 1 (BR) Corps organisation Scimitar

Top right *A FV105 Sultan.* **Above right** *FV106 Samson showing stowage towards rear.* **Right** *FV107 Scimitar showing the long barrel of the 30 mm Rarden.*

may be used in direct support of infantry combat teams or battle groups. Many of the mid-life changes planned for the FV101 Scorpion will also be applied to the Scimitar. Already many Scimitars used by the Royal Armoured Corps have had their wading screens removed.

FV721 Fox

Armament 1 × 30 mm Rarden L21 Gun, 1 × 7.62 mm L8A1 Machine-Gun and 2 × 4-barrel smoke dischargers; **Crew** 3; **Weight in action** 6,386 kg; **Length (gun forward)** 5.359 m; **Length of hull** 4.166 m; **Height** 2.2 m; **Width** 2.134 m; **Wheel track** 1.753 m; **Ground clearance** 0.3 m; **Maximum road speed** 104 km/h; **Range (roads)** 430 km; **Engine type** Jaguar J60 No. 1 Mark 100B; **Engine power** 195 bhp; **Engine capacity** 4.235 litres; **Fuel capacity** 145.47 litres; **Ammunition capacity** 30 mm—99 rounds, 7.62 mm—

2,600 rounds; **Main armament elevation** –14° to + 40°; **Main armament traverse** 360°.

During the early 1960s it was decided to produce a replacement for the Ferret reconnaissance vehicles and early studies and designs were evaluated at what is now the Military Vehicle Experimental Establishment at Chobham in Surrey. In 1965 the project, which was then known as the Combat Vehicle Reconnaissance (Wheeled), or CVR(W), emerged as a gradual development of the existing Ferret design incorporating such new technology as aluminium armour and a turret mounting the Rarden 30 mm gun. Prototype production was handled by Daimler at Radford, Coventry, who went on to complete a total of 15 prototypes, starting in 1966 with the first example being ready in late 1967. However, the main contract went to the Royal Ordnance Factory at Leeds, which completed its first production version during 1973.

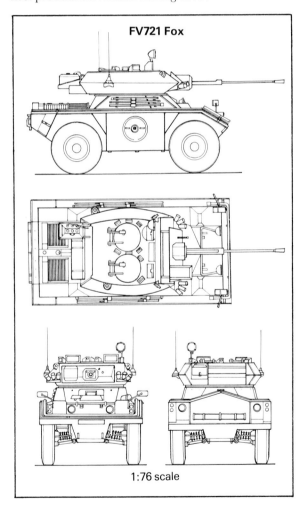

FV107 Scimitar

FV721 Fox

1:76 scale

1:76 scale

FV721 Fox is basically an updated version of the Ferret but every aspect of the former has been reworked and redesigned from scratch. The turret, produced by Alvis Limited, is the same as that used by the FV107 Scimitar but the internal stowage has been somewhat altered—for example the ammunition capacity is 66 rounds less. The Jaguar engine gives the Fox a lively performance, and its cross-country capabilities are such that it is likely to cross any type of terrain. Three Foxes can be carried in a single C-130 Hercules and two can be para-dropped together on a special platform. Early production models were fitted with wading screens for crossing deep water obstacles but these have now been removed and late production models have no provision for them.

During the early service career of the Fox some serious accidents occurred which caused some doubts to be expressed as to its stability, mainly in view of the seeming 'top-heaviness' of the design. Trials showed that the Fox was likely, in certain conditions to 'over-steer' and the driver's instinctive reactions only made the situation worse. A corrective course of training removed the likelihood of the 'over-steer' condition happening.

The early plans to replace the Ferret as a general reconnaissance vehicle have now been virtually completed (despite the fact that the Ferret continues its distinguished service career). At the time of writing there are three armoured reconnaissance regiments equipped with the Fox, one regular and two TA. The UK-based armoured reconnaissance regiment close reconnaissance troops are equipped with the Fox, while in the TA regiments, all the recce squadrons are so equipped. (The TA regimenments involved are the Royal Yeomanry and the Queens Own Yeomanry.)

One off-shoot of the FV721 Fox was the FV722 Vixen, which was a simplified Fox fitted with a small turret mounting a GPMG. The intention was to provide a liaison vehicle suitable for Infantry and Engineer units, but it was a victim of one of the many Defence spending cuts and only prototypes were made. But the idea of a cheaper version of the Fox is not yet dead (although it is unlikely to enter British Army service), as Peak Engineering have produced a GPMG turret suitable for installation on a production Fox.

Top right *FV721 Fox still fitted with wading screens and with the flag flying from the turret denoting that the main armament is loaded.* **Above right** *A standard FV721 Fox at speed, clearly showing the general layout.* **Right** *A Fox belonging to the 3rd Battalion, Royal Regiment of Fusiliers, on border patrol near Staaken, Berlin* (Army PR, Berlin).

FV432

Basic versions

Armament 1 × 7.62 mm L7A2 Machine-Gun, 2 × 3-barrel smoke dischargers; **Crew** 2 + 10; **Weight in action** 15,280 kg; **Length overall** 5.251 m; **Length of hull** 4.826 m; **Height overall** 2.286 m; **Height (to roof)** 1.879 m; **Width (overall)** 2.8 m; **Width (over tracks)** 2.527 m; **Track width** 0.343 m; **Ground clearance** 0.406 m; **Maximum road speed** 52 km/h; **Range (roads)** 580 km; **Engine type** Rolls-Royce K60 No. 4 Mark 4F; **Engine power** 240 bhp; **Engine capacity** 6.57 litres; **Fuel capacity** 454 litres; **Ammunition capacity** 1,600 rounds plus.

The FV432 is by far the most numerous of all the tracked vehicles used by the British Army, and exists in a wide variety of versions with an even greater variety of differing equipment installations. The FV432 is used by almost every branch of the British Army, and as every branch requires the vehicle to carry out a different role, this section of the book will deal with the FV432 as a basic vehicle, while I will deal separately with how it is used by the Infantry, the Royal Artillery and the Royal Engineers. Also included in this section will be those versions used by all branches of the Service.

The FV432 development cycle can be traced back to before 1939 when the Bren Gun and Universal Carriers were in widespread Army use. From these there gradually evolved a post-war family of carriers

Above left *FV432 in its muddy element.* **Left** *FV432s on the Suffield Ranges.* **Below left** *FV432 with GPMG mounted on the commander's hatch.* **Below** *FV432 ambulance.*

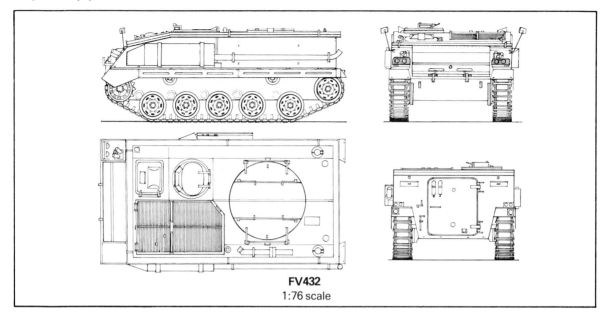

FV432
1:76 scale

known as the FV400 series which were further developed into the FV420 series. There were six different vehicles in the FV420 series with each one intended for a different role and, from these, after trials with several prototypes, evolved the FV430 series. The first of the FV430s was the FV431 Load Carrier, but only a prototype was built. However, it did provide the basis for the rest of the FV432 series, production of which began in 1962. The concern that built the FV432 was GKN Sankey of Wellington, Shropshire, which kept the range in production until 1971. There have been four basic types of FV432 starting with the Mark 1 which had a prominent exhaust system on the left-hand side of the vehicle. Then came the Mark 1/1, the Mark 2 and the Mark 2/2. The later versions all had their exhausts re-routed to over the roof, and the last versions can be recognised by the almost-flush NBC filter box on the right-hand side plate.

Construction of the FV432 follows that of a steel-plate box mounted on tracks with the engine at the front. The main access door is at the rear while the commander and driver both have their own hatches. Over the main compartment is a four-piece circular hatch, while the engine compartment has access via a front plate and through a roof hatch next to the driver who sits on the right-hand side. This simple structure provides the basis for a wide number of variants, and some of them, the FV433 105 mm Self-Propelled Gun, the FV434 Maintenance Carrier, the FV438 Swingfire and the FV439 Signals Vehicle, warrant their own separate entries. With the exception of the last-mentioned

vehicles, all the FV432 vehicles can be switched from one role or equipment fit to another.

Armoured Personnel Carrier: The APC role is the primary reason for the FV432's existence and as such it carries a crew of two and up to ten fully armed soldiers. The soldiers are carried in two rows of five along each side wall and face inwards. They have no external vision devices when the vehicle is closed down (only the driver and commander have these) and no way of using their own personal weapons unless a hatch is opened. The only weapon that is usually in use when closed down is the dismountable L7A2 GPMG by the commander's hatch, and to fire this the commander has to expose his head and shoulders to possible enemy fire. The inability of the soldiers to fire from the FV432, or even see anything from inside, is one of the FV432's most serious faults, as more modern APCs usually provide each soldier with a firing point and some form of vision device. From personal experience after a period of time spent travelling in a closed-down FV432, when the time comes to 'de-bus' and go into action, the most common reaction is one of serious disorientation while local conditions, directions and features are taken into account.

The FV432 is fitted with integral wading screens and has all the usual NBC air-cleaning equipment. Armour thicknesses vary from 6 to 12 mm over the vehicle. Any mark of FV432 is likely to be encountered in the basic APC role, but the very early Mark 1s with Rolls-Royce B-81 Mark 8F petrol engines are now used only at the Suffield Training Ground in Canada where they are gradually being worn out by repeated training exercises under all conditions of climate.

Command vehicle: The FV432 can be easily converted into a command vehicle by the fitting of a kit which includes sliding map boards, folding tables, fluorescent lamps and extra radios. However, many units have their own particular requirements and this 'fit' will vary accordingly. One feature on the command FV432s is a canvas 'penthouse' which extends from over the rear door. The dimensions of this are 3.66 × 2.74 × 1.98 metres. The usual weight in action of the command FV432 is about 15,500 kg, and the number of men carried is seven. A useful recognition feature of a command FV432 on the move is the stowage of the penthouse joists on the side.

Ambulance: Any FV432 can be easily converted to the ambulance role, and racks for four stretchers can be fitted, two to each side. If two stretchers are not fitted, up to five sitting casualties can be carried. When in the ambulance role, no armament other than the smoke dischargers is retained.

Cargo carrier: When the basic FV432 has its ten seats folded upwards, or removed altogether, the interior can accommodate a wide variety of different bulk cargos such as ammunition or fuel. Up to 3,670 kg can be carried.

Recovery vehicle: For the recovery role the FV432 can be fitted with an internal winch driven from the main engine, with a cable directed through the main rear door. The winch is a Plumett auto-capstan Type CA45 and uses a double capstan with a direct pull of 6,608 kg. If a three-part tackle is used, up to 18,300 kg can be moved. The winch alone weighs 470 kg and is fitted with 250 metres of heavy cable. An extra external spade is fitted to the rear bulkhead for the recovery role. Another special part for the role is a shortened rear door, the space being taken up by a pulley which directs the cable.

FV 432 with Wavell: During the late 1980s a number of FV432s will be converted to take the Wavell equipment needed to accommodate the front-line task force Wavell terminals and other associated equipment. In this version, power generators and air conditioning equipment will be fitted on the roof with the interior housing the two-man Wavell operators and racks holding the various 'black boxes'.

Above *Command FV432 with extra radio aerials erected.* **Below** *FV432 with GPMG turret.*

Infantry versions

81 mm Mortar: Each mechanised infantry battalion has on its support company strength a total of six FV432s fitted with the 81 mm Mortar L16A1 firing through the circular main roof hatch. The 81 mm Mortar can be fitted into any FV432 by the installation of a special turntable mounting which provides a full 360° traverse. Internal racks are fitted for the ammunition, and up to 160 bombs can be carried. When on the FV432 mounting only the barrel and the sighting unit are fitted—the baseplate and the bipod have been seen stowed both internally and externally, ready for possible dismounted use. In the mortar role, the normal FV432 crew complement is increased to six, and the weight in action is about 16,400 kg.

84 mm Infantry Gun: In order to fire the 84 mm Carl Gustav from the FV432 a special bar rest can be fitted across the main roof hatch.

7.62 mm GPMG turret: In order to give the FV432 commander some degree of protection when firing the 7.62 mm GPMG from his hatch, some FV432s have been fitted with a small GPMG turret in a new location over a permanently closed circular main roof hatch. The new turret, made by Peak Engineering Limited of Stratford-on-Avon, mounts a L37A1 Machine-Gun and has an extra four smoke dischargers on each side. When closed down the machine-gun is aimed by a periscopic sight. As well as having a full 360° traverse, the gun can be elevated to about 50° giving it a limited anti-aircraft or anti-helicopter capability. All traverse and elevation controls are by hand, and the gunner sits on a small seat fitted to the turret ring.

30 mm Rarden turret: Although this project has now been terminated, some conversions were made

to allow the FV432 to accommodate an FV721 Fox turret complete with the 30 mm L21 gun. A small batch of 13 conversions was carried out and demonstrated, these being used for troop trials in Germany until the project was ended during mid-1976. The converted FV432s were then issued to the Berlin Garrison where they remain.

The turret was placed over the circular roof hatch but, although the Rarden would undoubtedly give the FV432 a useful offensive and fire-support potential, the vehicle is no doubt top-heavy and unwieldy. Space inside the main compartment is also rather cramped. As the FV107 Scimitar was also being produced for the same role, the Rarden FV432 was no doubt thought to be too much of an expensive luxury with no precise operational task.

Radar GS No. 14 Mark 1: Battlefield surveillance is an Infantry responsibility and to enable it to carry out this task at night or in poor visibility, some FV432s have been fitted with the Radar GS No. 14 Mark 1 (the ZB 298). As mentioned in the section on this radar, the No. 14 detects movement and has a range of 10,000 metres. When in use in an FV432, the No. 14 can be recognised by its distinctive 'suitcase' aerial, usually mounted on the roof towards the rear.

Milan: Each mechanised infantry battalion is issued with the Milan anti-tank missile launcher and the corresponding missiles in their pre-packed tubes. The launcher and the missiles are carried inside an FV 432 stowed on special racks, but it is not intended that the missile be fired from the roof of the vehicle itself, although there is no reason why this should not be done if the tactical circumstances dictate such a

Top left *Cymbeline-equipped FV432 of the Royal Artillery.* **Below** *FV432 used by a REME workshop and fitted with extra stowage, attached to a Royal Engineer Field Squadron.*

method. Normally the Milan will be fired from a dismounted position.

Beach version: For some years the Army used a 'one-off' beach version of the FV432 for general use in beach training operations at a location in Devon. The FV432 had special waterproofing and exhaust re-location and was often used to tow boat-launching trailers. Its present status is not known.

Royal Artillery versions

Royal Artillery FV432s use the L4A4 Bren Gun as their main armament.

FACE: Every Royal Artillery battery has at least one, and sometimes two, FV432s equipped with a FACE fire control computer. Looking from the rear, the main computer is on the left-hand side—down the right-hand side are racks to take the books, tables and other paperwork associated with the computer. Also on the left is a teleprinter/typewriter used with the system. Extra racking is carried on the roof for the crew's bedding and belongings, and some are also fitted with the command 'penthouse'. The FACE FV432s cannot be easily converted to any other role.

Cymbeline: 105 mm field regiments of the Royal Artillery have a mortar-locating role and up to about 1976 the main radar used in this role was Green Archer. Some of these radars were fitted to a special FV432 variant, the FV436, but these have now passed from service as the current mortar-locating radar is Cymbeline. This equipment is carried in self-propelled mortar-locating batteries on converted FV432s where the folding radar aerial is mounted on the vehicle roof. On the move the aerial is folded and contained in a wire mesh cage for protection; when in action it is erected and rotates on a mounting fitted to the main circular roof hatch. The radar controls and displays are housed in the main compartment.

Sonic detection: Some artillery FV432s have been equipped as sonic detection vehicles and as such have all the appropriate aerials and detectors necessary for the role. The crew of this version is eight and the interior is equipped not only with sound recorders but also with map boards and extra radios. The sonic equipment concerned is the Sound Ranging Radio Link No. 2 Mark 1 which uses a line of up to seven carefully sited microphones transmitting, via radio, to the main equipment in the FV432. A forward observer switches on the microphones when necessary—at the same time he alerts the receiving and recording equipment. The resultant paper trace can be used to calculate the enemy position.

Royal Engineer versions

Royal Engineer FV432s also use the L4A4 Bren

Gun as their main armament.

Bar Mine Layer: The FV432 is used by the Royal Engineers as their usual towing vehicle for the Bar Mine Layer system. The Bar Mine Layer is towed behind the FV432 with the mine conveyor protruding into the main compartment. The Bar Mines can thus be loaded and sown with the FV432 crew being almost completely protected.

Ranger: The Ranger anti-personnel mine layer system can be fitted over the main roof hatch of the FV432. The Ranger launcher has a traverse to the rear of 180° and can be elevated from +5° to +35°. When fitted, the launcher weighs 630 kg fully loaded. One possible configuration for Engineer FV432s is to have the Bar Mine Layer towed from the rear with a Ranger launcher fitted to the roof. The combination is then able to render

Above left REME FV432 with awning over rear hatch. **Left** *One of the few FV432s fitted with a 30 mm Rarden turret.* **Below left** *A FACE FV432—note the extra stowage bins on the roof.* **Right** *Royal Artillery FV432 fitted for the sonic detection role.* **Below** *Royal Engineer FV432 fitted with an empty Ranger projector.*

whole tracts of country impassable to men or machines without time-consuming clearance measures.

Giant Viper: The Giant Viper mine-clearing system (L3A1) can be carried on a trailer behind a FV432.

MCV-80 Warrior

Armament see text; **Crew** 2 + 8; **Weight in action** 20,000 kg; **Weight in action (FV510)** 23,800 kg; **Length** 6.34 m; **Height (top of FV510 turret)** 2.74 m; **Width** 3.03 m; **Ground clearance** 0.5 m; **Maximum road speed** 75 km/h; **Range (road)** 500 km; **Engine type** Rolls-Royce 8V800 diesel; **Engine power** 800 hp.

During the early 1970s GKN Sankey were awarded a contract to develop a new armoured personnel carrier for the Army, a vehicle that eventually became known as the MCV-80 (Mechanised Combat Vehicle 80). As ever, defence budget restraints prompted the Ministry of Defence to consider alternatives for the Army's future APC and at one time considerable attention was given to

the American M2 and M3 Infantry Fighting Vehicles as possible future equipments. As it turned out, the decision went in favour of the UK-built MCV-80 and development is now proceeding apace to provide the next generation of APCs for the British Army, now called Warrior.

To date, only prototype development vehicles of Warrior have been produced and one of them, the FV510, is fitted with a two-man turret housing a 30 mm Rarden L21 gun and a co-axially mounted Hughes 7.62 mm Chain Gun. This latter weapon is a new one for the British Army and its operation relies on an externally powered electrical motor which drives all the machine-gun operations via a metal link chain—hence the name Chain Gun. The FV510 is intended to be a general squad vehicle with a crew of two and carrying eight fully armed troops who leave via two doors at the rear of the vehicle. There is no provision for the troops to use their weapons from inside.

The Warrior uses a torsion bar suspension, but there does not appear to be any provision for wading or amphibious equipment. A full NBC pack

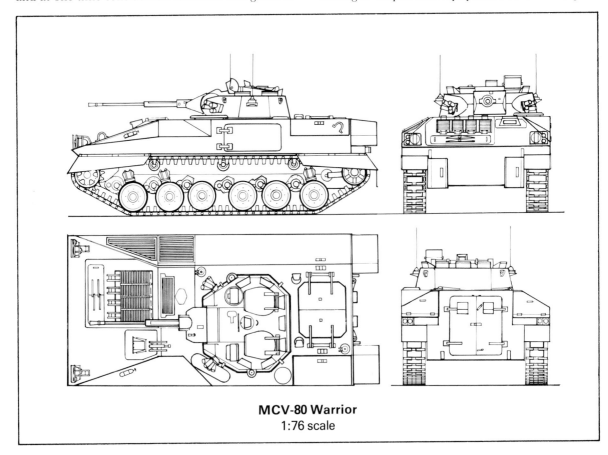

MCV-80 Warrior
1:76 scale

MCV-80 used for troop trials by the Irish Guards. This vehicle is fitted with VIRSS smoke projectors.

is provided and there will be a full range of night driving and other vision equipment provided.

As with the FV432 series, it is expected that Warrior will be developed into a range of specialised vehicles. The following are known to be under development for the British Army: **1** A platoon and command vehicle with a small turret mounting a GPMG; **2** A mechanised recovery vehicle with a dozer blade at the front, a winch and a cupola-mounted GPMG; **3** An 81 mm Mortar carrier firing through a roof hatch, and with a cupola-mounted GPMG; **4** An engineer combat vehicle mounting a Ranger mine launcher on the rear upper decking and with a cupola-mounted GPMG; **5** An artillery command vehicle; and **6** A combat repair vehicle with a roof-mounted hydraulic crane with an extending jib, and a cupola-mounted GPMG. Other developments, including forms of missile-launchers are anticipated.

In the short term, Warrior will only supplement the FV432 and it may be a long time before it will replace it. As it stands Warrior is a hefty and expensive-looking piece of equipment with seemingly few development or design advantages over the venerable box on tracks that it is intended to replace. But the FV 510 will provide the infantry with much-needed fire support under their own control, and it is to be hoped that Warrior will enter service as soon as possible.

FV433 Field Artillery, Self-Propelled (Abbot)

Armament 1 × 105 mm L13A1 Gun, 1 × 7.62 mm L4A4 Machine-Gun and 2 × 3-barrel smoke dischargers; **Crew** 4; **Weight in action** 16,556 kg; **Length overall** 5.84 m; **Length of hull** 5.709 m; **Height (top of cupola)** 2.489 m; **Width** 2.641 m; **Track width** 0.343 m; **Ground clearance** 0.406 m; **Maximum road speed** 48 km/h; **Range (roads)** 390 km; **Engine type** Rolls-Royce K.60 Mark 4G; **Engine power** 240 bhp; **Engine capacity** 6.57 litres; **Fuel capacity** 386 litres; **Ammunition capacity** 105 mm—40 rounds, 7.62 mm—1,200 rounds; **Main armament elevation** –5° to +70°; **Main armament traverse** 360°.

The FV433 Abbot is the field artillery component of the FV432 family of vehicles and the first prototype was completed in 1961. The first battery was issued with production Abbots in 1965 and ever since then the vehicle has been the principal self-propelled weapon of Royal Artillery field regiments both in Germany and the United Kingdom. Each regiment has four batteries of Abbots and each battery has two troops of three guns each, although in some battle groups this might vary.

The main production line for the Abbot was at the Vickers-Armstrong works at Elswick, Newcastle-upon-Tyne. Only the suspension components and the main engine are related at all closely to the FV432 for the Abbot differs in many

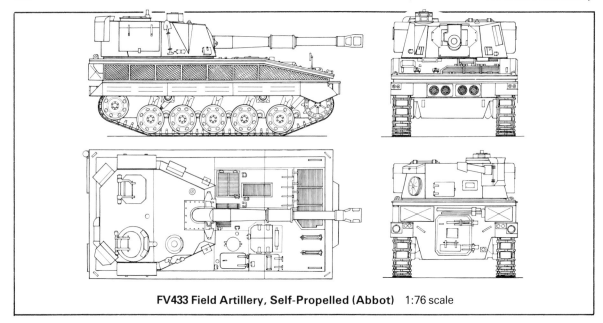

FV433 Field Artillery, Self-Propelled (Abbot)   1:76 scale

Above A factory shot of an FV433 Abbot (Vickers Ltd).
Below left *Camouflaged FV433 Abbots on exercise in Germany* (MoD). **Below right** *FV434 with a tilt for an awning over its rear.*

ways from the rest of that family. The most obvious difference is the large and roomy turret at the rear which mounts the 105 mm L13A1 gun. The turret also provides the main stowage space for the 40 rounds of ammunition carried, six of which have HESH warheads for the possible engagement of enemy AFVs. (For convenience the number of rounds carried under normal circumstances is restricted to 38.) For ease of loading the gun is fitted with a power rammer, and power is also available for traversing the gun—elevation is by hand. The layer sits to the right of the gun.

As with all the rest of the FV432 family, wading screens are fitted as standard, and the full NBC air-cleaning gear is a normal fitment. In action the turret can be rotated for a full 360° and the hull need not be moved for any rapid change in traverse.

For export, Vickers-Armstrong developed a simplified version of the vehicle known as the Value-Engineered Abbot. In order to keep down costs of this version several features of the FV433 Abbot were left off, such as the wading gear, power ramming and traverse, the full NBC pack, and so on. The engine was de-rated to 213 bhp (and runs on diesel fuel only) and anything that could be omitted, was omitted. The bulk of the Value-Engineered Abbots went to the Indian Army but the British Army obtained four for use at the Suffield Training Ground in Canada.

Operational experience in the various Middle East conflicts has shown that the smallest artillery calibre capable of breaking up massed armoured

formations is now 155 mm. Thus the 105 mm Abbot is obsolescent in its main field artillery role and the Abbot batteries are now mainly used as close support systems for battle groups. However, the Abbot will still remain as one of the most important items in the Royal Artillery gun park for many years to come and there are at present no immediate plans for its replacement unless it is to be by a substantially increased 'buy' of 155 mm equipment.

FV434 Carrier, Maintenance, Full Tracked

Armament 1 × 7.62 mm L4A4 Machine-Gun or 1 × 7.62 mm L7A2 Machine-Gun and 2 × 3-barrel smoke dischargers; **Crew** 4; **Weight in action** 17,750 kg; **Length overall** 5.72 m; **Height (top of crane)** 2.794 kg; **Height (roof)** 1.891 m; **Width (overall)** 2.844 m; **Width (over tracks)** 2.527 m; **Track width** 0.343 m; **Ground clearance** 0.419 m; **Maximum road speed** 47 km/h; **Range (roads)** 580 km; **Engine type** Rolls-Royce K60 No. 4 Mark 4F; **Engine power** 240 bhp; **Engine capacity** 6.57 litres; **Fuel capacity** 454 litres; **Ammunition capacity** 7.62 mm—336 rounds (12 magazines) for L4A4, 1,000 rounds for L7A2.

The FV434 is a specialised version of the FV432 developed for use by the REME in the field. It is an open-backed vehicle fitted with a crane capable of lifting such items as AFV engine packs, gun barrels and similar parts in need of care and attention. Early FV434 prototypes were simply FV432s with a crane on the roof but in time the specialised FV434 emerged with several features unique to it apart from the crane. One such feature is the ability to lock the torsion bars on the front and rear axles to give stability when using the crane. Other features

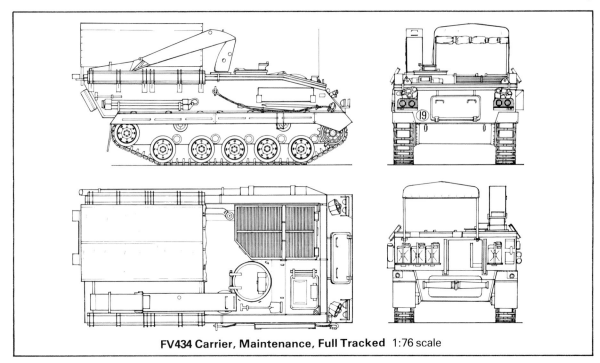

FV434 Carrier, Maintenance, Full Tracked 1:76 scale

are the tool bench, vice and tool kit for field repairs. The open rear can carry such large parts as a Chieftain engine pack, and the FV434 has a total carrying ability of 2,703 kg.

The most noticeable part of the FV434 is the hydraulic HIAB crane which has a two-piece jib.

FV438s at Sennelager, 7.7.77.

Mounted on the right-hand side and about half-way along, it is capable of lifting all manner of loads but its performance is affected by the radius at which the load is situated. For instance, at a radius of 2.25 metres it can lift 3,050 kg, but at about 4 metres the lift is limited to 1,250 kg.

The usual crew of the FV434 is four, the commander, driver/crane operator, and two fitters. While the FV434 rear is usually left open, it can be fitted with a canvas tilt for some measure of protection against the elements. The usual wading screens are fitted. If it is provided, the machine-gun is mounted on a pintle near the commander's hatch.

FV438 Swingfire launcher
Armament 14 × Swingfire missiles, 1 × 7.62 mm L4A4 Machine-Gun *or* 1 × 7.62 mm L7A2 Machine-Gun and 2 × 3-barrel smoke dischargers; **Crew** 3; **Weight in action** 16,200 kg; **Length overall** 5.105 m; **Height overall** 2.705 m; **Width (overall)** 2.972 m; **Width (over tracks)** 2.527 m; **Track width** 0.343 m; **Ground clearance** 0.406 m; **Maximum road speed** 52 km/h; **Range (roads)** 480 km; **Engine type** Rolls-Royce K60 No. 4 Mark 4F; **Engine power** 240 bhp; **Engine capacity** 6.57 litres; **Fuel capacity** 454 litres; **Ammunition capacity** 14 Swingfire missiles, 7.62 mm—1,200 rounds; **Main armament elevation** –20° to + 20°; **Main armament traverse** 90° (45° either side).

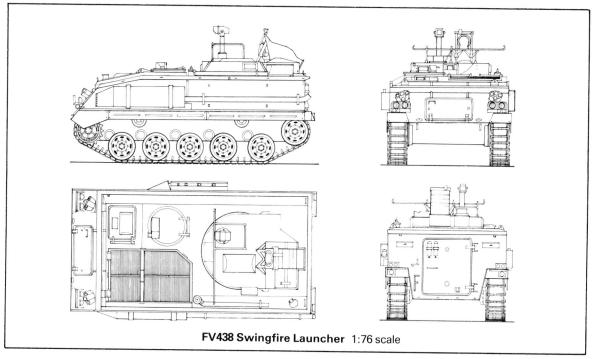

FV438 Swingfire Launcher 1:76 scale

The FV438 is a straightforward conversion of the basic FV432 to accommodate the Swingfire ATGW system, and although the appearance of the FV438 is distinctive from that of the FV432, there are few major differences between them. The main recognition point of the FV438 is its large rear-mounted cupola, the missile bins just behind it (to the left), and the periscopic sight.

In action, the missile bins are raised and the commander/layer selects his target using the periscopic sight. If a purely defensive position has been selected, the sight can be taken up to 50 metres away from the vehicle—which enables it to be concealed behind cover and the missiles fired without the launcher being exposed. Once fired, the missile bins can be reloaded from within the vehicle.

FV439 Signals vehicle
The Royal Signals use several versions of the FV432 series, the main one of which is a command type equipped with extra radios. A special version used only by the Royal Signals is the FV439 which acts as a mobile radio relay station. It is equipped internally with the necessary signals equipment, but externally the main differences from other FV432s is the large aerial mast which is carried partially dismantled ready for erection at the chosen station site. Extra stowage bins are provided on the roof and cable reels are also carried. For defensive pur-

poses there is provision for an L4A4 machine-gun on the commander's hatch.

Saxon
Armament 1 × 7.62 mm L7A2 machine-gun or Chain Gun; **Crew** 2 + 8; **Weight in action** 10,670

A Royal Signals FV439 on an exercise (MoD).

A Saxon APC complete with a DISA GPMG mount over the commander's cupola.

kg; **Length** 5.169 m; **Height** 2.628 m; **Width** 2.489 m; **Wheel track front/rear** 2.08 m/1.99 m; **Maximum road speed** 96 km/h; **Range (roads)** 510 km; **Engine type** Bedford 500 diesel; **Engine power** 164 bhp at 2,800 rpm; **Fuel capacity** 160 litres.

The vehicle now known to the Army as the Saxon was initially known as the GKN AT 105 and was developed as a wheeled armoured personnel carrier version of the AT 104, an internal security vehicle. The AT 105 was intended to be a useful all-round counter-insurgency vehicle which could be produced and used at relatively low cost with the first production vehicles being produced for export during 1976. In 1983 the Ministry of Defence placed an order with GKN Sankey for an initial batch of 50 Saxons and in January 1984 another order was placed, this time for a further 450.

The Saxon has been procured for the Army to provide the regular BAOR reinforcement units based in the United Kingdom with a means of travelling to West Germany in an emergency and providing them with armoured protection once they get there. Thus the main users of Saxon will be 19 Infantry Brigade who are headquartered at Colchester and form part of 3 Armoured Division in West Germany in time of war. The wheeled Saxons can travel long distances on roads at far higher speeds than any tracked vehicle and there is no attendant problem of track wear.

The Saxon is a fairly straightforward armoured personnel carrier with a 4 × 4 drive configuration and a fully armoured hull. Many of the components are based on readily available Bedford MK parts. The driver sits on the right-hand side next to the engine and behind and over him is the commander's position. The commander has a fixed cupola with vision devices on all four sides and provision for mounting a L7A2 GPMG on a DISA mounting that can be used in the anti-aircraft role. It is possible that a Hughes EX-34 Chain Gun will be fitted to late production models. Seating for an infantry section of eight men is provided at the rear and there are doors at the rear; there is a side door on the right-hand side. Stowage boxes are provided around the hull exterior and there is provision for more kit or equipment stowage on the roof.

Apart from the basic armoured personnel carrier, the Saxon is produced in recovery vehicle and command post versions. The recovery vehicle is equipped with a side-mounted 5,000 kg winch and the command post is equipped with map boards and all the other paraphernalia required for the role. A four-stretcher ambulance is another version.

At one time there was talk of extending the Saxon production run to provide vehicles for TA and other units, but it now seems that the costs involved will be too high for the defence budget to bear.

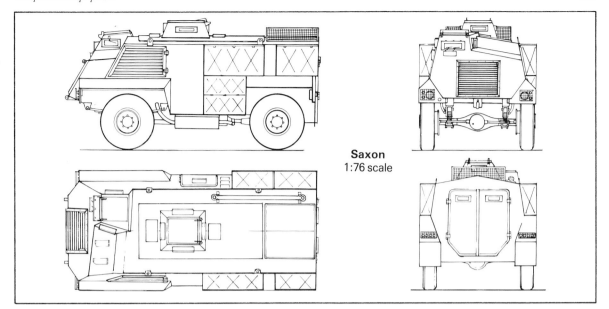

Saxon
1:76 scale

Some extra Saxons will be produced for use by the Royal Artillery's Rapier batteries. These versions will be used as command and control posts and will be equipped with extra radios, plotting tables and other such equipment.

FV1611 Pig

Armament Nil—see text; **Crew** 2 + 6 to 8;. **Weight in action (approx)** 7,000 kg; **Length** 4.926 m; **Height** 2.12 m; **Width** 2.044 m; **Wheel track** 1.713 m; **Maximum road speed** 64 km/h; **Range**

(roads) 402 km; **Engine type** Rolls-Royce B60 Mark 5A; **Engine power** 120 bhp; **Engine capacity** 4.25 litres; **Fuel capacity** 145 litres.

Exactly how the unlovely name of 'Pig' came to be bestowed upon this vehicle is unknown but it started life in the late 1940s. Originally it was a Humber 1-ton truck, the FV1601A, which was converted to the APC role by the addition of an armoured steel body as an expedient pending an adequate supply of the FV603 Saracen. The expedient turned into a production run of about 1,700 from both GKN Sankey at Wellington in Shropshire, and the Royal Ordnance Factory at Woolwich —the chassis came from the Humber Works at Maidstone. With the advent of the FV432 into

Below *Saxon at speed showing the commander's cupola and the driver's position relative to the rest of the hull.* **Below right** *A Pig on patrol in the centre of Belfast* (Army PR HQ NI).

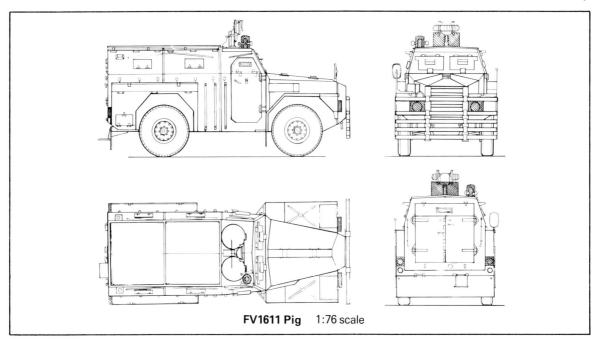

FV1611 Pig   1:76 scale

service the Pig was declared obsolete, but events in Northern Ireland enforced a return to active service, and numbers were brought out of storage and even re-purchased from civilian buyers.

In Northern Ireland the Pig has had a renewed service career. Being relatively small and innocuous it does not have the political 'tank' appearance that would arouse passions in civil unrest situations, yet it still provides a useful degree of protection and mobility to troops 'acting in support of a civilian power'. But in 1972 it was discovered that high-velocity armour-piercing bullets were in the hands of some of the dissenting groups operating in Ulster, and that these were capable of penetrating the armour of the Pig. In order to rectify this state of affairs, all the 500-odd Pigs in use in Northern Ireland were returned to various Royal Ordnance factories in the United Kingdom for additional armour plating to be applied (Operation Bracelet). At the same time the suspension was modified to accommodate the extra weight and the various vision blocks and ports were updated and an extra armoured shield added to the rear. On some vehicles smoke or CS canister dischargers were added to the roof.

With the withdrawal of the last Saracens from Northern Ireland in 1984, the Pigs have had to take over some of the functions carried out by those vehicles. This has led to a range of Pig variants, some of them with exotic-sounding names. Apart from the standard personnel carrier there is now the Kremlin Pig covered with wire mesh as a protection against RPG-7 rockets, the Flying Pig with large side-mounted riot screens, and the Holy Pig, a Pig with a roof hatch cut into the top and surrounded with forward-folding perspex screens. There is also an Ambulance Pig capable of carrying one stretcher and some Pigs operating in Armagh have had machine-gun turrets from Shorland armoured cars added to their roofs.

FV601(C) Armoured Car Mark 2 Saladin

Armament 1 × 76.2 mm L5A1 Gun, 1 × 7.62 mm L3A3 Machine-Gun, 1 × 7.62 mm L3A4 Machine Gun and 2 × 3-barrel smoke dischargers; **Crew** 3; **Weight in action** 11,583 kg; **Length (gun forward)** 5.27 m; **Length of hull** 4.93 m; **Height (top of cupola)** 2.39 m; **Width** 2.565 m; **Wheel track** 2.083 m; **Ground clearance** 0.426 m; **Maximum road speed** 72 km/h; **Range (roads)** 400 km; **Engine type** Rolls-Royce B80 No. 1 Mark 6D; **Engine power** 160 bhp; **Engine capacity** 5.67 litres; **Fuel capacity** 241 litres; **Ammunition capacity** 76.2 mm—42 rounds, 7.62 mm—3,500 rounds; **Main armament elevation** –10° to + 20°; **Main armament traverse** 360°.

Only a relative few FV601(C) Saladins remain operational—they are with the armoured reconnaissance squadron based in Cyprus—but the type is still used in the United Kingdom for a number of ancillary roles most of which involve training. Like so many post-war armoured vehicles, it had a long

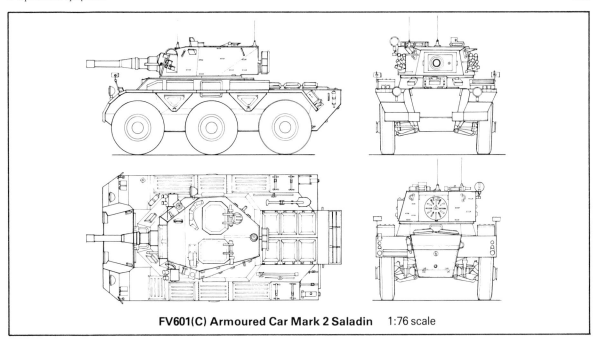

FV601(C) Armoured Car Mark 2 Saladin   1:76 scale

and protracted development history, but the Saladin's was rather longer than most as it had been under development for some 13 years before it went into production during late 1958. The first examples were issued during 1959 and thereafter served well in all sorts of climate and terrain. It has now been replaced by the FV101 Scorpion in the reconnaissance regiments of the Cavalry. Some are still used (in small numbers) by TA units, and a few soldier on in Cyprus.

In service the Saladin was often used as a 'wheeled tank', a role made possible by its 76.2 mm L5A1 gun. This is the progenitor of the L23A1 fitted to the FV101 Scorpion but both fire the same ammunition—the L5A1 is heavier than its successor and is 2.164 m long.

FV603 Saracen

Armament 1 × .30 L3A3 Machine-Gun, 2 × 3-barrel smoke dischargers; also see text; **Crew** 2 +

A Saladin, still retained for training purposes in the 1980s.

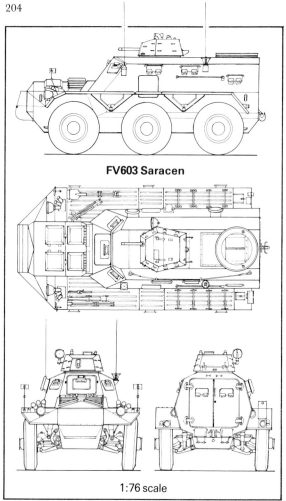

FV603 Saracen

1:76 scale

was in production by late 1952, well in advance of its progenitor.

The main assembly line for the Saracen was at Alvis Company Limited at Coventry. Progressive versions were the FV603(B) and the FV603(C), but the latter was the most numerous. As well as production for the British Army, the Saracen became a great export success and many still remain in service all over the world with several armies. As well as the APC version the Saracen family expanded into the FV611 ambulance and the FV610(A) artillery command vehicle for the Royal Artillery as well as the FV604 armoured command vehicle, some of which are still in service pending the delivery of the FV105 Sultan.

With the coming into service of the FV432 and its variants the Saracen gradually faded from the scene. Many were issued to TA units, driving schools and to various trials units. Some were even used as hard targets on firing ranges. But the coming of the disturbances in Northern Ireland changed all that. Saracens were taken out of their various stores and special-duty hiding places and sent to Ulster where they formed the APC backbone of the units on duty there. Their numbers were swelled by a batch of export Saracen Mark 3s, originally intended for sale to Libya but not delivered. They arrived in Northern Ireland with their desert camouflage still applied. Once in the province they were gradually uparmoured and fitted with various anti-riot equipment such as CS canister or smoke dischargers, anti-wire posts to protect the commander, loudspeakers, and the like

Waiting for the 'off'—a Saracen, fully equipped and ready for a training demonstration at Bovington.

10; **Weight in action** 10,170 kg; **Length overall** 5.233 m; **Height (top of turret)** 2.463 m; **Height (top of hull)** 2.0 m; **Width** 2.539 m; **Wheel track** 2.083 m; **Maximum road speed** 72 km/h; **Range (roads)** 400 km; **Engine type** Rolls-Royce B80 Mark 6A; **Engine power** 160 bhp; **Engine capacity** 5.67 litres; **Fuel capacity** 200 litres; **Ammunition capacity (approx)** 1,600 rounds; **Main armament traverse (if fitted)** 360°; **Main armament elevation (if fitted)** −15° to +45°.

The FV603 Saracen began life as a result of the Malayan emergency in about 1948 or 1949. It was then discovered that the need for an APC with some form of overhead cover for the passengers was very necessary and work began on the project with great haste to the extent that prototypes and production models were being constructed almost simultaneously. The basis for the new APC was the six-wheeled chassis of the FV601 Saladin armoured car, and the resultant APC, the FV603 Saracen,

(Operation Kremlin 1 and 2). Some Saracens had their turrets removed, while variants such as the FV 610 and FV 604 were pressed into use after their special equipment was removed.

In Northern Ireland the Saracens gave good service for many years but by 1984 the situation there had reached the stage where they were no longer needed. They were withdrawn from the Province and placed into store. They were not the last in Army service for many others are still used for training. Others are used by the EOD squadrons of the Royal Engineers for either reconnaissance or for the safe remote control of some special digging or earth-moving equipment. Few of these have any armament still fitted.

The Ferrets

One of the few armoured fighting vehicles to remain in production throughout the Second World War was the Daimler Scout Car, a remarkable little vehicle that was pressed into a variety of roles throughout the war years. After 1945 it was felt that the basic design was capable of further development, and Daimler Company Limited were given a development contract. They completed their first prototype in June 1950, and a production contract followed almost immediately. In 1952 the first production versions came off the Coventry lines and the new vehicle, soon known as the Ferret, remained in production until 1971 by which time a total of 4,409 had been completed, many for export to other nations.

The Ferret has been produced in several versions, not all of which remain in Army service. Over the years the Ferret has been gradually developed and updated and at the present time there is an ongoing programme to modernise all the Ferrets in service to enable them to remain in active use until the late 1980s. This longevity is necessary for the Ferret is one of those vehicles that the British Army deems it cannot do without. It fills a variety of roles. The Infantry use it for liaison, the Royal Artillery for general reconnaissance with their field batteries, the armoured regiments use it as a general run-about and again for reconnaissance, and just about every branch of the service seems to have a few somewhere around. It is in active service in Germany and Northern Ireland, and is one of the standard items pressed into use whenever the Army is involved in a local conflict or United Nations peace-keeping force.

The basic version of the Ferret is the Mark 1/1 or FV701(J). In this form it is an open-topped 4 × 4 vehicle with armour varying from 6 mm at the rear to 16 mm on the superstructure and hull front and sides. The open hull can house a crew of two or three men, and a machine-gun, usually a .30

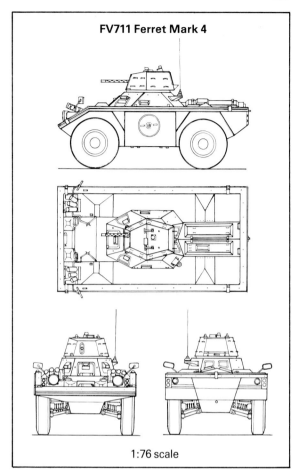

FV711 Ferret Mark 4

1:76 scale

Browning or 7.62 mm Bren, is mounted on a pintle. The suspension is the same as that of the older Daimler Scout Car but has been strengthened, while the engine is more powerful giving an increased cross-country performance. A canvas cover provides some protection against the elements.

The Ferret designations do not follow a particularly tidy pattern so the next version to be considered is the Mark 1/2 or FV704. This is almost the same as the Mark 1/1 but it has a small flat-topped turret with an external machine-gun pintle.

Perhaps the most commonly encountered version of the Ferret is the Mark 2/3 or FV701(H). Structurally and mechanically it is the same as the Mark 1/1 but has a small turret mounted on the superstructure. For armament the turret mounts either a .30 Browning or a 7.62 mm Bren but no doubt the GPMG will be mounted in one form or another.

The Ferret Mark 3 is an updated Mark 1/1 with bigger wheels, a flotation screen stowed all around the body and the suspension modified to support the

	Ferret Mark 1/1 FV701(J)	Ferret Mark 1/2 FV704	Ferret Mark 2/3 FV701(H)	Ferret Mark 4 FV711
Armament	1 × .30 L3A4 MG *or* 1 × 7.62 mm L4A4 MG	1 × 7.62 mm L4A4 MG	1 × .30 L3A4 MG	1 × .30 L3A4 MG
Crew	2 or 3	3	2	2 or 3
Weight in action	4,210 kg	4,370 kg	4,395 kg	5,400 kg
Length	3.835 m	3.835 m	3.835 m	3.962 m
Height	1.448 m	1.651 m	1.879 m	2.336 m
Width	1.905 m	1.905 m	1.905 m	2.133 m
Wheel track	1.549 m	1.549 m	1.549 m	1.75 m
Ground clearance	0.33 m	0.33 m	0.33 m	0.41 m
Maximum road speed	93 km/h	93 km/h	93 km/h	80 km/h
Range (roads)	300 km	300 km	300 km	300 km
Engine type		All: Rolls-Royce B60 Mark 6A		
Engine power	129 bhp	129 bhp	129 bhp	129 bhp
Engine capacity	4.26 litres	4.26 litres	4.26 litres	4.26 litres
Fuel capacity	96 litres	96 litres	96 litres	96 litres
Ammunition capacity	450 rounds	450 rounds	2,500 rounds	2,500 rounds

extra weight involved. Relatively few of these vehicles were made from new but it is the basis for the present updating programme of Mark 1s. It was originally the FV701(J).

The most modern of the Ferrets in service is the Mark 4 or FV711. It is a turreted Ferret with large wheels, an integral wading screen and strengthened suspension.

Right *A Ferret still serving with the Yeomanry during a TA exercise on Salisbury Plain.*

Below left *Ferret in use by a Royal Engineer unit in BAOR.*

The heaviest of all the Ferrets to date was the Mark 5 or FV712 which had a drastically modified turret with bins for four Swingfire missiles and a machine-gun mounting. Once again the suspension had to be strengthened to take the weight involved, but the Mark 5 was intended only as an interim and training vehicle until the FV438 and FV102 Striker could get into service in sufficient numbers. By the end of 1978 they were no longer in use and were re-worked into Mark 4 or similar status.

The Ferret has been used for many trials and experiments, some of which reached a form of service status. One of these was the Mark 2/6 or FV703 which had two Vigilant anti-tank guided missiles mounted, one to each side of the turret. With the missile equipment removed this version became the Mark 2/7. The FV701(H), the Mark 2/3 was at one time used for trials with the No. 14 radar (ZB298). There were various trials conducted in the search for swimming gear which involved at one time the use of external flotation bags. Another approach was the use of a 'bolt-on' polyurethane hull, but the final answer proved to be that now adopted for nearly all similar British vehicles, and that is the collapsible wading screen. Plastic stowage boxes add to the buoyancy.

155 mm Self-Propelled Howitzer M109A2

Armament 1 × 155 mm M185 Howitzer, 1 × 7.62 mm L4A4 Machine-Gun; **Crew** 6 + 2; **Weight in action** 24,070 kg; **Length (gun forward)** 9.042 m; **Length of hull** 6.256 m; **Height (less machine-gun)** 3.06 m; **Width (with fenders)** 3.295 m; **Width (less fenders)** 3.149 m; **Track width** 0.381 m; **Ground clearance** 0.467 m; **Maximum road speed** 56 km/h; **Range** 360-390 km; **Engine type** GMC Model 8V71T Detroit Diesel; **Engine power** 405 bhp; **Engine capacity** 9.3 litres; **Fuel capacity** 511 litres; **Ammunition capacity** 155 mm—34 rounds; 7.62 mm—1,200 rounds; **Main armament elevation** -3° to +75°; **Main armament traverse** 360°.

The M109A2 is an American self-propelled howitzer with a rather involved development history that at one point touched on that of the M113 APC. The development test vehicle was the T196 Howitzer Motor Carriage that went into production as the M109 in November 1962 but that vehicle was fitted with the 155 mm Howitzer M126. It entered British Army service in 1965 and during 1978 these vehicles were fitted with longer barrels known as the M185 to give their self-propelled carriages a new designation of M109A1, later M109A2.

The M109A2 is the standard equipment of the Royal Artillery's medium self-propelled batteries based in Germany. The first two vehicles were obtained for trials in 1975, and the barrel retrofit programme was scheduled to be completed by the end of 1978.

The M109A2 is a rather bulky vehicle but the turret is roomy and the vehicle has a limited swimming ability. As with many other self-propelled artillery pieces, the engine and transmission are at the front of the vehicle and the turret at the rear, where a large hatch is used for ammunition replenishment. On the move, the driver and five of the gun crew remain with the vehicle but for a full detachment another two ammunition numbers travel in an ammunition limber vehicle. Hatches in the roof provide not only vision but also access to the 7.62

An M109A2. Just visible on the rear hull side is the name 'Armageddon'.

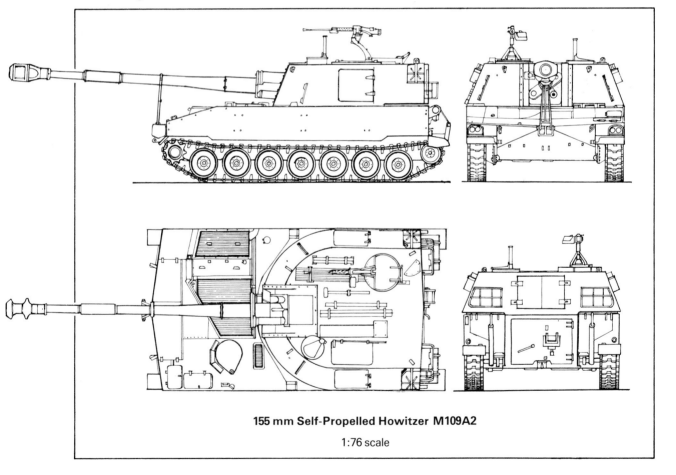

155 mm Self-Propelled Howitzer M109A2

1:76 scale

mm L4A4 Bren Gun mounting which is fitted for limited local and anti-aircraft defence. One rather unusual feature on such a large vehicle is that the hull and turret are of all-welded aluminium construction—which enables it to be more amphibious than similar vehicles of its bulk. To provide stability when firing two small recoil spades are fitted to the hull rear. Full night-driving and NBC equipment can be fitted.

The M109A1s now in service have been updated to a new standard known as M109A2 and new vehicles have been purchased from the United States with all up-to-date modifications incorporated. These 'new' vehicles are sometimes referred to as M109A3s.

There is no sign of the M109 being phased out of service for some time to come. Despite well-laid plans to phase in the 155 mm SP70 (see next entry), there is still little sign that this will happen as scheduled and in the meantime numerous changes can be made to the basic M109A2 to improve its range and all-round performance. Several concerns are now promoting new and longer barrels for the M109A2 and revised turrets to go with them. Autoloaders are another

available option and some of these may be incorporated into future British Army M109A2s.

SP70
(Data provisional)
Armament 1 × 155 mm howitzer, 1 × 7.62 mm machine-gun; **Crew** 5; **Weight in action** Approx 43,500 kg; **Length (gun forward)** 10.235 m; **Length of hull** 7.637 m; **Engine type** MTU MB 871 diesel; **Ammunition capacity** 32 rounds; **Main armament elevation** −2.5° to +70°; **Main armament traverse** 360°.

It would be nice to say something encouraging regarding SP70 for it has been in the offing for so many years that something should have been in the hands of the Army by now. The truth is that the development time scale of SP70 has now become so protracted and bedevilled by political considerations among its international sponsors that costs have risen through the roof and the whole programme now seems set to be overtaken by technical developments elsewhere.

SP70 is a parallel development to the towed 155

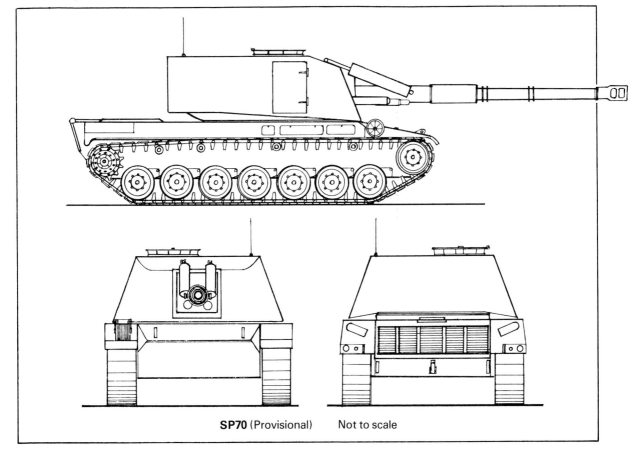

SP70 (Provisional)   Not to scale

Above *The latest form of SP 70* (Rheinmetall). **Below** *The 175 mm M107.*

mm FH70 and, like the towed weapon, has been developed by an international team involving West Germany, the United Kingdom and Italy. Full development of SP70 began in 1973 and trials involving prototypes at various stages of design development were still in progress at the time of writing. The earliest in-service date now possible seems to be 1988 with West Germany taking 400, the

United Kingdom 221 and Italy 90. As these words are written, not even the production centre has been announced and there is still discussion as to exactly what type of aluminium armour would be used for the hull and turret. Many of the SP70's complex mechanisms are still under development or undergoing troop trials in various countries.

If SP70 ever does get through all its pre-service stages, it will be a formidable piece of artillery. The main armament is virtually the same as the FH70 and will fire the same ammunition. The gun will be loaded from a magazine in the turret wherein are located four of the crew of five: the layer, the magazine operator and the charge loader; the commander oversees all the operations and is seated between the layer and magazine operator. The fifth crew member, the driver, sits in the front of the hull. The magazine holds 32 projectiles which are selected under microprocessor control and fed to the breech automatically and then rammed into the chamber; the charge is loaded by hand. Getting the projectile into the turret magazine is quite a complex process involving a device known as a SRG (shell replenishment gear) and once inside the projectile is taken to its place in the magazine rack by yet more handling equipment. In theory the magazine-loading system is admirable but many gunners are wondering what would happen to a battery once all the contents of the magazine have been expended. It is possible to load more ammunition directly into the system via a hatch in the turret but this will not provide much protection for the ammunition handlers involved. The only alternative is for the SP70s to leave the battle zone to reload under cover of some sort. This consideration has produced much thought in some gunnery circles and while non-magazine weapons such as the M109A2 have to be loaded by hand direct from internal racks, they can be replenished by hand fairly easily without always having to leave the battle.

The loading system is not the only complexity regarding SP70. The use of an all-aluminium hull and other components has given rise to much intersponsor arguing. The engine pack is a V-8 version of the V-12 engine pack used in the Leopard II MBT.

Perhaps the greatest factor now working against SP70 ever seeing service is that ballistic technology has now overtaken the possible performance of the armament fitted. The SP70 howitzer barrel is 39 calibres long but current thought is that an increase in barrel length to 45 calibres or even longer will provide a corresponding increase in possible range (albeit at a decrease in barrel life using conventional propellants). The current barrel can fire a standard projectile to 24,000 m but an L/45 barrel could increase this to 30,000 m or even more with enhanced-range projectiles. Even longer barrels up to 52 calibres in length are now in development. Thus, at a time when SP70 might be expected to come into service, it is very possible that it will be outranged by more modern equipments. Already Italy has undertaken a programme to re-barrel its M109A2s with L/45 barrels and several manufacturers are now offering barrel 'kits' to improve existing M109A2s. BMY of the USA and Royal Ordnance have combined to offer a package involving a L/45 or L/47 barrel in a new M109A2 turret known as the 'International Turret', and the costs involved are way below those involved in a relatively small quantity purchase of new SP70s. Thus it may well emerge that SP70 has been bypassed and its chances of ever reaching the front line gunners are growing more remote by the day. To counter this argument it has to be said that with so much finance and development expertise sunk into the SP70 programme, it would be even more wasteful if nothing was to emerge after all, so it may well happen that SP70 will still be pushed through. We will have to wait and see, but exactly how long that wait will be is still uncertain.

175 mm Self-Propelled Gun M107

Armament 1 × 175 mm M113 Gun; **Crew** 5 + 3;

Weight in action 28,168 kg; **Length (gun forward)** 11.246 m; **Length (hull only)** 5.72 m; **Height (top of mounting (0°) 2.809 m; Height (top of barrel, travelling)** 3.679 m; **Width** 3.149 m; **Track width** 0.457 m; **Ground clearance** 0.441 m; **Maximum road speed** 56 km/h; **Range (roads)** 725 km; **Engine type** GMC Model 8V-71T Detroit Diesel; **Engine power** 405 bhp; **Engine capacity** 9.3 litres; **Fuel capacity** 1,137 litres; **Ammunition capacity** 175 mm—2 rounds; **Main armament elevation** −2° to +65°; **Main armament traverse** 60°.

The M107 is one of a family of American self-propelled artillery vehicles that were the result of a design requirement put forward in 1956. The first prototypes appeared in 1958 and were built by the Pacific Car and Foundry Company at Renton, Washington. The version mounting the 175 mm gun was the T235 powered by a petrol engine, but when a diesel engine was substituted it became the M107. The first M107s entered British Army service in 1965-1966.

The M107s with 1 (BR) Corps come directly under HQ control as a Corps general support regiment. As they use the same self-propelled

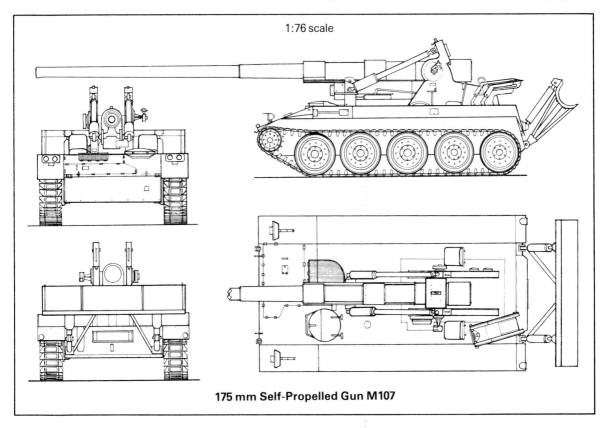

1:76 scale

175 mm Self-Propelled Gun M107

carriage as the 8-in M110s and the same engine as the 155 mm M109A1s, a great deal of spares commonality is possible. Indeed, the 175 mm gun and the 8-in howitzer are interchangeable. The changeover involves only about two hours' work, and if necessary, can be accomplished in the field. As the M107 is intended for use well behind the front lines, no armour or other protection is provided for the crew, but consideration is now being given to some form of canvas or nylon housing over the breech area. Even such a flimsy structure can provide some protection against the elements and nuclear fall-out.

On the move, up to five of the gun detachment can travel on the gun carriage, with a further three gun numbers on one of the ammunition limber vehicles. Ammunition space on the carriage is limited and only two rounds are normally carried. To assist the loading procedure a hydraulically operated ammunition lift and ramming mechanism is fitted to the vehicle rear. Hydraulic operation is

Left *The long 175 mm barrel can be well appreciated from this photograph, taken at Bovington.* **Below left** *M110A2 of 39 Heavy Regiment, RA.*

also used to power the large recoil spade which stabilises the gun when fired, and further stabilisation is provided by locking out the suspension cylinders.

8-in Self-Propelled Howitzer M110A2

Armament 1 × 8-in M201 Howitzer; **Crew** 5 + 8; **Weight in action** 28,350 kg; **Length (gun forward)** 10.7 m; **Length (hull only)** 5.72 m; **Height (top of mounting (0°)** 2.809 m; **Height (top of barrel, travelling)** 2.93 m; **Width** 3.149 m; **Track width** 0.457 m; **Ground clearance** 0.441 m; **Maximum road speed** 56 kkm/h; **Range (roads)** 725 km; **Engine type** GMC Model 8V71T Detroit Diesel; **Engine power** 405 bhp; **Engine capacity** 9.3 litres; **Fuel capacity** 1,137 litres; **Ammunition capacity** 8-in—2 rounds; **Main armament elevation** − 2° to + 65°; **Main armament traverse** 60°.

As the M110 had the same origins as the M107 it only remains to mention that its trial designation for the US Army was T236E1. Apart from the barrel and mounting it is almost identical to the M107, but

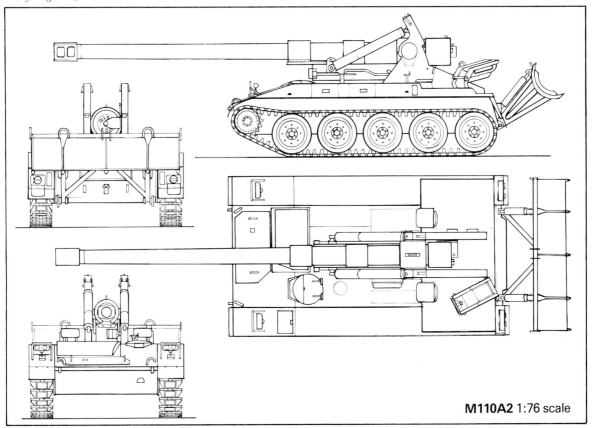

M110A2 1:76 scale

the heavier projectiles involved dictates the use of eight ammunition numbers travelling in the ammunition limber vehicles.

Operationally the M110A2s are used singly and from carefully pre-selected and prepared positions. They operate in a 'shoot-and-scoot' mode as it is well known that their nuclear capability marks them out for special attention by enemy counter-battery forces.

Tracked Rapier

Armament 8 × Rapier surface-to-air missiles, smoke dischargers; **Crew** 3; **Weight in action** 14,010 kg; **Length** 6.4 m; **Height (tracker raised)** 2.78 m; **Width** 2.8 m; **Track width** 0.381 m; **Ground clearance** 0.41 m; **Maximum speed (roads)** 48 km/h; **Range (cruising)** 300 km; **Engine type** GMC Model 6V-53T diesel; **Engine power** 210 hp at 2,100 rpm; **Fuel capacity** 398 litres.

Development of the Tracked Rapier can be traced back to 1974 when attempts were made to mount a Rapier launcher on to a M548 tracked cargo carrier. Subsequent development led to the use of a chassis known as the RCM 748 (a member of the M113 APC series) in place of the M548 and an order was obtained from the then Imperial Iranian Armed Forces. This version had eight missile launchers and the chassis were duly ordered from FMC in the United States. Unfortunately for British Aerospace, the Shah was then overthrown and the order was cancelled. This

left British Aerospace with a number of tracked carriers and nothing to show for a long and expensive development programme. However, the British Army carried out some trials with the Tracked Rapier and in June 1981 an order was placed for 50 examples, subsequently increased to 70.

Tracked Rapier is now in service with Royal Artillery air defence regiments in BAOR. It is used by two batteries each of 12 and 22 Air Defence Regiments, RA, with the other two batteries using towed Rapiers. Each of the Tracked Rapier batteries has 12 Tracked Rapiers organised into two sections of six together with a Land Rover-based reconnaissance section and all the necessary REME field workshop back-up. The first Tracked Rapiers were delivered to BAOR in January 1984.

Tracked Rapier is a great improvement over towed Rapier as far as BAOR air defence is concerned. One of its main advantages is that is can be ready for action within 15 seconds of arriving on site instead of the 30 minutes or so of towed Rapier. This makes the use of Tracked Rapier much more flexible in advanced battle areas where Tracked Rapier can also be much more mobile than towed Rapier (with its dependence on wheeled Land Rover tractors and support vehicles). It can also keep up with armoured units in the field and, as it is armoured, it is much less vulnerable to battle damage than the completely unprotected towed Rapier.

Tracked Rapier has its crew of three located in a

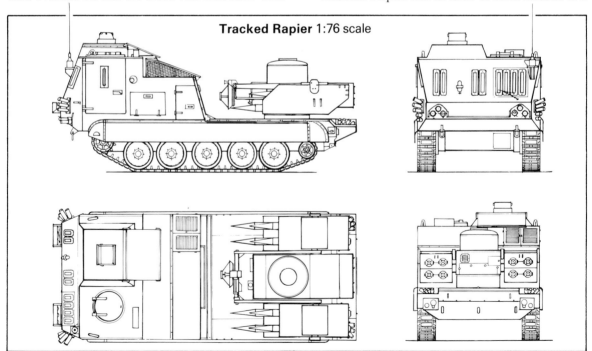

Tracked Rapier 1:76 scale

Above *A Tracked Rapier ready to fire with the commander wearing the helmet sight system.* **Right** *The interior of a Tracked Rapier cabin with the driver's position in the foreground.*

rather cramped, soundproofed forward control cabin. Normally a Sergeant is in charge and he wears a Ferranti helmet pointing system that allows him to spot a target and slew the launcher on to its heading within half a second. Slewing the launcher also moves the optical tracker head for the operator to carry out a normal Rapier tracking and firing sequence. It is possible to use a radar system for target search as well. Onboard microcomputers are used extensively for both surveillance and tracking operations and in the missile guidance, and they are also used for Built-In Test Equipment (BITE) to check out all parts of the system. The eight Rapier missiles are contained in an armoured launcher surrounded by 25 mm of aluminium armour and can be loaded (or reloaded) by hand in about five minutes.

There is still some development work to be done on Tracked Rapier apart from such all-round improvements as TOTE (or Tracker, Optical, Thermal-Enhanced), which allows the system to track targets on clear nights (TOTE is also known as Darkfire).

TOTE effectively introduces a thermal imager into the optical system and is fitted to a variant of Tracked Rapier known as Mark 1B, early versions without this equipment being known as the Mark 1A. The Mark 1B will also introduce a Ferranti Argus M700 series computer to assist in signal processing for the search radar. On a more mundane level, however, the track life is too short for comfort (although a new design is being trialled) and the Auxiliary Power Unit (APU) that powers the system when Tracked Rapier is in action is at present far too 'dirty' since its exhaust can compromise concealment, even at a distance. One feature of Tracked Rapier that will not make it very popular with its support personnel is the engine pack. The position of this on the vehicle is such that to change it involves no less than 29 hours of work including removal of the cab and much of the contents.

Supporting the Tracked Rapier batteries means a major effort on the part of the REME. Each battery has a support troop which travels with it and each regiment has a REME workshop which takes to the field with eight tracked vehicles, 80 trucks and Land Rovers, 64 trailers and 14 generators. The battery support troop has three teams used for forward repair and known as Carrier Fire Units Repair (CFUR). It is these teams which employ M548 tracked carriers

with forward-mounted cranes (see next entry). Each troop also has two automotive repair teams, one with a M578 tracked armoured recovery vehicle and the other with a 4-tonne truck equipped with a winch. It is easy to see that maintaining Tracked Rapier in the field is going to be a major task, and this is without even considering the various facilities provided at Dortmund for training and general support. Training for Tracked Rapier is carried out at Larkhill and Dortmund and every year each battery moves to the Hebrides for a training camp where most missile operators get to fire one Rapier missile.

The Tracked Rapier regiments have their own RAOC store platoons with 20 trucks and trailers that supply the missile resupply vehicles (covered in the next entry).

M548 Missile Re-supply Vehicle

Armament 1 × 7.62 mm L7A2 machine-gun; **Crew** 2; **Weight fully loaded** 12,880 kg; **Length** 5.892 m; **Height** 2.81 m; **Width** 2.69 m; **Track width** 0.381 m; **Ground clearance** 0.6 m; **Maximum road speed** 64 km/h; **Range** 483 km; **Engine type** GMC Model 6V-53T diesel; **Engine power** 215 hp at 2,800 rpm; **Fuel capacity** 397 litres; **Missiles carried** 20.

Re-supplying Tracked Rapier in the field is something of a problem for the tracked vehicles are able to

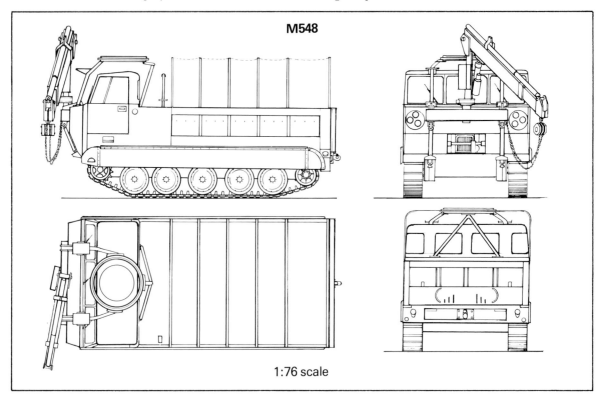

M548

1:76 scale

traverse terrain which would be impassable to wheeled supply vehicles. The Army's solution has been to procure a number of American M548 tracked cargo carriers and configure their load-carrying area to accept 20 Rapier missiles in their transport containers. The M548 can easily keep pace with the Tracked Rapier units and many of the mechanical components are compatible with those used on the Tracked Rapier chassis. The cab of the M548 is designed for three men but in the Rapier re-supply role it will only have a crew of two, giving them plenty of space. At present no radio is fitted to keep the M548 crew in contact with the vehicles they are meant to supply.

The M548 is also used for various repair functions in the field, such as removing the Tracked Rapier cab roof to gain access to some components. These M548s are equipped with front-mounted cranes and are used by the REME Carrier Fire Unit Repair (CFUR) teams, at one time known as Forward Area Support Teams (FAST). The cargo area of these CFUR M548s is used to carry spares, tools and other equipment.

Above right A M548 missile re-supply vehicle showing the Rapier storage. **Below** *The forward-mounted crane on a CFUR M548.*

FV180 Combat Engineering Tractor

Armament 1 × 7.62 mm L4A4 Machine-Gun, 2 × 4-barrel smoke dischargers; **Crew** 2; **Weight in action** 17,010 kg; **Length overall** 7.544 m; **Length of hull** 5.334 m; **Height overall** 2.667 m; **Height (top of hull)** 2.286 m; **Width of bucket** 2.896 m; **Width of hull** 2.793 m; **Width over tracks** 2.769 m; **Track width** 0.508 m; **Ground clearance** 0.457 m; **Maximum road speed** 56 km/h; **Range (roads)** 480 km; **Engine type** Rolls-Royce C6TFR; **Engine power** 320 bhp; **Engine capacity** 12.2 litres; **Fuel capacity** 430 litres; **Ammunition capacity** 336 rounds (12 magazines).

The FV180 Combat Engineering Tractor, or CET, is a unique vehicle which has been developed from the outset for the combat engineering role, a duty that is usually fulfilled by converted AFVs. Starting as an international project with the West German Army and the French involved, early design studies were carried out at the Military Engineering Experimental Establishment (MEXE) at Christchurch, now part of the MVEE. In time, both France and West Germany withdrew to foster their own comparable projects, but the Christchurch work continued, and in 1968 two test rigs were completed to test the basic concepts. As a result seven prototypes were built in 1973 and 1974, and these underwent extensive trials before production got under way at the Royal Ordnance Factory, Leeds during 1977.

As its name implies, the CET is used by the field engineer regiments of the Royal Engineers. In action it fulfils a variety of roles from preparing or clearing obstacles, digging vehicle or gun pits, path-finding river crossings, preparing river banks for

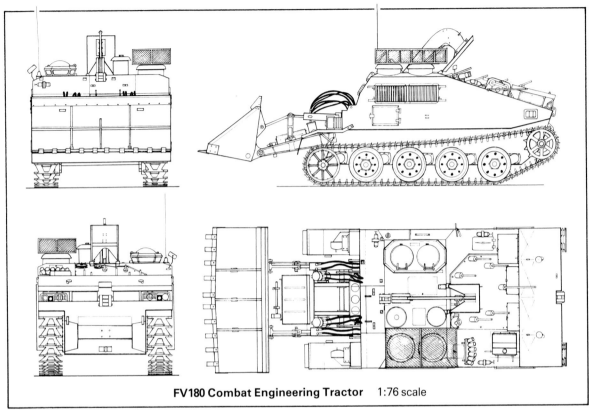

FV180 Combat Engineering Tractor   1:76 scale

crossings, recovering disabled vehicles from water or other obstacles, and so on. Having been developed specially for these tasks, the CET can carry out the bulk of them with surprising facility and efficiency. As it is intended to spend a fair amount of its working life in or near water, the CET has been built as lightly as possible and the hull is largely constructed from aluminium alloy, as are many other parts and sub-assemblies. The CET can be rendered amphibious after about ten minutes' work, and once in the water it is driven by two Dowty water jets. Normally, the CET is driven with

Left *A CET carrying out digging operations on a range in Germany.*

Above right *A CET being used to carry a length of Class 60 Trackway in its digging bucket.*

Right *A Bovington-based CET carrying an extra passenger.*

its large earth-moving bucket to the rear and the crew of two sit on the left of the hull. Both crew positions have driving controls and the CET can be driven in either direction by either crew member—both their driving seats are reversible. To assist the CET out of water obstacles with steep banks, the CET can be equipped with a Laird rocket anchor which can be fired over them. Once dug-in, the anchor is used to tow the CET upwards as the vehicle is fitted with a two-speed winch with a towing capacity of up to 8,000 kg. This can also be used to tow other vehicles out of difficulties, and then the earth bucket doubles as a winch anchor— the winch has 107 metres of cable.

On dry ground the CET still has a multitude of uses. The 1.72 cubic metres capacity earth-moving bucket can be used for either earth-moving or digging, and is powered from hydraulic pumps driven from the main engine. When a small jib

crane is fitted into the bucket it can also be used for loading and unloading stores. Other extras which can be fitted are a pusher bar for launching bridging spans or pontoons, track-laying equipment, and other Engineer stores such as the Giant Viper mine-clearer can be towed.

The CET gave sterling service in the Falklands' campaign of 1982 when two made the journey from San Carlos to Port Stanley, only for one of them to be subsequently lost when it struck a land mine. However, there are now chances that this CET will be replaced for—although the vehicle went out of production some years ago—a recent order from the Indian Army has meant that the production line at Leeds will be re-opened. It will be very surprising if further CETs are not ordered by the British Army as well.

FV4003 Centurion Mark 5 AVRE 165

Armament 1 × 165 mm Demolition Gun, 1 × .30 L3A3 Machine-Gun, 1 × .30 L3A4 Machine-Gun and 2 × 6-barrel smoke dischargers; **Crew** 5; **Weight in action** 51,810 kg; **Length** 8.686 m; **Height** 3.009 m; **Width (over blade)** 3.962 m; **Width (over hull)** 3.39 m; **Track width** 0.61 m; **Ground clearance** 0.46 m; **Maximum road speed** 34.6 km/h; **Range (roads)** 176 km; **Range (cross-country)** 113 km; **Engine type** Rolls-Royce Meteor Mark IVB; **Engine power** 650 bhp; **Engine capacity** 27 litres; **Fuel capacity** 1,037 litres; **Ammunition capacity (approx)** 165 mm— 20 rounds, .30—3,000 rounds; **Main armament elevation** −10° to +20°; **Main armament traververse** 360°.

The FV4003 is a specialised version of the Centurion Mark 5 MBT for use by the Royal Engineers, hence the designation Assault Vehicle Royal Engineers, or AVRE. The first prototype was built in 1957 and the bulk of the production run was undertaken by the Royal Ordnance Factory, Leeds, during the early 1960s. Ever since then the AVRE has been part of the equipment of the armoured engineer squadrons serving in Germany.

The three squadrons are 26, 31 and 77 Armoured Engineer Squadrons, which combine to form 32 Armoured Engineer Regiment based at Munster-lager. In each squadron there are three Armoured Engineer Troops, each with three AVREs (in addition to the AVLBs), but there are now two types of AVRE. The original AVRE is known as the AVRE 165 as its main armament is a 165 mm demolition gun. These have been joined by the AVRE 105 which is basically a converted battle tank once used by the Royal Artillery for forward observation. These AVRE 105s retain their 105 mm L7A2 gun. At

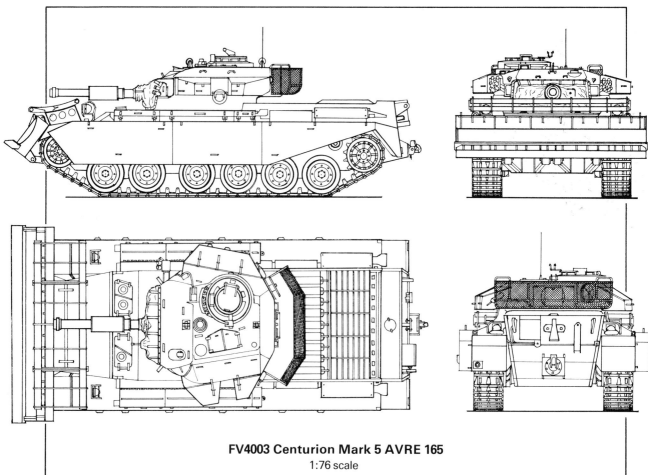

FV4003 Centurion Mark 5 AVRE 165
1:76 scale

present the plans are that each troop will have two AVRE 165 sections and one AVRE 105 section.

The 165 mm demolition gun of the AVRE 165 is a powerful weapon firing a 29 kg HESH projectile accurately at ranges up to 2,400 m. This is powerful enough to bring down structures such as bridges. The AVRE 105 gun fires a HESH projectile weighing 11.26 kg which, while not as powerful as the 165 mm projectile, is still a potent demolition device. The guns are not the only difference between the AVRE 165 and AVRE 105. The former is at present fitted with a front-mounted dozer blade and a fascine carrier while the latter will, for a time at least, be fitted

Above left A Centurion AVRE 105 towing a Giant Viper trailer and with its mine ploughs raised. **Below** *The FV4006 Centurion ARV Mark 2.* **Bottom** *A Centurion AVRE 165 showing the stubby 165 mm demolition gun and the front-mounted dozer blade with the fascine carrier above.*

only with the mine plough. However, the AVRE 105 and 165 can tow Giant Viper and carry out various other tasks. On the AVRE 165 the fascines used have traditionally been wooden stakes that are used to fill ditches and similar obstacles. These are now being replaced by bundles of plastic piping that perform the same function but are much lighter and can be re-used many times. The fascine carrier can also be used to carry and lay lengths of Class 60 Trackway. Normally, these lengths of trackway are held in place by cables secured by explosive bolts and are laid by simply moving forward and releasing them at the correct point. They then unravel to provide a firm road over soft ground.

Apart from the Giant Viper trailer, both types of AVRE can be used to tow a special stores-carrying trailer known as the FV 2721 Trailer 7½-ton Centurion AVRE. This trailer can travel behind an AVRE anywhere the AVRE can go and can be used for all manner of tasks from simple load-carrying to towing a Bar Minelayer with the Bar Mines stacked ready for use on the trailer. Full details are: **Weight empty** 7,316 kg; **Capacity** 7,500 kg; **Length** 6.59 m; **Height** 2.16 m; **Width** 2.972 m.

It is easy to appreciate exactly what the combat role and importance of many items of Army equipment will be. With the AVRE it is not so easy, but in combat the vehicle will be invaluable. It will be able to clear obstacles, carry out demolitions, lay trackway, enable ditches to be crossed, lay minefields, move forward combat engineer supplies and undertake a variety of other tasks. The list of potential combat roles is seemingly endless and the fact that this has been appreciated is shown by the addition of AVRE 105s to the existing AVRE 165s. Despite their age, there is no sign of the Centurion AVREs being replaced and in the near future some modifications such as the replacement of the old Browning machine-guns by various forms of L7A2 GPMG is scheduled. There are whispers of a future requirement for some form of 'counter obstacle vehicle' but it is a long way off yet, if it ever materialises in British Army service, and in the meantime the current AVREs are set for a long service life to come.

FV4006 Centurion ARV Mark 2

Armament 1 × .30 L3A4 Machine-Gun, 2 × 5-barrel smoke dischargers; **Crew** 4; **Weight in action** 50,295 kg; **Length** 8.966 m; **Height** 2.895 m; **Width** 3.39 m; **Track width** 0.61 m; **Ground clearance** 0.45 m; **Maximum road speed** 34.6 km/h; **Range (roads)** 102 km; **Engine type** Rolls-Royce Meteor Mark IVB; **Engine power** 650 bhp; **Engine capacity** 27 litres; **Fuel capacity** 1,045 litres; **Ammunition capacity** .30—2,000 rounds.

Developed from the Centurion ARV Mark 1

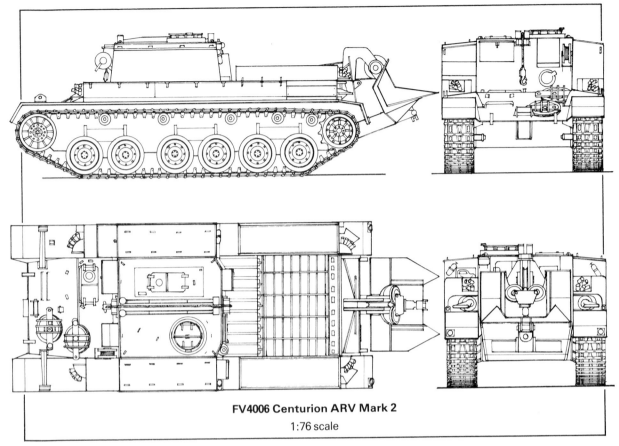

FV4006 Centurion ARV Mark 2

1:76 scale

(which was little other than a specialised tractor), the Centurion ARV Mark 2 is now nearing the end of its service life as it is gradually replaced by the FV4204 Chieftain ARV. The first Centurion ARV Mark 2s entered service circa 1956 and were produced at the Royal Ordnance Factory, Leeds. The main improvement over the Mark 1 was that the Mark 2 had a large-capacity winch capable of towing a load of up to 31,000 kg. To take advantage of this facility the Centurion hull was modified to take a large earth anchor at the rear. The internal winch was electrically driven with the power generated from an auxiliary engine, also internally mounted. The engine used in this operation is a Rolls-Royce B80 petrol engine with an output at 3,750 rpm of 160 bhp. Using various blocks and tackle the ARV Mark 2 winch can pull up to 90,000 kg, and is supplied with a cable length of 137 metres. For lifting purposes a crane jib with a lifting capacity of 10,000 kg can be erected. Like most ARVs, the FV4006 carries a wide variety of extra equipment, stowage bins and tools, including a hand vice mounted on the front hull glacis.

Armoured Recovery Vehicle M578

Armament 1 × 7.62 mm L4A4 Machine-Gun; **Crew** 3; **Weight in action** 24,470 kg; **Length overall** 6.42 m; **Length of hull** 5.937 m; **Height (top of cupola)** 2.921 m; **Width of hull** 3.14 m; **Track width** 0.457 m; **Ground clearance** 0.47 m; **Maximum road speed** 60 km/h; **Range (roads)** 725 km; **Engine type** General Motors Model 8V71T; **Engine power** 405 bhp; **Engine capacity** 9.3 litres; **Fuel capacity** 1,137 litres; **Ammunition capacity** 7.62 mm—1,200 rounds.

When the British Army adopted the American M109 self-propelled howitzer it was placed in something of a quandary in that existing recovery and repair vehicles would be unable to lift the large and heavy engine pack from these vehicles. The answer was to purchase a relatively small number of the American M578 armoured recovery and repair vehicles direct from the USA (three more were purchased during 1979). The M578 is the recovery

Right *M578 armoured recovery vehicle.*

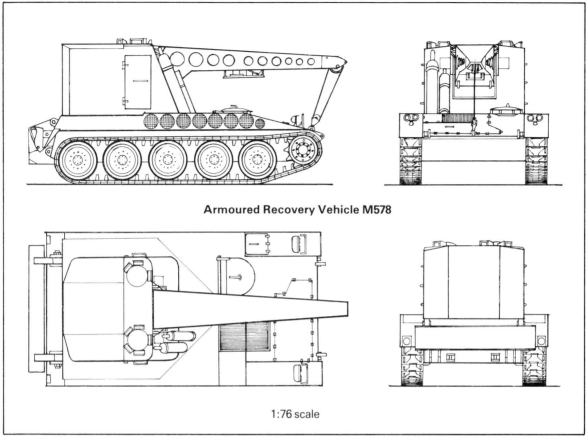

Armoured Recovery Vehicle M578

1:76 scale

vehicle counterpart to the M107 and M110 self-propelled artillery carriages but in place of the gun there is an armoured turret mounting a crane. The turret houses the hoisting gear and winch, while a towing winch is fitted at the rear—this can also be used in conjunction with the rear-mounted spade. In use the turret can rotate through a full 360°. While the M578 has a good cross-country performance it has only a very limited wading capability.

Operationally the M578's role is not limited to the M109A1 batteries as it is also used with the M107 and M110 regiments where it is employed when field changes of barrels are carried out, as well as engine pack changing.

Carrier, Full Tracked, Articulated, LHD, Bv202E

Armament 1 × 7.62 mm L7A2 Machine-Gun (if fitted); **Crew** 2 + 8-10; **Weight in action** 4,200 kg; **Length** 6.172 m; **Height** 2.21 m; **Width** 1.759 m; **Ground clearance** 0.3 m; **Maximum road speed** 39 km/h; **Range (roads)** 400 km; **Engine type** Volvo type B18 petrol; **Engine power** 91 bhp; **Engine capacity** 1.78 litres; **Fuel capacity** 156 litres.

The Bv202 is a Swedish over-snow vehicle

Below *Royal Artillery Bv202 in a non-Arctic setting at Larkhill.* **Below right** *The Bv206 all-terrain carrier* (Hägglund and Söner).

designed under the aegis of the Swedish Army, the first prototypes being constructed in 1958. Volvo of Eskilstuna became the overall project leader and the production line was set up by Bolinder-Munktell, also at Eskilstuna, with the first examples coming off the production line during 1962 and 1963. When the British Army took over its NATO role of flank defence in Norway, the Bv202 was selected for British Army service and ever since it has been a maid-of-all-work with a number of important Army roles.

The Bv202 was designed from the start with an over-snow performance in mind, and the final design used an articulated configuration. The engine and driving compartment are in the front half while the main load carrier is at the rear with a driving shaft imparting drive to the rear section track. The two tracks, front and rear, are one-piece rubber with steel reinforcing inserts. They are wide enough to spread the loads involved and consequently the Bv202 has a very lively cross-snow performance which is far better than its performance across snowless terrain. The rear compartment has a number of configurations. It can have either a hard or soft cover, or it can be left open to provide an area of 2.3 × 1.56 metres. As a personnel carrier it can accommodate eight men but ten can be carried at a squeeze. It has been used as an artillery tractor towing the 105 mm Light Gun and in the artillery role, some were altered to carry the battery FACE computer. In the Infantry support

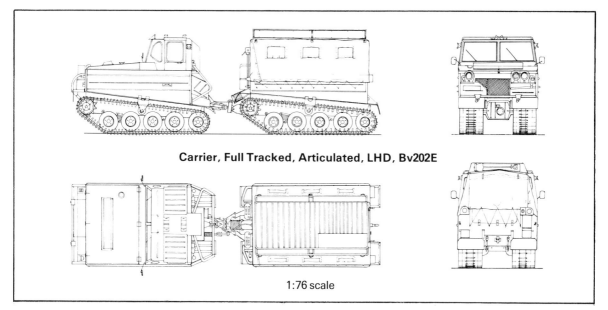

Carrier, Full Tracked, Articulated, LHD, Bv202E

1:76 scale

role, the Bv202 is used as a carrier for the 81 mm Mortar. There is a REME fitters' version, and a command version. Some have also been converted to the ambulance role. A fairly common fitment is that of a GPMG to a ring over the driver's compartment, but this is not universal.

As well as being a versatile over-snow vehicle, the Bv202 is also amphibious, and uses its tracks for propulsion to reach a water speed of 3.3 km/h. The bulk of the Bv202s in British service were obtained between 1968 and 1970. About 150 were bought at that time although more have been purchased since.

Bv206 All-terrain Carrier
Armament 1 × 7.62 mm L7A2 machine-gun (if fitted); **Crew (front unit)** 2 + 3; **(Rear unit)** 10 or

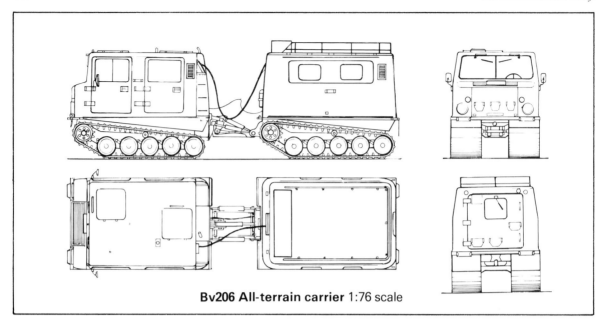

Bv206 All-terrain carrier 1:76 scale

11; **Weight loaded** 6,340 kg; **Length** 6.86 m; **Height** 2.4 m; **Width** 1.85 m; **Track width** 0.62 m; **Ground clearance** 0.35 m; **Max speed (roads)** 55 km/h; **Range** 330 km; **Engine type** Ford Model 2658 E V-6 petrol; **Engine power** 136 bhp at 5,200 rpm.

The Bv206 all-terrain carrier is a Swedish design produced by AB Hägglund and Söner. The first of them was developed for the Swedish Army during the mid-1970s and, unlike the earlier Bv202, had been designed as an all-terrain vehicle rather than an over-snow vehicle. Intended for use over the rugged Swedish terrain and under all Swedish climatic conditions, the Bv206 has attracted a great deal of attention and has even been ordered by the US Army for units located in Alaska. When the British Army started to consider a replacement for the Bv202 (now out of production), the Bv206 was thus a likely candidate and an initial batch of four was ordered in 1981 for the usual tests and trials. It is expected that more will be ordered to replace the full Bv202 fleet for service in Norway.

The Bv206 consists of two tracked units linked by a steering unit. Both are fully tracked and the four suspension units are completely interchangeable. Each unit consists of a central beam on to which the drive unit and the suspension are fitted. The beam unit also carries the glass fibre-reinforced plastic (grp) body. It is expected that in British Army service these bodies will be fully enclosed. The front unit carries the driver, commander and three men. The rear unit can carry up to 12 men but it is expected that ten will be more comfortable. As with the Bv202, various body

forms for special purposes will be developed and it is expected that the Bv206 will be used as an artillery tractor. The rear unit can be easily converted for the ambulance role.

The Bv206 has a remarkable cross-country performance and is amphibious, being driven in the water by the tracks. Steering is accomplished by changing the direction between the front and rear unit by two hydraulic cylinders, servo-controlled from a steering wheel. Performance across snow is almost the same as that across clear terrain and in the water the tracks drive the vehicle at 3 km/h.

'B' vehicles

Bombardier Motor Cycle
Crew 1; **Length overall** 2.3 m; **Height** 1.14 m; **Width** 0.86 m; **Ground clearance** 0.23 m; **Engine type** Bombardier-Rotax 2-stroke; **Engine power** 26 hp at 7,500 rpm; **Fuel capacity** 16 litres.

The motor cycle is back in the British Army. For many years the motor cycle vanished from the tactical scene and was used only for vehicle escort purposes and some ceremonial or display duties, but, by about the mid-1970s, it was once more appreciated that the motor bike could still fulfil many useful roles such as supply convoy escort, scouting, liaison, message-carrying and so forth. Well over 3,000 250 cc Bombardier motor cycles have therefore been ordered from Bombardier Inc, of Quebec, Canada.

Not all these Bombardiers are actually in service. Most of them have been stockpiled pending combat use, for the Army has no wish to see their motor bikes subject to the everyday hazards of Army life. Those that are ridden under normal circumstances are used for training or during specific exercises. In service most would be used by headquarter or reconnaissance units, but the motor cycle is a standard item for the Royal Military Police.

The Bombardier has not been an unqualified success in British Army use although it is a rugged and nippy run-about. The main problem appears to lie in the fact that the design is a conglomeration of components from various sources. The engine is an Austrian product, the frames are made in Canada, some of the electrics are British, and so on. The end result is not as reliable as it might have been and there are rumours that the Army is looking for a replacement—the Armstrong Military Motorcycle is a likely candidate.

The ½-tonne Land Rover

Crew 1 + 2; **Weight loaded** 2,018 kg; **Length** 3.632 m; **Height** 1.95 m; **Width** 1.524 m; **Wheel**

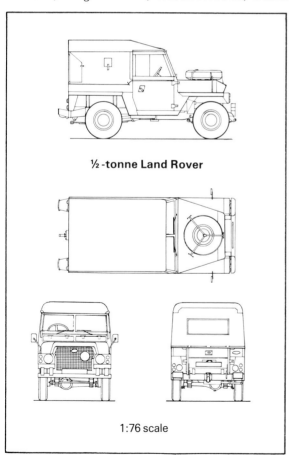

½-tonne Land Rover

1:76 scale

Top *A Bombardier 250 cc motor cycle in its Army element.* **Above** *A ½-tonne Land Rover on Gibraltar.*

track 1.308 m; **Ground clearance** 0.21 m; **Maximum road speed** 105 km/h; **Range on roads** 560-600 km; **Engine type** Rover 4-cylinder OHV; **Engine power** 77 bhp; **Engine capacity** 2.286 litres; **Fuel capacity** 91 litres.

The ½-tonne Land Rover was designed to a

Right *Land Rover equipped for laying land lines on Gibraltar.*

general military requirement for a version of the Land Rover that could be carried slung under a helicopter—originally the specified helicopter was the RAF Wessex but this was later changed to include the Puma. Using the 88 in/2.235 metre wheelbase chassis as a basis, the first prototypes were ready in 1965 but it was not until 1968 that the new model was introduced into service.

Despite some rather drastic modifications to the Land Rover design it was not possible for the new version to be airlifted by the Wessex without further stripping of items such as the windscreen, all the doors, the tarpaulin and its support, and many of the internal fittings. But as the Puma has now taken over many of the lifting roles of the Wessex such stripping, although desirable, is now no longer strictly necessary. For more general use, the ½-tonne Land Rover has now almost entirely replaced the earlier ¼-tonne version (although some are still in limited use).

There are at present only two basic versions in use. One has a normal 12 volt electrical system, while the other has a 24 volt system for use with radios. Although some of these small Land Rovers have been altered to suit local requirements the changes involved have not been so drastic or varied as they have been with the larger ¾-tonne version, and the only major fitting likely to be seen is that of racks for two stretchers to convert the ½-tonne Land Rover into an emergency ambulance.

With the advent of the Land Rover 110, a new Land Rover 90 has also been introduced. This may be regarded as the future version of the ½-tonne Land Rover and, although no orders have been announced as yet, it seems very likely that the Land Rover 90 will

soon be seen in Army markings. The Land Rover 90 has the same coil-spring suspension as the 110 allied to a wheelbase of 2.36 m. The 4 × 4 drive configuration is permanent.

The ¾-tonne Land Rovers

Crew 1 + 2-8; **Weight loaded** 2,620 kg; **Length** 4.648 m; **Height** 2.057 m; **Width** 1.689 m; **Wheel track** 1.308 m; **Ground clearance** 0.228 m; **Maximum road speed** 90 km/h; **Range (roads)** 450/500 km; **Engine type** Rover 4-cylinder OHV; **Engine power** 77 bhp; **Engine capacity** 2.286 litres; **Fuel capacity** 91 litres.

Without a doubt the Land Rover has been one of the outstanding production feats of the British automotive industry since 1945. It has been produced in hundreds of thousands and it is used all over the globe. It is still in production in 1980 and it will probably remain so for years yet—there seems to be no replacement for it, and many competitors have come and gone during the years the Land Rover has reigned supreme.

The Land Rover was first mooted in the lean years following 1945. Rover, long a leading light in the British automobile ranks, were unable to continue their high-cost saloon car range and searched for a new product. They chose the all-purpose cross-country vehicle and the Land Rover was the result. It soon became an immediate commercial success and the production line at Solihull got under way in 1948.

The first models had an 80 in/2.032 metre wheelbase, and some of these were ordered for the British Defence Forces as early as 1949. Gradual production changes and increases in engine power

led to two models being in production, one with a wheelbase of 88 in/2.235 metres, and the other with a wheelbase of 109 in/2.768 metres. Both were officially adopted for British Army service in 1956 but by them there were many already in widespread use. In time the smaller wheelbase version became the ¼-tonne Land Rover. There are few in service today as they have been replaced by the ½-tonne version.

The long wheelbase version became the ¾-tonne Land Rover. Over the years there have been many variations in engine power and such details as the headlamp positioning but the general appearance has remained the same, as has the layout. The main problem for a book of this nature is that no two service Land Rovers appear to be the same. They are issued to every branch of the Army and every unit seems to have its own particular 'fit'. Some have radios, some do not. Some are used only as troop carriers and thus have seating for two in the front, apart from the driver, and bench seats for up to eight at the rear. Some carry battery charging equipment. Some are used as mobile command posts. Some are equipped as miniature workshops. Some are used as signals or telephone switching vehicles. Others have very specialised installations such as FACE computers. Many units convert the Land Rover to their own particular requirements by using Dexion or similar racking.

The basic Land Rover is usually fitted with a canvas tilt but some units use them fully open and others have 'hard' tops, especially if they have signals or similar equipment installed. Land Rovers intended for use in really cold climates have extra heating fitted as well.

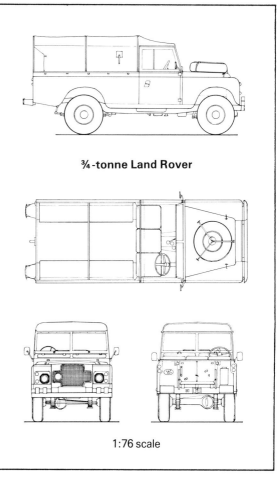

¾-tonne Land Rover

1:76 scale

Left *Typical of the 'hard-topped' Land Rovers is this Royal Engineers EOD example.*

Right *A 1-tonne Land Rover towing a 105 mm Light Gun.*

Left *One of the most recent additions to the Land Rover stable is the Tactical Command Post variant produced by Carawagon Coachbuilders of Sunbury-on-Thames. 35 have been ordered by the Army and the Command Post interior has all the usual map tables, extra lighting and impedimenta needed for the role. Extra stowage is supplied over the cab and a 'penthouse' can be fitted to provide more space. There is even provision for folding bunks inside.*

As well as being used to carry things, Land Rovers are also used to tow various loads such as Cymbeline Mark 1 radars and components of the Rapier missile system. Numerous other types of trailer are used, from ordinary general service types to special ones containing water filtration equipment, and some small water or fuel tanks. The listing of all the possible trailer types would be a very long one. The following list gives details of but three trailer types in widespread use. All are manufactured by GKN Sankey, and are general purpose models. The FV2361 and FV2381 are both box-type trailers for general use and are equipped with canvas covers. The FV2380 is a flat-bed trailer

for carrying such items as generators and water tanks.

Weight empty 404 kg (FV2361)/390 kg (approx) (FV2380)/408 kg (FV2381); **Length** 2.92 m/2.92 m/2.851 m; **Height** 0.94 m/0.8 m/1.113 m; **Width** 1.425 m/1.6 m/1.676 m; **Wheel track** 1.2 m/1.416 m/1.416 m.

The Land Rover has been the subject of some rather drastic modifications, to the extent that they have virtually become new vehicles. One of these drastically modified Land Rovers is known as 'Piglet' and is used only in Northern Ireland. This has added armour proof against armour-piercing bullets, and should not be confused with the 'ordinary' Northern

Ireland Land Rovers which are protected by Macralon armour. The extra armour on the Piglet is very heavy and almost overloads the suspension, making the vehicle slow and awkward to drive, so they are due to be replaced in the near future.

Land Rover 110

Crew 1 + 2-8; **Weight** 3,050 kg; **Length** 4.669 m; **Height** 2.035 m; **Width** 1.79 m; **Wheel track** 1.486 m; **Ground clearance** 0.216 m; **Maximum road speed (approx)** 90 km/h; **Engine type** Rover 4-cylinder; **Engine power** 67 bhp at 4,000 rpm; **Engine capacity** 2.495 litres; **Fuel capacity** 79.5 litres.

By 1983 Land Rover were beginning to phase their standard ¾-tonne model out of production in favour of a new model known as the 110 from the length of the wheelbase (110 in/2.794 m). The Army had for long anticipated this production change and referred to the new model as the Land Rover Stage 2. At the time of writing the new model, which will be referred to here as the Land Rover 110 pending an 'official' designation, is still under various stages of testing but a production order seems likely.

The Land Rover 110 is an amalgam of the usual Land Rover body with the chassis and coil spring suspension of the Range Rover. The new vehicle is thus even stronger than the previous model and has the advantage of providing a smoother and more comfortable ride over rough ground. In appearance the Land Rover 110 is similar to the earlier models but can be distinguished by the 'eyebrows' over the wheel arches and the revised radiator grill. The windscreen is a one-piece component and the four-wheel drive is permanent. There are many other detail changes but overall the 110 is a great improvement over the earlier version.

The British Army Land Rover 110 will have a 2½-litre diesel engine allied to a new five-speed gearbox, known as the LT77, which provides the 110 with a lively cross-country performance. It is only to

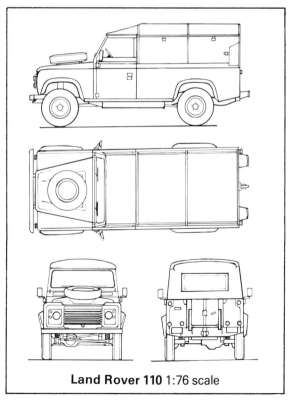

Land Rover 110 1:76 scale

based on the 110 and intended for use in Northern Ireland. It is produced by Glover Webb Ltd of Hamble who have a contract to produce over 100 of these armoured vehicles, no doubt to replace the current overloaded 'Piglets' and some of the elderly Pigs in service. The Glover Webb vehicle closely resembles the existing Northern Ireland Land Rovers but uses metal armour that is presumably proof against armour-piercing small-arms ammunition, while the suspension has been up-rated to carry the extra weight. There is a roof hatch at the rear for the commander and double rear doors provide access to the interior.

The 1-tonne Land Rover

Crew 1 + 1-8; **Weight loaded** 3,120 kg; **Length** 4.127 m; **Height** 2.138 m; **Width** 1.842 m; **Wheel track (front)** 1.524 m; **Wheel track (rear)** 1.549 m; **Ground clearance** 0.254 m; **Maximum road speed** 120 km/h; **Range (roads)** 560 km; **Engine type** Rover V8; **Engine power** 128 bhp; **Engine capacity** 3.5 litres; **Fuel capacity** 109 litres.

The 1-tonne Land Rover was a joint venture, being designed not only by Rover but also by the MVEE at Chobham. The original requirement called for a 1-tonne vehicle capable of towing a power trailer but in the event the latter was not adopted by the Army. Other demands on the design which had to be met were that there should be seating for eight soldiers in lieu of the 1-tonne payload, and that it should be light enough to be airlifted by helicopter or aircraft. After the usual prototypes were made in 1968 a pre-production run for further trials was completed at Solihull in 1972 with the full production run starting in 1974.

One of the first tasks assigned to the 1-tonne Land Rover once it was in service was to tow the 105 mm Light Gun. In this role the towing vehicle carries the gun crew and other following vehicles carry the ammunition. Another role is that of carrying the 81 mm Mortar and in this form the 1-tonne Land Rover has been issued to the TA. It is also used to carry and pull part of the Rapier guided missile system. Other 1-tonne Land Rover conversions are being made to provide hard-tops as cover for electronics equipment to be used for specialised purposes in BAOR.

One more involved conversion of the 1-tonne Land Rover's 101 in/2.565 metre wheelbase chassis was ordered during 1976, the Marshall of Cambridge-built lightweight ambulance.

be expected that there will be as many versions of the 110 as there have been of the earlier models. It is known that a version of the 'Pink Panther' model festooned with machine-guns has been ordered for the SAS and an ambulance model has been shown. Other versions forecast include fire tenders and command posts. Solid and soft-topped versions have already been seen. With the Land Rover 110, the Army will be provided with its standard runabout and general-purpose vehicle for the next couple of decades. One wonders how many variations the troops will be able to produce on the basic theme over the next 30 years. . .

In fact, the variants have already started to appear. One is a new 'low profile' internal security vehicle

FV18067 Ambulance 2/4 Stretcher (Rover 0.75-tonne 4 × 4)

Crew 1-2; **Weight in action** 2,670 kg; **Length** 4.826 m; **Height** 2.146 m; **Width** 1.905 m; **Wheel**

Left *A Land Rover 110 equipped with a forward-mounted winch and fitted for radio (FFR).*

Below left *The Glover Webb internal security vehicle based on the Land Rover 110, over 100 of which have been ordered for the Army.*

Right *The 1-tonne Land Rover ambulance conversion produced by Marshall of Cambridge.*

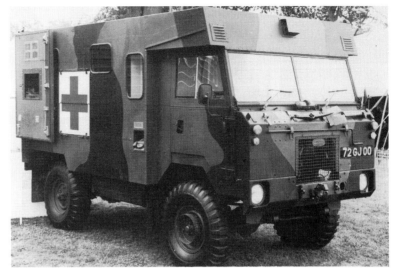

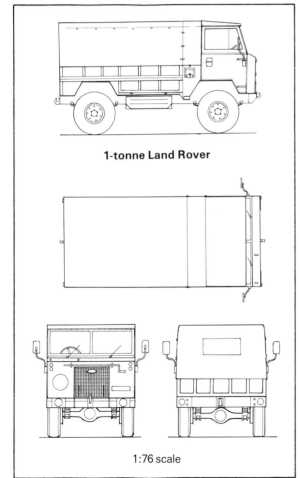

1-tonne Land Rover

1:76 scale

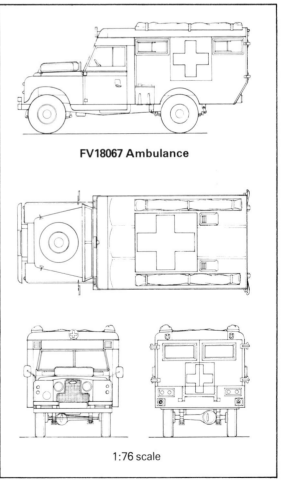

FV18067 Ambulance

1:76 scale

track 1.308 m; **Maximum road speed** 96 km/h;
Range (roads) 450 km; **Engine type** Rover 2.5;
Engine power 77 bhp; **Engine capacity** 2.286
litres; **Fuel capacity** 90.86 litres.

The FV18067 is a conversion of the long wheelbase Land Rover to take a new aluminium ambulance body constructed by Marshall of Cambridge. The first developments to meet an Army
requirement for a light vehicle capable of
evacuating casualties from forward battle areas
began in 1963 and production started in 1968. Ever
since then the Land Rover ambulance has been a
common sight wherever the Army has been posted
or in action—it has even become a fairly common
sight on public roads, especially during the ambulance drivers' strikes of early 1979.

The FV18067 has a large hard-topped body
equipped with extra heating and ventilation.
Casualty accommodation is variable and can vary
from two or four stretchers, to two stretchers and
three seated casualties. As another alternative the
stretchers can be folded away and six seated
casualties carried. There is also a small seat for a
medical orderly, and if necessary extra casualties
can be seated next to the driver.

Mercedes-Benz Unimog

Crew 1 + 1; **Weight loaded** 4,200 kg; **Length** 4.74
m; **Height (cab)** 2.25 m; **Width** 1.825 m; **Wheel
track** 1.396 m; **Ground clearance** 0.39 m;
Maximum speed (roads) 73 km/h; **Engine type**
Daimler-Benz OM 616; **Engine power** 60 hp at
3,500 rpm; **Engine capacity** 2.404 litres; **Fuel
capacity** 90 litres.

The first British Army Unimogs (Universal Motor
Gerät) were delivered to the Berlin Garrison but their
use spread to other parts of BAOR. Many of these
early vehicles were the S-404 model but these have
now all passed from use to be replaced by small numbers of a later model, the U 600 L. Whereas the earlier
Unimogs were used as general purpose vehicles, the
latest have a more specific task. They are retained at
various depots and other installations to keep the
roads clear of snow in winter and debris all the year
round. For this task they are fitted with a front-
mounted plate that can carry either a snow-clearing
device or a rotary brush. The U 600 L is the smallest of
the Unimog series and is also used by the Royal Air
Force.

Truck, Cargo, 2½-ton M35CDN (GMC)

Crew 1 + 1 or 2; **Weight loaded (approx)** 8,200
kg; **Length** 6.477 m; **Height (top of cab)** 2.032 m;
Height (tarpaulin) 2.667 m; **Width** 2.235 m;
Wheel track 1.755 m; **Maximum road speed** 93

Top *An FV18067 Ambulance.* **Above** *Mercedes-Benz Unimog.*
Right *A 'deuce-and-a-half' on the Suffield Ranges.*

km/h; **Range (roads)** 480 km; **Engine type**
General Motors 302 M; **Engine power** 130 bhp;
Engine capacity 4.942 litres; **Fuel capacity** 212
litres.

The General Motors (GMC) trucks in British
Army service are all used on the Suffield Training
Area in Canada, and nowhere else. They were obtained locally from Canadian Army stocks in an attempt to keep down the costs involved in
establishing the area, as to bring 4-tonne and other
trucks over from Europe would have been a very
expensive operation (even so, a few MKs have
made the journey). To the British soldier, as to
many others, this truck is known as the 'deuce-and-

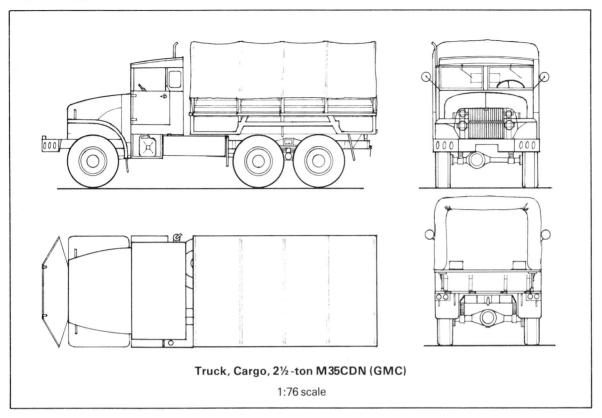

Truck, Cargo, 2½-ton M35CDN (GMC)

1:76 scale

a-half' from its weight rating. As far as can be determined, all the vehicles involved in the Suffield operation were built in Canada by the General Motors plant at Oshawa, Ontario. They are used as general service cargo trucks, and are fitted to tow water tankers and other trailers. A few have been fitted with ammunition-handling cranes behind the cab, while others have winches. Nearly all the trucks involved show the signs of extensive and hard use.

Bedford RL (4 × 4) 4-tonne Truck

Crew 1 + 1; **Weight loaded** 8,800 kg; **Length** 6.36 m; **Height (top of cab)** 2.602 m; **Height (tarpaulin)** 3.11 m; **Width** 2.39 m; **Wheel track** 1.854 m; **Maximum road speed** 75 km/h; **Range (roads)** 400 km; **Engine type** Bedford 6-cylinder OHV; **Engine power** 130 bhp; **Engine capacity** 4.93 litres; **Fuel capacity** 118 litres; **Load area** 4.267 × 2.178 m.

The Bedford RL series of 4-tonne trucks can be said to be among the Army's veterans as the first examples were delivered for service back in 1952. Ever since then they have been the workhorses of the Army and have been produced in a wide range of variants for an almost equally wide range of purposes. When they were first issued they were designated 3-tonne vehicles but this was uprated to 4-tonne in 1968.

The RL series was based on a commercial chassis and, although gradually numerous changes were made to suit the exacting military role, the range was so successful that they remained in production until 1969 by which time 73,135 had been made for military and civilian use, many for export. By the early 1970s the RLs began to be replaced by the Bedford MK series, although large numbers remain in service in many roles, and the last of them is not likely to be seen for a long while yet. They soldier on in many guises and the table below can give only a rough outline of the many variants that have been used by the Army. Not all remain in use, and several of the following types have long since passed from service and been disposed of, but it is likely that just as many more have been stockpiled against some likely future employment.

FV13101 GS Cargo Truck; **FV13102** Container Stores, Binned; **FV13103** Charging Vehicle—Signals; **FV13104** Charging Vehicle—MT Batteries; **FV13105** Cargo—with winch (Dropside); **FV13106** Tanker—3,636 litres; **FV13109** GS Cargo Truck; **FV13110** Signals Truck; **FV13111** Tipper—short wheelbase; **FV13112** Truck, Cargo, Dropside; **FV13113** MT Repair Shop Truck; **FV13115** Recovery Vehicle, Wheeled; **FV13120** Tanker—1,728 litres; **FV13136** Container, Flatbed; **FV13142** Cargo, Dropside (Airportable);

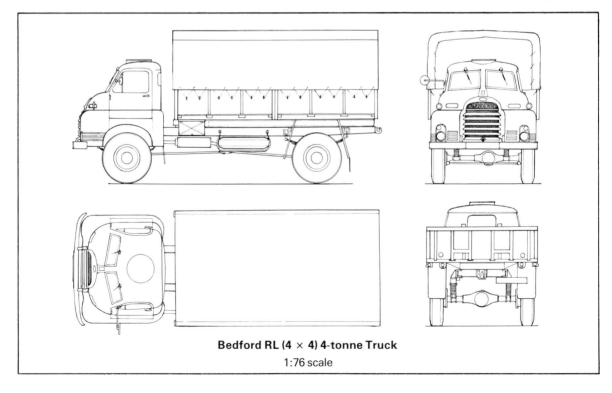

Bedford RL (4 × 4) 4-tonne Truck

1:76 scale

FV13143 Cargo (LH Drive); **FV13149** Tanker, Fuel Dispensing, 2,730 litre; **FV13152** Container Truck; **FV13165** Dental Truck; **FV13197** Water Tanker (4 × 2).

5,000 kg winches were fitted to many of the above variants. Apart from these specialist roles, many RLs were used as artillery tractors, and some were converted as Midge drone launchers. Some may still be found in use as Laird Class 30 Trackway carriers and layers. One role that has now been passed to the newer Bedford MK is that of carrier for Medium Girder Bridge components, although some are still used for training in this capacity.

Several types of trailer have been developed for use with the Bedford RL, some of which are now being used by the MK. A small selection of these are included below along with the relevant data: **FV2501(A)** Trailer, Cargo, 2-tonne Mark 2; **FV2505(D)** Trailer, Flat Platform (2-tonne); and **FV2508** Trailer, Low Platform, Earth Moving Ancillaries (2-tonne). **Weight laden** 3,734 kg (FV2501(A))/5,270 kg (FV2505(D))/4,650 kg (FV2508); **Length** 4.902 m/7.671 m/7.645 m; **Height** 1.55 m/0.775 m/1.473 m; **Width** 2.159 m/ 2.362 m/2.134 m; **Wheel track** 1.702 m/2.057 m/ 1.702 m.

The CB 101 container bodies were produced for the Bedford RL by Laird (Anglesey) Limited, and many are still used for a wide range of purposes which can vary from mobile offices to small workshops. They are carried on flatbed versions of the RL and have the following dimensions: **Weight empty** 590 kg; **Length** 2.756 m; **Height** 1.854 m; **Width** 2.235 m.

Bedford MK (4 × 4) 4-tonne Truck

Crew 1 + 2; **Weight loaded** 9,650 kg; **Length** 6.579 m; **Height (top of cab)** 2.501 m; **Height (tarpaulin)** 3.404 m; **Width** 2.489 m; **Wheel track (front)** 2.05 m; **Wheel track (rear)** 2.03 m; **Maximum road speed** 73 km/h; **Range (roads)** 560 km; **Engine type** Bedford 6-cylinder; **Engine power** 106 bhp; **Engine capacity** 5.42 litres; **Fuel capacity** 150 litres; **Load area** 4.28 × 2.01 m.

The Bedford MK was the successful entry in a three-sided contest to meet the Army's requirement for a new 4-tonne 4 × 4 truck to replace the Bedford RL. The requirement was issued during the early 1960s, and the unsuccessful entries were made by Austin and Commer. The Bedford entry was a 4 × 4 version of the commerical 4 × 2 TK model, and

Top right *This RL load is a mobile office-workshop used at the AAC Centre, Middle Wallop.* **Above right** *Looking rather battered is this FV13111.* **Right** *A standard Bedford MK (4 × 4) 4-tonne truck.*

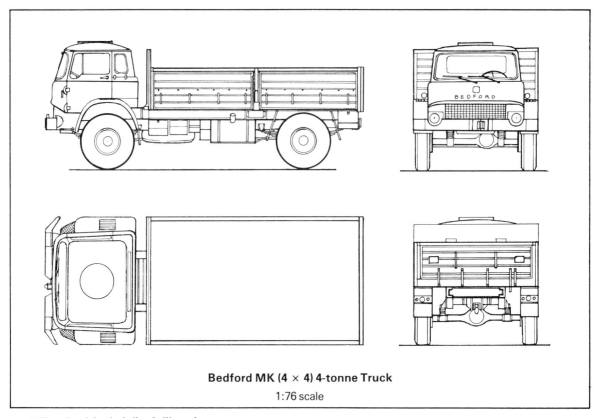

Bedford MK (4 × 4) 4-tonne Truck

1:76 scale

An MK equipped for the bulk refuelling role.

Above *A Royal Signals Bedford MK carrying a radio container/shelter.* **Below** *An MK and trailer carrying MGB components.*

was so successful that by the end of 1977 a total of over 11,700 MKs had been produced, although not all of these went to the British Army for the truck has proved to be a very successful export to many overseas military forces.

Like the Bedford RL that preceded it, the MK has been produced in many versions. There are two basic variants, one of which is the FV13801/13802 cargo truck and the other the FV13803/13804; this is essentially the same vehicle but with the addition of a winch having a pull of 3,500 kg and 76 metres of cable. Both vehicles can be converted into flat-bed versions and another variation is the changing of the single-tyred rear wheels to two-tyred wheels to give extra traction for cross-country work.

Although the earlier RL is still in service in appreciable numbers, the MK has by now assumed the role of general workhorse for the Army. Apart from its general purpose stores-carrying role, the removal of the dropside and rear panels easily converts the MK into a flatbed truck for the carrying of containers and container bodies. The usual container bodies carried are manufactured by Marshall's of Cambridge as their CB.300 series. In this series are all manner of bodies ranging from simple rest-rooms to computer terminals (as with Wavell). The CB.300 containers are produced or converted into numerous configurations such as command centres, workshops, offices, simulator housings, repair and testing shops, signal stations, post offices

and for many other similar functions. Any MK can be thus converted into any number of specialist roles.

More complex conversions have been made to turn the MK into the carrier/launcher for the Midge drone system or the carrier/layer for the Laird Class 30 Trackway. The MK is also used to carry Medium Girder Bridge components and bulk refuelling dispensers. A tipper version is also in use. The list of different roles the MK is called upon to perform is beyond the scope of this book but most of them are based on the two main truck versions.

The 4 × 2 Bedford TK is also used in large numbers for general stores carrying and driver training.

Basic details of the CB.300 series of container bodies are as follows: **Weight empty** 952 kg; **Length** 4.674 m; **Height** 1.905 m; **Width** 2.515 m.

FV622, Truck, Cargo, High Mobility Load Carrier, Stalwart Mark 2

Crew 1 + 2; **Weight loaded** 14,480 kg; **Length** 6.356 m; **Height (with tilt)** 2.64 m; **Height (top of cab)** 2.312 m; **Height (rear floor)** 1.5 m; **Width** 2.616 m; **Wheel track** 2.03 m; **Maximum road speed** 63 km/h; **Range (roads)** 515 km; **Engine type** Rolls-Royce B81 Mark 8B; **Engine power** 220 bhp; **Engine capacity** 6.522 litres; **Fuel capacity** 455 litres; **Load area** 3.6 × 2.4 × 925 m.

The very first member of the Stalwart family was

Above left *Bedford MK carrying a standard workshop/shelter body.*

Left *A flatbed MK with crane.*

Right *A Stalwart laden with fuel and a bulk refuelling pack.*

built by Alvis Limited of Coventry in 1959 and was based on the chassis of the FV652 Salamander used by the Royal Air Force as a fire tender. Continued development resulted in the amphibious Stalwart Mark 1, or FV620, from which the present FV622 Stalwart Mark 2 evolved. Production started in 1966 and continued until 1971.

The Stalwart is a very mobile load-carrying vehicle which can cross almost any type of country and is amphibious as well. All six of its wheels impart drive; while in water, driving jets can propel a loaded vehicle at speeds up to 9.6 km/h. The large load area can carry a wide range of stores and a special pack has been produced which can convert the Stalwart into a bulk fuel carrier. Alternatively, the Stalwart can carry up to 38 fully equipped soldiers. The load-carrying capacity is 5,000 kg and if trailers are attached up to 10,000 kg can be towed. For use in self-recovery, or the recovery of other vehicles, a 4,990 kg-capacity winch is fitted to the front.

Apart from the amphibious load carrier there are two variants in service. The first of these is the

A FV623 Stalwart showing the loading crane.

FV623, fitted with a hydraulic crane behind the cab. This is used as an ammunition limber vehicle with the Artillery regiments based in Germany, where its crane is used to handle ammunition packed on to pallets. The all-up weight of the FV623 is 15,600 kg and the height is increased to 3.124 metres. Second of the Stalwart variants is the FV624 which is a repair vehicle used by the REME.

For all the success of the Stalwart as a cross-country vehicle, it has shown itself to be rather prone to mechanical breakdowns, and as the engine and main fuel tank are under the load area, something of a fire hazard. If the Stalwart is carrying fuel and an engine fire results, the end product is likely to be a very expensive blaze. Its fuel consumption of a steady 71 litres for every 100 road kilometers is considered by many to be rather high.

Bedford TM 4-4 (4 × 4) 8,000 kg Truck

Crew 1 + 2; **Weight loaded** 16,300 kg; **Length** 6.604 m; **Height (top of cab)** 2.997 m; **Width** 2.476 m; **Wheel track** 2.078 m; **Ground clearance** 0.352 m; **Maximum road speed** 88 km/h; **Range** unknown; **Engine type** Bedford 500 OHV; **Engine**

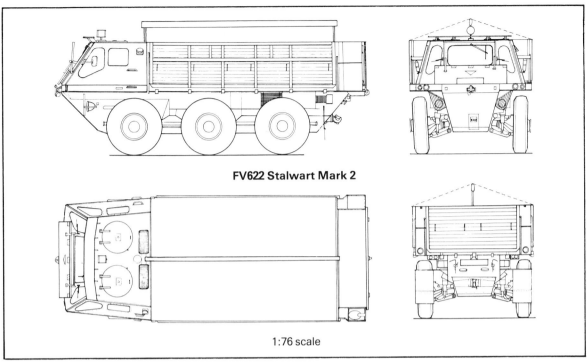

FV622 Stalwart Mark 2

1:76 scale

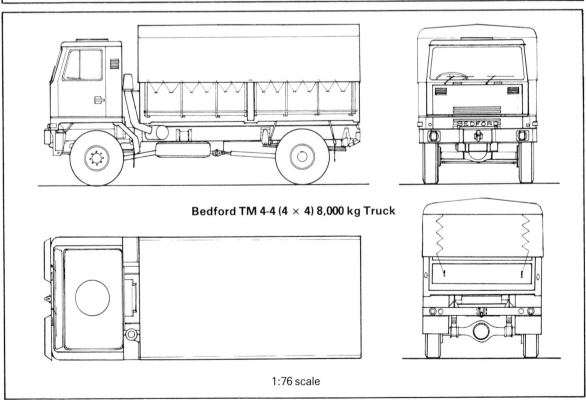

Bedford TM 4-4 (4 × 4) 8,000 kg Truck

1:76 scale

power 202 bhp; **Engine capacity** 8.198 litres; **Fuel capacity** 150 litres; **Body plus cargo payload** 10,000 kg.

During 1970 an Army requirement for a new 8-tonne truck was issued with an expected into-service date of 1980. Three concerns entered designs for the requirements and the result was a series of trials that began as soon as the first prototypes emerged during 1976. The three firms involved were Foden, Vauxhall Motors and Leyland, and the successful contestant emerged in 1977 as Vauxhall Motors of Luton. Their entrant was the Bedford TM 4 × 4, based on a commercial model but suitably modified to suit the needs of its exacting military role, namely that of being the main component of the Army's Medium Mobility 8-tonne range. A production contract worth £40 million was duly signed for around 2,000 vehicles. The first examples came off the Luton production lines during 1978 and these were subsequently subjected to a rigorous programme of tests and trials ready for the main production run starting in late 1979.

Four main versions have been ordered by the Army. The first will be a straightforward cargo truck, with its loading bed height compatible with that of existing 4-tonne trucks. Then will come two slight variants of the basic cargo truck, one with an 8,000 kg winch and the other with an Atlas AK 3500 crane mounted behind the cab. The fourth version will be a tipper truck with a shorter wheelbase of 3.883 metres as opposed to the normal 4.325 metres. Other versions that have been mentioned

are a tanker and a recovery vehicle. An airportable version has also been suggested.

Once in service the Bedford TM will be an important part of the Army's front-line logistic support. Starting in 1982 it will begin to replace some of the existing 4- and 10-tonne trucks at second and third-line level, but at whatever level it is used the Bedford TM will no doubt prove to be as capable as its 4-tonne RL and MK forebears.

AEC Militant Mark 1 (6 × 6) 10,000 kg trucks

Crew 2; **Weight loaded** 21,200 kg; **Length** 9.14 m; **Height** 3.6 m; **Width** 2.49 m; **Wheel track (front)** 1.99 m; **Wheel track (rear)** 1.91 m; **Maximum road speed** 40 km/h; **Range (roads)** 480 km; **Engine type** AEC 6-cylinder diesel; **Engine power** 150 bhp; **Engine capacity** 11.3 litres; **Fuel capacity** 218 litres.

The AEC 10-tonne range has been in British Army service for many years now and, although they are scheduled for replacement by 1983, they are still an important part of the Army's heavy-lift logistic range. The first of them were developed from existing commerical models by AEC during the early 1950s and ever since the first cargo versions were produced the basic design has been used for a variety of purposes. Some of these have been 6 × 4 vehicles and different wheelbase versions are still in service. The wheelbases built were either 3.92, 4.49 or 4.887 metres. Some vehicles have been fitted with HIAB cranes, and most examples in service

Left *A Bedford TM 4 × 4 with canvas tilt.*

Right *AEC Militant Mark 1 with load-ing crane used in Germany by Royal Engineers.*

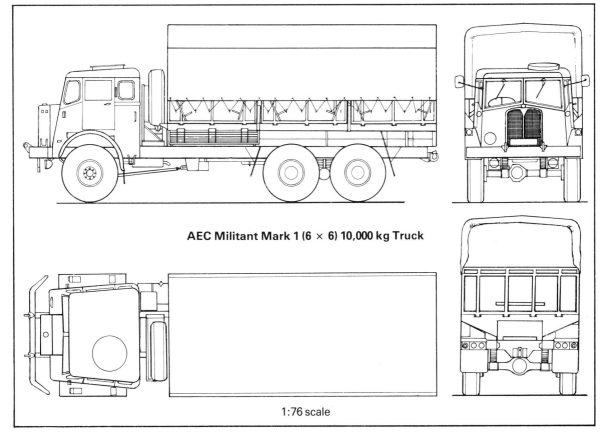

AEC Militant Mark 1 (6 × 6) 10,000 kg Truck

1:76 scale

are fitted with a 7,000 kg winch. A listing of the main variants is given below but not all are still in service and many have been converted to flat-bed trucks for carrying stores and ammunition pallets. All are due to be replaced by the new Bedford TM 8-tonne range but the old AECs will not be finally replaced for some time yet.

FV11001 Artillery Tractor, 6 × 4, w/b 3.92 m; **FV11002** Artillery Tractor for Bofors, 6 × 6, w/b 3.92 m; **FV11003** Crane Bridging, 6 × 6, w/b 4.493 m; **FV11005** Tipper, 6 × 4, w/b 3.92 m;

Above AEC Militant Mark 1 with cargo body. **Below** *Militant Mark 3. Few of these cargo trucks serve in the United Kingdom—nearly all were delivered direct to West Germany.* **Above right** *Foden FH70 gun tractor.* **Below right** *Side-on shot of a FH70 Tractor (Fodens Ltd).*

FV11008* Cargo Truck, 6 × 6, w/b 4.877 m; **FV11009** Fuel Tanker, 6 × 4, w/b 4.877 m; **FV11010** GS Semi-trailer, 6 × 6, w/b 3.92 m; **FV11013** Crane GP, 6 × 4, w/b 3.92 m; **FV11014** Excavator Carrier, 6 × 6, w/b 3.92 m; **FV11041** AEC Mark 2—trials only.

AEC Militant Mark 3 (6 × 6) 10,000 kg cargo truck

Crew 2; **Weight loaded** 22,000 kg; **Length** 9.07 m; **Height (to tarpaulin)** 3.5 m; **Width** 2.44 m; **Wheel track (front)** 2 m; **Wheel track (rear)** 2.06 m; **Maximum road speed** 53 km/h; **Range (roads)** 483 km; **Engine type** AEC AV760 diesel; **Engine power** 226 bhp; **Engine capacity** 12.473 litres; **Fuel capacity** 218 litres; **Load area** 6.248 × 2.337 m.

The AEC Mark 3 10-tonne truck was developed during the mid-1960s in answer to an Army requirement for a new 10-tonne general cargo truck. Production took place at the AEC factory at Southall in Middlesex and most of the output (the

*The data refers to this version.

FV11046/11047) are now used in Germany. The cargo body has drop sides for fork-lift loading, and most vehicles are fitted with a 7,000 kg winch. They are scheduled to be at first supplemented, and finally replaced, by the Bedford TM 8-tonne trucks. A variant is the FV 11044 Medium Recovery vehicle (qv).

Foden 6 × 6 Medium Mobility FH70 vehicles

Crew 1 + 8 (tractor)/1 + 2 (limber); **Weight loaded** 26,570 kg/28,488 kg; **Length** 9.15 m/9.046 m; **Height** 3.75 m/3.607 m; **Width** 2.489 m (tractor and limber); **Maximum speed (roads)** 109 km/h (tractor and limber); **Maximum speed (cross-country)** 54.5 km/h (tractor and limber); **Range** Unknown; **Engine type** Rolls-Royce Eagle 305 Mark III (tractor and limber); **Engine power** 305 bhp (tractor and limber); **Engine capacity** 12.17 litres (tractor and limber); **Fuel capacity** 409 litres (tractor and limber); **Ammunition capacity (155 mm)** 68/136 rounds.

The Foden 6 × 6 Medium Mobility vehicles share many of their components with the 8 × 4 Low

**Foden 6 × 6
Medium Mobility range**

1:76 scale

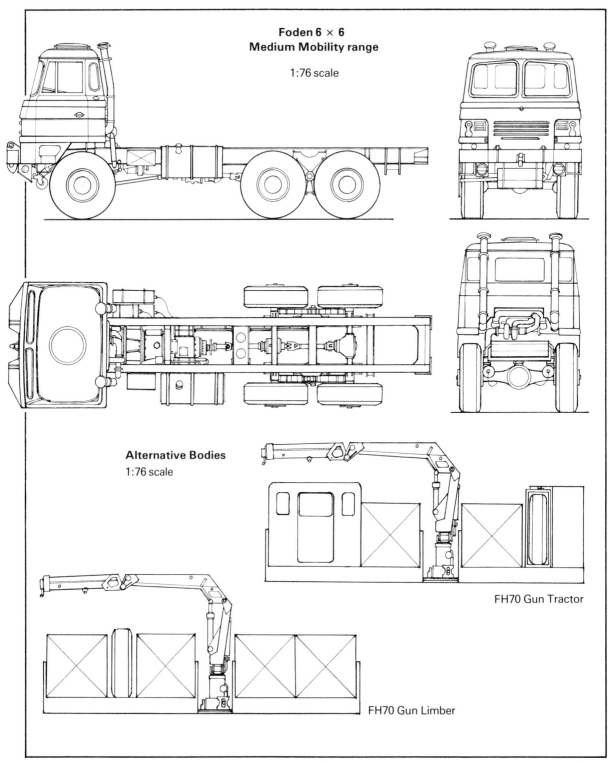

Alternative Bodies

1:76 scale

FH70 Gun Tractor

FH70 Gun Limber

Mobility range (perhaps the most obvious being the tilting S90 cab). The Medium Mobility range was developed primarily to provide towing and limber vehicles to service the 155 mm FH70 howitzer. Foden produced the 23 prototype vehicles used during the early howitzer trials and as a result were awarded the production contract for 111 vehicles during 1977. All the vehicles were produced at the Foden Works at Sandbach, Cheshire.

The FH70 tractor and the limber vehicle both use the same basic chassis and body, each of which has an auxiliary gearbox for use when crossing rough ground—this can be switched in or out as required. Both use the same articulated suspension and are equipped with an Atlas hydraulic crane for lifting the ammunition pallets. The tractor version carries a heated cabin pallet which can accommodate the eight-man howitzer crew, which is situated just behind the driver's cab. Also on the tractor are two standard NATO ammunition pallets each containing 34 rounds. At the rear is space for some of the howitzer spares and stores. The limber vehicle carries four ammunition pallets. Controls for the lifting crane are on the side of the vehicle.

Exactly how successful the FH70 vehicles will be in their role remains to be seen. The turbo-super-

charged Eagle engines will certainly have enough power for prolonged cross-country travelling but the view of some serving gunners is that they will prove to be too bulky and too high. Even at the ranges at which FH70 will be employed, the bulk of the tractor or limber will prove difficult to hide.

Bedford TM 6-6 (6 × 6) 14,000 kg Truck

Crew 1 + 1 or 2; **Weight loaded** 24,390 kg; **Length** 8.597 m; **Height (cab)** 2.997 m; **Width** 2.476 m; **Maximum speed (roads)** 89.7 km/h; **Range** 500 km; **Engine type** Bedford turbocharged diesel; **Engine power** 206 bhp at 2,500 rpm; **Engine capacity** 8.2 litres; **Maximum load** 14,000 kg.

The Bedford TM 6-6 may be regarded as a 6 × 6 version of the TM 4-4 8-tonne truck and both vehicles have many components in common. The first prototype TM 6-6 was ready in late 1981 and was followed by a further three prototypes in 1983. During 1984 eight more test vehicles were produced and if all is well the TM 6-6 will go into production for the Army in September 1986.

The TM 6-6 is seen as the replacement vehicle for the ageing AEC Militants and some of the other old trucks still in use such as the Leyland 10-tonne vehicles. Once in service the similarities between the

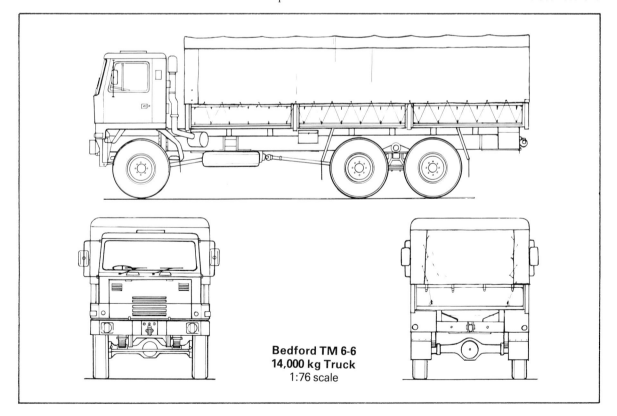

**Bedford TM 6-6
14,000 kg Truck**
1:76 scale

two TM vehicles will make servicing and spare part supply that much easier. The two trucks use the same engine, cooling system, exhaust, front axle and suspension, steering wheel and tyres. New equipment for the TM 6-6 relates mainly to the 6 × 6 configuration but includes a new transmission and transfer box.

Three versions of the TM 6-6 are planned: one with a standard cargo body; a second with the same body but equipped with a centrally-mounted recovery winch for loads up to 10,000 kg; and a third version with a platform body equipped with an Atlas crane behind the cab.

FV11701/11702 cargo truck

Crew 1 + 2; **Weight loaded** 29,553 kg; **Length** 10.278 m; **Height** 3.137 m; **Width** 2.497 m; **Maximum road speed** 76 km/h; **Range** Unknown; **Engine type** Rolls-Royce Eagle 220 Mark III; **Engine power** 220 bhp; **Engine capacity** 12.17 litres; **Fuel capacity** 227 litres; **Payload** 20,000 kg; **Body area** 8.23 × 2.5 m.

The Foden Low Mobility range has been produced to meet a British Army requirement for a new family of vehicles that could supply the various needs of service units, not only when travelling on

Left The Bedford TM 6-6 14-tonne truck fitted with a standard cargo body.

Below Foden 8 × 4 cargo truck.

roads but also on rough tracks. The Army vehicles are all based on commerical models which not only lowers the overall procurement costs but also makes provision for spare parts that much easier. Production of the Foden Low Mobility range began in 1976 and was substantially complete by 1978, and an indication of the importance of the range is that 70 per cent of the total run of 1,007 units were built with left-hand drive for use on the continent.

The most numerous of the range is the 8 × 4 cargo truck of which 703 were produced. Each vehicle has a payload of 20,000 kg and has drop sides and a dropping tailgate. A tilt can also be fitted

when required. The engine, transmission, cab, suspension and many other features are shared with the other vehicles in the Low Mobility range. Ease of accessibility is a feature carried over from the commercial models—for instance the cab can be tilted forward to expose the engine for removal without the cab being removed entirely. One item of note regarding the cab is that 20 were enlarged for driver training.

Foden 8 × 4 Low Mobility tanker
Crew 1 + 2; **Weight loaded** 28,888 kg; **Length** 10.27 m; **Height** 3.25 m; **Width** 2.502 m;

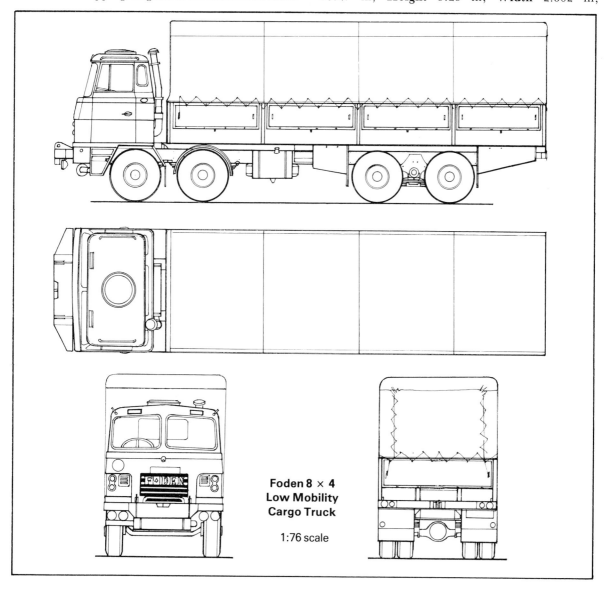

**Foden 8 × 4
Low Mobility
Cargo Truck**

1:76 scale

Above *Foden 8 × 4 Low Mobility Tanker.*

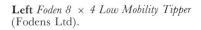

Left *Foden 8 × 4 Low Mobility Tipper (Fodens Ltd).*

Left *Foden 6 × 4 Low Mobility Tanker.*

Right *Antar Mark 3 towing a trailer loaded with a Chieftain.*

Maximum road speed 76 km/h; **Range** Unknown; **Engine type** Rolls-Royce Eagle 220 Mark III; **Engine power** 220 bhp; **Engine capacity** 12.17 litres; **Fuel capacity** 227 litres; **Tank capacity** 22,500 litres.

The Foden Low Mobility 8 × 4 tanker is the second most numerous of the Low Mobility range as 134 were produced. The large tank body is sectioned off internally into five compartments, each holding 4,500 litres. The tank itself was produced by Clarke Chapman of Bilston, Cheshire. It is expected that fuel will be the normal load for this tanker.

FV11703 Truck Tipper 11m³

Crew 1 + 2; **Weight loaded** 29,705 kg; **Length** 8.09 m; **Height** 3.139 m; **Width** 2.497 m; **Maximum road speed** 76 km/h; **Range** Unknown; **Engine type** Rolls-Royce Eagle 220 Mark III; **Engine power** 220 bhp; **Engine capacity** 12.17 litres; **Fuel capacity** 227 litres; **Body capacity** 11 m³.

The Low Mobility tipper was produced in smaller numbers than the rest of the range as only 70 were delivered. This version differs from the other 8 × 4 vehicles as it has a shorter wheelbase.

Foden 6 × 4 Low Mobility tanker

Crew 1 + 2; **Weight loaded** 22,786 kg; **Length** 8.75 m; **Height** 3.124 m; **Width** 2.497 m; **Maximum road speed** 87 km/h; **Range** Unknown; **Engine type** Rolls-Royce Eagle 220 Mark III; **Engine power** 220 bhp; **Engine capacity** 12.17 litres; **Fuel capacity** 227 litres; **Tank capacity** 12,000 litres.

One hundred of the 6 × 4 Low Mobility tankers were delivered to the British Army. Like their larger 8 × 4 counterparts, they will be used mainly for the carriage of fuel. (NB: Foden is now part of Paccar UK Ltd.)

FV 12004 Tractor Wheeled Semi-Trailer (Thornycroft Antar Mark 3, 30 tonne 6 × 4)

Crew 3; **Weight (with ballast)** 23,040 kg; **Weight (less ballast)** 21,900 kg; **Length** 8.7 m; **Height** 3.15 m; **Width** 3.2 m; **Wheel track (front)** 2.25 m; **Wheel track (rear)** 2.286 m; **Maximum road speed** 32.18 km/h; **Range (roads—laden)** 702 km; **Engine type** Rolls-Royce C8SFL-843 diesel; **Engine power** 333 bhp; **Engine capacity** 16.2 litres; **Fuel capacity** 910 litres.

The Thornycroft Antar was originally a commercial design that originated during the late 1940s, and was subsequently adopted by the Army for towing tank transporter trailers. The first service

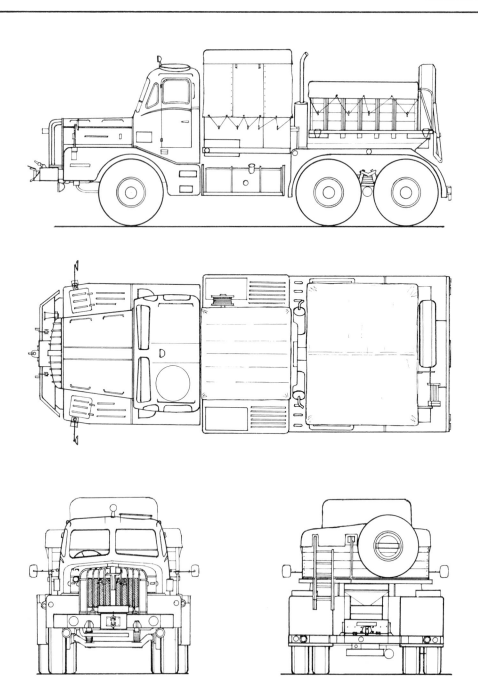

FV12004 Tractor Wheeled Semi-Trailer
(Thornycroft Antar Mark 3, 30 tonne 6 × 4)

1:76 scale

Antar was the FV12001 which was used for pulling trailers only. The FV12002 could be converted to pull semi-trailers as well, as could the next version, the FV12003. With the FV12004 Antar Mark 3 considerable improvements were made over the earlier marks. The ability to tow either trailers or semi-trailers was retained but a new and more powerful engine was fitted along with a new transmission, and some alterations were made to the cab. In this form the Antar Mark 3 is the current tank-towing tractor in service today. Originally the Antars towed Centurions but now they tow Chieftains, and many are being driven by their second generation of drivers. To assist with the loading of disabled vehicles on to their trailers, the Antars are fitted with a 20,000 kg winch.

The Antar Mark 3 is usually employed to tow a semi-trailer when Chieftains are the main load, but a trailer, the origins of which can be traced back to the Second World War, is still an alternative. The types involved and their relevant data are as follows: FV30011 Semi-trailer Tanker-transporter (50 ton-tonne) and FV3601 Trailer, Tank Transporter No. 1 Mark 3 (50 tonne). **Weight laden** 66,360 kg (FV30011/68,640 kg (FV3601); **Weight unladen** 16,360 kg/18,640 kg; **Length** 11.925 m/10.211 m; **Height** 3.086 m/2.21 m; **Width** 3.353 m/3.2 m; **Wheel track (outer)** 2.692 m/2.4 m.

Scammell Commander tank transporter
Crew 1 + 3 or 4; **Weight empty** 19,920 kg; **Gross combination weight** 104,000 kg; **Length (tractor unit)** 9.01 m; **Height** 3.5 m; **Width** 3.25 m; **Wheelbase** 5.03 m; **Maximum road speed (loaded)** 61 km/h; **Engine type** Rolls-Royce CV12 TCE turbocharged diesel; **Engine power** 625 bhp at 2,100 rpm; **Fuel capacity** 817 litres.

Design work on the Scammell Commander began in 1976 with the first examples being ready in 1978. At that time it was uncertain exactly what engine would eventually be required by the Army so some of the early prototypes were fitted with the Rolls-Royce CV12 TCE diesel and another by an American Cummins KTA 600 diesel—in the end the Rolls-Royce engine was selected. However, that selection

The imposing bulk of a Scammell Commander tractor with the trailer carrying a Chieftain MBT.

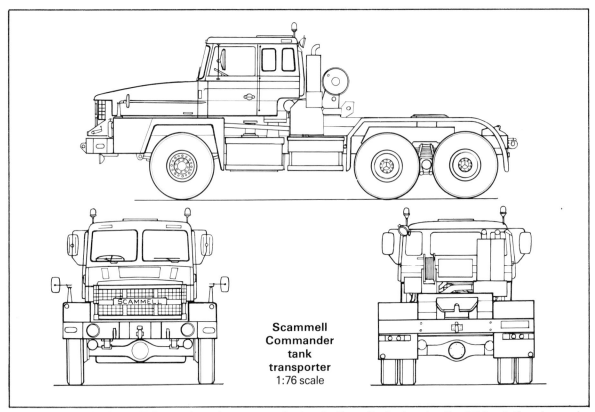

**Scammell
Commander
tank
transporter**
1:76 scale

Below *An unloaded Scammell Commander tank transporter showing the Crane Freuhauf semi-trailer.* **Right** *A Crusader carrying construction equipment.*

took time for, although a General Staff Requirement for the Commander was issued in 1981, it was not 'endorsed' at the time due to defence spending cuts. It was not until late 1982 that a definite order was placed for 125 units. It was mid-1984 before the Commander officially entered service with 7 Tank Transporter Regiment, RCT, at Fallingbostel, and with its UK-based 414 Tank Transporter Troop, RCT, at Bulford.

The Commander was ordered as the elderly Antars are unable to carry the weight of the new Challenger MBT. They will be used to carry the Challenger only which means that the Antars will have to be retained in service to pull the Chieftains. 7 Tank Transporter Regiment will have 91 Commander tractors and 83 trailers. 414 Tank Transporter Troop will have 22 Commanders and trailers and there is a war reserve of ten tractors and trailers. A further two Commanders and trailers will be based at Emblem, near Antwerp.

The Commander is a prodigious beast that is not only twice as fast as the Antar but also takes a much shorter time to load. It is used to pull a new Crane Freuhauf trailer and loading can be assisted by a heavy duty Rotzler winch with a 20,300 kg line pull. The cab has many driver comforts with full interior heating and ventilating equipment but what will be most appreciated on long journeys is the provision for one or two crew bunks at the rear of the cab.

FV12006/FV12007 Scammell Crusader

Crew 1 (20,000 kg version)/4 (35,000 kg version); **Weight empty** 9,200 kg/10,567 kg; **Length** 6.661 m (both versions); **Height** 3.3 m (both versions); **Width** 2.502 m (both versions); **Wheel track (front)** 2.05 m (both versions); **Wheel track (rear)** 1.845 m (both versions); **Maximum road speed** 85 km/h/66 km/h; **Range (roads—approx)** 500 km (both versions); **Engine type** Rolls-Royce Eagle Mark III (both versions); **Engine power** 305 bhp (both versions); **Engine capacity** 12.17 litres (both versions); **Fuel capacity** 318 litres/455 litres; **Load capacity** 20,000 kg/35,000 kg.

The Scammell Crusader is a commercial vehicle used by the Army mainly as a tractor for trailers carrying heavy plant and equipment. Most of the Crusaders in service are used for towing Royal Engineer low-loader trailers carrying such items as dozers, graders and the FV180 CET. There are two versions in service, the smallest of which is the 20,000 kg type with a two-man cab, and the other the 35,000 kg version with a four-man cab. Both vehicles can double as tank transporter tractors if so required but the 20,000 kg version will not be able to tow MBTs. There are various trailers in use but one has been specially developed for use with the 20,000 kg version by Crane Fruehauf. It is a 10-tonne tilt trailer with the following dimensions: **Length overall** 8.535 m; **Height of platform (unladen)** 1.118 m; **Width** 2.438 m; **Wheel track** 1.82 m.

Other special trailers towed by the Crusader include the No 9 AVLB bridge trailer which can, under certain circumstances, unload the bridge directly across damaged road bridges. Another trailer can be used to carry spare 175 mm M107 gun barrels and there are also a few used to transport disabled M2 ferry units. Other plant trailers include one model (the Craven Task 37-tonne RE Plant-carrying Semi-trailer) that uses a detachable goose-neck to aid the loading of large or bulky loads.

Tractor, Wheeled, Fork Lift 4,000 lb— Eager Beaver Mark 2

Crew 1; **Weight complete** 2,961 kg; **Weight airportable** 2,560 kg; **Length** 5.461 m; **Height (fork raised to maximum)** 3.708 m; **Height (top of mast)** 2.388; **Height (airportable)** 1.829 m; **Width** 1.854 m; **Wheel track** 1.55 m; **Maximum road speed** 64 km/h; **Range (roads)** 644 km; **Range (cross-country)** 322 km; **Engine type** Perkins 4-236 diesel; **Engine power** 78 bhp; **Engine capacity** 3.8 litres; **Fuel capacity** Unknown; **Maximum lift** 1,814 kg.

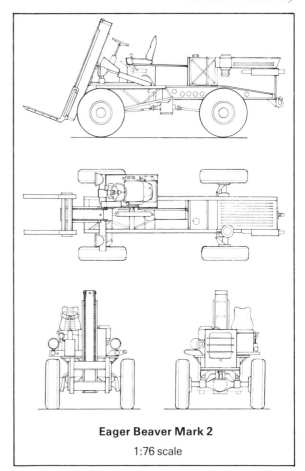

Eager Beaver Mark 2
1:76 scale

Eager Beaver Mark 2.

The Eager Beaver is a rough terrain fork lift tractor specially designed for the needs of the modern Army. It is very much a 'go-anywhere' vehicle capable of carrying a wide range of loads from ammunition and fuel pallets to engine packs and spares. A product of the Royal Ordnance Factory, Nottingham, the Eager Beaver is used by many branches of the Army for rapid loading of trucks and vehicles under a range of conditions. It can be either a 4 × 2 or a 4 × 4 vehicle, and can ford up to 0.76 metres of water.

The fork lift itself is mounted on an adjustable mast which can be tilted 13° forward and 20° backwards—for air transport it can be laid back at an angle of 60°. The lift can be raised to a maximum of 2.737 metres. Extras are a small crane and an enclosed cab to protect the driver from really inclement weather.

Experiments have been made with some Eager Beavers to allow them to be operated by radio remote control. These experiments went on through

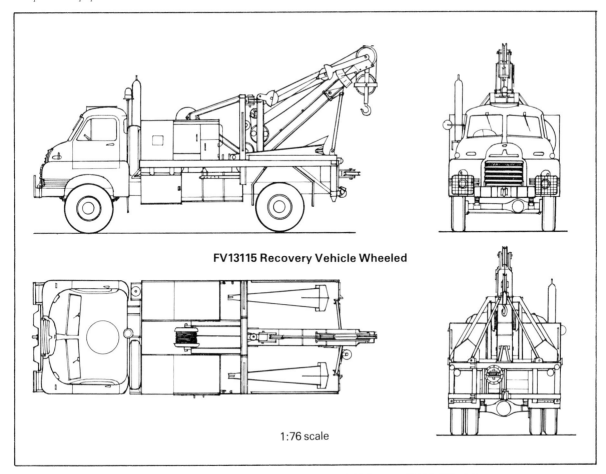

FV13115 Recovery Vehicle Wheeled

1:76 scale

1978 in an attempt to counter the use of car bombs in Northern Ireland and elsewhere. The idea is to lift a suspect car bomb and remove it to a position where its possible destructive effect will be minimised or where bomb clearance crews can use their specialised equipment to better effect.

FV13115 Recovery Vehicle Wheeled— Light (Bedford 4-tonne 4 × 4)

Crew 2; **Weight loaded** 8,128 kg; **Length** 7.976 m; **Height** 2.705 m; **Width** 2.324 m; **Wheel track (front)** 1.854 m; **Wheel track (rear)** 1.708 m; **Maximum road speed** 80 km/h; **Range (roads)** 400 km; **Engine type** Bedford 6-cylinder OHV; **Engine power** 130 bhp; **Engine capacity** 4.93 litres; **Fuel capacity** 118 litres.

The FV13115 is the recovery vehicle variant of the Bedford RL family, and mounts a jib crane at the rear. The crane, like the vehicle winch, is powered by a power take-off from the main engine, and can lift up to 3,000 kg. The winch can be used

FV13115 Recovery Vehicle Wheeled.

to either the front or rear, but in the latter case an earth anchor is provided which can increase the maximum pull from 7,000 kg to 13,000 kg.

The FV 13115 is now on its way out after many years of service and will be replaced by a Reynolds Boughton (4 × 4) 6,000 kg recovery vehicle. This has a Bedford M-type chassis combined with a Bedford TK-style cab. The recovery hamper is a Reynolds Boughton design and has a traversing jib mounted on a turret. When this crane is in use four legs situated at each corner of the top hamper are used to stabilise the vehicle. The top hamper is well supplied with tool boxes and other stowage space. Not much information has been issued regarding this new vehicle, but it has a wheelbase of 3.962 m, length is 6.452 m, height 2.591 m and width 2.438 m.

FV11044 Recovery Vehicle Wheeled— Medium (AEC Mark 3 6 × 6)

Crew 3/4; **Weight loaded** 21,019 kg; **Length** 8.23 m; **Height** 3.1 m; **Width** 2.502 m; **Wheel track** 2 m; **Maximum road speed** 78 km/h; **Range (roads)** 483 km; **Engine type** AEC AV 760 diesel; **Engine power** 226 bhp; **Engine capacity** 12.47 litres; **Fuel capacity** 218 litres. (See plans on page 227.)

The AEC Mark 3 recovery vehicle was developed during the 1960s as a replacement for the old FV11301 Scammell 6 × 6. Only the chassis and engine are actually AEC-produced, and emanate from their Southall factory. The recovery equipment came from the Thornycroft works at Basingstoke, and the crane from Coles of Sunderland.

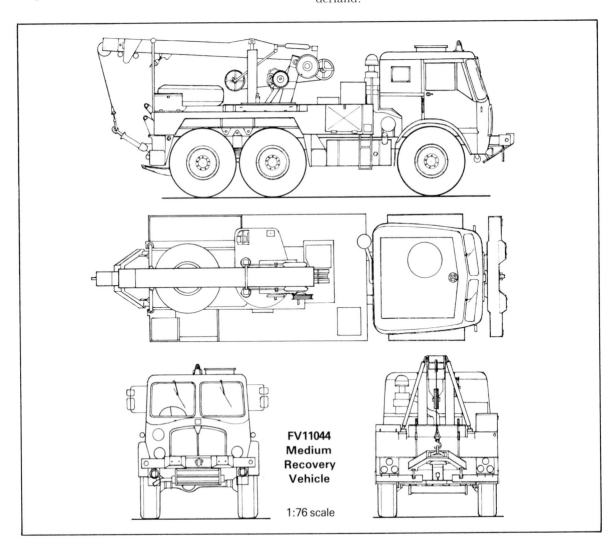

FV11044
Medium
Recovery
Vehicle

1:76 scale

Top *FV11044 in action towing an FV101 Scorpion.* **Above** *The new Reynolds Boughton 6,000 kg recovery vehicle which will replace the FV13115.*

The AEC Mark 3 can be used to recover vehicles up to the 10-tonne class, its main lifting component being the Coles hydraulic crane fitted to the rear chassis. The crane has a jib which can extend from 3.124 to 5.563 metres. The jib can also be slewed through 240°. Outrigger jacks can be used to stabilise the vehicle and crane when it is used to lift up to 2,600 kg at maximum jib extension. A winch fitted to the rear can pull up to 15,000 kg but when a

hydraulically-operated earth spade is lowered, this can increase the pull up to 30,000 kg. There are towing hooks at the front and rear, and the vehicle is well provided with all the special tools required for the recovery role.

FV1119 Recovery Vehicle Wheeled— Heavy (Leyland 10-tonne 6 × 6)

Crew 3; **Weight loaded** 21,604 kg; **Length** 8.89 m;

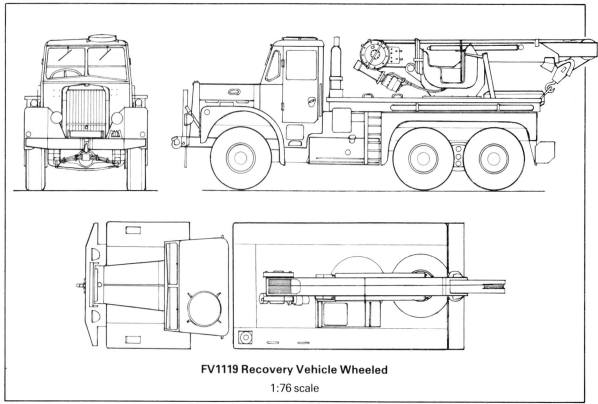

FV1119 Recovery Vehicle Wheeled

1:76 scale

Height 3.1 m; **Width** 2.591 m; **Wheel track (front)** 2.089 m; **Wheel track (rear)** 2.096 m; **Maximum road speed** 56.2 km/h; **Range (roads)** 562 km; **Engine type** Rolls-Royce B81 Mark 5K; **Engine power** 195 bhp; **Engine capacity** 6.62 litres; **Fuel capacity** 446 litres.

The Leyland 10-tonne recovery vehicle is based on the chassis of the FV1103 cargo truck, but the main difference is the provision of a swivelling hydraulic crane with a lifting capacity of up to 15,000 kg. The crane can swivel through 240° and has a jib which extends from 3.048 to 5.486 metres. A two-speed hydraulic winch is fitted which, in conjunction with the hydraulically operated rear earth spade, can pull up to 39,000 kg. As with all other similar vehicles, rear and front towing eyes are fitted. A special low-loader trailer was developed for this vehicle and is designated FV3221 Trailer Recovery (10-tonne). The FV1119 uses its winch to load the trailer. Dimensions for the trailer are as follows: **Weight loaded** 20,067 kg; **Weight empty** 7,130 kg; **Length** 7.28 kg; **Height** 1.9 m; **Width** 2.74 m; **Wheel track** 2.057 m.

Left *FV1119 Recovery Vehicle Wheeled.*

Crusader/EKA 6 × 4 Recovery Vehicle

Crew 1 + 3; **Weight loaded (approx)** 46,700 kg; **Length** Unknown; **Height** 3.25 m; **Width** 2.502 m; **Wheel track (front)** 2.166 m; **Wheel track (rear)** 1.845 m; **Maximum road speed** 78 km/h; **Range (roads—approx)** 500 km; **Engine type** Rolls-Royce Eagle 305 Mark III; **Engine power** 305 bhp; **Engine capacity** 12.17 litres; **Fuel capacity** 454.5 litres.

Based on the Crusader 35,000 kg tractor, the Crusader 6 × 4 Recovery Vehicle was ordered by the British Army in late 1977. At that time it was announced that 130 were to be delivered. It uses the Swedish EKA hydraulic recovery equipment mounted on the rear of the vehicle and, as well as being used as a recovery hoist, the jib can also be used as a crane. As with all other recovery vehicles the Crusader version is well equipped with winches. The main one is at the rear and, in conjunction with a hydraulically operated spade, has a pulling power of up to 22 tonnes—50 metres of cable is supplied for it. The front winch is mainly used for self-recovery and has a maximum pull of 7.7 tonnes with 40 metres of cable. Carried over from the Crusader tractor are the four-man cab and the 15

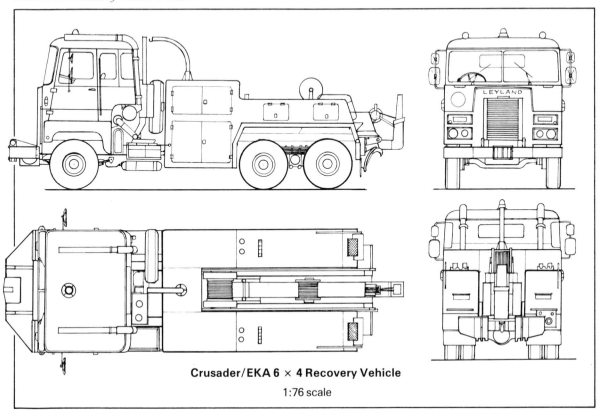

Crusader/EKA 6 × 4 Recovery Vehicle

1:76 scale

forward-speed gearbox.

The main feature of the Crusader Recovery Vehicle is its main lifting gear. This is a most adaptable piece of equipment that can be fitted with a variety of attachments to make it an extremely versatile hoist capable of tackling many recovery tasks. It has a maximum lifting capacity of 22 tonnes, power for the hydraulic mechanism coming from the vehicle's main engine.

Foden (6 × 6) Recovery Vehicle

Crew 1 + 3; **Weight loaded** 25,338 kg; **Length** 9.055 m; **Height (cab)** 3.55 m; **Width** 2.492 m; **Wheelbase** 4.728 m + 1.516 m; **Track (front/rear)** 2.029 m/2.06 m; **Engine type** Rolls-Royce Eagle 390 turbocharged diesel; **Engine output** 300 hp at 1,950 rpm; **Fuel capacity** 360 litres.

The Foden (6 × 6) Recovery Vehicle was ordered for the Army in September 1984 and in time 333 will be delivered. This recovery vehicle is an off-shoot of

Below left *Scammell Crusader/EKA with the lifting jib stowed.* **Below right** *1-5 tonne Dummy Axle.* **Bottom left** *The Foden (6 × 6) recovery vehicle showing the recovery top hamper (Fodens Ltd).* **Bottom right** *10-30 tonne Dummy Axle.*

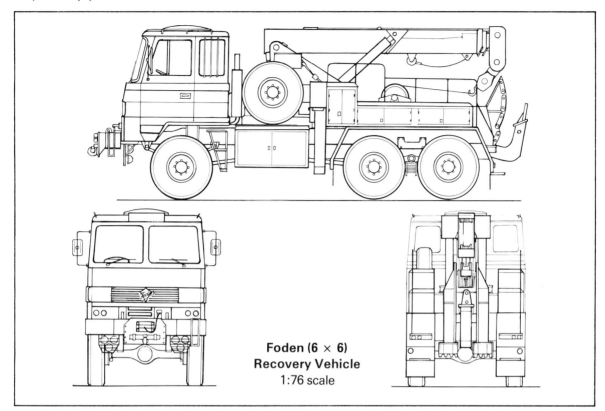

**Foden (6 × 6)
Recovery Vehicle
1:76 scale**

the Foden FH70 tractor and limber vehicle range and inherits many of their features, the cross-country performance also being similar. It is thus a large vehicle with a recovery performance to match. It carries a top hamper known as the AK6500 EA 12 with the usual form of EKA support/tow jib. This is a folding boom with a maximum lift capacity of 11,000 kg that allows it to recover any in-service logistic support vehicle. There is also a Rotzler winch with a single line pull capacity and 80 m of wire rope. However, the main and most prominent item of recovery equipment is a slewing crane with a maximum lift capacity of 12,000 kg. When this is in use two extensible hydraulically operated outriggers are used. In addition to all this equipment there is the usual stowage for tools and other equipment and a NATO towing hook.

FV2692 Trailer, Dummy Axle, Recovery, 1-5 tonnes

Weight unladen 1,183 kg; **Length** 3.47 m; **Height** 2.31 m; **Width** 2.362 m; **Wheel track** 1.816 m.

Developed from the earlier FV2691, the 1-5-tonne Dummy Axle is used in the recovery role for the rapid transport of disabled vehicles up to a weight of 6.25 tonnes. In use, the vehicle is lifted by the Dummy Axle's crane, and after being secured, the axle can then be towed carrying its load. The lifting crane, or winch, does not carry the load once it has been secured to the Axle by spreader bars. The FV2692 is produced by Rubery Owen (Warrington) Limited, of Darlaston.

FV3561 Trailer, Dummy Axle, Recovery, 10-30 tonnes

Weight unladen 2,900 kg; **Length** 3.658 m; **Height** 3.226 m; **Width** 2.388 m; **Wheel track** 1.778 m; **Engine type** Hatz air-cooled diesel; **Engine power** 7.5 bhp; **Engine capacity** 0.433 litres.

The FV3561 Trailer follows the same general lines as the lighter FV2692 but, due to the extra weight it will have to raise, it is fitted with a small diesel engine to drive the hydraulic pump for the winch. This has a lifting capacity of 10,400 kg, and a small hand winch is used to position the A frame and towing bar which actually carries the load. Almost any wheeled vehicle up to the size of an Antar can be carried on the 10-30 tonne Dummy Axle. Production is carried out by Royal Ordnance factories.

Miscellaneous vehicles

Left *The Mini, the Army's universal runabout for junior officers and others, now in the process of being supplemented by the Metro. Further up the scale comes the Ford Escort/Vauxhall Chevette while the standard staff car is the Vauxhall Cavalier.*

Below left *A Ford Granada used by the Royal Military Police Special Patrol Group in Germany for escort duties and autobahn traffic control (MoD).*

Bottom left *The Leyland Sherpa is one of the Army's 'universal' vehicles used for all manner of utility tasks from delivering light loads to being used as a minibus. This minibus version was photographed on Gibraltar.*

Above right *110 of these 6 × 6 Scammell self-loading dump trucks were ordered for the Royal Engineers in late 1984 and mid-1985. Although they are intended mainly for the construction role they can carry a load of 9,168 kg and the self-loading crane behind the cab has a maximum lifting capacity of 2,000 kg (Scammell Motors).*

Right *One of 135 Dodge buses ordered for the Army in early 1985. These buses can be used as ambulances and can also be converted for the NBC decontamination role.*

Above *The Supacat is a 6 × 6 all-terrain vehicle with a load capacity of 1,000 kg which is used by the Army for range duties and other such tasks. It can carry up to six men, including the driver, and can tow a special trailer.*

Left *The Rolba Goblin is one of the Army's more unusual vehicles for it is used in Northern Ireland to carry EOD equipment to rural sites. It is carried to a location near the EOD task by helicopter and is intended for use over short distances only. It weighs 390 kg but can carry a load of 410 kg. Driven by a 28 hp Citröen petrol engine, it uses chain drive to provide a full 4 × 4 drive (Rolba Limited).*

Still going strong

Not all the vehicles in the Army are as modern as many would like for some veterans are still in use. Only a few of these are illustrated here.

Right *A FV13209 Commer Q4 fitted with a workshop body still used by a REME workshop in Germany.*

Right *The FV1103(A) 6 × 6 tractor was developed during the early 1950s as a medium artillery tractor and was used for a variety of artillery tasks. Its last major towing role was as tractor for the 5.5-inch gun-howitzer but the few now left are used mainly for driver training.*

Right *Dating from the early 1950s is the Truck, 10-ton, 6 × 4, Machinery RE, FV11102, an Albion WD/HD/23N. These trucks are still used by the Royal Engineers for the simple reason that they are too costly to replace and are thus kept going.*

Another veteran still in service. The Leyland FV1110(A) 10-ton trucks date from the early 1950s but are still likely to be encountered. They are well overdue for replacement by the Bedford TM 6-6.

Bridges

M2

Crew 1 + 3; **Weight** 22,000 kg; **Length** 11.35 m; **Height** 3.7 m; **Width (road)** 3 m; **(water)** 5.92 m; **Wheel track (front/rear)** 2.13 m/2.161 m; **Wheelbase** 5.35 m; **Maximum road speed** 60 km/h; **Speed in water (single rig, no payload)** 8 knots; **(3-rig ferry, 60-ton load)** 6 knots; **Range (road)** 1,000 km; **(water)** 6 hours; **Engine type** 2 × Deutz Model F 8 L 714a diesels; **Engine power** 2 × 178 hp.

The M2 is a West German amphibious ferry and bridging system that is also used by the West German Army. The first of them were produced during the late 1960s and today they are used by only one British Army regiment, 28 Ampibious Engineer Regiment, RE, (the 'Rubber Ducks').

No 28 Amphibious Engineer Regiment, RE, has one of the most complicated internal organisations in the Army. It consists of a Regimental Headquarters controlling two Amphibious Engineer Squadrons (23 and 64) supported by 71 Amphibious Engineer Support Squadron and 28 Amphibious Engineer Regiment Workshop (REME). Each of the Amphibious Engineer Squadrons has two Troops and in peacetime each Troop has four sections, each with three M2s, known as 'rigs'. However, in time of war each Troop would have an extra section. Some of the rigs for these extra sections come from within the regiment's own resources and some from outside. 71

Amphibious Engineer Support Squadron has a Troop that simply holds the spare rigs ready for use while more are held in a central engineer park. 71 also has a training function with a single Training Troop that in time of war would immediately add its weight to the operational total. Normally this Troop has four three-rig sections with another added in war. The rest of the Support Squadron is made up of a Diving Section (for reconnaissance), a Plant Section with CETs and Light Wheeled Tractors (for approach preparation) and a Resources Section with CSBs (for safety) and heavy trucks.

No 28 Amphibious Engineer Regiment Workshop (REME) is one of the largest establishments of its kind within the Army for the M2s take some looking after. The Workshop has a main element close to 28's main base at Hameln (Hamelin) on the River Weser. This Workshop Main runs very much along factory lines. It controls three Workshop platoons that would move out into the field with the squadrons and keep them going in the field.

The above is only an outline of the M2 organisation for when one delves, it does become very complex. There are over 100 M2 rigs in service with the regiment in all, but at any one time several will be away undergoing what amounts to a total re-build at the EWK/KHD facilities. Such attention is made necessary because of the stressed alloy construction used on these amphibious vehicles coupled with the hydraulic systems needed to raise and lower the

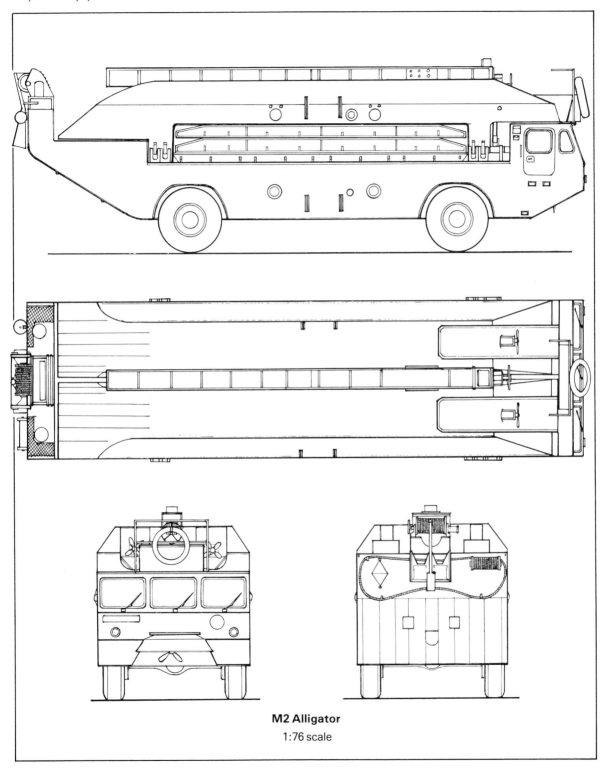

M2 Alligator
1:76 scale

Above *M2s forming a bridge with a Challenger MBT crossing* (RSME).

Left *An M2 ready for the road.*

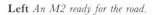

Left *An M2 rig about to leave the River Weser near Hameln.*

hinged buoyancy tanks. Before each rig enters the water these tanks are lowered into position each side of the vehicle and a hand-operated crane is used to position vehicle ramps. The rigs can act either as single-vehicle ferries or be joined together to act as floating bridges. Once in the water the rigs are driven by two engines, one powering propellers for sideways propulsion and the other powering a single steering propeller. The road wheels are raised when in the water. The training for these water-borne skills is provided within 28 Regiment by 71 Amphibious Engineer Support Squadron.

For many years the version used by the Army has been the M2B but this is changing to a new version known as the M2D, another result of the introduction of the Challenger MBT into BAOR since the M2B has a load classification of Class 70 only. The M2D has a classification of Class 93 which can accommodate the Challenger comfortably. The extra load capacity comes from the addition of extra engine-inflatable bags along the sides with more powerful hydraulics to cope with the increased weight. The modifications are factory-introduced.

The Medium Girder Bridge

The Medium Girder Bridge is an important component of the British Army's planned mobility in Europe and for this reason is here considered in some detail. Rapid bridging of defiles, river or water obstacles and other terrain gaps is an important factor in the consideration of fluid modern warfare, and to keep large armoured formations moving the military bridge is thus an essential item.

With a wealth of experience gained in combat by the exploits of the Royal Engineers, consideration of a new bridge led to an extensive design and development programme at the MVEE at Christchurch during the 1960s. The result was what is now known as the Medium Girder Bridge, the first examples of which were introduced into service during 1971. Production was, and still is, by Fairey Engineering Limited at Stockport, for the Medium Girder Bridge (MGB) has proved to be a tremendous export success and has been sold to over 25 countries, including the USA.

There are several factors involved in the success of the MGB, one of which is the material employed for most of the components. It is a novel alloy of aluminium, zinc and magnesium which is not only weldable and tough but also very light. As a result the bridge is constructed from components that can be manhandled, and no mechanical aids are necessary in the assembly of the bridge itself—everything can be accomplished by manpower alone. Another important factor is that any type of

Chieftain on a single-span MGB.

bridge can be constructed using only seven types of component, rather in the manner of an oversize Meccano set. The largest of these components is capable of being handled by six men—others only require four. These parts and their weights are as follows: **Top panel** 175 kg; **Bottom panel** 197 kg; **Junction panel** 182 kg; **End taper panel** 272 kg; **Ramp unit** 120 kg; **Bankseat beam** 258 kg; **Deck unit** 74 kg. They are stored and carried on standard pallets, and can be used to assemble several types of bridge, as outlined below.

Single span: This is the most basic of all the MGB structures and can be up to 31 metres long if a Chieftain tank is to be the heaviest vehicle to cross—lighter vehicles can cross longer spans. The construction can be either single- or double-storey with the double-storey method being capable of carrying the heavy loads. A building party of 25 men is needed to construct a double-storey single-span bridge 30 metres long, but they can complete the task in about 45 minutes. One of the most useful features of the MGB is that it can be constructed by relatively untrained personnel.

Assembly of all the various bridge types follows the same basic pattern. Working from one bank only, a building frame is constructed on which the various components are fixed. As construction progresses, the frame supports the completed portions and holds them as they are progressively pushed out over the gap—rollers on the frame enable this to be done. As the lengthy completed portions hang over the gap, counterweights made from unused bridge components counteract the completed weight, and at the front of the completed portion a launching nose unit is fitted. Small bridges can be pushed by manpower alone but bridges over about 30 metres require the use of some form of pusher vehicle.

Chieftain crossing a double-storey MGB (MoD).

Link reinforcement set: The addition of a link reinforcement set to a single-span bridge enables much longer spans to be made capable of carrying up to Class 60 vehicles such as Chieftain. The longest single span capable of carrying such a vehicle is 31 metres—by the addition of the rein-forcement set this can be substantially increased. For instance, single spans up to 49.4 metres capable of carrying a Chieftain can be built. An extra eight men are needed in addition to the normal 24/25 needed for single span construction. The reinforcing links are fitted beneath the bridge girders.

Multi-span: For really wide gaps or water crossings it may not be possible to construct a single

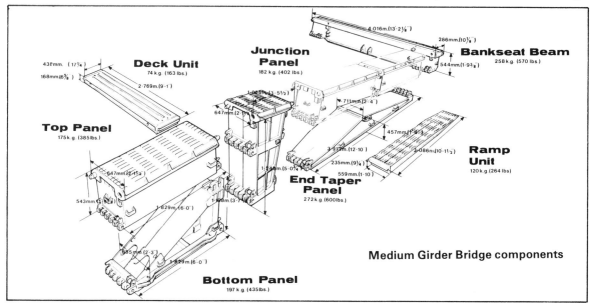

Medium Girder Bridge components

span long enough so multi-spans have to be used. These are made up of single spans utilising one or more intermediate piers. Piers may be formed from the remains of demolished bridges or specially constructed parts made up from whatever can be gleaned locally—spare MGB components are one possibility. The separate single spans are joined by a span junction set, which consists of a linking component which can be set to any suitable angle, and other parts such as capsills. If required, a portable pier set can be used to provide custom-made piers. When multi-span bridges are used the length of each single span is limited to 26.5 metres, so a two-span bridge will be up to 51 metres long and a three-span bridge up to 76 metres long.

Although MGB components are stored and carried on pallets, the make-up of each pallet varies. There are eight different pallet 'kits', each type of bridge being assembled from differing kits. Whatever the bridge type, the components are usually carried on 4-tonne trucks, each of which tows more components on a special trailer known as the FV2842; this has the following dimensions: **Weight unladen** 1,461 kg; **Length** 5.867 m; **Height overall (loaded)** 2.616 m; **Width** 2.565 m; **Wheel track** 2.261 m.

One small detail worth mentioning regarding the MGB is that a special training model has been produced that exactly duplicates the construction and handling methods used on the real thing in 1:12 scale. It is made by Miltra Training Aids of Harrow.

The range of different types of military bridge that can be formed from MGB and special MGB components is enormous, and its versatility and ease of adaptation to almost any military bridging need makes the MGB an important part of the Army's equipment. It will remain in service for a very long time. Considering that the old World War 2 Bailey Bridge is still a fairly common engineering tool, the MGB may continue in service in the year 2000 and long beyond.

Class 16 Air-portable bridge

The Class 16 Air-portable bridge is yet another design product of the Military Engineering Establishment at Christchurch, and is constructed from the same aluminium-zinc-magnesium alloy as that used on the Medium Girder bridge. Like the larger bridge, the air-portable version is made up of a number of standard components.

For a straightforward clearspan bridge capable of spanning a gap of up to 15.2 metres only two standard parts are necessary: deck boxes and ramps, the dimensions of which are as follows: **Weight** 305 kg (deck box)/346 kg (ramp); **Length** 3.6 m/3.6 m;

Height 0.38 m/0.38 m; **Width** 1.2 m/1.8 m.

For a 15.2-metre clearspan bridge seven deck boxes and four ramps are required. Such a bridge can be constructed by 16 men in about 20 minutes. The complete bridge can be carried on three ¾-tonne Land Rovers pulling special trailers. The trailer used is the FV2420 with the following details: **Weight unladen** 340 kg; **Length** 3.81 m; **Height** 0.711 m; **Width** 2.006 m; **Wheel track** 1.752 m.

A more general application of the Air-portable bridge is as a floating structure but for this role extra components are needed. These are articulator boxes and float and support units. The deck boxes are laid across the float and support frames and the articulator boxes are fitted at each end. The floating bridge can be up to 58 metres long. The floats themselves are collapsible and are inflated by the exhausts of the Land Rovers used to carry the bridge. Five Land Rovers and trailers can carry a floating bridge and the assembly takes 24 men about 45 minutes.

One extra application of the Air-portable bridge is as a powered raft. Such a raft uses all the components of a floating bridge with the addition of sponsons, each of which carries an outboard motor. A standard powered raft measures 22 metres overall (with a 12.2 metre long deck) and has four sponsons, and thus four motors. Longer rafts up to 28 metres long overall can be constructed but need six outboard motors and sponsons. Production of the Class 16 Bridge is carried out by Laird (Anglesey) Limited.

A US Army Chinook carrying a Class 16 Bridge into a Royal Engineer demonstration.

Aircraft

Lynx AH Mark 1

Crew 1 + 1 or 10; **Armament** 6 × TOW missiles, 2/4 × 7.62 mm L20A1 Machine-Guns, and reconnaissance flares; **Length (rotors turning)** 15.164 m; **Length (fuselage)** 11.665 m; **Height (to rotor hub)** 3.43 m; **Width (fuselage)** 1.78 m; **Rotor diameter** 12.8 m; **Maximum speed** 333 km/h; **Cruising speed** 296 km/h; **Range** 885 km; **Engine type** 2 × Rolls-Royce BS 360/07/26 turbo-shafts; **Engine power** 2 × 850 bhp; **Fuel capacity** 909 litres; **All-up weight** 3,620 kg.

The Lynx is a product of Westland Aircraft Limited of Yeovil, Somerset, and was originally designed as a general purpose and transport helicopter. When the prototype first flew in March 1971, it was known as the WG.13 and was developed at first in two marks. The first became the Lynx AH Mark 1 for the Army while the second became the Lynx HAS Mark 2 for the Royal Navy. More were scheduled to be delivered to the French Navy as the Lynx was one of the three helicopters involved in the Anglo-French helicopter deal of the mid-1960s.

The Lynx is now in the process of gradually replacing the Scout AH Mark 1 as the Army's standard general utility helicopter. As such it has to be able to undertake a wide variety of roles which vary from troop transport (carrying ten soldiers), to anti-tank guided missile launcher (using TOW missiles), fire support (using L20A1 podded machine-guns), casualty evacuation (up to three stretcher cases in the cabin), general liaison, cargo-carrying, tactical airborne command post, air-to-ground photography, and a hundred-and-one other tasks. To add to all the above the Lynx is also used for pilot training.

As it is a very advanced design, the Lynx has a lively battlefield performance, and despite its relative bulk should prove an effective weapons platform. The choice of anti-tank missiles for the Lynx was an involved contest with three missile systems involved—the Franco-German HOT, the British Hawkswing and the American TOW. The TOW system was finally selected and will be carried on the Lynx, three to each side in 2.2-metre-long launching tubes over the landing skids. As a gunship, the Lynx should prove a formidable opponent as it can carry up to two machine-guns firing either out of the side hatches or mounted firing directly forward.

The first Lynx AH Mark 1 flew during 1973 and 100 were ordered for the Army. But, as with so many other weapon programmes, the machine ran into troubles as the main contractors, Westland, encountered financial problems, and made a loss on

A Lynx in its battlefield environment (Westland Helicopters Ltd).

each item built. Thus the Lynx became a political problem for a while, but the first production examples were issued for full service during 1978.

Gazelle AH Mark 1

Crew 1 + 4; **Armament** 2 × 7.62 mm L20A1 Machine-Guns and reconnaissance flares; **Length (rotors turning)** 12.09 m; **Length (fuselage)** 9.519 m; **Height (to rotor hub)** 3.02 m; **Rotor diameter** 10.5 m; **Maximum speed** 265 km/h; **Cruising speed** 240 km/h; **Range** 650 km; **Engine type** Turbomeca/Rolls-Royce Astazou 111N; **Engine power** 592 shp; **Fuel capacity** 445 litres; **All-up weight** 1,800 kg.

The Gazelle was originally a French design produced by Aerospatiale but the British Army version was produced by Westland at Yeovil in Somerset. The original French design was produced

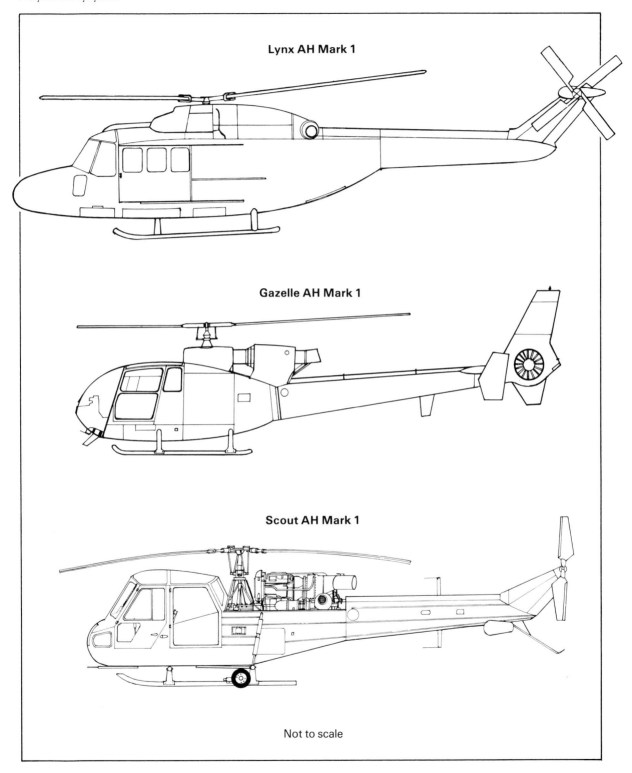

Lynx AH Mark 1

Gazelle AH Mark 1

Scout AH Mark 1

Not to scale

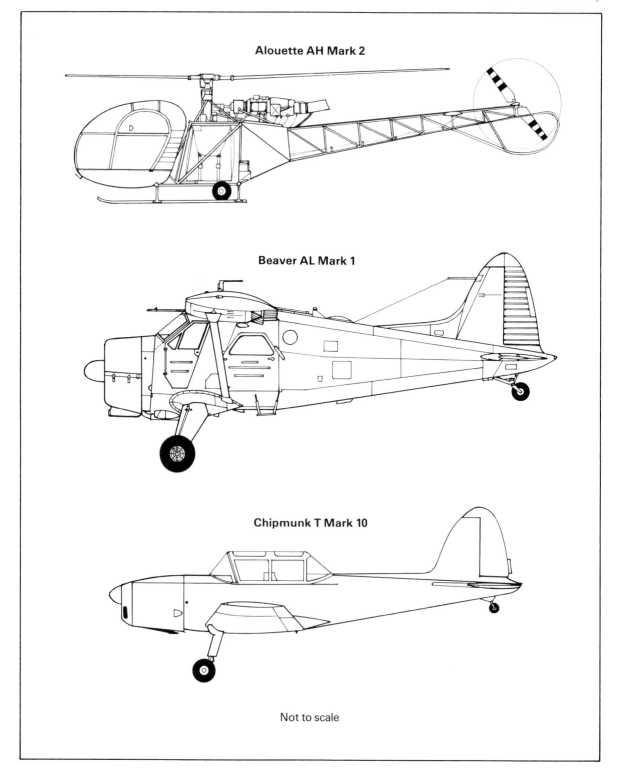

Alouette AH Mark 2

Beaver AL Mark 1

Chipmunk T Mark 10

Not to scale

in a number of versions but the designation for the Army model was SA 341B, and it has now replaced the earlier well-known Sioux AH Mark 1 as the light general purpose helicopter of the Army Air Corps. Within the AAC it fulfils a number of roles from general battlefield observation to ambulance, and can also be employed as a light mobile command helicopter and runabout. In most roles armament is not carried, although a machine-gun can be mounted in the area behind the pilot, firing out to the side. Machine-gun pods can alternatively be fitted over the landing skids. Pilot training is also carried out on the Gazelle.

One optional function for the Gazelle is as the carrier for the 'Skyshout' airborne loudspeaker equipment. This is used for crowd and disaster control or for the airborne command role.

Scout AH Mark 1

Crew 1 + 4; **Armament** 4 × SS11 missiles; 2 × 7.62 mm L20A1 Machine-Guns and/or 2 × 7.62 mm L7A2 Machine-Guns and reconnaissance flares; **Length (rotors turning)** 12.29 m; **Length (fuselage)** 9.335 m; **Height (to rotor hub)** 2.718 m; **Width (fuselage)** 1.65 m; **Rotor diameter** 9.83 m; **Maximum speed** 210 km/h; **Cruising speed** 196 km/h; **Range** 507 km; **Engine type** Rolls-Royce Bristol Nimbus 102 or 105; **Engine power**

Right *Skyshout fitted to a Gazelle.* **Below** *Gazelle AH Mark 1.*

Top *Alouette AH Mark 2 seen here at Middle Wallop* (Peter F. Guiver). **Above** *The Scout AH 1.* **Right** *Beavers para-dropping supplies.*

710 shp; **Fuel capacity** 709 litres; **All-up weight** 2,404 kg.

The Scout has had a fairly protracted existence as the very first prototype first flew in mid-1958. At that stage is was known as the P.531, but it was not until 1962 that the first deliveries were made of the final service version. Even then, service trials further delayed the full in-service date and it was not until the mid-1960s that the Scout became fully integrated into the Army. Originally the P.531 was a Saunders-Roe design but it was produced even-

tually by Westland Aircraft at Yeovil in Somerset.

The Scout is now due for replacement by the Lynx AH Mark 1 but no doubt it will soldier on for some years yet. Throughout its service career it has proved rugged and versatile. It has been used in a wide variety of roles. Originally it was designed as a general purpose helicopter runabout but it has also been used as an ambulance, a trainer, a gunship, and eventually as an anti-tank missile carrier. In the latter role, which was taken over in 1970, the Scout carries four SS11 anti-tank missiles aimed and guided by a roof-mounted AF 120 sight over the front left-hand seat. As a gunship the Scout is not in the same class as the specialised American armed helicopters, but it has been used to try out many of the installations that will be used on the Lynx.

Alouette AH Mark 2

Crew 1 + 4; **Armament** None; **Length (rotors turning)** 12.06 m; **Length (fuselage)** 9.677 m; **Height (to rotor hub)** 2.769 m; **Width (fuselage)** 1.803 m; **Rotor diameter** 10.82 m; **Maximum speed** 185 km/h; **Cruising speed** 167 km/h; **Range** 500 km; **Engine type** Turbomeca Artouste 11C; **Engine power** 460 shp; **Fuel capacity** 578 litres; **All-up weight** 1,598 kg.

The Alouette AH Mark 2 is a French helicopter which was originally the Sud Aviation SE-3130 Alouette II. During the early 1960s development of the Scout series was becoming protracted so the French helicopter was procured in limited numbers to tide the AAC over until the fully developed Scout became available in appreciable quantities. The Alouette AH Mark 2 was intended only as a stop-gap, but once in service it proved to be a first-class helicopter and a pleasure to fly, so much so that it remained in service long after its original withdrawal date. Today only a handful remain, all of them based in Cyprus where they will remain for an appreciable period until their replacement by Scouts—once the Lynx re-equipment programme has been completed.

Beaver AL Mark 1

Crew 6 or 7; **Length (fuselage)** 9.27 m; **Height** 2.896 m; **Wing span** 14.63 m; **Maximum speed** 262 km/h; **Cruising speed** 202 km/h; **Range** 1,078 km; **Engine type** Pratt and Whitney Wasp R-985 Junior; **Engine power** 450 bhp; **Fuel capacity** 505 litres; **All-up weight** 2,450 kg.

The Beaver is the Army's only operational fixed-wing aircraft but as it has been in service for many years, few are now left, and by the time these words are read the last of them may well have been phased out of service. The Beaver prototype, a Canadian design, first flew in 1947. Ever since, this rugged and dependable aircraft has been used for a variety of purposes. With the British Army it serves as a general purpose liaison and communications machine, but it has been used as an airborne ambulance, for dropping supplies and small groups of paratroopers, and as an airborne photographic platform. It has even been fitted with loudspeakers for 'voice from the sky' missions. The last complete Beaver unit is the Beaver Flight based at Aldergrove in Northern Ireland, but other AAC units occasionally add a Beaver to their strength. One

example has even found its way back to its country of origin for it is on the strength of the BATUS unit at Suffield.

While the original Beavers were designed by de Havilland Aircraft of Canada Limited, the Beavers for the British Army were assembled by de Havilland at Hawarden, Chester, in the United Kingdom.

Chipmunk T Mark 10

Crew 2; **Length (fuselage)** 7.823 m; **Height** 2.16 m; **Wing span** 10.465 m; **Maximum speed** 222 km/h; **Cruising speed** 191 km/h; **Range** 483 km; **Engine type** de Havilland Gipsy Major 8; **Engine power** 145 hp; **Fuel capacity** 82 litres; **All-up weight** 908 kg.

Ever since the Army Air Corps took over the responsibility for training its own pilots in 1957, pilot training has been carried out in the initial stages using the Chipmunk T Mark 10. The Chipmunks were all taken over from the Royal Air Force who up till then carried out the training for the Army (all pilots have to learn to fly fixed-wing aircraft before they graduate to helicopters).

The Chipmunk is a Canadian design, the DHC1,

Chipmunk T Mark 10.

which was built by the de Havilland works at Chester between 1949 and 1953. Ever since then they have been used to train generations of pilots for all the British Services although they are now used by only the Army for flying training proper. All the Army's Chipmunks are based at the AAC centre at Middle Wallop. One of these has been given a camouflage colour scheme for use in air observation training and is known as the 'Spitmunk' (unofficially), but its lavish paint scheme has made it some 20 kg heavier than standard Chipmunks.

Water craft

Armament Ship Logistic *St George*
Crew 22 + 10; **Length** 70.5 m; **Displacement (full load)** 1,968 tons; **Engines** 2 × Mirrlees-Blackstone diesels; **Speed** 14 knots; **Range** 5,000 miles.

The *St George* (A382) is the flagship of the RCT's fleet and is used as an ammunition and stores carrier between United Kingdom ports and those serving BAOR as well as the outlying ranges in the Scottish islands. The *St George* was commissioned in July 1981. She has two holds and is slightly different from the other two ships in her class that are used by the Royal Navy (HMS *Kinterbury* (A378) and HMS *Throsk* (A379)). The normal crew is 22 men but there is provision for a further ten bunks to allow personnel to use the vessel for some journeys that would otherwise have to be undertaken by other means of transport.

Landing Craft Logistic
Crew 36 + 34; **Length** 73.1 m; **Displacement**

(standard) 884,755 kg; **Displacement (loaded)** 143,695 kg; **Engines** 2 × diesels; **Engine power** 2 × 2,000 bhp; **Speed** 10.6 knots; **Range** 6,435 km.

HMAV *Ardennes* (L4001) and *Arakan* (L4003) were both ordered during 1974 from Brooke Marine Limited of Lowestoft. The first to be commissioned, during 1977, was the *Ardennes*, soon followed by the *Arakan* during 1978. Both ships are used for store, supply and equipment carrying, usually from Marchwood to the BAOR port at Antwerp, but both have been used to carry supplies and equipment among the various bases and ranges in the Scottish islands. Both ships have the distinction of being the single most expensive items ordered for the Army. They can each carry five Chieftain tanks apiece and have accommodation for 34 troops in addition to their 36-man crews. Both vessels are operated by 20 Maritime Regiment, RCT.

Ramped Powered Lighters
These vessels are mainly used for short-haul stores-carrying over approaches to ports and beaches after being loaded from RFA Logistic Landing Ships. Not all are in use at any one time. All are powered by twin diesel engines.

RPL 03 *Clyde*, RPL 04 *Dart*, RPL 05 *Eden*, RPL 06 *Forth*, RPL 10 *Kennet*, RPL 11 *London*, RPL 12 *Medway*.

Landing Craft Marine
Length 25.7 m; **Displacement (light)** 76,272 kg; **Displacement (loaded)** 178,985 kg; **Engines** 2 × Paxman YHXAM diesels; **Engine power** 2 × 624 bhp; **Speed** 10 knots.

The LCMs are normally carried in the well of HMS *Intrepid*, but as this ship can only carry four of

Top *The Armament Ship Logistic (ASL) St George* (MoD).

Above *HMAV* Arakan (UKLF PR).

Right *RPL 09* Itchin (MoD).

these large ramped landing craft, not all the vessels remain in use. They are used to carry lorries and other large vehicles from the ship to the shore, and each can carry up to 100 tonnes of vehicles, including tanks. They are numbered L700-711, L3507 and L3508.

Landing Craft Vehicles and Personnel

Length 41.5 m; **Displacement (light)** 8,644 kg; **Displacement (loaded)** 13,730 kg; **Engines** Foden diesel; **Engine power** 200 bhp; **Speed** 10 knots.

These ramped landing craft (LCVP142-149) were at one time operated by the Royal Navy before being handed over to the RCT. There are eight of them, carried between the Assault Ships HMS *Intrepid* and *Fearless*, and as a result of their use in the Falklands, the planned withdrawal from service of *Fearless* has been postponed. Each LCVP can carry up to 35 troops or two Land Rovers.

Range Safety Craft

As their name implies, these vessels are mainly used for range safety patrol but their size and general handiness also makes them suitable for many other tasks. There are two types of vessel in this general

bracket, the first which has a displacement of 70 tons and a length of 23.7 m. The two vessels in this class are the *Alfred Herring VC* and *Michael Murphy VC*. The former is used at the Royal Artillery Missile Range in the Outer Hebrides and the latter serves off Cyprus.

To confuse matters somewhat, the second small class of range safety craft (with a displacement of 19 tons and a length of 15 m) were originally given the class name of 'Honours' and include *Samuel Morley VC*, *Joseph Hughes VC*, *Richard Masters VC* and *James Dalton VC*; a second batch of these craft ordered in late 1981 are known as the 'Sirs' class. They include the *Sir Paul Travers*, *Sir Cecil Smith*, *Sir John Potter*, *Sir William Roe*, *Sir Reginald Kerr* and *Sir Humfrey Gale*. All these vessels have a crew of three. Two of them are based in Hong Kong (*Joseph Hughes VC* and *Sir John Potter*).

Work Boat Mark 2

These small craft used to be known as General Service Launches and are used in harbours and ports as general-purpose workboats. They can be used as light tugs, firefighting vessels and ferries. Only five now remain in use, one of them (WB07 *Pike*) in Cyprus and one in the Falklands. The names of the other four

Above *A Mark IV assault boat on Horley Lake, near Aldershot* (MoD).

Right *A Mark 5 assault boat in use by Royal Engineers.*

are WB03 *Bream*, WB04 *Barbel*, WB05 *Roach* and WB06 *Perch*.

Command and Control Craft

With the withdrawal of the Army's amphibious role, not all the following craft still remain in use, but as their name implies they are intended as general control craft during a landing. Each one is 12.5 metres long, and in the past some have been used for target-towing. L 01 *Petrel*, L 03 *Fulmar*, L 04 *Skua*, and L 05 *Shearwater*.

Assault Boat Mark IV

Weight 190 kg; **Length** 5.3 m; **Beam** 1.8 m; **Weight capacity** 1,130 kg; **Load area** 7 m².

The Mark IV Assault Boat was designed and developed by the Military Engineering Establishment at Christchurch, but production began in 1961 under the aegis of Laird (Anglesey) Limited. The boat was designed to carry a load of 1,130 kg or a crew of two plus 11 fully equipped soldiers. Construction is basically aluminium with some steel parts but the weight is kept low so that it can be easily manhandled over land. To increase the carrying capacity of the design, two boats can be secured together, stern to stern. For silent use each boat has stowage points for paddles but the more usual power source is an outboard motor.

Assault Boat Mark 5

Weight 181 kg; **Length** 4.88 m; **Beam** 1.68 m; **Weight capacity** 1,043 kg; **Depth (hull moulding)** 0.602 m; **Depth (under keels)** 0.641 m.

In 1979 it was announced that the MoD had placed a contract for 624 assault boats to replace the existing Assault Boat Mark IV. The new design was originally known as the Sea Jeep and was designed by A.E. Freezer and Company of Hayling Island, but the service designation is Assault Boat Mark 5. The production run was carried out by Fairey Allday Marine. The Mark 5 is constructed from aluminium alloy overall and has built-in buoyancy tanks which render the craft virtually unsinkable. The boat can carry up to 12 fully-armed men or 1,043 kg of supplies, and it can be carried overland by four men or dragged by two. Under the hull are three prominent keels which act as stabilisers in water and double as 'runners' when the boat is beached. Integral grab rails are provided

Above *A CSB being launched from its special transport trailer with the aid of a CET* (Fairey Engineering). **Left** *A laden Mexeflote awaiting the tide* (MoD).

all round the craft and the overall design is such that the boats can be stacked six high for storage or carriage.

Combat Support Boat

Length 8.2 m; **Beam** 2.5 m; **Maximum draught (laden)** 0.66 m; **Weight** 4,080 kg; **Engine type** 2 × Sabre 212; **Engine power** 2 × 180 hp; **Fuel capacity** 277 litres; **Maximum speed (laden)** 30 km/h.

Development of the Combat Support Boat, or CSB, began in 1975 and the first example was delivered for trials in 1977. An order for 56 was placed in 1980 and, as a result of the Army's involvement in the Falklands, a further 12 were ordered in 1983 (some of these were replacements for CSBs lost with

the *Atlantic Conveyor*).

The CSB is very much a maid of all work as far as the Army is concerned. They are used in the assembly of the MGB and are also used as safety boats during M2 ferry operations. They can be used as supply carriers for cargo or personnel, and as general liaison vessels. They have been used to carry Ranger anti-personnel mine launchers. In the Falklands they were used for landing supplies right over the beaches for their propulsion system uses water jets driven by the twin Sabre engines. These enable the CSB to operate in very shallow water and they make the craft very manoeuvrable as well as being able to drive the CSB in reverse—they also act as very efficient brakes. The CSB has a small cab well forward that can be removed if required—CSBs in the 1983 batch have extra 'winterisation' kits for operations at low temperatures. A roll bar acts as a mast and on the bow are fenders (or 'knees') that can be used to nudge bridging components or other vessels. Two standard NATO supply pallets can be carried.

Mexeflote

Mexeflote is a multi-purpose pontoon equipment that has been specifically designed for operation in salt-water maritime conditions. It can be made up into rafts, jetties, causeways and can even be used for rudimentary breakwaters. Despite the large number of possible applications and configurations possible, Mexeflote is constructed from only three basic components, namely the bow, centre and stern pontoons, which are all connected by special linkages. The dimensions of the three pontoon types are as follows: **Length** 7.92 m (bow)/ 6.1 m (centre)/ 6.1 m (stern); **Width** 2.44 m/2.44 m/2.44 m; **Depth** 1.45 m/1.45 m/1.45 m; **Weight** 59.09 kg/46.54 kg/ 44.18 kg.

For most applications, Mexeflote consists of the centre pontoons only, joined together by pontoon connectors, each of which weighs 73.94 kg. When rafts are needed, the bow and stern pontoons are added. The rafts concerned are powered by their own specialised power units in the shape of 5-cylinder Dorman 5LB diesel engines, derated to 75 bhp. The engine units have a capacity of 7.98 litres and the complete units weigh 3,162 kg. The larger the rafts, the more engine units will be required.

Mexeflote is widely used by the Army but as the accent is now being changed away from amphibious towards conventional land warfare, the Mexeflote units are more and more being employed for docking facilities. The RCT Logistic Carriers often carry ready-assembled jetties along their sides ready for launching once near a landing position, and Mexeflote jetties are used during some NATO exercises.

Production of Mexeflote was originally carried out by the Gloster Railway Carriage and Waggon Company, but the licence for production is now held by Fairey Engineering. More have been ordered to replace units in use in the Falklands.

Uniforms and insignia

When dealing with the insignia of the British Army one is on fairly safe ground for the cap badge of any particular regiment or corps is well established and the only variations that might be encountered between dress and service forms are in the materials used, ie, cloth or metal. When it comes to uniforms, however, things are much more varied and included below are the many dress variations. Individual regimental distinctions are jealously guarded by all who wear them with such pride, and these are described in detail in David Griffin's companion volume to this book, *Encyclopaedia of Modern British Army Regiments,* also published by Patrick Stephens. However, it must be stressed that the guidelines provided below are general and cannot deal with every tiny variation that might be encountered. Changes are constantly being introduced, both official and individual, and despite all the efforts of overall guidelines there are variations to be seen in nearly every unit of the Army.

Before going into detail it must be mentioned that there are several types of dress in everyday use. No 2 Dress is normal khaki service dress. No 6 Dress is lightweight and a stone-coloured warm weather version of the No 2 Dress. No 8 Dress is the temperate combat dress with disruptive patterned material (DPM), while No 9 Dress is the tropical version. No 12 Dress is Coveralls, and No 13 Dress is known as Barrack Dress. No 14 Dress is shirt-sleeve order. In addition to these there are a number of more splendid and exotic forms of dress such as No 10 Dress which is worn by officers and senior NCOs and known as Mess Dress; No 11 Dress is its tropical equivalent. No 1 Dress (Blues) is worn by the Household Division and certain officers as well as by many of the regimental bands with No 4 Dress (in white) being its tropical equivalent. The old No 5 Dress (Battle Dress) is no longer used and has been replaced by No 2 Dress.

There are many other forms of formal dress such as the Household Division's Full Dress described in David Griffin's book. But they nearly all have a common point of origin in the Stores and Clothing Research and Development Establishment (SCRDE) at Colchester. This establishment is charged with all manner of Army clothing and uniforms from the selection and testing of the materials involved to the actual design—'the cut of the cloth'. The SCRDE's range of activities is extremely wide and includes such items as camouflage netting and even dummy tanks but here we must concentrate on the clothing aspects only.

In recent years the SCRDE has been instrumental in providing the Army with what amounts to an entirely new range of clothing and personal equipment. Some of the new kit is merely changed in colour. For instance, it has been stated that the current dark blue berets worn by many of the Arms and Services will be replaced by khaki berets. This will not affect the regiments and corps who wear distinctive coloured headgear such as the Paras who prize their 'red' berets (actually maroon—the RMP have red berets) or the AAC with their distinctive light blue berets.

This is all as nothing compared with the changes being made to current combat gear. This new range of clothing is from the skin outwards. Starting with a new form of sock there will also be a new pattern of olive green thermal underwear. As a result of combat experience in the Falklands new boots will be issued which will differ in several respects from the old familiar boot, not least in their leg height. A new combat suit is to be introduced, still with a form of DPM but with 'concertina' type pockets and revised closures. For cold weather use there will be a new padded inner jacket. The current multi-purpose poncho will be replaced by a new waterproof smock and trousers. Northern Ireland-pattern combat

Right *The soldier on the left is wearing the new pattern combat suit together with the new grp helmet, new webbing and boots. The soldier on the right is wearing full NBC protection including the S10 respirator, a Mark IV NBC suit and overshoes. He is also wearing the new webbing with a single combat pack, and both soldiers are carrying the IW (UKLF).*

gloves with their padded outer finger panels will become a general combat issue.

All this new kit will be worn together with a new pattern of webbing. After a great deal of research carried out by the SCRDE, the new webbing will use a fine meshed nylon-based material and at first sight appears to be very similar to existing webbing. There are many detail differences though, not the least of which are new types of rapid-release buckles. As before the belt is used to hang all manner of pouches and containers including the now-universal respirator pouch. In the centre of the back is secured a new three-piece entrenching tool, which can also be used as a very effective close-quarter weapon, carried in a shaped pouch. The belt is supported at the front by braces but at the back a nylon mesh panel is used for support. On to these braces goes the back-pack which is to be of a new internally-braced type. The main pack can be used together with two side-mounted smaller packs and another on the top. These three packs can be detached and one worn as a single combat pack or as two packs for more stowage. When the full kit is worn an overall waterproof cover encloses the top of the load which could also include a sleeping bag and an olive green foam 'kip mat'.

On top of the head goes a new pattern of grp helmet that can also be worn by parachutists, but an alternative will be a woollen-like garment known as a 'head-over' that can be worn in a number of ways, including as a scarf. NBC clothing also has to be considered and the Mark IV NBC suit will be the future standard, replacing the present unloved Mark III 'Noddy' suit. The Mark IV resembles in many ways a conventional combat suit but is made from a charcoal-impregnated cloth and makes extensive use of Velcro closures. It is to be expected that a flame-proof version of the Mark IV will emerge in the near future.

Other detail changes are in the pipeline, including a new set of trade and other qualification badges. It seems extremely likely that, in order to save money on tailoring costs, many forms of dress-type uniforms will be manufactured to a single pattern and the various colour patches and other individual regiment and corps distinctions will be added using Velcro panels—this could even extend to rank badges.

It must be re-stressed that the descriptions in this entry are overall guides only. Any observer at any Army occasion will find all manner of rule-bending or personal changes introduced by officers and men of all ranks and almost every corps and regiment has some small detail of dress that they guard fiercely as their own. These variations are a study in their own

Left *Soldier of the 1st Battalion, the Royal Regiment of Wales, wearing temperate DPM combat dress and carrying a GPMG* (Major R.P. Smith, RRW).

right and those readers requiring more detailed information are recommended to read David Griffin's excellent book mentioned above.

Officers' bages of rank

(Worn on the shoulder straps, usually gold but there are regimental exceptions.)

General Officers

Field Marshal: Crown over crossed batons within a wreath; scarlet gorget patches* with gold oakleaf embroidery and button; red hat band with cap badge of gold crowned lion over a crown over crossed batons within a laurel wreath; gold oakleaf embroidery to top and edge of black peak.

General: As for Field Marshal except shoulder badges are a crown over a four-pointed star ('pip') over a crossed baton and sabre.

Lieutenant General: As for General except that the shoulder badge is a crown over a crossed baton and sabre.

Major General: As for General except that the shoulder badge is a pip over a crossed baton and sabre; cap badge is a lion over a crown over a crossed baton and sabre within a laurel wreath.

Brigadier: Cap badge is a crowned lion over a crown, red hat band, gold oakleaves to edge of peak; shoulder badge is a crown over three pips in triangular formation (point up). Scarlet gorget patches with crimson lace and gold button.

Field Officers

Colonel: As for Brigadier except the shoulder badge is a crown over two pips all in line.

Lieutenant Colonel: Regimental cap; cap badge, collar badges and buttons; shoulder badge is a crown over a pip.

Major: As for Lieutenant Colonel except that the shoulder badge is a crown.

Junior Officers

Captain: As for Major but three pips in line on the shoulder.

First Lieutenant: As above but only two pips.

Second Lieutenant: As above but only one pip.

Officer Cadets: White collar patches with white cord and a gold button.

Warrant Officers (WOs): There are many different regimental deviations from the rank titles shown here, particularly among the Guards, but brevity forces their exclusion. The badges are

* Most General Officers wear scarlet gorget patches but some wear them in the colour of their corps. Examples are: RAMC—dull cherry, RAChD—purple, RAPC—primrose, RAVC-maroon, RAEC—Cambridge blue, RADC—emerald green, ACC—grebe grey and WRAC—beech brown.

The new form of combat webbing with the full pack and side packs.

usually either white woven or brass, but there are several regimental exceptions.

Conductor (RAOC only): The Royal Coat of Arms worn on the forearm within a blue laurel wreath within a red ring.

Warrant Officer First Class (WOI): The plain Royal Coat of Arms (WO1s of technical corps have the coat of arms outlined in the regimental colour).

Warrant Officer Second Class (WOII): A crown on the forearm (certain technical appoinments have the crown within a laurel wreath).

NCOs

(Rank distinctions worn on the upper arm.)

Staff Sergeant: A crown over three chevrons, point down.

Sergeant: Three chevrons, point down.

Drum (Pipe/Bugle) Major: Four chevrons, point up, on the *forearm* and surmounted by a drum or bagpipe or bugle, except in the Foot Guards.

Corporal: Two chevrons, point down.

Lance Corporal: One chevron, point down.

No 2 Dress (Service Dress)

A variety of hats is worn with the uniform. Officers can wear a khaki peaked cap with brown leather chinstrap, two 'gold' buttons and the regimental cap badge; this is the No 2 Dress Cap. The next possibility, for more formal occasions, is the No 1 Dress Cap in regimental colours with black patent leather chinstrap and peak (the latter edged in gold braid for Field Officers, on top and bottom for Colonels). Some regiments (Royal Tank Regiment, Parachute Regiment, Special Air Service) do not wear either of the above hats but always wear their regimental berets which other corps only wear sometimes. The last possible headgear to be worn with No 2 Dress is the regimental side cap.

Other ranks wear the No 1 Dress Cap, beret or side cap with No 2 Dress; the exceptions to this rule are the Guards and the Royal Military Police who have stiff-topped all-khaki peaked caps, 'gold' buttons and brown leather chinstraps with brass buckles.

The new high combat boot (top) compared with the former pattern.

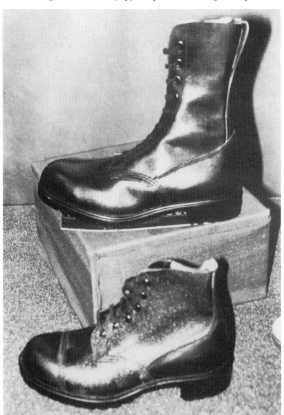

The jacket—Officers: There are various minor regimental differences in style to this garment, the main ones being the 'Highland' pattern with its cutaway front skirts (to give access to the sporran) and two rear vents, the 'Lowland' style with slightly longer skirts and the 'English' pattern with single rear vent and full skirts. All varieties have four pockets with buttoned flaps of various regimental designs and four front button except for officers of the Foot Guards who wear buttons according to regiment (Grenadiers—singly; Coldstream—in pairs: Scots—in threes; Irish—in fours; Welsh—in fives). For most regiments the top pockets have a central pleat and the skirt pockets are of the patch type. The top pocket flaps are usually trident shaped, those on the skirt pockets square. The shoulder straps run up beneath the collar and the cuffs are usually pointed (Polish) with buttons to the rear according to regiment.

Most regiments wear collar badges—the Guards wear none—and certain regiments wear shoulder titles, eg, Other Ranks in the Guards.

The jacket—Other Ranks: Four-button front (three-button with cutaway skirts and two rear vents for Highland and Lowland regiments; slightly longer skirts for Lowland regiments); two breast pockets with buttoned flaps having a single point, inset skirt pockets, no buttons on the rectangular flaps. No decoration to cuffs; single rear vent for all except above-mentioned regiments. The shoulder straps do not reach the collar and have rounded top ends. For most regiments all the buttons are of one size.

The trousers: These are narrow in the leg (bottoms about 42.5 cm) and match the colour of the jacket except for the Royal Hussars who wear crimson trousers, the 5th Royal Inniskilling Dragoon Guards who wear dark green and the Royal Irish Rangers who wear piper green trousers. The Highland regiments wear kilts or trews, the Lowland regiments wear trews.

The shirt and tie: Both are khaki.

The shoes: Most officers wear brown; Light Infantry and Scottish regiments wear black brogues as do the Royal Irish Rangers. Other ranks wear black shoes, WOIs wear officer-pattern brown shoes.

The Sam Browne Belt: (Worn by officers and RSMs.) This anachronistic item is brown with brass fittings for most dismounted regiments and is always polished to a mirror-like finish. Officers of Cavalry regiments frequently wear brown leather bandoliers with brown leather pouches instead of the Sam Browne.

Gloves: Brown leather for officers of most regiments and corps; black for Light Infantry and Highland regiments. Other ranks wear khaki, dark green or black woollen gloves according to regiment.

Canes: Another anachronism; most Infantry officers and those from dismounted corps carry a short cane in various regimental patterns. Officers of the Royal Tank Regiment carry 'Ashplant' walking sticks (a tradition dating from World War 1).

Senior NCOs and Warrant Officers wear red worsted sashes from right shoulder to left hip (under the shoulder strap) when on parade or on certain duties. The sash has long red tassels hanging at the left hip.

Regimental Distinctions worn in No 2 Dress and sometimes No 13 and No 14 Dress

(All berets dark blue initially, but now being replaced by khaki in Infantry, and all jerseys olive green unless otherwise stated.)

Collar badges, buttons, shoulder titles, No 1 Dress caps and side caps are not included due to lack of space. Each regiment or corps wears its own individual cap badge (officers of the Royal Hampshires wear a different badge from soldiers in the same regiment). Coveralls are olive green for all regiments except the Royal Tank Regiment which wears black. All service parade belts are white unless otherwise stated.

The Household Division

The Life Guards: Cap badge—gold cypher 'EIIR' within a crowned ring; red lanyard on right shoulder; stable belt red over blue; black polonecked jersey sometimes worn under olive green coveralls.

The Blues and Royals: Cap badge—bronze 'EIIR' within a crowned ring; red lanyard on left shoulder; on upper left arm a gold Napoleonic eagle on black cloth backing; stable belt blue with a red central stripe.

Royal Horse Artillery: (See Royal Artillery.)

The Foot Guards: (All berets khaki; all stable belts blue with red central stripe.)

Grenadier Guards: Cap badge—a flaming brass grenade in various forms according to rank.

Coldstream Guards: Cap badge—a gold, eight-pointed Star of Order of Garter.

Scots Guards: Cap badge—a gold, four-pointed Star of Order of St Andrew.

Irish Guards: Cap badge—a gold, eight-pointed Star of Order of St Patrick.

Welsh Guards: Cap badge—a gold leek.

The Royal Armoured Corps

Where an item is marked with an asterisk (*) this indicates that it is only worn by part of the regiment,

usually officers and senior NCOs.

1st The Queen's Dragoon Guards: Cap badge—'silver' Imperial Austrian double eagle; white lanyard on right shoulder; royal blue stable belt; brass crowned wreath enclosing 'BAYS' in Gothic script on blue cloth backing on upper left arm.

The Royal Scots Dragoon Guards (Carabiniers and Greys): Cap badge—'silver' Napoleonic eagle over crossed 'brass' carbines on a plinth inscribed 'WATERLOO'; Light grey beret; on the upper left arm is the silver Prince of Wales' plumes.

4th/7th Royal Dragoon Guards: Cap badge— brass, eight-pointed star on red patch; white lanyard on right shoulder; brown leather waist belt for Service Dress; stable belt dark red over dark

A driver of the RCT based in the Falklands and wearing the well-known 'Woolley-Pulley'. On his webbing belt he is wearing a universal Falklands piece of kit, a standard field dressing, worn at all times. Behind him is a Mercedes-Benz 4 × 4 light vehicle captured from the Argentinians in 1982 and used now by the garrison as a Captured Vehicle (CV). This CV is now used as a staff car.

A Royal Artillery Bombardier and a RCT Lance Corporal both wearing the crossed swords badge of an Assistant Physical Training Instructor (R.J. Marrion).

blue with narrow central yellow stripe; on the upper left arm a black diamond bearing one gold over two maroon chevrons (dating from World War 1).

5th Royal Inniskilling Dragoon Guards: Cap badge—crowned, interlocked 'VDG' in silver on dark green cloth backing (shamrock shaped on beret); white lanyard on left shoulder; silver Hanoverian horse on dark green cloth backing on upper right arm; stable belt red over yellow with narrow dark green central stripe.

The Queen's Own Hussars: Cap badge—silver Hanoverian horse over brass scroll bearing reigmental title; on lower left arm silver 'Maid of Warsaw' badge (a mermaid carrying a round shield and scimitar) on crimson cloth backing (World War 2); stable belt—equal stripes of blue-yellow-blue each with a narrow red central stripe; officers wear a lovat green, V-necked jersey with white 'QOH' on khaki epaulettes.

The Queen's Royal Irish Hussars: Cap badge—crowned lion over a crowned Irish harp within a brass ring resting on a scroll; the blue beret has a green headband; yellow lanyard on right shoulder; crowned, silver harp badge on upper arm* (Lance Corporals wear two chevrons without the badge); stable belt green with narrow central stripes yellow over dark blue; dark green, V-necked jersey.

9th/12th Royal Lancers (Prince of Wales's): Cap badge—crossed lances under the crowned

Prince of Wales's plumes over a scroll bearing 'IX-XII'; red and yellow lanyard on left shoulder; red stable belt with two yellow stripes.

The Royal Hussars (Prince of Wales's Own): Cap badge—the Prince of Wales's silver plumes over a brass scroll bearing 'THE ROYAL HUSSARS'; reddish brown beret with round-topped crimson patch behind the badge; stable belt—three equal stripes yellow-red-yellow, each yellow stripe edged in narrow dark blue lines on the outer side only; officers wear dark green, V-necked jerseys with crimson epaulettes.

13th/18th Royal Hussars (Queen Mary's Own): Cap badge—silver, entwined 'QMO' under a crown and behind a 'Z' shaped scroll; white lanyard on right shoulder; silver entwined 'QMO' on upper sleeve for NCOs; on upper left arm a diamond halved vertically white and dark blue; stable belt dark blue-white-dark blue-white; officers wear dark green, V-necked jerseys.

14th/20th King's Hussars: Cap badge—officers—a gold Prussian eagle; senior NCOs wear a black Prussian eagle with gold crown, orb and sceptre on blue over yellow cloth backing*; junior NCOs and privates have the black eagle on a blue over yellow patch divided diagonally; on each upper sleeve small crossed kukris in silver (an honour dating from World War 2); stable belt—blue-lemon yellow-blue; officers wear dark green, V-necked jerseys with khaki epaulettes.

15th/19th The King's Royal Hussars: Cap badge—a crowned lion on a crown within a brass ring over 'XV.XIX' over a brass scroll; red cloth patch behind badge; silver lion over crown badge on right arm*; stable belt—dark blue with narrow central stripe yellow over red.

16th/5th The Queen's Royal Lancers: Cap badge—crowned gold crossed lances behind silver '16' over a gold scroll; stable belt—equal stripes red over yellow over blue.

17th/21st Lancers: Cap badge—silver skull and crossbones with scroll bearing 'OR GLORY'; on upper right arm the cap badge*; stable belt dark blue with twin central white stripes.

1st Royal Tank Regiment: Cap badge—silver World War 1 tank within crowned laurel wreath over a scroll bearing 'FEAR NAUGHT'; black berets; white cloth World War 1 tank badge on upper right arm; stable belt equal stripes green over red over brown; officers and senior NCOs wear black, V-necked jerseys with black epaulettes; red lanyard.

2nd Royal Tank Regiment; As above except—yellow flash around base of shoulder straps with brown, red and green vertical central stripes; yellow lanyard.

3rd Royal Tank Regiment: As for 1 RTR except—green shoulder strap flash and green lanyard.

4th Royal Tank Regiment: as for 1 RTR except—blue shoulder strap flash and lanyard.

Royal Regiment of Artillery

Cap badge—a brass cannon under a crown and over a scroll; white lanyard on left shoulder*; red stable belt with dark blue central band having a central yellow stripe; officers wear dark blue jerseys with dark blue epaulettes having brass buttons and 'RA' shoulder titles; Royal Horse Artillery officers have a silver cap badge of the royal cypher ('EIIR') within a crowned oval garter over a scroll with 'ROYAL HORSE ARTILLERY'; stable belt light blue with narrow yellow central stripe.

Corps of Royal Engineers

Cap badge—'EIIR' within a gold, crowned ring within a silver laurel wreath over a gold scroll; blue lanyard on right shoulder; red stable belt with two narrow dark blue stripes.

Royal Corps of Signals

Cap badge—silver Mercury under a gold crown over a gold scroll bearing 'Certa Cito'; senior NCOs wear cap badge (minus crown) over rank chevrons; blue lanyard on right shoulder; black SD belt; stable belt light blue over dark green with narrow dark blue central stripe; dark blue jersey.

The Scottish Division

(All stable belts are made of a strip of that tartan of which the regimental trews are made.)

The Royal Scots (The Royal Regiment); 1st Foot: Cap badge—silver, four-pointed star with St Andrew's cross; as centrepiece St Andrew with his cross within a ring; no beret; dark blue glengarry with scarlet, green and white diced band and scarlet Toorie; trews in No 8 Hunting Stuart tartan.

The Royal Highland Fusiliers (Princess Margaret's Own Glasgow and Ayrshire Regiment); 21st, 71st and 74th Foot: Cap badge—a crowned, flaming grenade in gold with superimposed, entwined cypher 'HLI'; no beret, glengarry as above; trews in No 5A Mackenzie tartan (HLI sett).

The King's Own Scottish Borderers; 25th Foot: Cap badge—large silver thistle wreath enclosing a castle on a St Andrew's cross over a scroll, all under a crowned lion on a crown; glengarry as above; trews in No 7 Leslie tartan.

The Black Watch (Royal Highland Regiment); 42nd and 73rd Foot: Cap badge—a large, four-pointed star with a St Andrew's cross, in the centre a crowned oval enclosing St Andrew and his cross, around the oval a thistle wreath; khaki bonnet (blue for parades) with scarlet toorie and red hackle over badge (over left ear); kilt and trews in No 1 (42nd or Black Watch) tartan.

Queen's Own Highlanders (Seaforth and Camerons); 72nd, 78th and 79th Foot: Cap badge—a crowned thistle over a stag's head over a scroll; blue glengarry as above with blue cut-feather hackle behind badge; kilt in No 2, Mackenzie tartan (Seaforth sett); trews in No 4, Cameron of Erracht tartan.

The Gordon Highlanders (75th and 92nd Foot): Cap badge—a silver stag's head rising from a mural crown within a wreath and over a scroll; glengarry as above but with scarlet, blue and white dicing; kilt and trews in No 3 (Gordon) tartan.

The Argyll and Sutherland Highlanders (Princess Louise's); 91st and 93rd Foot: Cap badge—a large silver wreath enclosing the boar's head and wild cat separated by the reversed cypher 'L'; glengarry as above but with scarlet and white dicing; kilt and trews in No 1 (42nd) tartan; senior NCOs and officers wear grey shirts and grey V-necked jerseys.

The Queen's Division

The Queen's Regiment; 2nd, 3rd, 31st, 35th, 50th, 57th, 70th, 77th, 97th and 107th Foot: Cap badge—in silver the Prince of Wales's plumes over a winged dragon within a brass ring and over a scroll; lanyards* on left shoulder—1st and 2nd Battalion dark blue; 3rd Battalion royal Dutch orange; stable belt dark blue.

The Royal Regiment of Fusiliers; 5th, 6th, 7th and 20th Foot: Cap badge—a gold flaming grenade bearing St George and the dragon within a crowned ring; a white over red hackle is worn over the badge; stable belt—equal stripes of crimson-yellow-crimson.

The Royal Anglian Regiment; 9th, 10th, 12th, 16th, 17th, 44th, 48th, 56th and 58th Foot: Cap badge—a small, eight-pointed silver star bearing a gold castle over a scroll; khaki beret with oval-topped black patch behind the badge; lanyard*—1st Battalion yellow; 2nd Battalion black; 3rd Battalion purple; 4th Battalion grey-red-black stripes; stable belt—dark blue with red central band having narrow yellow central stripe; dark green jersey.

The King's Division

The King's Own Royal Border Regiment; 14th, 34th and 55th Foot: Cap badge—within a crowned gold laurel wreath a lion guardant worn on a red, diamond-shaped patch; stable belt blue with narrow central yellow stripe; at top of right arm a gold glider badge (World War 2).

The King's Regiment; 8th, 63rd and 96th Foot: Cap badge—a gold fleur-de-lys bearing a silver prancing horse over a scroll on a square scarlet cloth patch; officers wear grey shirts in shirt-sleeve order; lanyard*—dark green on left shoulder; dark green, V-necked jersey*; dark green stable belt with narrow central maroon stripe.

The Prince of Wales's Own Regiment of Yorkshire; 14th and 15th Foot: Cap badge—a running silver horse over a scroll; maroon stable belt with narrow central yellow stripe and black edges; dark green jersey.

The Green Howards (Alexandra, Princess of Wales's Own Yorkshire Regiment): Cap badge—a crowned silver cross entwined with the cypher 'A' over a scroll, on a 5 cm square grass green patch; grass green lanyard on left shoulder; grass green stable belt with narrow central white stripe; dark green, V-necked jersey* with grass green epaulettes.

The Royal Irish Rangers; 27th (Inniskilling), 83rd and 87th Foot: Cap badge—crowned Irish harp and scroll on piper green bonnet with matching hackle behind the silver; piper green stable belt.

The Queen's Lancashire Regiment; 30th, **40th, 47th, 59th, 81st and 82nd Foot:** Cap badge—a crowned rose within a gold oval and over a scroll, worn on a diamond-shaped primrose yellow patch; maroon lanyard* and stable belt.

The Duke of Wellington's Regiment (West Riding); 33rd and 76th Foot: Cap badge—a rampant lion rising from a mural crown and bearing a flag, all over two scrolls; worn on a scarlet patch; red lanyard*.

The Prince of Wales's Division

The Devonshire and Dorset Regiment; 11th, 39th and 54th Foot: Cap badge—a silver castle and key behind a sphinx with brass scrolls top and bottom; grass green lanyard*; grass green stable belt with orange central stripe; at the top of each sleeve a strip of 1914-1918 pattern French Croix de Guerre ribbon (World War 1).

The Cheshire Regiment; 22nd Foot: Cap badge—an eight-pointed silver star enclosing an oak apple sprig within a ring; red lanyard*; cerise stable belt with buff central stripe.

The Royal Welch Fusiliers; 23rd Foot: Cap badge—a gold, flaming grenade bearing in silver the Prince of Wales's plumes within a ring under a white feather hackle; maroon and dark blue stable belt; at rear of SD collar five black silk ribbons about 22.5 cm long by 5 cm wide, each with a swallow-tailed end.

The Royal Regiment of Wales; 24th/41st Foot: Cap badge—the silver Prince of Wales's plumes behind a mural crown with scroll on a grass green patch; grass green stable belt with wide white central stripe having narrow red edges; grass green jersey.

The Gloucestershire Regiment; 28th and 61st Foot: Cap badge—a large silver sphinx on laurel leaves over a scroll; dark blue stable belt with narrow red central stripe and narrower yellow stripes near outer edges; black jersey; on the back of all headdress is a small silver sphinx within a wreath (Battle of Alexandra, 1800); at the top of each sleeve is the gold edged, royal blue US Presidential citation ribbon (Korean War).

The Worcestershire and Sherwood Foresters Regiment; 29th, 36th, 45th and 95th Foot: Cap badge—an eight-pointed star enclosing an antelope within a ring, worn on Lincoln green patch; Lincoln green lanyard* on right shoulder; Lincoln green stable belt with narrow maroon central stripe.

The Royal Hampshire Regiment; 37th and 67th Foot: Cap badge—officers'—a crowned, eight-pointed silver star enclosing a red rose within a blue and gold ring and over a blue and gold scroll; Other Ranks'—within a crowned laurel wreath a tiger over a rose over a scroll; stable belt—black

Left *The Goat Major of the 1st Battalion Royal Welch Fusiliers (RWF) with the Regimental Goat (never called a mascot). The ornate silver headpiece was presented by Queen Victoria; the breast plate is worn only by the Regimental Goat of the 1st Battalion* (R.J. Marrion).
Right *Sergeant Bandsman and Fanfare Trumpeter of the Royal Highland Fusiliers (RHF) in Full Dress* (R.J. Marrion).

with stripes of yellow, red, green and mauve; black jersey.

The Staffordshire Regiment (The Prince of Wales's); 38th, 64th, 80th and 98th Foot: Cap badge—the Prince of Wales's plumes over the Staffordshire knot on a buff backing of 'Holland Cloth'; black lanyard* on left shoulder; black stable belt; gold glider at top of right arm (World War 2).

Duke of Edinburgh's Royal Regiment (Berkshire and Wiltshire); 49th, 62nd, 66th and 99th Foot: Cap badge—a small, gold Maltese cross bearing a dragon within a ring, worn on a square red cloth backing; blue lanyard*; blue stable belt with two narrow red stripes.

The Light Division
The Light Infantry; 13th, 32nd, 46th, 51st, 53rd, 68th, 85th, 105th and 106th Foot: Cap badge—a silver stringed bugle badge with red backing; rifle green beret and lanyard on left shoulder; rifle green stable belt.

The Royal Green Jackets; 43rd and 52nd Foot, The King's Royal Rifle Corps, Rifle Brigade: Cap badge—a silver Maltese cross within a crowned laurel wreath; rifle green beret; green and black lanyard*; rifle green stable belt.

The Parachute Regiment
Cap badge—a silver winged parachute under a crown under a lion; maroon beret and stable belt; light blue and white parachutists' badge at top of right sleeve; lanyard*—1st Battalion red; 2nd Battalion blue; 3rd Battalion green.

The Brigade of Gurkhas
All regiments wear the khaki Gurkha hat (really two sewn together) with flat brim and light khaki pagree, the badge being on the left side. Alternative

parade headgear is the black Kilmarnock (pill box) with cap badge in front and toorie in the regimental colour; rifle green berets are worn on fatigues and for training.

2nd King Edward VII's Own Gurkha Rifles (The Sirmoor Rifles): Cap badge—Prince of Wales's plume, scroll and coronet (silver for officers, black for ORs) worn on red backing; black toorie and black and red diced band to Kilmarnock; black lanyard* on left shoulder; stable belt—rifle green central band edged in narrow red stripes; black outer edges.

6tn Queen Elizabeth's Own Gurkha Rifles: Cap badge—two silver kukris in saltire (hilts and cutting edges down) over '6' all ensigned with the crown; scarlet toorie to Kilmarnock; rifle green and black lanyard; rifle green and black stable belt.

7th Duke of Edinburgh's Own Gurkha Rifles: Cap badge—two silver kukris in saltire, points and

A Lance Bombardier of the Royal Artillery wearing a brassard with his rank and unit insignia (R.J. Marrion).

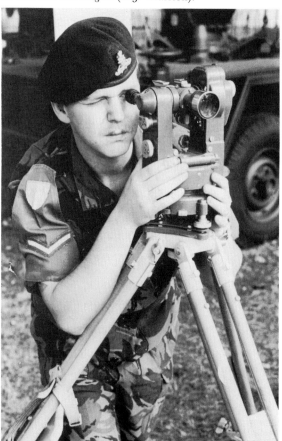

cutting edges up; between the points '7', between the hilts the reversed crowned cypher 'P'; black toorie to Kilmarnock; rifle green and black lanyard; rifle green and black stable belt.

10th Princess Mary's Own Gurkha Rifles: Cap badge—silver, a stringed bugle horn interlaced with a kukri fesswise, the blade to the sinister; above the kukri the cypher of HRH Princess Mary (The Princess Royal) and below it '10'; black toorie to Kilmarnock; black lanyard; rifle green and black stable belt.

Gurkha Engineers; Cap badge—two silver kukris in saltire, blades up, cutting edges out under a gold flaming grenade; over kukri hilts a gold scroll bearing 'UBIQUE'; yellow toorie and head band to Kilmarnock; lanyard and stable belt as for Royal Engineers.

Gurkha Signals: Cap badge—as for Royal Corps of Signals but with addition of two kukris in saltire, blades up, cutting edges in, behind the globe; dark blue toorie to Kilmarnock, lanyard and stable belt as for Royal Corps of Signals.

Gurkha Transport Regiment: Cap badge—as for Royal Corps of Transport but scroll bears 'GURKHA TRANSPORT REGIMENT' and the royal cypher is over two kukris in saltire (silver blades, gold hilts), hilts down, cutting edges out; black toorie to Kilmarnock.

Special Air Service Regiment
Cap badge—silver dagger with light blue wings and scroll bearing 'WHO DARES WINS' on dark blue patch; beige beret.

Army Air Corps
Cap badge—silver eagle within a crowned wreath on a square dark blue patch; light blue beret; senior NCOs wear a light blue eagle edged dark blue above their chevrons.

Royal Corps of Transport
Cap badge—brass, eight-pointed star under a crown and enclosing 'EIIR' within a scroll; dark blue lanyard (left); dark blue stable belt with twin narrow central white lines, two narrow red stripes towards outer edges.

Royal Army Medical Corps
Cap badge—within a gold, crowned laurel wreath a silver snake and staff, below the wreath a gold scroll; dull cherry lanyard (left); stable belt in three equal stripes; crimson over dark blue over yellow.

Royal Army Ordnance Corps
Cap badge—silver shield bearing three antique cannon under three balls, all within the crowned,

A Gunner Farrier and a Lance Bombardier of the King's Troop, RHA, wearing the horseshoe and bit badges of their respective trades (farrier and saddler & collar maker) (R.J. Marrion).

gold garter wreath over a scroll; red and dark blue lanyard on left shoulder; stable belt dark blue with three narrow red stripes.

Corps of Royal Electrical and Mechanical Engineers

Cap badge—under a gold crown and scroll a silver, prancing horse chained to a globe, all superimposed on a gold lightning flash; stable belt dark blue with two narrow stripes each red over yellow.

Corps of Royal Military Police

Cap badge—brass 'EIIR' within a crowned laurel wreath; below the wreath a scroll; red beret; red lanyard on left; red stable belt.

Royal Pioneer Corps

Cap badge—silver piled rifles, pick axe and shovel behind a wreath, all under a crown and over a scroll; red and green lanyard on left shoulder; dark blue stable belt with narrow central stripe red over green.

Intelligence Corps

Cap badge—a crowned rose between laurel leaves over a scroll; Cypress green beret.

Royal Army Veterinary Corps

Cap badge—within a gold crowned wreath a centaur; all over a scroll.

Royal Army Education Corps

Cap badge—gold crown over a scroll, all superimposed on a silver flaming torch; light blue and dark blue lanyard (left) and stable belt.

Army Catering Corps

Cap badge—on a gold crowned circular disc a silver flaming bowl all over a gold scroll; lanyard* grey and yellow (left); grey and yellow stable belt.

Women's Royal Army Corps

Cap badge—within a crowned gold wreath a rampant silver female lion; dark green beret with beech brown patch behind the badge; Lovat green, single-breasted four-buttoned jacket with dark green piping to shoulder straps; lovat green skirt; black gloves, shoes and handbag; white blouse, black 'tie'.

Queen Alexandra's Royal Army Nursing Corps

Cap badge—brass cross within a crowned laurel wreath over a scroll; grey beret; grey jacket and skirt, as for Women's Royal Army Corps with crimson piping to shoulder straps; white blouse; black 'tie', gloves, shoes and handbag.

Temperate Combat Dress

This consists of hat, jacket and trousers in DPM (olive drab, black, brown, green and buff). The jacket has four patch pockets with buttoned flaps, buttoned cuffs and is fitted with draw-strings at waist and hem. The front has a full length, double-ended zip and a buttoned fly flap. The collar is only about 3 cm high and can be buttoned up. Under this jacket can be worn an olive green, quilted liner in sleeveless jerkin style. The olive-green trousers have a double-ended fly zip and draw-strings at the ankles. Around the waist are loops to take the web belt. The lower ends of the trousers are enclosed in khaki puttees which replaced web gaiters in the period 1974-76. For normal wear black Direct Moulded Sole (DMS) boots are worn but for extreme cold special boots with thicker soles and thermal insoles are worn.

The heavy, olive green woollen jersey with crew neck may be worn under or instead of the combat jacket. Beneath this is worn the combat shirt ('Shirt Hairy Mary' to the soldiers) in flannel-like material. In 1976 black leather 'combat gloves' were introduced into Northern Ireland and they are now being issued to all soldiers to replace the unsatisfactory khaki knitted gloves.

Combat headdress is still the steel helmet of 1950s vintage but is is being replaced by a composition 'Combat Helmet' with increased ballistic and shock protection and a much firmer sit. This item has been troop-trialled in Northern Ireland. A variation of this item is the new parachutist's helmet.

Cold Weather Clothing

This consists of temperate combat clothing with the following additions: string vest; 'long johns' in olive green for the legs; a quilted, sleeved under-jacket; quilted under-trousers; a DPM parka reaching to the knees and special, thick-soled boots with thermic insoles. In snowy conditions this is worn under a windproof, white-hooded smock and trousers together with special sheepskin mittens and ski-boots. For non-skiing duties in deep snow Canadian-pattern white Mukluks are worn over the cold weather boots.

Tropical Combat Wear

Special lightweight cotton DPM hat, 'safari jacket' and trousers, with or without shirt of same basic style as temperate combat dress; either DMS boots or special jungle boots of US Army Vietnam pattern (commercial hockey boots have also been used). For desert conditions suede boots of commercial pattern are very popular, as are plimsolls.

New equipment developments

Helmet: Until recently the British army wore a steel helmet with single chinstrap and curved bottom edge coming low over ears and neck. This was designed to give protection only against shell splinters; a helmet protecting against small arms projectiles at close range would have been far too heavy for a man to wear for more than a few minutes at a time.

This helmet had four main disadvantages: it was unstable and fell off easily; it provided minimal protection against blows to the head (rocks, clubs, etc): its shape over the eyes made it difficult for the wearer to operate some of the newer weapons without considerable inconvenience and contortions; and it was difficult to wear earphones with it.

In about 1975 a new 'Northern Ireland Combat Helmet' made of glass reinforced plastic was introduced. It weighed less than the steel model, fitted more closely to the head and had a chinstrap which was anchored at four points to the helmet and thus gave a much firmer fit. It also afforded 'bump' protection and had less pronounced front and rear peaks, thus permitting easier operation of many weapons in various positions. Facilities were included for the rapid fitting of a plastic visor for internal security duties. This helmet proved to be a great improvement on the old steel model and is now being introduced into general use. A variation of this basic pattern is the new parachutist's helmet.

The combat glove: Northern Ireland has proved to be a comprehensive testing ground for all items of Army combat clothing and it soon became obvious that the knitted khaki glove was totally inadequate. It was thus replaced with (initially) a commercial pattern, black leather ski glove which, with added padding strips along the knuckles, has become the new combat glove.

Windproof waterproof clothing: To protect soldiers from adverse weather in situations where they are exposed to the elements but must remain stationary for long periods, an olive drab smock and overtrouser suit was developed. It is completely proof against wind and rain and thus preserves body heat.

The disadvantage of such clothing is that if the wearer has to engage in strenuous exertion while wearing it, it becomes a very efficient sauna and the man is rapidly soaking in his own sweat. Subsequent inaction leads to considerable loss of body heat in most uncomfortable conditions. These garments are now being issued with the DPM camouflage print.

Tank crew clothing: Two items of interest have recently been developed; first is a waterproof, olive green, one-piece coverall to protect the crews of armoured fighting vehicles from inclement weather when carrying out maintenance in the field such as track changing. This garment has the inherent disadvantage of all waterproof clothing—it catches

Member of 20th Maritime Regiment, RCT, wearing the Royal Naval No 8 working rig with the black beret and badge of the RCT. The insignia worn by all ranks of the Maritime Regiment is just visible on the left shoulder but it is worn on both upper arms (R.J. Marrion).

fire relatively easily. As fire is a constant hazard in a tank in a combat situation, a fire-resistant coverall is also being developed.

As the Chieftain tank has no heating when in 'silent watch' mode, crew efficiency and comfort suffers considerably in winter in north-west Europe. Experiments were made with a coverall containing electrical heating wires all over the body and designed to be plugged into the tank's battery system. The device worked but the drain on the batteries was too great so it was rejected and instead development is proceeding on electrically heated insoles for the men's boots and electrically heated mittens which will plug into the tank battery system with quick-release snatch plugs.

NBC clothing: Since the German gas attacks of World War 1, the British Army has been careful about chemical warfare defence. The current S6

respirator, of black rubber with built-in filter, is the latest in a line of continuously developed items. It provides complete protection for the optical and respiratory systems against known Soviet NBC warfare agents.

To protect the rest of the body each soldier is issued with a two-piece Mark III NBC suit in olive drab, charcoal impregnated paper. This suit offers complete protection against NBC agents for several hours. It then has to be removed and replaced by a new suit. Three are given to each soldier.

No country has the complete answer to protection against the NBC threats. The grey rubber suit of the Warsaw Pact forces has the advantage of being more robust than the British paper model but it acts as a dreadfully efficient sauna bath and leads to rapid exhaustion of the wearer. It has to be decontaminated—an operation not required with the disposable British suit—and is not proof against certain NBC agents for more than a few hours.

The British NBC suit is worn with disposable rubber and paper-charcoal overboots and black disposable rubber gloves with white cotton inner gloves.

Web Equipment (WE): Even today, a large proportion of the British Army wears '1937 Pattern' WE (much hated because of the constant need to blanco it) but this is now being replaced by '1958 Mark II WE' with heavy shoulder yoke and with the ammunition pouches, water bottle, respirator and small pack being attached to the waist belt. The bayonet is held in its scabbard on the side of the left-hand ammunition pouch and the equipment is made of olive drab synthetic material which is resistant to both water and NBC agents. All metal fittings are in matt black finish. A folding entrenching tool is carried on the back.

For tropical wear a special type of WE was developed during the war and called '1944 Pattern'. Its advantages were that it absorbed very little water in its olive green fabric and thus did not greatly increase the soldier's load in the 'rain forest' environment. It was usually worn with two water bottles. 1944 Pattern WE is characterised by broad shoulder straps with two narrower straps falling to the rear of each and crossing to attach to rear and sides of the belt.

Parachutist's smock: Since World War 2 the British airborne forces have worn the 'Denison Smock' with its peculiar camouflage pattern, ribbed woollen cuffs and crutch strap. It has become enshrined almost as a ceremonial item (particularly since Arnhem) and only with great reluctance could the Parachute Regiment be persuaded recently to accept the introduction of a new smock in standard DPM colours.

Barrack Dress trousers: These dark green, 100 per cent synthetic textile items were introduced in 1974-76. With their permanent creases they were designed to smarten up the soldiers' appearance at less cost than Service Dress would incur. The Scottish regiments were extremely reluctant to adopt them as they suspected the introduction of these items as the 'thin end of the wedge' of a plan to deprive them of their trews.

Many units prefer to wear the light olive drab 'Trousers Lightweight' for barrack wear as these contain a percentage of natural fibres and present more resistance to oils in the dirty job situation such as vehicle maintenance. Coveralls ought to be worn for this work but are unpopular, particularly in summer.

Special combat clothing: The terrorist war in Northern Ireland has led to the development of a range of protective clothing which at first glance may seem novel but on reflection is merely an updated selection of historic items of personal armour using

Sergeant of the Royal Corps of Signals wearing the badge of a Qualified First Aid Instructor (R.J. Marrion).

modern materials instead of the more conventional wood, steel and leather.

In the early stages of the most recent 'Troubles' in 1969-70 the troops and police were frequently called upon to stand firm for hours under a hail of stones, bottles and molotov cocktails with no protective clothing at all. To give them at least a degree of protection they were issued with cricket pads and light metal shields. As the situation continued to deteriorate the Stores and Clothing Research and Development Establishment (SCRDE) began to develop special items. The 'Combat Helmet Northern Ireland', of glass reinforced plastic (GRP) with improved ballistic and bump protection, firmer sit and optional plastic visor, was one such item. GRP leg greaves and light, transparent plastic riot shields were others. When the threat of being picked off by an IRA terrorist with a rifle became greater, the British government authorised the purchase of a quantity of US pattern 'Flak Jackets' to protect the upper body. These were made of multiple layers of 'Kevlar'—a synthetic fibre much stronger than steel in certain respects and a substance tested in the US space programme. These Flak Jackets afford protection against normal projectiles from pistols and sub-machine-guns from close range (about 5 m) and from soft-cored rifle and machine-gun bullets from about 400 m (depending upon strike velocity and angle).

Of course, this armour, as in the Middle Ages, had the conventional disadvantage—its protection could only be bought at the high price of its weight. The wearer was very limited in his movements, tired much more easily when wearing it and moved much more slowly than if he had not worn it. Mobility itself is protection and the age-old tussle between mobility and armour continued its maddening spiral.

A British company (Bristol Composite Materials Engineering Ltd) has recently developed an armoured vest which is in use with the Royal Ulster Constabulary and with some British Army units in Northern Ireland. Kevlar has the disadvantage of suffering a great reduction in its ballistic protective properties if wet (it regains them when dried out again). In order to cut down the weight of a vest designed to protect against armour-piercing projectiles fired from a Kalashnikov assault carbine at close range to acceptable limits, this company has developed 'composite armour' plates (ceramic and GRP) which for any given level of ballistic protection are much lighter than armoured steel.

Vests of this type were used by the West German elite anti-terrorist group 'Grenz-Schutz-Gruppe 9' (GSG9) in their successful raid on the Lufthansa jet held by hijackers in Mogadishu in 1977. To give the

GSG9 men greatest mobility within the close confines of the plane's cabin, they used the vests
without the ceramic-GRP plates. One GSG9 man
was shot from a range of about 3 m by a terrorist
using a Makarov pistol, the bullet lodging in the
side of the armoured vest, and the policeman reported that all he felt was a slight bump 'as if someone
had poked me in the ribs with a finger'! He shot the
terrorist.

The Explosive Ordnance Disposal (EOD) suit:
Ammunition Technicians (ATs) and Ammunition
Technical Officers (ATOs) of the Royal Army Ordnance Corps have the unenviable task of attempting to disarm IRA terrorist bombs. To give them
some degree of protection in this hazardous job and
EOD suit was developed at great speed and
produced partly by SCRDE Colchester and partly
by the British firm of Galt Glass. It consists of a
helmet with massive plastic visor and built-in inter-
communication facilities, a two-piece smock of
Kevlar in an olive green cover and Kevlar leggings
in olive green covers. The chest is protected by a
GRP plate shaped to deflect shock waves from a
bomb away from the head and the lower abdomen
is protected by another such shield. On the back of
the equipment is a small two-way radio with a range
(under suitable conditions) of several hundred
metres.

The suit is, of course, extremely heavy (over
30 kg) and severely limits the movements of the
wearer. It is designed to be worn only for a few
minutes at a time while the ATO carries out his
initial examination of the bomb and so this disadvantage is of limited validity. As one ATO said to me
'at least it enables you to be buried in one piece'.
Since the introduction of this suit (1974) various international firms have come up with improvements
which are easier to don and to take off than the in-
service EOD suit and which afford greater ballistic
protection without increasing the limitations to the
wearer's mobility.

Specialist badges

The British army is traditionally extremely niggardly
with the award of medals and badges of achievement and skill when compared to other armies and
this was also the case in the Napoleonic era. Highly
qualified soldiers of the British army, who have seen
action in World War 2, Africa, Cyprus, Aden,
Dhofar and Northern Ireland frequently wear far
fewer medals and badges than their equivalents in
other armies who have never heard a shot fired in
anger or been involved in any more perilous
situation than the Nijmegen marches. In the British
army the purple and dark green 'General Service
Medal' covers a span of campaigns which would fill

many a chest in another army.

Badges for skill at arms or for technical skills are
usually worn only by NCOs and privates. Exceptions (worn also by officers) are: pilots' badge—a
crowned lion over a crown between light blue
wings, all on a dark blue ground—worn on the left
breast; fully trained parachutists' wings—a white
parachute between light blue wings on khaki—on
the upper right arm; parachutists' badge (known
as the 'Edward Bear Badge' after the custom
of the RMAS of always throwing a battered
Teddy Bear (with a parachute) out of an airplane
before the officer cadets follow it on their first
jump). The 'Edward Bear Badge' is worn on the
lower left arm.

'A' Class Tradesman: (Various corps.) An 'A'
between laurel leaves, all in white, worn on the upper arm (privates and junior NCOs only).

Aircraft Technician, REME: Within a
crowned, winged yellow ring the yellow letters
'AT'; around the yellow ring the black letters
'REME'.

Air Despatcher, RCT: Within a crowned,
winged yellow ring the letters 'AD'.

Air Gunner: On a dark blue ground a yellow 'G'
within a crowned ring with a single light blue wing
to the left side, worn on the left breast.

Air Observer: As above but the 'G' is replaced
by an 'O'.

Ammunition Technical Officer: Black, gold
and yellow flaming bomb worn on the lower left
sleeve.

Ammunition Technician: A larger version of
the above in black, yellow and red worn above the
rank chevrons or below the warrant badge.

Anti-Tank Gunner: 'AT' within a laurel wreath
in regimental colours or brass.

Armament Artificer: Crossed hammer and
pincers, but this badge also covers a number of
other trades including blacksmith, fitter, etc.

Army Parachute Jumping Instructor: A small
white parachute within light blue wings, below the
parachute 'APJI' in yellow within a green laurel
wreath.

Artificer, REME: (Staff Sergeants and Warrant
Officers.) White crossed hammer and pincers on
khaki worn over the chevrons or under the warrant
badge.

Assault Pioneer: Crossed axes.

'B' Class Tradesman: (Various corps.) A 'B'
between laurel leaves, all in white, worn on the upper arm (privates and junior NCOs only).

Bugler: A white cloth or brass bugle on the upper
arm.

Bugler (Light Infantry.) As above but a stringed
bugle horn.

Corps badges: (In regimental colours or in brass, worn by senior NCOs of the following corps above their chevrons.) *Royal Artillery:* a Napoleonic cannon side view; *Royal Engineers:* a white, flaming grenade; *Royal Corps of Signals:* the figure of Mercury on a globe.

Diver, Royal Engineers: An old-fashioned brass diver's helmet over the letters 'SW' (shallow water).

Driver: A five-pointed white star worn on the left upper arm (privates and junior NCOs only).

Drummer: Representation of a white cloth or brass drum worn on the upper arm (also over the four chevrons of a Drum Major).

Farrier: A white horseshoe on khaki on the upper arm (privates and junior NCOs only).

Gun Layer: 'L' within a laurel wreath in regimental colours or brass.

Marksman (Light Machine-Gun): 'LMG' within a laurel wreath in regimental colours or brass.

Marksman (Rifle): Crossed rifles. (A similar badge is worn by WOs and senior NCOs of the Small Arms School Corps in white on khaki as a technical qualification.)

Mortarman: 'M' within a laurel wreath in regimental colours or brass.

Musician: A white cloth or brass lyre worn on the upper arm.

Physical Training Instructor: Crossed sabres, points up.

Pilot, AAC: A crowned lion standing on a crown between light blue wings, worn on the left breast.

Piper: White cloth on brass bagpipes worn on the upper arm.

Radar Technician, REME: 'R' between lightning flashes in white on khaki.

Royal Engineers Bomb Disposal: A yellow bomb under a blue cross on a red oval worn on the cuff.

Saddler and Harness Maker: A bit worn on right upper arm. Usually only worn by the King's Troop, Royal Horse Artillery, but may be worn by Household Cavalry.

Signaller: Crossed flags in white, yellow and dark blue worn on the lower arm (privates and Lance Corporals) or over the chevrons (Corporals).

Sniper: Crossed rifles under an 'S' in regimental colours or brass.

Special Air Service: A white parachute and wings on a dark blue ground worn on the upper right arm.

Telecommunications Technician, REME: 'T' between lightning flashes in white on khaki.

Trumpeter: White cloth or brass crossed trum-

Right *The Explosive Ordnance Disposal (EOD) suit.*

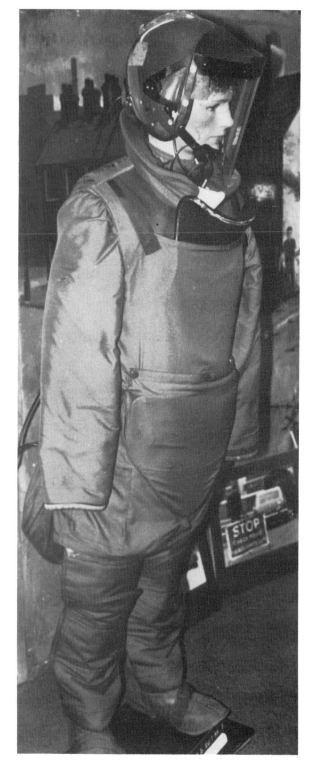

pets worn on the upper arm.

Wheelwright: An old-fashioned cartwheel.

From January 1984 a number of new qualifications for skill at arms were introduced, prompting some completely new badges and altering others by the addition of a star, a common practice in the years up to 1939. At the time of going to press none of these new badges appear to have entered general use.

Instructor's Badges

Crossed gun barrels: Assistant Instructor in Gunnery (AIG), Royal Artillery.

'QI' in wreath: Qualified Instructor in Field Engineering, Royal Engineers.

Crossed rifles: Weapon training instructor. Worn on right arm, position depending on rank.

Crossed swords: Assistant Physical Training Instructor.

Crossed semaphore flags: Assistant Instructor of Signalling, Royal Signals.

A spur: Roughrider, or Equestrian Instructor. Worn on right arm with the position depending on rank.

Good conduct stripes

These are awarded for ascending periods of 'undetected crime' and are worn only by privates and

Right *Sergeant of the King's Troop, RHA, in Full Dress wearing the badge of Equestrian Instructor* (R.J. Marrion). **Below** *The interior of a Berlin strongpoint with soldiers of 3RRF demonstrating how current webbing is worn* (Army PR Berlin).

Lance Corporals on the lower left sleeve. They take the form of chevrons in the regimental colour, point up. One chevron = two years' service; two chevrons = five years; three = eight years.

Variations in rank titles

Usual title	Foot Guards	Household Cavalry	Royal Artillery	Cavalry of the Line and other mounted corps
Regimental Sergeant Major (RSM)	RSM and Superintending Clerk	Regimental Corporal Major	RSM	RSM
Company Sergeant Major (CSM)		Squadron Corporal Major	Battery Sergeant Major	Squadron Sergeant Major
Regimental Quarter Master Sergeant (RQMS) (badge with wreath)	RQMS or Orderly Room QMS	Regimental Quarter Master Corporal *or* Farrier Quarter Master Corporal. Squadron Quarter Master Corporal *or* Staff Corporal of Horse (*NB* These NCOs wear a crown over 4 chevrons)	RQMS	RQMS
Staff Sergeant (SSgt) or Colour Sergeant (CSgt) or Company Quarter Master Sergeant (CQMS)	Sgt or CSgt or CQMS	Corporal of Horse	Battery QMS (BQMS)	Squadron QMS (SQMS)
Sergeant (Sgt)	Sgt	Lance Corporal of Horse	Sgt	Sgt
Corporal (Cpl)	Cpl	Cpl	Bombardier	Cpl
Lance Corporal (LCpl)	LCpl	LCpl	Lance Bombardier	LCpl

Index

The following index combines a glossary of abbreviations. Where an abbreviation is common, eg, AFV, it is not indexed as it would be of no value as a reference. **Bold** type denotes a main or major entry.

M2s starting to form a bridge over the Weser (Soldier Magazine/MoD).